The Lesbian Myth

The Lesbian Myth

Bettie Wysor

RANDOM HOUSE  *New York*

Library of Congress Cataloging in Publication Data

Wysor, Bettie.
  The Lesbian myth.

  Bibliography: p.
  1. Lesbianism.   2. Homosexuality.   3.   Gay   Liberation   Movement—United States. I. Title.
  [DNLM: 1. Homosexuality. WM615 W994s 1974]
  HQ76.W93   301.41′57   73–17392
  ISBN 0–394–48190–9

Manufactured in the United States of America
98765432
First Edition

Grateful acknowledgment is made to the following for permission to reprint previously published material:

American Association for the Advancement of Science and Dr. Judith Blake: For excerpts from "Population Policy for Americans: Is the Government Being Misled?" by Judith Blake, reprinted from *Science*, Vol. 164 (May 2, 1969), pp. 522–29.
Djuna Barnes: For excerpts from *The Ladies' Almanack* by Djuna Barnes. Copyright © 1972 by Djuna Barnes (Harper & Row, 1972).
The British Journal of Psychiatry and June H. Hopkins: For excerpts from "The Lesbian Personality" by June H. Hopkins, from *The British Journal of Psychiatry*, Vol. 115, No. 529, December 1969.
Faith and Freedom: For excerpts from "Christian Society and the Homosexual," by Anthony Grey, from *Faith and Freedom*, Vol. 19, No. 56, Spring 1966.
Femina Books Ltd. and A. S. Barnes & Co., Inc.: For excerpts from *Radclyffe Hall: A Case of Obscenity* by Vera Brittain. Copyright © 1968 by Vera Brittain.
Jeannette H. Foster: For excerpts from *Sex Variant Women in Literature* by Jeannette H. Foster (Vantage Press, 1956).
Grune & Stratton, Inc., and Drs. Gundlach and Riess: For excerpts from *Self and Sexual Identity in the Female: A Study of Female Homosexuals,* by Ralph H. Gundlach and Bernard Riess (New Directions in Mental Health, New York, 1968).

Harper & Row Publishers, Inc.: For excerpts from *Ethics in a Christian Context* by Paul Lehmann (Harper & Row, 1963).

Indiana University Press: For excerpts from an article by Frank A. Beach, from *Perspectives in Reproduction and Sexual Behavior*, edited by Milton Diamond (University of Indiana Press, 1968).

International Mental Health Research Newsletter (Postgraduate Center For Mental Health): For excerpts from "Who Is A Lesbian?" by Ralph H. Gundlach and excerpts from "A New Psychology of Women or a Psychology for the New Woman, Active or Passive" by Bernard Riess, from *International Mental Health Research Newsletter*, Vol. XIV, No. 4, Winter 1971.

Journal of the American Medical Association: For excerpts from "Normal and Deviant Sexual Behavior" by Judd Marmor, from *Journal of the American Medical Association*, 217 (2): 1965.

KTAV Publishing House: For excerpts from *Sex Laws and Customs in Judaism* by Louis M. Epstein.

The Ladder: For portions of the Bibliography from *The Lesbian in Literature* by Gene Damon and Lee Stuart, published by *The Ladder*, P.O. Box 5025, Washington Station, Reno, Nevada.

J. B. Lippincott and Company and Dr. Frank A. Beach: For excerpts from "Masculine Copulatory Behavior in Intact and Castrated Female Rats" by Frank A. Beach and Priscilla Rasquin, published in *Endocrinology*, Vol. 31, No. 4, October 1942.

Little, Brown and Company and Drs. William Masters and Virginia Johnson Masters: For excerpts from *Human Sexual Inadequacy* by William Masters and Virginia Johnson (Little, Brown and Company, 1970).

Liveright: For excerpts from *The Collected Works of Pierre Louys*. Copyright © 1960 by Liveright Publishing Corp.

Longman Group Limited: For excerpts from *Homosexuality and the Western Christian Tradition* by Derrick Sherwin Bailey.

The Month: For excerpts from an article by William Dempsey from the *Dublin Review* (now incorporated in *The Month*), No. 504, Summer 1965.

The New York Times: For excerpts from "Episcopal Clergymen Here Call Homosexuality Morality Neutral," *The New York Times*, November 29, 1967. Copyright © 1967 by The New York Times Company.

Peter Pauper Press: For excerpts from *The Songs of Sappho*, translated by J. M. Edmonds. (Peter Pauper Press, Mt. Vernon, N.Y.)

W. B. Saunders Company: For excerpts from *Sexual Behavior in the Human Female* by Alfred Kinsey et al. (W. B. Saunders Company, 1953)

United Church Press: For excerpts from *Making Sexuality Human* by W. Norman Pittenger (Philadelphia: Pilgrim Press). Copyright © 1970 United Church Press. For excerpts from *The Same Sex: An Appraisal of Homosexuality*, edited by Ralph W. Weltge (Philadelphia, Pilgrim Press). Copyright © 1969 by United Church Press.

It is only with the heart that one can see rightly; what is essential is invisible to the eye.

Antoine de Saint-Exupéry
The Little Prince

Acknowledgments

No one writes a book such as this without being greatly in the debt of many people who gave freely of their expert knowledge and valuable time. I would here like to express my particular gratitude to the following:

Dr. Joseph Fletcher, University of Virginia; Reverend Dr. Herbert Rodgers, S.J., Fordham University; Dr. Paul Lehmann, Union Theological Seminary, New York; Rabbi Charles Sheer, Columbia University; Dr. Theodore H. Gaster, Barnard College; Dr. Robert Johann, Fordham University; Reverend Howard Wells, Metropolitan Community Churches, New York; Reverend Father Robert Clement, Church of the Beloved Disciple, New York; Reverend Canon Walter D. Dennis, The Cathedral Church of St. John The Divine, New York; John V. P. Lassoe, Jr., Assistant to the Bishop, Episcopal Diocese of New York.

Equal gratitude goes to Dr. Margaret Mead; Dr. Carol Diakow, The Rockefeller University; Dr. Judith Blake, University of California at Berkeley; Dr. Lester Aronson, American Museum of Natural History; Mrs. Lee Mackler, Postgraduate

Center For Mental Health, New York; Barbara Bronson Fox, Postgraduate Center for Mental Health, New York; Dr. Bertha Harris, University of North Carolina at Charlotte; Dr. Barry Ulanov, Barnard College; Dr. Esther Newton, New York University; Frederica Leser, American Museum of Natural History.

Additionally, I am much indebted to: Dr. Judd Marmor, University of Southern California at Los Angeles; Dr. Martin Hoffman, University of California at San Francisco; Dr. John Money, The Johns Hopkins University and Hospital; Dr. Lewis Wolberg, Postgraduate Center for Mental Health; Dr. Bernard F. Riess, Postgraduate Center for Mental Health; Dr. Ralph Gundlach; Dr. Laura Perls; Dr. Jean Mundy; Dr. William T. Bourke; Bernice Goodman, M.S.W. of The Institute for Human Identity, New York; Dr. Elaine Marks, University of Massachusetts; Richard Tedesché, University of Massachusetts.

A very special thanks goes also to the groups of women who graciously allowed me to attend and record their group discussions. A particular appreciation is also expressed to Dr. Jeanette H. Foster for the unique and pioneer work done in her book *Sex Variant Women In Literature,* and to Gene Damon and Lee Stuart who prepared an exhaustive bibliography entitled *The Lesbian In Literature,* published by *The Ladder.* Without these two splendid reference sources the literature chapter would have been very difficult indeed.

Contents

Introduction

In 1971 a national woman's magazine (not *Ms*) asked me to write an article on lesbianism. Since I had done many articles on psychology and medicine as they relate to contemporary family life and social attitudes, the subject interested me. I was concerned, however, that the magazine might try to use the article exploitively. With assurances that I would have a free hand to report the subject honestly and sensitively as I found it, I agreed. After several weeks of extensive research and interviews, I wrote the article. The magazine then began to hedge on their agreement—the idea of sensationalism was too tempting—and I withdrew the article.

The things I had discovered, however, in the course of my research—the shocking misinformation that is circulated in the areas of medicine, psychology and social anthropology, and the outrageous misinterpretations of religious material—were of such importance and so fascinating that I felt only a book was adequate to present the true picture, and I also felt there was a real need for an honest and thorough exploration of the subject. My research into the subject had convinced me that there is actually no such thing as heterosexuality or homosexuality; there is only *sexuality,* upon which has been imposed a social and moral structure which demands sharply defined sex roles and ritual sexual behavior. Studies in animal behavior, psychology and anthropology have showed that most of the mammalian species, including man, can and do respond sexually to a variety of stimuli without respect to sexual differentiation.

I learned from Biblical scholars just how effective religious doctrine and its followers have been in selecting obscure passages which were often taken out of context and misinterpreted to justify condemnation or inhibit sexuality in general and homosexuality in particular. This material was not only questionable in meaning and interpretation, but in some instances represented nothing more than interim ethics: ethics applicable to that time and that place and totally irrelevant to this day and age; ethics which were calculated to preserve and protect the strength and unity of the Hebrew people in exile in a pagan land. The logical place to begin unraveling the maze of misinformation, misunderstanding and misinterpretation which has surrounded the subject of sexuality and homosexuality seemed to be where it originated—with the Bible and the church.

My research led me to explore several of the strategic popular myths: the Sodom Myth, the Genesis Myth, the Original Sin Myth. Perhaps the motivation for most of our moral condemnations and much of our social prejudice stems directly or indirectly from one of these three. For example, many fine scholars do not believe the sin of Sodom and the cities of the plains was homosexuality; they believe the sin being identified there was that of idolatry. Idolatry was, of course, the most serious of sins; it would make much more sense to think that God might destroy cities so violently for such a crime against Him. The Genesis Myth involves the order of creation—Adam first, then from Adam's rib to Eve. Many scholars claim that man, Adam, was not created first—that Adam and Eve were one and the same, having both sexes and no sex, a sort of hermaphrodite, until they were separated at a later date for purposes of companionship. Even then Eve was not a child-bearing woman in the conventional sense and did not become so until God decided that they should "be fruitful and multiply, and replenish the earth and subdue it." How else could the earth be subdued unless populated, and unless populated how else could the grand and divine experiment be carried out; for God had chosen man to be the most superior of his created creatures and had created him in His own image. But to construe this necessity for population in the beginning of the world into a moral law and sexual ethic for all time seems absurd, and particularly absurd in terms of the population crisis presently facing mankind.

As for the Original Sin Myth—that Adam in the incident at Eden demonstrated man's true nature—it is erroneous in the first place, and irrelevant in the second, in view of the doctrine of the Second Adam. The Second Adam, or Christ, wiped the slate clean and brought universal forgiveness to all men through His martyrdom—as clearly documented by St. Paul himself in Romans 5. According to St. Paul, man takes his nature not from primal Adam but from the Second Adam, Jesus Christ—an altogether different proposition. For one thing, it gives man back his dignity and respect; he need no longer bear the burden of original sin—that sin presumably bequeathed to him by primal Adam.

What is the overall significance of the exploration of these myths? The realization that these rigid concepts so long preached and accepted are myths, not facts, and in being myths are subject to interpretation and distortion and therefore open to question. Myths are not facts, and when exploration reveals that the questioning and scholarship of renowned Biblical scholars supports a different interpretation and viewpoint, one is obliged to alter one's own viewpoint to see the long-accepted interpretations as applicable to myths and not to facts, and therefore to be considered in the realm of theory. Wherever there is one theory being held, it is the nature of intellect and reason to explore an opposing theory. Much of the Bible was handed down by word of mouth, and across the centuries interpretations and theories have been applied to most of it—that too is the nature of mind and individuality. Additionally, certain later passages in the New Testament seem to alter or contradict interpretations of passages in the Old Testament—as in the case above mentioned of St. Paul's reference to the Second Adam. The knowledge of scholarly opposition to accepted interpretations strips the church of weapons long used for power over and therefore control of man. These realizations eliminate Biblical justification for the oppression or harassment of people who may be different, or do not conform to the same ideas as some other people. They may also, hopefully, encourage the prejudiced to think for themselves . . . to question why they believe the things they do, and where their ideas came from. As Dr. Judd Marmor has said: "Being prejudiced is being down on something you're not up on."

As a result of my explorations of this entire subject, I came to despair of religious orthodoxy and psychiatric orthodoxy as well. It is my belief that neither institution will accept reform in this area until and unless it is forced upon them. Perhaps it is too much to expect the church to be in touch with reality, but certainly one has the right to expect it of psychiatry. The new and exciting theories and studies that have been done in the field of psychology and sexuality are totally ignored by many of orthodox persuasion. In some instances, doctors are not even aware of the new innovative work that has been and is being done. But, every field has its reactionaries, and alas, it seems that psychiatry is not an exception.

Even though I despair of the institutions of orthodoxy, I also find reason for hope in the independent and enlightened people working within the confines of the establishment, and in the younger people who will someday control. I came to respect and admire courageous individual clergymen who have elected to act independently in administering to congregations and parishes in terms of need and relevancy, opposing their religious hierarchy. They say they "haven't time to wait for institutional reform—the need is now." I also have the same respect and admiration for questioning, innovative, realistic and aware therapists who are breaking new ground, and not only coming up with theories, but with clinical evidence to support the theories.

Fiction was also explored for incidents of lesbianism or sexual variance. From Sappho onward, an astounding number of books have been written which involve homosexual characters and relationships. Some are amusing, some sophisticated, some worldly, some tragic, some banal, but all are fascinating from one standpoint or another. Many fine writers, and a great many not-so-fine writers, whom we are familiar with in literature have produced works containing overt, covert and even unconcious acts of variance. Many works were uncovered that have never been heard of except by literary scholars, works from the sixteenth, seventeenth, eighteenth and nineteenth centuries. Tracing the course of this fiction over the centuries, we can observe the change which has occurred in literature as our society has become more sophisticated and aware. Lesbian characters begin to be presented more realistically, more sympathetically and more humanly.

Thus, having explored the areas out of which the old shibboleths on homosexuality have grown—Biblical, psychological, genetic, anthropological and literary—I also thought that an exploration could not be complete and valid without exploring the subject with persons of homosexual life style. Since few studies have been done on the female homosexual, and quite a lot have been done on the male homosexual, I chose to concentrate on the lesbian life style. Too many theories have been advanced in the past without truly representative cross sections of homosexuals—ostensibly healthy, constructive, successful, and making it out in the everyday world. Hours were spent in group discussions with Lesbians on their life styles and verbatim tapes of those discussions are presented here without editing. They represent the raw gut feelings—the subtleties, sensitivities, pressures, sorrows, loves, hates and hostilities of women who know what it's all about.

Hopefully this exploration will help create a more constructive climate for mutual coexistence. People fear what they do not know about, and when they do not know, what they imagine is always distorted. As will be stated by experts in the context of the book, only when people of varying life styles feel free to come into the open—where they can exhibit their humanness, their worth and their usefulness to society—can people get to know them, stop mis-imagining, and realize that they can accept people who chose a different way of life without any threat to themselves or society. Then they will realize the truth of Dr. John Money's statement: "Homosexuals are just like everybody else, only more so." That is why I have written *The Lesbian Myth.*

Bettie Wysor

10 January 1973
New York City

PART ONE

The Scholars:
Theology, Science,
Literature

Chapter 1

The Word,
the Church
and Sexuality

> Mark you this, Bassanio,
> The devil can cite Scriptures for his purposes,
> An evil soul, producing holy witness,
> Is like a villain with a smiling cheek;
> O, what a goodly outside falsehood hath!
>
> William Shakespeare
> *The Merchant of Venice*

In this, the last quarter of the twentieth century, which has seen fantastic advancements in science, medicine and technology, and some progress in civil rights, the United States of America remains morally naïve, sexually adolescent, spiritually impoverished and humanely antiquated. We have excelled in the development of our exterior life, all too often leaving our interior selves to develop without direction or adequate nourishment. We are peoples alienated from ourselves, our fellows, our God, and especially from the church.

The blame for much of our condition lies at the door of the church and organized religion. The moral precepts and social values that restrict and confuse our lives have their basic foundation in religion. To many, the church seems remote and very nearly irrelevant to contemporary life, while paradoxically remaining an insidious influence that prevents us from gaining the emotional and sexual maturity necessary for the building of more meaningful and rewarding lives.

At the root of the church's influence is its amazing success at convincing man of his basic unimportance as a creature on earth, and of his base and evil nature. This has robbed man of his basic respect for himself, left him uncertain of even his spiritual nature, and saddled him with guilts and fears that have sent him floundering into the arms of psychoanalysis. The fact is, the church left man, all but driving him away with its inhumane irrelevancy. In its struggle for power, orthodoxy constructed an episcopacy of awesome rule, and a theology of rigid and complex legalistics that strangled spiritual progress and understanding, and imprisoned the minds of men and women, making possible a world in which confusion, prejudice, bigotry and man's inhumanity to man could fester and grow.

Steeped in Old Testament laws and New Testament Epistles, formal religion has forbade prospective examination of these laws in terms of contemporary relevancy and the interim ethics which they represented. In all probability the early laws were reasonable and necessary, given the times and conditions for which they were made, but what do they mean to us in the hydrogen-bomb, industrial, contraceptive twentieth century?

Those same early laws, however, are still being stubbornly shoehorned onto contemporary life, and both the church and society have consistently invoked them to restrict, to condemn, to whitewash what might otherwise appear to be inhumane, selfish and possibly reprehensible acts. Some excellent examples of its irrelevancy are the church's positions on birth control, legalized abortion, divorce reform, equality of women, legalized homosexuality between consenting adults. All of these have been opposed by the formal church body while it cited scriptures as the justification for its actions. When these issues have come before governing bodies for revision, individual legislators quite frequently have tried to vote out of humane and intelligent conviction, while others have bowed under the "righteous" pressures of their constituencies or out of their own prejudices. Because of their convictions, some courageous and civilized legislators have found themselves the victims at the polls in the next election.

On many of the issues of reform, if the church had lent its support, it would have swayed the tide, and helped to give individuals their civil rights, their dignity and the freedom to direct their own lives. Sane, mature and just attitudes, rather than fear and so-called righteous emotion, would have prevented much human agony—in some cases, even criminal exploitation—and would have made the church relevant to contemporary life.

However, that is not the name of the game. Our lives continue to be dogged by repressive laws of religious origin. Where do they come from? Many reach back to the ancient Jews, especially under the post-exilic Maccabean and Pharisaic leadership. These peoples lived by the law of the Torah, and its oral tradition (Halakah). It was a code of 613 (or 621, depending on the scholar) precepts, amplified by an increasingly complicated mass of Mishnaic interpretations and applications, all tremendously complex, as has been pointed out by Dr. Joseph Fletcher in his book *Situation Ethics:*

> Statutory and code laws inevitably pile up, ruling upon ruling, because the complications of life and the claims of mercy and compassion combine—even with code legalists —to accumulate an elaborate system of exceptions and compromise, in the forms of rules for breaking the rules! It leads to that tricky and tortuous now-you-see-it, now-you-don't business of interpretation that the rabbis called pilpul—a hairsplitting and logic-chopping study of the letter of the law, pyramiding from codes (e.g., the Cove-

nant and Holiness) to Pentateuch to Midrash and Mishna to Talmud. It was a tragic death to the prophets' "pathos" (sharing God's loving concern) and "ethos" (living by love as *norm,* not progress). With the prophets it had been a question of sensitively seeking "an understanding of *the situation.*" (1)

The stage was set, then, for the certain mystification of man, and there has been little willingness since that time to relinquish that power over man. Even the Christian Church is still dogged to death by legalistic machinations of a church hierarchy drunk on the unquestioning power of the Middle Ages.

There are, however, many enlightened, questioning, thinking scholars and clergymen today. In a personal interview in the spring of 1972, Dr. Paul Lehmann, professor of systematic theology at Union Theological Seminary in New York City, spoke about the laws contained in the Old and New Testaments: "There are two points to consider when one speaks of the laws and precepts of the Old and New Testament. One point is the simplistic way in which it has often been suggested that all a person has to do is read the Old Testament and then he knows what to do. And the corollary of that is the kind of literalism in which one reads all the New Testament as though it were the telephone directory. Then the obvious predicament occurs, if you really do read the New Testament, and you still remain puzzled, then the answer is, you haven't tried hard enough. So you are rather damned if you do, and damned if you don't.

"In thinking this over, it occurs to me that that really wasn't the way the thing came about within the New Testament itself. It seems to me that one of the things that the higher criticism of the scriptures freed us for was understanding the Bible within the original context out of which it emerged. Accordingly, if one tried to remember that the commandments of the Decalogue or the teachings of Jesus were as problematical for the people who first received them or heard them as they are to us today. . . .

Then, you see, one is free from certain simplistic readings of the New Testament criteria for what Christians are up to. But, more important, one is freed for a kind of relationship with the people back there, and can begin to share a predicament."

Dr. Lehmann describes a reasonable attitude of reference that we can relate to, the New Testament. Basically, our New Testament is a guide for or method of relating to the people back there: seeing them as sharing a predicament with us, trying to catch a clue as to how to deal with a contemporary problem, and how to understand the commandments and the teachings of Jesus. This is a reasonable point of view which one can credit, whereas the idea of applying two-thousand-year-old commandments literally to our day and age is totally unreasonable. No intelligent, rational person would consider applying an agrarian-economy procedure of two thousand years ago to the industrial, hydrogen age. Nor are the emotional circumstances of our lives today any more similar to those of that period; yet many people try to make ancient ethics and morality apply literally to today's varied life styles.

Dr. Lehmann stated emphatically that in his opinion the Ten Commandments were not a prescription for right and wrong actions. Why then, one wonders, is it so difficult to get people to question with an eye to relevancy? Are people's brains paralyzed by Biblical trappings? Certainly there is no area of life where there is more Biblically induced paralysis than in the area of human sexuality. The sternest prohibitive laws of the church relate directly or indirectly to human sexuality. Sexuality is almost irrevocably hitched up to the Bible and morality. Putting it mildly, from the church's standpoint sex is dirty, wicked and sinful unless it is engaged in for the purpose of procreation; then it is a holy act—provided, of course, one doesn't enjoy it too much. But then this fact doesn't surprise us because sex is an important ingredient in the concept of man's *supposed* baseness. We've always been led to believe that without strong sexual prohibitions mankind would resort to outrageous sexual orgies. Why does the church have such a strong, almost psychotic, reaction to sex? Let's explore the issue.

In 1966 Dr. Joseph Fletcher, advancing a theory for a New Morality in his book *Situation Ethics,* wrote: "Judaism, Catholicism, Protestantism—all major Western religious traditions have been legalistic. In morals as in doctrine they have kept to a spelled-out, 'systematic' orthodoxy." (2) Certainly as far as sex is concerned this is true, and it is almost laughable in the face of extensive psychological findings on man's many and varied sexual problems. The church simply buries its official head in the sand and pretends that man is not a sexual being; therefore, there is no problem. This, despite Freud, Kinsey, Masters and Johnson, Havelock Ellis, Dr. David Rubin and others who have done studies and written about sexuality. All have attested to the existence of any number of sexual problems in people which have their foundation in religion and the church. Problems of sexual inadequacy, frigidity, impotency, lack of enjoyment and satisfaction in sex—as a result of inhibitions, guilts and so forth. Freud would have us believe that many, if not all, of man's emotional ills are of sexual origin. The truth is man is just plain uncomfortable with his sexuality, and why wouldn't he be? His sexuality has been moralistically assaulted since well before puberty. The reluctance of the church to accept the fact that man is a sexual being, and normally so, that sexual expression is a natural phenomenon and an integral part of human personality, has made it attach such a stigma to sexual activity that man is damned by the church if he does, and damned by his psyche if he doesn't.

Fortunately, one has an occasional faint feeling of hope when independent, aware clergymen speak out:

> In the realm of human sexuality I, as a churchman, feel moved to confess that a great deal of the blame for preserving, if not indeed creating, the fears and guilt of sex

which permeate our culture, lies at our feet. The failure
to see sexual relationships in any other light but the functional one of reproduction has resulted in the limitation of
sex to the purely physical with no concept at all of the
depth of significant interpersonal trust, empathy and love
of which sexual intercourse, at best, is the expression. Of
course our generation in the Church has modified these
ancient views, but the pall of centuries of sin-obsessed
taboos and misanthropic caricatures of human nature
still blankets our culture and informs our mores. The current reduction of sexuality to the status of experience
devoid of relationship and responsibility, to a biological
function needing only satisfaction, to a medium for mass
marketing, seems to me to be only the expected result—
the acting out of a low view of sex which we have
fostered. (3)

So wrote Dr. Robert L. Treese, assistant professor of practical
theology, Boston University School of Theology. Scientists have
continually given specific data which supports Dr. Treese's
contention. In their studies of sexual inadequacy—specifically
those concerning the occurrence of primary impotency in males
—Masters and Johnson state:

Negation of the young man's potential for effective sexual
functioning has been thought to originate almost entirely
in derogatory influences of family background. Without
denying the importance of familial investment, the natural
social associations of the adolescent as he ventures from
his security base are statistically of major importance. The
etiological factors that are in large measure responsible for
individually intolerable levels of anxiety either prior to or
during initial attempts at sexual connection are untoward
maternal influence, psychosocial restrictions originating
with religious orthodoxy, involvement in homosexual functioning and personal devaluation from prostitute experience. (4)

Of thirty-two men treated for primary impotency, Masters and Johnson cite six histories with primary impotency "relating to tribulations of virginal men restricted from any form of overt sexual activity during the teenage courting years by family adherence to demanding forms of religious orthodoxy. The six men grew up in households (two Jewish and four Catholic) where strict religious orthodoxy was a way of life. These men, struggling with the repressive weight of an incredible number of behavioral *thou-shalt-nots,* were supported by a negligible number of *thou-shalts.* They uniformly approached their wedding night tragically handicapped by misinformation, misconception, and unresolved sexual taboos." (5) From these studies, Masters and Johnson drew the following conclusion: "Severe religious orthodoxy may indoctrinate the teenager with the concept that any form of overt sexual activity prior to marriage not only is totally unacceptable but is personally destructive, demoralizing, degrading, dehumanizing, and injurious to one's physical and/or mental health." (6)

Correspondingly, of the twenty-nine cases of vaginismus in women studied, Masters and Johnson found twelve examples of "religious orthodoxy as a major etiological factor in the onset of vaginismus. The presence of this syndrome contributed to 9 unconsummated marriages and 3 in which coitus was infrequent. Of the female partners with vaginismus 4 were oriented to restrictive orthodox Jewish background, 6 were products of psychosexually repressive Catholic background, and 2 had the religious orientation of strident Protestant fundamentalism." (7) One cannot help wondering if the hierarchy of the church or the moralistic members of society who damn sexual expression have ever read the books by Masters and Johnson, Kinsey, or anyone else who has written authoritatively on sexual and emotional problems.

The Reverend Ronald Mazur, author of *Common Sense Sex* and *The New Intimacy: Open-Ended Marriage and Alternative Lifestyles,* and director of the Sex Education Consulting and

Counseling Services in Salem, Massachusetts (a Unitarian minister raised a Catholic), put his opinion of the whole issue in language very much to the point: "Unfortunately, most of us have been mindfucked by religion and have been shamed into waiting for sex in the sky by and by. The sterile morality of organized religion continues to blind people in a state of sexual immaturity, denying them joy in the basic pleasures of the flesh, pleasures which make it worthwhile to be human and alive." (8)

The number of persons in psychotherapy due to emotional problems stemming from an inability to form constructive and fulfilling relationships, the astounding number of emotionally disturbed persons not even in therapy, and the increasing number of divorces tell us something, and it certainly isn't that we are more sinful, more subject to the wrath and harsh judgment of God than any other generation.

It is obviously not more blessed to refrain from sinning by refraining from involvement in life. Sexuality is an involvement in life and sex itself is not sinful. "Sin and sex are not identical. To have assumed that they were was the great mistake of many thinkers who wrongly believe that they were stating 'Christian' principles," says Reverend Norman Pittenger in *Making Sexuality Human.* (9)

Over the centuries, however, a lot of people have contributed to our "mindfucking." St. Augustine did his bit by equating sexuality with human sin and guilt, yet Augustine, like St. Paul, very often seemed to be saying two things at once, as Reverend Pittenger points out when he calls attention to Augustine's contention that "human sexual instincts, drives, and desires are utterly central and enormously important as indicative of what man *is,* what God purposes for man, and what is the highest and best human possibility." (10)

Absolutely germane to the whole sexual/procreative patchwork is St. Paul's often-quoted statement: "It is better to marry than to burn." The statement gets all tangled up in various interpretations with sexual connotations and has sometimes been construed to mean that if you must marry to satisfy sexual desires, then Paul is saying that sex is only permissible within the context of marriage. Dr. Lehmann disagrees with that interpretation, as do some other scholars and individual clergy. Given, however, the times and the conditions under which Paul was living, Dr. Lehmann suggests that Paul's statement was not referring to sexuality at all, but to a then-current practice prohibiting Christians from marrying non-Christians. In this instance Paul was being unusually liberal and realistic in recognizing the destructiveness that might attend a situation of sexual burning. Paul was actually saying that if you were going to burn to the extent that the burning would intensify emotional frustration and thus contribute to self-destruction, then it would be better to marry the non-Christian.

The amazing part of all this biblical haranguing about sexuality lies in the fact that a great deal of sex of all kinds was going on among the ancient Hebrews, even in Old Testament times. It did not seem to be a very complicated matter. Somewhere along the line, sexuality got extremely complex, and it's been getting more so all the time. In fact, Dr. Fletcher points out that we find nothing in the teachings of Jesus about the ethics of sex, except concerning adultery. While in *Sex Laws and Customs in Judaism,* Louis M. Epstein writes that "the Jew of the First Commonwealth was not morbid on sex matters. He did not treat sex offenses as though they belonged to a special department of human psychology. They were sins like every other sin." (11)

According to Dr. Epstein the radical change of this attitude came about during the Second Commonwealth, which was ushered in with the exile of the Jews. Prior to that time their civilization was characterized by a certain "naïveté and innocence." With the exile they found themselves surrounded by new and strange customs, beliefs, and economic circumstances of which they were suspicious. They found themselves city dwellers engaged in commerce, whereas they had been rural farmers before the exile. This "broader civilization" created a sense of uncertainty in the Jews, "a sense of uncertainty, culminating in pessimism," says Dr. Epstein, "and from pessimism there is but one step to asceticism." Dr. Epstein also points out that uncertainty often produces a "tightening [of] inner bonds, drawing in one's sails, so to speak, resulting in rigorous discipline and legalism. These four, worldiness, pessimism, asceticism, and legalism, had their combined bearing on the sex morality of the day." (12)

Dr. Epstein goes on to expound on the characteristics of asceticism, "which condemns all legitimate sexual pleasure as sinful." He also tells us that these ascetic tendencies had an "unsavory and unreasonable influence upon the contemporary code of sex morality" of the Jews of the Second Commonwealth period. He quotes the historian Josephus, who reported that the Essenes " 'reject pleasures as an evil, but esteem continence and the conquest over passions to be virtue. They neglect wedlock . . . they do not absolutely deny the fitness of marriage, and the succession of mankind thereby continues; but they guard against lascivious behavior of women and are persuaded that none of them preserve their fidelity to one man.' That attitude is also reflected in the Wisdom of Solomon: 'Happy is the barren that is undefiled, she who hath not conceived in transgression. She shall have fruit when God visiteth souls. And happy is the eunuch which hath wrought no lawless deed with his hands, nor imagined wicked things against the Lord.' (Wisdom of Solomon 3:13–14)

"Christianity has perpetuated the old ascetic philosophy and brought it down to this very day," continues Dr. Epstein. "There is no legitimate pleasure altogether, and certainly no legitimate sexual pleasure. It is all of the flesh and as such a defiance of the kingdom of heaven. Celibacy is a virtue in Christian teaching, binding upon the priesthood and recommended to every faithful follower." (13) It requires a very regressive and rigid person to even consider such concepts seriously today. Just such ideas, however, are largely responsible for the sexual discomfort and confusion which breeds guilt and plagues our society.

Equally injurious to both male and female are the attitudes toward women which come from this same period, and remain more than subconsciously with us today. Dr. Epstein tells us that during this period women were considered the perpetrators of sexual evil, tempting and ensnaring man. This same idea can also be traced to ancient taboos of primitive societies. The anthropologist Ernest Crawley brings it out in his monumental work *The Mystic Rose,* as does Dr. Erich Neumann, the distinguished Jungian analyst, who writes of taboos and myths and their bearing on the position of women in his book *The Origins and History of Consciousness.* Take, for example, this passage:

> Blood also plays a decisive part in feminine taboos, which from earliest times until far into the patriarchal cultures and religions have caused men to turn away from all feminine matters as though from something numinous. The blood of menstruation, defloration, and birth proves to men that women have a natural connection with this sphere. But in the background there is the dim knowledge of the blood affinity of the Great Mother who, as chthonic mistress of life and death, demands blood and appears to be dependent upon the shedding of blood. (14)

This alone is enough to frighten a man into impotency, or to present him with a challenge to overwhelm and conquer the women. In either case the results can be catastrophic to meaningful sexuality. This excerpt also illuminates another curious thing: the supposition that men and women are natural enemies, each subconsciously—and sometimes not so subconsciously—fearing the other.

Early Jewish law was quite specific regarding proper behavior between men and women during the woman's menstruation, after childbirth, and so forth. In short, the prescription was
that the male stay away from her because she was unclean.
This was frightening to the male, self-devaluating and inhibiting to the woman. These sexual attitudes can be seen in varying degrees in our culture today; they have gone a long way
toward creating an attitude of uncleanliness about sex, a discomfort with normal biological functions and our bodies in
general. Undoubtedly they played some part in organized religion's rigid attitudes toward sexuality.

They also influenced attitudes toward women in general, and
toward their sexuality in specific. Sex laws were made by men
and have been consistently upheld by men. Since women have
historically been considered the evil ensnarers of men, unclean
and all-consuming, it is quite natural that men would prescribe
quite rigid rules for the *acceptable* behavior of women, both in
bed and out of it. This of course gave men the freedom to behave pretty much as they wished. After all, everyone knew that
the woman was the evil ensnarer; men were upright, stalwart
and clean. No one ever heard of a man being stoned for committing adultery.

Many people still consider it loose and reprehensible for a
woman to visibly enjoy sex. Until fairly recently no one was
concerned—except possibly the woman herself—about a woman
really being satisfied during sexual intercourse. The woman
had been brainwashed not to expect it, and the man felt no
obligation toward her in that respect. A woman was, after all,
an object to be used for male satisfaction. Small wonder, then,
that under such circumstances many women rejected their
husbands, dreaded sexual relations, and were too uptight to
reach orgasm. Submission to the male's needs was a wifely duty.
Now that women have begun to revolt against the chattel role,
have begun to feel that they too have a *right* to expect sexual
satisfaction, a very interesting phenomonon has occurred. Men

have acquired fears of sexual inadequacy and impotence, have become excessively preoccupied with sex, and *advertise* inflated ideas of their sexual prowess. In many instances, and as a result of the extreme attitudes on both sides, sex has become a mechanical, purely physical activity, constituting an end in itself. One wonders, given all the misunderstandings, unrealistic expectations, and hostility between the sexes, how any two people manage to make it work at all.

Women, however, have a long way to go to effect a rational equality in the sex act, and in attitudes toward sexuality in general. Men have had it too good too long, and they can hardly afford to give up easily. Even the law is against the woman. For example, when a prostitute is "busted," *she* is prosecuted, not her male partners. She is the source of evil, not her customer or the racketeer who sometimes profits from her work. This one-sided law must surely have its origin in primitive taboo, mythology, and ancient religious laws. Suffice it to say that prostitution would not exist if there were not a market for it—and the market not infrequently has included the most avid supporters of the strict sexual codes. In discussing the hypocrisy of Victorian morality and the "bourgeois morality, rooted in the bourgeois mentality so dominant in English-speaking lands," Dr. Norman Pittenger offers a specific illustration of it: "The other illustration is the now fairly well established fact that during the latter part of the nineteenth century there were more prostitutes, used by distinguished public leaders who in the eye of the people were supposed to be ardent defenders of 'purity' in sexual affairs, than anyone had thought likely. London was filled with them, and so was New York. Well-furnished brothels, with inmates prepared to give satisfaction to a wide variety of sexual tastes, were part of the scene in the great cities. They provided amusement for the rich and powerful; and it was precisely those men who were generally taken to be stalwart supporters of the conventional sexual code." (15) Fathers sometimes secretly took their young sons to prostitutes to learn what *it* was all about, but girls had no such outlet.

Probably from the beginning of time, boys and girls have been finding out about the pleasure and release of masturbation, yet the sexual code strictly forbade that as well. Both Reverend Pittenger and many psychologists have attested to the damage done by the myths and old wives' tales told youngsters concerning masturbation. "Boys were told that if they indulged in masturbation they would go crazy or damage their physical health. Odd devices were invented and sold to make it impossible to engage in self-stimulation. The harm done to young people was enormous, creating a sense of guilt which was often very serious and might lead to the mental disturbances or physical upset which the practice itself never produces but which fear and guilt can create in any young person." (16)

There is a precedent for this prohibition, of course, in the Old Testament: masturbation was forbidden to prevent the spilling of the seed or the waste of nature. Reference is made in Genesis 38:9–10, the story of Onan's refusal to take his brother's widow unto himself, as was the custom. "And Onan knew that the seed should not be his; and it came to pass, when he went in unto his brother's wife, that he spilled *it* on the ground, lest that he should give seed to his brother.

"And the thing which he did displeased the Lord: wherefore he slew him also." It is from this that the term "onanism" originates which, according to Dr. Epstein: "The rabbis describe . . . euphemistically as 'threshing within and winnowing without.' " He further adds: "There is no definite inference from the Bible itself that onanism as such was considered a severe sin, for the death penalty suffered by Onan was not due to his waste of nature, but for refusing to raise seed for his deceased brother in accordance with the levirate requirement. But the rabbis treat such an act as moral depravity in and for itself, a wasting of nature. They prescribe no penalty, but account the offender as under automatic excommunication until he ceases the practice." (17)

Dr. Epstein discusses later Jewish law and teaching concerning the waste of nature, or the seed:

> The worst offense in this category is self-abuse, or waste of nature without sexual contact. R. Ishmael taught that the command, "Thou shalt commit no adultery," includes lewdness by means of the hand as well. Another tanna applied to those who practice self-abuse: the Biblical phrase, "Your hands are full of blood." (This is found in Isaiah 1:15 in reference to practices by the men of Sodom and Gomorrah.) More explicit is R. Johanan, a Palestinian amora, who says he is "guilty of a capital crime." The Zohar, quoted in our code, accounts it the severest sin of all recorded in the Scriptures. The ethical literature of post-Talmudic days, down to the latest centuries, endlessly harps on the severity of this sin, exhorts its avoidance, points out its dangers to health, threatens dire punishment in the day of reckoning, and pleads for penitence and expiation. (18)

Yet Jesus, the most exalted rabbi of all, said nothing of masturbation. The early laws were predicated upon the ethic that the purpose of intercourse is procreation. Says Dr. Epstein: "Nature has so ordained it by witholding complete satisfaction in copulation until it produces the seed of reproduction. By human design, nature's purpose may be frustrated by the deliberate waste of nature's power." (19)

The spilling of the seed spoken of in early Jewish law is an almost amusing and melodramatic point of emphasis in the light of our twentieth-century contraceptive society. The very acceptance of the use of contraceptives precludes the belief that the exclusive purpose of sex should be procreation; with sexual activity thus detached from procreation, one should be able to accept any sexuality as permissible.

Psychologists have been telling us for a long time that

masturbation is often helpful and therapeutic for persons unable to obtain sexual release for one reason or other: i.e., religious prohibitions, lack of a partner, illness of a partner, or unsatisfactory relations between partners, or whatever. Psychologically speaking, "jerking off" does seem to be a successful release for boys and men. The subject of women masturbating, on the other hand, generates an argument from the so-called sex experts (mostly men), who like to question the possibility of clitoral response to self-stimuli resulting in orgasm.

However, of the nearly 8,000 females who participated in the sample used in the Kinsey report,

> some 45 percent of all those females in the sample who had ever masturbated reported that they usually reached orgasm in three minutes or less, and another 25 percent in something between four and five minutes. The median for the whole group was a few seconds under four minutes. Many of those who took longer to reach orgasm did so deliberately in order to prolong the pleasure of the activity and not because they were incapable of responding more quickly.
>
> The data on the female's speed in reaching orgasm provide important information on her basic sexual capacities. There is a widespread opinion that the female is slower than the male in her sexual responses but the masturbatory data do not support that opinion. The average male may take something between two and three minutes to reach orgasm unless he deliberately prolongs his activity, and a calculation of the median time required would probably show that he responds not more than some seconds faster than the average female. It is true that the average female responds more slowly than the average male in coitus, but this seems to be due to the ineffectiveness of the usual coital technique. (20)

As for the reasons for and significance of masturbation by females, the Kinsey report states that "most females masturbate for the sake of the immediate satisfaction which they may obtain, and as a means of resolving the physiologic disturbances which arise when they are aroused sexually and are restrained by the social custom from having socio-sexual contacts." (21)

In terms of claims of physical harm resultant from masturbation, the Kinsey group found it to be without foundation. The report also discussed masturbation in relation to religious background: "Since masturbation has always been severely condemned in Orthodox Jewish codes, and is similarly condemned in Catholic and some Protestant codes, it is not surprising to find in the case of the female, just as we did in the case of the male, that adherence to a religious faith may lower the incidence of masturbation." (22)

The prohibition against the spilling of the seed, and the messianic pact of procreation between the Jews and God for the purpose of maintaining a strong and sturdy nation for the coming of the Messiah, account for the laws against male masturbation. In the Jewish patriarchal system, men, not women, were responsible for conception. Women didn't really count in any important way, and since men made laws, there were adequate taboos to prevent women from enjoying sex, from receiving satisfaction without male instigation or desire. Therefore, it is not hard to understand how the idea of a woman masturbating would be unthinkable. There is no law about women masturbating as such. That we still cling to these archaic sexual ideas today is astonishing, and especially so when we have the benefit of scientific knowledge, the sane practicality of new morality, and advanced theological thinking storming the ·bastions of rigid, legalistic morality.

Winding up the question of prohibitive sexuality, one is still left with the moral dilemma of adultery. There are strong and stern warnings against it, naturally, and the question may be a lost and futile one. Given the prohibitions of the Old Testament, Talmudic law, the warnings of Peter, Christ and the New Testament in general, and canon law, the church and organized religion are light-years away from accepting the new morality espoused by Reverend Mazur, or the situation ethics of Dr. Fletcher. Within the context of committed and trusting marriages, and constructive and deepening relationships, one cannot defend it. However, one does recognize that there are situations in which it is justified and permissible, i.e. long-term illness of a partner, estranged and unsatisfactory relations, or a circumstance in which both parties agree it is desirable and helpful to their relationship. It is and should be a personal and private affair between individuals.

Perhaps, however, it is by comparison that one does not condemn the adulterer as having committed a reprehensible and unforgivable sin. The late Bertrand Russell summed it up when he said: "To this day Christians think an adulterer more wicked than a politician who takes bribes, although the latter probably does a thousand times as much harm." (23) The inequity of judgment is meaningful. One sometimes forgets that in the church the only sin worse than idolatry is a sin involving sexuality.

Abstinence from sexual expression, within whatever context, the failure to develop total personality and human potential, to give and to receive, to share human warmth, expression, and comfort—to retire from life, as it were—is a regression to infantile existence. The human experience is one of struggle and achievement, ignorance and revelation, questioning and spiritual exploration to expand personal potential and the spiritual capacity. Anything that stops this process is injurious and inhibiting.

Dr. Fletcher has said: "Whether any form of sex (hetero, homo, or auto) is good or evil depends on whether love is fully served." (24) But what our religiously dominated society can not seem to accept is the fact that romantic love and sex are really inseparable, and that it has nothing whatsoever to do with morality or religion.

Chapter 2

The Word, the Church and Homosexuality

In a world in which life so perfectly responds to life, where flowers mingle with flowers in the wind's eye, where the swan is familiar of all swans, man alone builds his isolation. What a space between men their spiritual natures create!

Antoine de Saint-Exupéry
Wind, Sand and Stars

If the church and society have problems with sexuality in general—heterosexuality, that is—think what problems homosexuality presents. Homosexuality constitutes what hundreds of generations have considered an unnatural difference that is intolerable. After all, the Bible, the church, and the civil law have told us exactly what we should think about homosexuality, and do about it. Since it all begins with the Bible, let's look at the Bible. There are exactly seven references in the entire Bible to what is interpreted by some as activity involving homosexuality. Six of these seem to refer to such activity among men, and one appears to refer to women. However, these have been quite sufficient to help generate over two thousand years of condemnation and judgment against persons who express their emotional and sexual natures man to man or woman to woman.

The first mention of homosexuality occurs in Leviticus 18:22:

> Thou shalt not lie with mankind, as with womankind: it is abomination.

Later on in Leviticus 20:13 the judgment and punishment for the practice is prescribed:

> If a man also lie with mankind, as he lieth with a woman, both of them have committed an abomination: they shall surely be put to death; their blood *shall* be upon them.

There are five other references to the practice, some rather vague, others more specific. All seem to be based on the premise that God once and for all time pronounced his condemnation of homosexuality by the destruction of the Cities of the Plain, Sodom and Gomorrah, because the inhabitants of these cities presumably practiced homosexuality. However, nowhere in the Bible does it specifically identify Sodom's sin as that of homosexuality. Perhaps it is important to review the incident at Sodom which precipitated the final judgment.

Abraham, knowing of God's intention to destroy Sodom, pled with Him to spare it, saying: "Wilt thou destroy the righteous with the wicked?" As it happened, Abraham's nephew Lot also dwelt in Sodom. After considerable bargaining, Abraham got from God the promise that if ten righteous men could be found in the city, he would spare it for the sake of the ten righteous. God therefore dispatched two male angels to Sodom at evening in search of the ten righteous. On reaching Sodom the emissaries were met by Lot, who pressed them to lodge in his house. The text runs as follows:

But before they lay down, the men of the city, *even* the men of Sodom compassed the house round, both old and young, all the people from every quarter:

And they called unto Lot, and said unto him, Where *are* the men which came in to thee this night? Bring them out unto us, that we may know them.

And Lot went out at the door unto them, and shut the door after him.

And said, I pray you, brethern, do not so wickedly.

Behold now, I have two daughters which have not known men; let me, I pray you, bring them out unto you, and do ye to them as *is* good in your eyes; only unto these men do nothing, for therefore came they under the shadow of my roof.

And they said, Stand back. And they said *again,* This one *fellow* came in to sojourn, and he will needs be a judge: now will we deal worse with thee, than with them. And they pressed sore upon the man, *even* Lot, and came near to break the door.

Genesis 19:4–9

The visiting angels caused the men to be struck blind; and Sodom's doom was sealed. Lot and his family departed Sodom in the morning and the city was destroyed by fire.

As one can see, the crime is not specifically identified, but the assumption of homosexuality is based upon the use of the phrase: "that we may know them." The sexual implications of the verb "to know" (in the Biblical sense) were established by the account of Adam and Eve as related in Genesis 4:1: "Now Adam *knew* Eve his wife and she conceived and bore Cain." The assumption has therefore been made that the men of Sodom, in requesting that Lot bring the men out that "we may know them," had it in mind to assault the men sexually. But there are theological scholars who take exception to this assumption. The phrase derives from the Hebrew verb *yadha* (to know), and according to Dr. Robert Treese, it appears no less than ten times in the Old Testament to denote sexual intercourse. Derrick Sherwin Bailey, an Anglican minister and author of *Homosexuality and the Western Christian Tradition*, points out that this same verb was used 943 times in the Old Testament, of which fewer than a dozen uses denoted coitus, and that furthermore these latter always refer to heterosexual coitus. Dr. Bailey also points out that another Hebrew verb, *shakhabh,* is used directly to describe "both homosexual and bestial coitus, in addition to that between men and women. Thus there is no necessity linguistically to see the verb *yadha* as implying a desire for homosexual acts, in fact it could well be translated 'get acquainted with.' " (1)

It is not realistic to suppose that people who have long cherished the Sodom story as one of absolute proof of homosexual debauchery, and God's stern condemnation of it, will be convinced by a linguistic argument. It is, as they have been taught, *God's* law, and that is not to be questioned—especially if it provides righteous justification for a *witch hunt* for the homosexual. If anyone thinks the term "witch hunt" is melodramatic, or that the story of Sodom has no modern impact, then they've only to review the civil law and the behavior of some civic officials when confronted by open homosexuality.

For example, in January 1965 ministers involved in the Council on Religion and the Homosexual in the city of San Francisco announced to the police department of that city their intention of allowing homosexuals to hold a ball on their premises. In protesting the occurrence, a member of the police department stated, "If you aren't going to support God's law, we are."

On Monday, November 15, 1971, Barbara Trecker and Leo Standora of the *New York Post* reported a citizens' protest at a meeting of the City Council on a bill banning discrimination against homosexuals:

> Most of the witnesses today voiced opposition to the legislation because of religious reasons.
>
> Cecil Brauniger of Staten Island, who held a Bible while testifying, told the hearing: "God is love and God loves every one of us . . . but God has certain standards."
>
> He said that if the bill was passed, "the same thing that happened to Sodom and Gomorrah will happen here."
>
> Earlier Brauniger's wife had warned: "God has poured out fire and brimstone for this kind of (homosexual) behavior."

But reactions have not always been confined only to words. In his April 17, 1972, *New York Post* column Pete Hamill reported an incident which occurred at the annual dinner and show of the Inner Circle, an organization of New York political writers. Near the end of the second act, Hamill said, "A small group of gay activists began to drift through the audience, handing out leaflets protesting press coverage of their movement. One of them took over the microphone, which was backstage, and started to speak. He was jumped. One eyewitness described to me how six grown men stood over one of the gays kicking and punching him." Further on in the article he reports:

> The City Hall cops—a good bunch of men—intervened. They escorted the demonstrators out of the ballroom, calming things down, planning no arrests. One of the gays was on his way down the escalator, being led by a uniformed cop, when Michael Maye, head of the fireman's union, suddenly came charging after them.
>
> Maye took the gay from the cop, began punching him down and then repeatedly stomped him in the genitals as eyewitnesses told it to me. His duty done, he returned

to dinner. Mickey Maye was once one of the hardest punching Golden Gloves heavyweights ever seen in this town.

Hamill reported that Maye was not arrested, and the incident was not reported in the late Sunday editions of the newspapers. On May 23, 1972, however, *The New York Times* reported that a hearing had been held on the incident before a Manhattan grand jury and that Maye had been charged with harassment: he had allegedly "struck, shoved and kicked" a demonstrator. Maye pled not guilty and was released. Harassment is not legally a crime but is only a violation, such as speeding and disorderly conduct, and conviction carries a maximum penalty of fifteen days in jail. In *The New York Times* of July 6, 1972, Joseph Berger reported that Maye was acquitted.

We all read about countless incidents of harassment of homosexuals by both private citizens and civic authorities; it is not unreasonable to assume that people feel free to persecute homosexuals without fear of civil law or social judgment. After all, don't the Bible, the church and the law seem to offer justification? It's God's work!

This digression into press accounts hopefully serves to illustrate what injustice a few verses from the Bible "often wrenched out of context and interpreted with doubtful accuracy"—as Dr. Roger L. Shinn, a professor of applied Christianity and dean of instruction at Union Theological Seminary in New York, put it in the book *The Same Sex*—can be used to produce.

Let's return to those verses in the Bible and hear the scholars examine that accuracy. Dr. Derrick Sherwin Bailey's speculation on Sodom does not rest on linguistics alone. He develops his theory with the scriptures as well. Although the Old Testament depicts Sodom as a symbol of utter destruction (Isaiah

13:19), and its sinfulness of such magnitude "as to merit exemplary punishment, nowhere does it identify that sin explicitly with the practice of homosexuality." (2)

Dr. Bailey goes back to the sixth-century prophets to shed some further light.

> But in the prophets of Jerusalem I have seen a horrible thing: they commit adultery and walk in lies; they strengthen the hand of the evil doers, so that no one turns from his wickedness; all of them have become like Sodom to me. (Jeremiah 23:14)

> Behold, this was the guilt of your sister Sodom: she and her daughters had pride, surfeit of food, and prosperous ease, but did not aid the poor and needy. They were haughty and did abominable things before me; therefore I removed them when I saw it. (Ezekiel 16:49–50)

There is no mention of homosexuality—men with men, or women with women. But as Dr. Bailey points out, "In the latter verses the words *abominable things* could lend themselves to homosexual interpretations in light of later attitudes toward Sodom, but in the Old Testament *abomination,* or *abominable things,* is the conventional term for idolatry." (3)

This intelligence still leaves one dissatisfied about how homosexuality got fastened onto Sodom. Dr. Bailey believes the origin can be laid to the non-Biblical writings of the Jews in the second century B.C. The Greeks ruled in Palestine during that time; there existed a life-and-death struggle between the more orthodox Jews, who did not want Judaism contaminated with Greek ideas and practices, and the more liberal Jews, who embraced Hellenistic customs and manners. It is no secret to most fairly well-read persons that homosexuality was accepted by the Greeks, but it was one of the most objectional of Hellenistic customs to the Jews. Therefore, according to Dr. Bailey it is during this period that we find the first allusions to homosexuality. He quotes from the Testament of Haphtali, "that ye became not as Sodom which changed the order of nature."

During the first century B.C. and on into the first century A.D. these allusions continued to appear in the writings of Philo Judaeus and Josephus. Philo conjectured dramatically in his description of the men of Sodom:

> [They] threw off from their necks the law of nature and applied themselves to deep drinking of strong liquor and dainty feeding and forbidden forms of intercourse. Not only in their mad lust for women did they violate the marriages of their neighbors, but also men mounted males without respect for sex nature which the active partner shares with the passive. (DeArb. 26:1340136).

Obviously bisexuality is not a modern discovery. It is also interesting to see just how far back and how entrenched is the damning of the active sexual role of women.

It is the Jewish historian Josephus who rises to the heights of soap-operishness in his account of Sodom:

> Now when the Sodomites saw the young men (the angels) to be of beautiful countenance, and this to an extraordinary degree . . . they resolved themselves to enjoy those beautiful boys by force and violence. (Antiquities I, xi. 3:200).

One wonders a bit about Josephus, for he is the same Josephus who defected to the Romans (who also practiced homosexuality) while Masada lay under siege, leaving his comrades, the zealots, to perish. It is paradoxical that a man of such questionable character should set down an account of Sodom that would be accepted and remain to bear witness and to indirectly contribute to two thousand years' worth of persecution.

"Yet," says Dr. Bailey, "Rabbinical literature reflects scarcely anything of this development. With the single exception of an allusion to adultery in the Midrash on Genesis, no sexual (let alone homosexual) implications can be read into these conceptions (Rabbinical interpretations) of the sin of Sodom . . . Traditionally, the offense of the Sodomites was supposed to be that of the dog in the manger . . . The early Church Fathers, taking Philo and other Hellenistic–Jewish writings at face value, set the tradition in the Church for homosexual interpretations of Sodom's destruction." (4)

Dr. Bailey concludes with the following emphatic statement:

> It has always been accepted without question that God declared his judgment upon homosexual practices once and for all time by the destruction of the cities of the Plain. But Sodom and Gomorrah, as we have seen, actually have nothing whatever to do with such practices; the interpretation of the Sodom story generally received by Western Christendom turns out to be nothing more than a post-Exilic Jewish reinterpretation devised and exploited by patriotic rigorists for polemical purposes. Thus disappears the assumption that an act of Divine retribution in the remote past has relieved us of the responsibility of making an assessment of homosexual acts in terms of theological and moral principles. It is no longer permissible to take refuge in the contention that God himself pronounced these acts "detestable and abominable" above every other sexual sin, nor to explain catastrophes and human disasters as his vengeance upon those who indulge in them. (5)

It would be less than thorough to let the matter of Biblical treatment of homosexuality rest upon one disputation of Sodom's sin or upon the linguistic reasoning of one fine scholar. It would hardly satisfy the doubting mind, and there *are* other psychological, sociological and nationalistic factors which should be taken into account. Let's examine a few.

Having fled Egypt, the Jews were a people in exile in

Canaan during the time of the giving of the laws of Sinai which constitute the Levitical text, and out of which ultimately grew the Ten Commandments, the Decalogue. These laws suggested that the Canaanites, a pagan people, practiced homosexuality, as did the Egyptians. Supposedly the Jews did not take to the practice; the mention of it in the Bible is in reference to the "bad habits" of the pagans surrounding the Jews, as a deterrent to prevent them from falling into pagan practices, thus weakening them as a people in exile. In his paper "Toward a Theology of Homosexuality," Dr. Treese refers to these nations: "The fact that homosexual acts appear in a listing of offenses which are attributed to Egypt ('where you dwelt') and Canaan ('to which I am bringing you'), and are considered an abomination raises the question of underlying meaning." In a discussion of the meaning of *To ebhah* (abomination), Dr. Bailey further amplifies on this point:

Research fails to establish any satisfactory positive support for the allegation that homosexual practices were customary among the nations surrounding the Hebrews . . . it is not impossible that the attribution in question (*i.e.* of homosexual practices in Egypt and Canaan) is simply a piece of rhetorical denigration . . . designed to intensify Israel's sense of *national holiness* or separation as a peculiar people dedicated to Yahweh. Supposing this to be the case, it would seem that the significance of *To ebhah* (abomination) in these verses has often been misunderstood. This term, as we have seen, is closely associated with idolatry and designates not only false gods but also the worship and conduct of those who serve them . . . By a natural extension of meaning, however, it can also denote whatever reverses the proper order of things and this seems to be the connotation [of abomination in those verses] . . . Such acts are regarded as *abomination* not . . . because they were permitted by Egyptian or Canaanite idolators (for of this there is not proof) but because, as a reversal of what is sexually natural, they exemplify the spirit of idolatry which is itself the fundamental subversion of true order . . . [these laws] condemn homosexual acts . . . between males as typical expressions of the ethos of heathenism which Israel must renounce no less than religious and cultural syncretism with the nations which bow down to idols. (7)

If one accepts Dr. Bailey's interpretation of the sin referred to as that of idolatry, then the laws become even more inapplicable to contemporary times, and makes the persecution suffered by many homosexuals even more tragic. Psychological studies have shown that much guilt and emotional distress is suffered by homosexuals not only because of society's attitude in general, but because of the harsh treatment they have received from the clergy. If the homosexual feels alienated from God, it is not because he rejects God; his alienation from God is church produced. Case histories have illustrated this repeatedly. Many homosexuals, troubled by their discovery about themselves, have gone to priests and ministers for help and guidance; instead, they have been met with anger and condemnation, and have been made to feel evil, unclean and subhuman. Some relate stories of having been driven from the church by heated and angry rhetoric, the memory of which has taken years to erase, and the damage caused by it even longer to undo.

Discouraged and distressed by the rejection of the formal church, movements have sprung up to form homosexual congregations; many progressive theologians, acting independently, have been working to get oppressive laws rescinded so the homosexual may find his or her way back into the church. Their movements clearly indicate that many homosexuals desire to live their lives in relation to formal religion. Therefore, even if one interpreted homsexuality itself as a form of idolatry, the moves to embrace religion would prove the charge erroneous. Once again, it must be said that it is the church that has come between man and his God. The homosexual has not left the church, the church has left him.

Scholars, however, are still trying to bring some relevant and realistic understanding of these laws to the fore so that the church and society can and will accept the homosexual. Helmut Thielicke, for example, points an accusative finger when he writes in *The Ethics of Sex:* "It would never occur to anyone to wrench these laws of cultic purification from their concrete situation and give them the kind of normative authority that the Decalogue, for example, has." (8)

But it *has* been done. The church has chosen to extract many of the moral laws and precepts from the ancient texts and continues to stuff them into the heads of little children in Sunday school in order that they may grow up sound and bona-fide bigots. The adherence to these so-called wise laws of the ancient past offer a convenient justification for not dealing intelligently and compassionately with elements within the society which because of their *supposed difference* seem threatening. The mass of people will rarely make the effort required for emotional and spiritual growth. It is much easier to accept a package of rules handed out by the unquestionable, powerful institution of the church. What the church and the Bible say—or what some think it says, regardless of how uneducated and inaccurate what it says is—offers a powerful stamp of approval for any number of oppressive and bigoted acts. What is amazing, however, is how careful both church and society have been in selecting the laws that offer convenient weapons. If anyone doubts it, let them read all 640-odd prohibitions, covenants and precepts of the Sinaitic laws. Why have some been so carefully preserved and some so carefully dropped?

Consider the Ten Commandments. Most of us break several of them every single day, and accept the fact with a kind of fatalistic sophistication, conceding that no one could possibly keep them in this day and age. Here, for example, is a list of eight of the ten:

> Thou shalt not take the name of the Lord thy God in vain.
> Remember the sabbath day and keep it holy.
> Honour thy father and thy mother.
> Thou shalt not kill.
> Thou shalt not commit adultery.
> Thou shalt not steal.
> Thou shalt not bear false witness.
> Thou shalt not covet thy neighbor's wife.

How many of us can stand the test of all those commandments? Directly or indirectly we repeatedly violate them, yet we are not outcast and persecuted by society for our violations. If we do murder and are caught, we stand trial, yet we kill in war, and are equally as guilty if we condone wars that kill, even if we do not pull the trigger or release the bomb lever. We will be prosecuted if we are caught stealing, yet we cheat on our income tax and commit other seemingly harmless acts of theft. Adultery has all but disappeared as a punishable sin—except if we get caught . . . and lose our bargaining power in a divorce action. We work on Sunday; few of us are to be found in church with any kind of regularity. All of us tell lies—little ones, big ones, harmful and harmless ones. Coveting our neighbor's wife or husband, envying our neighbors' material possessions—both are fairly common acts.

Finally, in examining the New Testament attitudes toward homosexuality, we find it most strongly stated by St. Paul in his Epistle to the Romans:

> Wherefore God also gave them up to
> the uncleanness through the lusts of
> their bodies between themselves:

Who changed the truth of God into a lie,
and worshipped and served the creature
more than the Creator, who is blessed
for ever. Amen.

For this cause God gave them up unto vile
affections; for even their women did change
the natural use into that which is against
nature:

And likewise also the men, leaving the natural
use of the women, burned in their lust one
toward another; men with men working that
which is unseemly, and rejecting in themselves
that recompense of their error which was meet.

Romans 1:24–27

The same old question presents itself. What did Paul actually mean? Some scholars believe that he was looking for an illustration of man's impaired spiritual relationship with God, and he simply made an unfortunate choice in his use of homosexuality as an example. Dr. Treese believes that was St. Paul's intention, and that he was talking more about man's honoring God as his creator, when Paul refers to man's turning instead to "images resembling mortal man or birds or animals or reptiles (thus God has abandoned them) . . . to the dishonoring of their bodies among themselves because they 'exchanged the truth about God for a lie and worshipped and served the creature rather than the Creator' (verses 23–25). Then follows the verses which concern us: This would-be-autonomous man's refusal to accept his creatureliness by honoring the Creator is exemplified by disorders in the natural relationship of man to woman."

Treese refers to Helmut Thielicke's statement in reference to this question and quotes him: "Because the lower and the higher, the creature and the Creator are exchanged (perverted), the result is a perverse supremacy of the inferior desires over the spirit." In other words, because the Romans had exchanged God for the worship of the creatures, birds, animals and the like, in the eyes of Paul this represented the triumph of physical desires over the elevation of the spirit—God.

Dr. Treese suggests that "Paul could have chosen other examples of human behavior as a means of illustrating the distortions of the Creator's purposes by man's refusal to acknowledge his dependent status: pride or accidie (sloth) would have served as well to point out [what Thielicke had described as] . . . 'the hidden connections between the Fall, as a disordering of creation, and the pathological changes in existence in the world as a whole.' " Original sin is implied by Paul's statement: "Therefore God gave them up in the lusts of their hearts to impurity," which he believed was expressed by their acts contrary to the Creator's purpose. Dr. Treese believes that it is important to remember that "Paul is talking about concrete libidinous acts of a homosexual nature, and is not discussing the predisposition to homosexuality or what could be called constitutional homosexuality, which characterizes some persons"—meaning those persons born with a seemingly natural inclination toward homosexuality, and not those persons who engage in it for purposes of sexual lust and general debauchery. Dr. Treese points out, however, that "the theological issue here is not in the concrete acts, but in the meaning of the homosexual condition, as empirical fact, in light of God's order of creation. It would have been out of place for Paul to have discussed this issue in this particular context, even had he known of the reality of constitutional homosexuality. But the common interpretation of these verses 26–27 of [the first chapter of] Romans I indicating that the homophile has been abandoned by God (unless he becomes heterosexual) is certainly not consistent with Paul's purpose in this whole passage."

Yet that interpretation has been sufficient to motivate the

church to insist that the homosexual conform to heterosexuality or remain in a state of sin and condemnation, and very probably is largely responsible for early psychological notions that the purpose of therapy for a patient who happened to be homosexual was to make him or her into a heterosexual and all would be well. Some therapists, as we shall see later on, still believe in this outmoded and unrealistic concept.

The fuss about homosexuality in the Bible, therefore, is based on the charge in verse 22 of Leviticus 18: "Thou shalt not lie with mankind as with womankind: it is an abomination"; the judgment pronounced in verse 13 of Leviticus 20: "If a man also lie with mankind, as he lieth with a woman, both of them have committed an abomination: they shall surely be put to death; their blood *shall* be upon them"; the Sodom story from Genesis 19:4–9, as quoted in the beginning of this chapter . . . and the brief mention of its destruction in Isaiah 13:19; and the statement of St. Paul from Romans 1 just discussed.

Dr. Treese sums up his attitudes and interpretations on the Biblical materials thusly:

> Even though the two Old Testament verses (Leviticus 18:22 and 20:13) can be considered as of historical interest but not of contemporary relevance because of their setting in the rules for cultic purification, and the lack of clarity in their underlying meaning; and even though the Sodom story has been shown to have been used fallaciously in condemnation of homosexuality; the four verses cited from the New Testament (I Romans 1:26–27; I Corinthians 6:10 and I Timothy 1:1) indicates with no possibility of qualification that homosexual practices were considered by Paul (and the writer of I Timothy) as concrete sins on a par with adultery and murder, as evidence of the original sin with which the human race is infected. The moral question has been clouded rather than clarified by these verses because Paul has indiscriminately painted

all homosexual acts with the same brush with which he paints adultery and murder as acts of infidelity and violence. The theological issue of homosexuality remains unopened in the New Testament.   (9)

This theory might shed light on why there is no listing of homosexuality or lesbianism—in fact, not even sex or sexuality —in the Concordance, that book which is used to assist Biblical scholars in finding instantly any subject they want to find in the Bible. This fact opens the question of why? Is it not there because it really isn't in the Bible in that sense, but passages have been construed purposely to imply it? Certainly there is some reason why the subject has been omitted.

As for St. Paul's mention of women in Romans I, which, of course, has been construed to imply homosexuality among women, he never actually says women *are* lying with women. He says, "For even their women did change the natural use into that which is against nature." For all anyone knows, he was talking about masturbation or frigidity, or God only knows what.

Some scholars do not believe that Paul was talking about actual sexual acts between women and women or men and men in those verses at all. Dr. Lehmann, for example, suggests that Paul, coming out of his rabbinical background, may have been talking about spirituality altogether. He says: "Paul may have been talking about exaltation of the homosexual as the ideal platonic love as against the Hebrew-Christian life style."

If the truth be known, it is very likely that this is the common fear today. One occasionally hears that homosexuals want to make everyone like them. An absurd idea, of course, but what people do not understand, they very often fear. It is unlikely, as has been previously pointed out, that people can come to understand homosexuality in perspective as long as it is illegal and forced underground.

Dr. Lehmann pointed out that Paul would, of course, have

found a conflict with the idea of homosexuality being exalted. "But," said Dr. Lehmann, "to take that conflict and transpose it to another social situation, is not given in the Pauline text. What Paul is really saying, I think, is that the inordinate character of any sexual relationship, which is related to a fundamental distortion about man's relation to God, and leads to the breaking of the covenant, the violation of the First Commandment ('Thou shalt have no other gods before me.')." If so, we're back to the idea that to indulge in homosexuality was to indulge in idolatry. For man to love man seemed to constitute a kind of worship. Man should love God. Where this puts women is difficult to say. Were men not supposed to love women either? Or were women unimportant, and what men did with them insignificant? Was it what men did with men that counted? Yet, it is very interesting and somewhat contradictory to find Paul supporting Jesus' statement: "If you don't love God, you can't love your neighbor as yourself, and if you don't love your neighbor as yourself, you don't love God." According to Dr. Lehmann that was also Paul's view.

What is really being talked about is that the idea of men with men precludes the procreative process, which is part of the true order of things—or the great master plan—and that is a defiance of God's commandment to "be fruitful and multiply and replenish the land and subdue it." One supposes that God did say that in the beginning; obviously this was necessary if there was going to be any population of the land he had created. Faced with the possibility of extinction from overpopulation today, that does not seem a very meaningful or desirable commandment to keep. That contemporary relevant fact seems to let the homosexual somewhat off the religious procreative hook.

Dr. Lehmann was careful to point out, however, that while he couldn't argue that Paul approved of homosexuality, regardless of what Paul seems to be saying in his text, Dr. Lehmann felt that "You couldn't argue that the Christian view of sexuality excludes from the range of Christian freedom a homosexual relationship. What it does is raises a fairly persistent question about whether that mode of relatedness can be humanly fulfilling in the sense of wholeness, and it is implying, rather, I think, the negative answer to that. But it is one thing to have that perspective and another to make all sorts of legal arrangments and social taboos which drive people inside, to intensify their own struggles and agonies, which would be destructive. The problem is, what is the human reality? The human reality is the integrity and the freedom of human beings for each other that is either assisted by or obstructed by any given pattern of relationships." One needs to remember that St. Paul did not have the benefit of what the psychoanalytic world or the anthropologists have learned, of what we are aware of today. The present-day church, however, is at least superficially aware of it, and it has not made a great deal of difference. It has chosen to ignore the facts and its *moral* responsibility toward alleviating human suffering. One point to be considered is the fact that the overlay of social, legal and moral confusion about homosexuality has perpetuated the prejudice. Until recently homosexuals have not dared come into the open, the only way they can come into their own and have their life style assessed fairly and reasonably, along with the rest of society. (There are still psychologists who stubbornly refuse to accept and apply the findings of scientists who have done recent and extensive work in the field.)

To return again briefly to St. Paul, Dr. Lehmann stated that in light of present-day psychoanalytic findings regarding homosexual life styles, he believed that St. Paul might have said something rather different about it. "I don't want to put words in Paul's mouth, but I rather think he would be on the side of freedom and openness for the homosexual and not on the side of oppression, as he is, for the most part, understood as being." (Personal interview, New York, 1972) Dr. Lehmann insisted that while he thought he would not have liked St. Paul as a person, he did, in fact, respect his wisdom and found him a profound interpreter of the human condition. The homosexual clergymen I spoke with shared Dr. Lehmann's attitude toward St. Paul. In a personal interview in the spring of 1972, Father Robert Clement, pastor of The Church of the Beloved Disciple, New York (an American Orthodox Church), and himself a homosexual, put it this way: "My overall opinion of Paul is that he was a great man. He obviously had some hangups about sex in general and homosexuality in particular. We don't anywhere hear of him having been married, having a sweetheart, or anything of that kind which would indicate that he had any close, emotional relationships, but he did a great and marvelous work for the church, in a particular period, of adapting Christianity to the needs of the society all around him. He may have done some damage in doing this, but he had marvelous things to say about love, the whole concept of love, and it should not be disregarded, in context, because we find that he also mentions the prohibitions of things which *he* felt about sexual relationships which have come ringing down through the ages. Unfortunately, almost more held onto than the greater things that Paul had to say. And even if he were convinced of what he had to say, and this has been seen in the light of a man who had gone through a personal reformation—and of course, the reformed person is always one hundred and fifty per cent *more* extreme than a person who accepts something from their own background. And although he had a great many beautiful and wonderful things to say about love—and he was a great man—we must remember, after all, that he *was not God*. A great saint, but not God. He was commenting on what took place around him. But I do not believe that the works of Paul should be considered greater than or should supersede the works of the Gospels.

"The four Gospels show so clearly the beauty of the love of Christ and are certainly not condemnatory. The works of one man, Paul, should be understood in context. It is really like a very simple British phrase—you have to be careful not to throw the baby out with the bathwater. An awful lot of Christians in letting their religion become legalistic, and following the letter of the law rather than the spirit of the law, and using St. Paul in particular to amplify this, are the kind who have lost the Christianity and kept the wrong part—so that everything gets misconstrued. What was important went out of their faith."

In discussing St. Paul, Father Herbert Rodgers, S.J., Professor of Systematic Theology at Fordham University (a man who has worked long and hard for peace, who was instrumental in the beginning of the peace movement at Fordham; a man who has worked equally as diligently for the reform of certain Catholic attitudes toward morality, especially amongst the young priests coming on), took the viewpoint of the relevance of St. Paul's remarks in the same light as he considered the early Sinaitic laws. "The general interpretation of the sin of Sodom is that of homosexuality, but I don't think it is necessarily specific. Of course, Sodom was a Canaanite city, and they apparently allowed homosexuality. They were the enemy, and of course you say the worst thing you can think about the enemy. It's like the old English-Irish thing: 'Tell me what the English are doing, and I'll tell you what the Irish don't like.' I think something of this was going on all through the texts concerning homosexuality. When one goes back to the Sinaitic Covenant there's every indication that here you are dealing with a nomadic people who are oppressed, and outnumbered. A class which wants very much to survive—this above all else. Obviously then you're going to stress multiplying the race. This is the first law. Therefore, sex has to appear predominantly as procreative. Anything else is going to be morally sidetracked, or even condemned."

"The situation then in Canaan was that almost everything was anti-Jewish, or the other way around. So, you find a strong anti-Canaanite feeling among the Jews. This feeling quite probably entered into the law at Sinai about men lying with men. The law was saying: 'Don't be Canaanites.' This of course is speculation on my part. As for St. Paul's charges against homosexuality, you have the same thing occurring. They had the Greeks and Romans to contend with—and homosexuality was accepted among them. Paul was saying what the Greeks and Romans do, we don't do. They are pagans and we are Christians; for at this point St. Paul became a Christian and follower of Jesus." (Only incidently, it might be interesting to know that St. Paul was the only Apostle who never actually met Jesus.)

Christian theologians have discussed the interpretations of the ancient laws concerning homosexuality, but the Jewish interpretation also seems extremely important to explore; after all, the laws began with the Jews.

> Sodomy, or copulation between male and male, was an evil practice in ancient times more prevalent than buggery with beasts. It belonged to the same class of sex perversion, but evidently it was accepted as a pardonable indulgence for licentious rulers and as a natural form of debauchery for pleasure-seeking common folk. Its prevalence comes to light in the biblical stories of the atrocities of Sodom and those of the town of Gibeah, in both of which the mob demanded to be given the visiting strangers for male copulation. (10)

So writes Louis M. Epstein in *Sex Laws and Customs in Judaism*. Dr. Epstein seems certain of what other scholars do not, if they are correct in saying that the Bible makes no specific mention of Sodom's atrocities, nor does it actually state that the mob demanded the visiting angels for male copulation. The Biblical text itself reads "that we may know them"; both Dr. Treese and Dr. Bailey take issue with the common interpretation of "to know," while other scholars decline to take the text literally. Therefore, one might as well conclude, philosophically, that disagreement makes scholarship, and let it go at that.

Dr. Epstein, however, does take it a step further when he states that "it may be taken for granted that therefore from very ancient days sodomy was considered among the Hebrews a severely immoral act." That seems quite clear, but it is somewhat mystifying when he goes on to say: "Yet, no direct legislation is found against it either in the Covenant Code or Deuteronomy. It is only in Leviticus that the law specifically prohibits sodomy and declares it a capital crime." He later discusses the severity of punishment for the act, and the emphasis of it as a form of idolatry:

> In the Bible and the Talmud sodomy and buggery are treated as similar sex crimes, and the assumption is that the one like the other had its origin in the licentiousness of the heathen Canaanites. Again, both from biblical and talmudic evidences, we should be inclined to say that sodomy was also one of the vices which the Hebrews did not adopt to any extent from their heathen neighbors. This statement might be true, were it not for the fact that sodomy was sometimes part of the heathen worship, with male sacred prostitutes known to the Hebrews as *kedeshim* (*s. kadesh*), ministering sexually to the worshipers; and the Hebrews who refused to accept immorality in secular form succumbed to it more readily when draped in religious garb. Thus sacred sodomy, alien and hateful to the ancient Hebrew cult, penetrated into Judea at the time of the early kings from the idolatry of the Canaanites. (11)

The issue becomes slightly more clouded when Dr. Epstein discusses the connotation of *kadesh* at that time:

> In rabbinic times, the *kadesh* in the original connotation, as a sacred sodomite, was entirely out of existence. The deuteronomic law was sometimes understood as prohibi-

tion against marriage with a slave (Targum Onkelos, Deut. 23:18), but more often as containing nothing more than what is implied in the levitical law against secular sodomy. To the Rabbis, therefore, sodomy is sodomy no matter what the circumstances, and the law applies in all cases, sacred as well as secular, condemning both male participants to death." (12)

There seem to be a lot of declarations, disclaimers and prohibitions concerning the practice among the Jews, perhaps too many to substantiate the idea that all the writing on the subject related only to the Canaanite preoccupation with homosexuality, and fear of outside infestation of the Jews. For example, listen to the extent to which the law went to make certain that even the opportunity for such expression should not present itself.

The superior morality of the Jews, thus, is grounded on the rabbinic principle that "Jews are above suspicion of committing sodomy." If the law prohibits an unmarried man to be a teacher of boys, it is because of the visits of their mothers to the schoolhouse, not because of this association with the boys themselves. Post-talmudic authorities, however, advised as a matter of special piety, that there be no solitary association between males without chaperonage, and R. Joseph Karo, the famous codifier, adds: "Especially in this generation, when immoral persons have become more numerous, it is proper to avoid unchaperoned association between males." "It is more than mere piety but actually moral necessity," some rabbis teach, not to permit young people to sleep together in one bed, because it is putting temptation in their way. (13)

That statement seems to imply that there was more to be concerned about than the Egyptians and the Canaanites. It also raises the question of whether or not the rabbis and prophets didn't recognize that under given circumstances, homosexuality was as natural a sexual response as heterosexuality? After all, as we will see, it is only the Judeo-Christian culture which is so irrationally concerned about it. Although in both ancient and contemporary writings, and in fact in those of the present day, the major emphasis is placed on homosexuality among men, there are mentions of the practice among women other than that in the epistle of St. Paul. Dr. Epstein apparently dismisses St. Paul's mention of lesbianism (I Romans 1:26) when he writes:

> Amours between females is not prohibited in the Bible. The rabbis record it as a practice among the heathens and find it implied in the general levitical injunction. "After the doings of the land of Egypt wherein ye dwelt shall ye not do; and after the doings of the land of Canaan whither I bring you shall ye not do, neither shall ye walk in their ordinances." (Lev. 18:3) R. Huna, a Babylonian amora, considered such homosexual practices equal to harlotry and would declare a woman who indulged in it unfit for marriage with a priest. The law, however, does not treat the practice so severely, but accounts it an unseemly, immoral act, which Maimonides advises should be disciplined by flagellation, declaring also that women known to be addicted to this vice should be excluded from the company of decent women. It is reported that Samuel's father, a saintly Babylonian amora of the third century, did not permit his daughters to sleep together, probably to avoid homosexuality among them. The final halakah, however, condemning the act and disposing disciplinary penalties, did not recognize the restriction of Samuel's father or any other restriction against the private association between woman and woman. (14)

The lack of emphasis on female homosexuality may have something to do with the position of the female in general in that culture as previously discussed. Additionally, given the emphasis on procreation, the strong prohibition against the spilling of the seed, and the fact that in the Jewish patriarchal system men, not women, were responsible for conception, it is understandable why there is more concern with the male. Despite the fact that men apparently did find homosexuality attractive, they also must have used women to beget children, for women did, in fact, produce and rear children. Then too, women seem to have lived rather isolated lives, always in semi-seclusion and having no real influence on the society; whatever took place among them could easily be ignored. Feeling isolated from the exalted male society, they quite probably did pretty much as they wished among themselves without being noticed.

It is reasonable to speculate that the serious preoccupation with prohibitions against male homosexuality indicates that a considerable amount of it was going on—and small wonder, given the stern taboos concerning association between the sexes, against women in general and against sexual gratification. These laws and customs show an unrealistic view of the nature of creature man, as well as unrealistic expectations of nature itself. As Dr. Margaret Mead has pointed out, wherever there has been a society which advocates the extreme separation of the sexes, there has been homosexuality.

Yet the Bible speaks of love between man and man and woman and woman. The story of the great love between David and Jonathan, for example, or between Ruth and Naomi, is related with great tenderness, and all the world approves. So far as we know, of course, the relationship between David and Jonathan was a great spiritual love; there is no hint that it might have encompassed physical or sexual expression. Yet both relationships were intense, and our more aware age could be inclined to read more into them. In I Samuel 18:1 it is recorded "that the soul of Jonathan was knit with the soul of David, and Jonathan loved him as his own soul." Further testimony is included in verses 3 and 4: "Then Jonathan and David made a covenant, because he loved him as his own soul. And Jonathan stripped himself of the robe that was upon him and gave it to David, and his garments, even to his sword, and to his bow and his girdle." Later on when Saul would become envious of David and wish his death, it is his son Jonathan who warns David. In chapter 20, verses 16 and 17: "So Jonathan made a covenant with the house of David saying, let the Lord even require it at the hand of David's enemies. And Jonathan caused David to swear again, because he loved him: for he loved him as he loved his own soul." In verses 41–42 Jonathan goes to David in hiding: "And as soon as the lad was gone, David rose out of a place toward the south, and fell on his face to the ground, and bowed himself three times: and they kissed one another, and wept one with another, until David exceeded. And Jonathan said to David, Go in peace, for as much as we have sworn both of us in the name of the Lord, saying "The Lord be between me and thee, and between my seed and thy seed forever." In chapter 23, verses 16–18, Jonathan again goes to David in the wilderness: "And Jonathan Saul's son arose, and went to David into the wood, and strengthened his hand in God. And he said unto him. Fear not: for the hand of Saul my father shall not find thee; and thou shalt be king over Israel, and I shall be next unto thee; and that also Saul my father knoweth. And they made a covenant before the Lord: and David abode in the wood, and Jonathan went to his house." In II Samuel 1:26 David laments the slaying of his friend Jonathan: "I am distressed for thee, my brother Jonathan: very pleasant has thou been unto me: thy love to me was wonderful, passing the love of women." The two men clearly loved each other, but whether this was ever expressed physically, the Bible certainly gives no indication. If their relationship had physical elements, apparently God either condoned or forgave these, as he forgave David many things, even Bathsheba.

In the first chapter of the Book of Ruth, verses 14–22, we read of the great love of Ruth and Naomi. After the husbands of Ruth and her sister-in-law Orpah had died, their mother Naomi instructs her daughters-in-law to return to their people, but Ruth refuses saying: "Entreat me not to leave thee, or to return from following after thee: for whither thou goest, I will go; and where thou lodgest, I will lodge: thy people shall be my people and thy God my God: Where thou diest, will I die, and there will I be buried: the Lord do so to me, and more also, if ought but death part thee and me. When she saw that she was steadfastly minded to go with her, she left off speaking unto her. So they two went until they came to Bethlehem, that all the city was move about them, and they said, Is this Naomi? And she said unto them, Call me not Naomi, call me Mara: for the Almighty hath dealt very bitterly with me. I went out full, and the Lord hath brought me home again empty: why then call ye me Naomi, seeing the Lord hath testified against me, and the Almighty hath afflicted me? So Naomi returned, and Ruth the Moabitess, her daughter-in-law, with her, which returned out of the country of Moab: and they came to Bethlehem in the beginning of the barley harvest."

The sentiments expressed in these Biblical passages are beautiful and noble, and we are moved by them. But there is no reason to believe that in relationships between two men or two women that *include* physical expressions of love, equally as beautiful and noble sentiments are not felt. The human potential for love and nobility is not precluded by the physical expression of love; if this were so, then we would have to say that the same would hold true for physical relationships between men and women, and I don't think any of us are prepared to concede that. It is inhuman to attempt to rule the physical out of love.

We have examined the ancient laws and the historical church position, and we have heard arguments as to interpretation of these laws and the relevance of their application to contemporary life, but exactly where does the church stand today on the issue of homosexuality? What role is it going to play in the rational and realistic acceptance of not only the homosexual life style, but other varying sexual life styles common in life today? How long will it take for that second, and most important, reformation . . . the sexual reformation of man?

Perhaps that reformation is already in progress, and evidence of it will be shown in a later chapter. But before going on to evidence of some clergymen's efforts to bring about a reformation of the church's position on homosexuality, we should explore another theory postulated by some scholars which questions the Genesis myth of creation—the very foundation on which the concept of heterosexuality has been built—the story of Adam and Eve. If this theory, which is discussed below, were to win general acceptance, it could make any other Biblical discussion academic, and would put the question of the accepted "normal" purpose of life to serious question.

The Reverend Neale A. Secor, priest in charge of St. Mary's Episcopal Church, New York City, puts the argument very articulately:

> The temptation of recent moral investigation has been to move on to interpretations of Levitical statutes and of Pauline statements on sexual relations (especially I Corinthians 5 and I Romans 1), and to overlook the basic assumption upon which such later interpretations rest. It does not suffice to demythologize and liberalize later biblical words without first coming to terms with the biblical assumptions upon which the later words depend— thus, the crucial importance of the Genesis myths of creation.
>
> "Male" he created them. "Female" he created them. And in his own image! Male and (a separate) female. Traditional Christian ethics has tended to interpret the conjunctive "and" as a disjunctive "or," so that sexual dif-

ferentiation has become part of the essential definition of man.

So strong has been this conviction of polarity that it has not only been deemed theologically normative for human relationship (a thou to a thou), but it has also assumed metaphysical significance in the very constitution of "man." To be human becomes, by hypothesis, to be purely male or purely female. Only in monogamous marriage desirous of reproduction is this essential duality preserved in proper balance.

In contrast to this understanding, however, one might recall that also in biblical mythology Adam (man) was created by God prior to Eve's separation from Adam; one might therefore postulate that the "essential" quality of the God-designed image is a mixture, or combination, of *both* sexes rather than a strict sexual duality. One might urge that, although the Genesis stories point to an *existential* biological separation of sexual relational *function,* the *essential* mythological separation was of the androgynous "male-female" Adam from God, and not Eve from Adam. (15)

Whatever reason God chose to effect a separation—either of Adam from God, or of Eve from Adam—becomes secondary to understanding the nature of the creature first created. Those of us who were sent to Christian Sunday School were taught that God created Adam and then created Eve from Adam's rib. One was led to envision a sturdy and stalwart man—the master creation of the master creator—who submitted to the extraction of a rib from which the creator might fashion him a wife, Eve; these elements make up a fairy tale to impress any child. A careful investigation of this tale, however, reveals that things just didn't happen quite that way. Granted, the specification of Adam's rib is only symbolic, but the order of the creation is what is significant. The scholars tell us that Adam did not precede Eve, nor was Adam a man: the first creature of creation was both man and woman. "According to one opinion in the Midrash—a collection of rabbinic comments to the Bible—the first human God created was a male-female, a hermaphrodite," said Orthodox Rabbi Charles Sheer, Jewish chaplain at Columbia University. "Man was not created first, woman then coming out of him. Adam was a bisexual creature later subdivided into two sexes. Also, note that Genesis contains two presentations of human creation. In the first sequence (Genesis 1:24–31), man appears as a higher species among all the other species of creation. Although he is to dominate and rule over the lesser creatures, he is simply the last step in the biological chain of living creatures. Like the other animals, he is commanded to reproduce, to preserve his species. The second presentation (Genesis 2:18–25) opens with a soliloquy. God observes that 'it is not good for man to be alone.' Loneliness is the motivation for the creation of distinct male and female species. Man is not merely a biological, natural animal with greater powers and roles in the world, he is depicted as a social or spiritual being who has needs distinct from his biological functions. God therefore creates a second sex to fulfill these unique human needs. At the end of this sequence the text states that man will leave his parental setting and cling to his wife and 'they will be as one flesh.' " This, Rabbi Sheer pointed out, further implies that they were one unit, subsequently subdivided and ultimately reunited.

God then proceeds to instruct his subdivided creatures to "Be fruitful and multiply and replenish the land and subdue it." Doubtless this was the purpose of the other creatures as well. Then what was *man's* very special purpose for being?

Rabbi Sheer continues: "Genesis suggests two motivations for marriage: 1) biological, and 2) social/spiritual. The first function allows for the propagation of the species. Sexuality preserves the human race. (Would this then make birth control prohibitive?) The second function is to conquer loneliness, and here is where the social, interpersonal sexual relationship comes into play. (In this instance, birth control might enhance the relationship between man and woman.) The two presentations of the creation of mankind offer differing, contradictory implications regarding birth control. Here you have, in a word, the basic source of the tension which exists throughout the Judeo-Christian ethic regarding birth control."

This is relevant to the discussion of homosexuality if one accepts man's purpose as only that of procreation. Clearly the homosexual is not fulfilling that purpose. But the spiritual concept of loneliness, the introduction of pairing for companionship, and the very natural development of sex under those circumstances has to be valid for the homosexual as well. He too gets lonely. God has said it is not good for man to be alone. It would seem that the inclination to dismiss the homosexual's need for companionship and sexual expression is the basis for some of the tensions that exist between homosexual and heterosexual, although it is extremely difficult to see why it must be either/or. Aside from the very human need and right of every individual to love, and to find sexual expression, there is the very real question of overpopulation—which as was stated previously, makes the charge of Genesis obsolete today, and again illustrates that many Biblical references, particularly those in the area of sexual relations, represent interim ethics not applicable to this time and this place.

Will this argument satisfy the literalistic mind, or solve the fundamental dilemma of those who must understand man's essential purpose on earth, God's grand plan for man? Dr. Paul Lehmann suggests that God's purpose for man is to make human life more human, and to become more human is to be more mature. While Dr. Pittenger suggests that to be human means to be a *lover* and not merely a heterosexual acting-out-identifiable-object.

Reverend Secor expounds on the Genesis myth, and poses several questions for scholars when he writes:

It well may be revealed by further work by those scholars that Genesis does indeed presume an essential, God-willed strict polarity between male and female, and not just a God-willed functional, relational, rational differentiation. It even may be that a literal interpretation of the Genesis myth will be considered primary for a firm foundation of ethics. It must suffice to say that these issues of biblical interpretation are not fully considered by otherwise thoughtful explorers into the ethical content of homosexuality even though they are very much considered by the very same explorers when they treat the ethics of heterosexuality! At this point, conclusions simply have been drawn too hastily from predetermined biblical assumptions.

Should an understanding of the Genesis myth requiring an essential male "or" female polarity be agreed upon, ethical students in the days of study ahead must still face the next ethical issue: whether the failure of persons to rejoin as man and woman in monogamous marriage (henosis) for the presumed purpose of propagation is a sin which is susceptible to easy Christian "acceptance."

The resolution of this issue is of concern to more persons than just those of homosexual preferences. It is of concern to the bachelor, the unmarried woman, the divorced person, the separated couple, the widow, the widower, and to those young people who in increasing numbers are "living together" or who after a sanctified marriage purposely decide to remain childless. The resolution of this issue likewise has consequences for the behavior patterns of masturbation, sexual abstinence, premarital relationships, extramarital relationships, and nonmarital relationships. Are all of these relationships and all of these sexual practices—along with gender identification and behavior which prefers the same sex—results of the fall? Are only monogamous child-filled relationships expressive of God's essential divine will for man in relationships? (16)

Dr. Secor's penetrating questions illustrate how poorly thought through are our prejudices: how subjective, how discriminating, how infantile. Perhaps one could forgive the mentally deficient for their ignorance, but how can one forgive so-called learned theologians, guardians of decency and humanity, or so-called educated sophisticates, or for that matter, *Christians* (providing they understand the significance of the word Christian)? The Reverend Ralph W. Weltge of the United Church Board of Homeland Ministries, who specializes in the church's ministry to the new generation, views the Genesis myth thusly:

In terms of literature the creation stories are prehistoric sagas, and they include a basic affirmation of the mystery of man and woman. One could summarize the theme this way: God created man as male and female and "it was good." Sexuality is a good gift to be gladly received and duly celebrated. For "it is not good that . . . man should be alone." God intended man to be fully human within his primordial distinction. Man and woman are created for each other, to be one flesh. But they do not exist for each other alone; together they are created for others and for God. Therefore, their existence as one flesh is a prototype of man's love for his fellow-man, and a human parable of God's love for all men. (Genesis 1–2, and Mark 10:6–9)

The creation stories are not descriptive facts, not science or any explanation of nature and its origins. The Bible does not begin with creation but with exodus. These stories are *flashbacks* originating after the exodus for slavery, after the identity of Israel was first formed by the liberation movement. As C. A. van Peursen has noted, "Man acquires his identity by the stories he tells about God." . . . "The stories represent Israel positioning the meaning of sexual identification of God, in the same liberating power who meets his people in the events of their history. Faith transforms old facts with the proclamation that sexual distinction is normative for man. The daily refrain of creation is "it was good." Man also acquires his sexual identity by the stories he tells about God. For on the basis of that narrated norm the family and society will teach and model out the defined sexual roles. (17)

It would appear then that the Bible is not so much what God has said, as what man has wanted God to say. Whatever was said, whether by God or by man speaking for God, the Bible has gone through translations and interpretations, even interpretations of interpretations; it seems likely that each era has left its marks, expressing its unique needs and requirements. One concludes that the Bible is a fascinating book through which we learn about predicaments of peoples of other times and places, their ethics and laws; as Rabbi Eugene Borowitz defines it later on, it is "a book of history," but not a book by which to construct contemporary laws, nor can it be used literally to conduct life in the 1970's. We have seen examples of the different ways in which each significant passage concerning sexuality and homosexuality has been interpreted. It matters little, however, whether it is God, or man as he perceives God, being expressed in the Bible. What does matter very much is the use religious institutions have made of the Bible to forge an instrument of power and oppression.

It was stated in the beginning of the book that the church's basic power over man was attained by convincing him of his unimportance as a creature on earth by virtue of his base and sinful nature, as illustrated by Adam's fall from grace in the incident in the Garden of Eden. Adam's sin was every man's sin, calling down a curse upon all men forever. According to the church, man is born in sin and lives in sin and dies in sin . . . unless he confesses his sinfulness and proclaims Jesus Christ his savior and redeemer. Only in this fashion can he be cleansed of his sins. It is a sermon so familiar to every Christion Sunday school-bred person that without some infiltration of doubt, it can hang as a heavy cloud over our lives hampering us as we attempt to construct a healthy self-image and a code of ethics. Almost no Christian, however, is significantly aware that this so-called curse of the primal Adam was removed by the life and martyrdom of Jesus Christ. Not only was it removed, but God reaffirmed his faith in man as a worthy creature created in His image, by the choice to present himself in the world in the form of the flesh-and-blood man Jesus. This concept is known as the doctrine of the Second Adam. I Romans 5:8–19 gives us a clue to the doctrine when Paul says:

> But God commendeth his love toward us, in that while we were yet sinners, Christ died for us.

> Much more than, being now justified by his blood, we shall be saved from wrath through him.

> For if, when we were enemies, we were reconciled to God by the death of his Son, much more, being reconciled, we shall be saved by his life.

> And not only *so,* but we also joy in God through our Lord Jesus Christ, by whom we now received atonement. Wherefore, as by one man sin entered the world, and death by sin; and so death passed upon all men, for that all have sinned:

> (For until the law sin was in the world: but sin is not imputed when there is no law.

> Nevertheless death reigned from Adam to Moses, even over them that had not sinned after the similitude of Adam's transgression, who is the figure of him that was to come.

> But not as the offence, so also is the free gift. For if through the offence of one many be dead, much more the grace of God, and the gift by grace, which is by one man, Jesus Christ, hath abounded unto many.

And not as it was by one that sinned, so is the gift; for
the judgement was by one to condemnation, but the free
gift is of many offences unto justification.

For if by one man's offence death reigned by one; much
more they which receive abundance of grace and of the
gift of righteousness shall reign in life by one, Jesus Christ.)

Therefore as by the offence of one judgement came upon
all men to condemnation; even so by the righteousness of
one the free gift came upon all men unto justification of
life.

For as by one man's disobedience many were made sinners,
so by the obedience of one shall many be made righteous.

Why were we not taught this marvelous humanity on the
part of God toward his creature? We have been taught that a
man's sins will be forgiven and washed away if he accepts
Jesus as savior, yet nowhere in the fifth chapter of I Romans
V is a condition for forgiveness and grace given; here there is
no inkling of divine blackmail. It is a blanket, universal forgiveness. The slate was wiped clean; man was restored to dignity, and his divine potential reaffirmed by God. In this revelation one realizes that man can justifiably hold up his head and
believe in his divine potential, even relate to his creator directly
without begging leave of church doctrine or clergy. How then
did man become so brainwashed and cowed about himself?

As the young Christian Church grew it came under the influence of Rome, the mightiest empire of the known universe,
and its concept of temporal power. Rome had a very poor idea
of man in general, and magnificent organizational powers. The
church fell under the spell of the empire, and man lost himself
to the church; for the church knew very well that the way to
control men was to take away their dignity and respect, to
make them believe in their unworthiness, in the curse and
wrath that God had caused to be visited upon them. Hadn't Adam
demonstrated man's unworthiness and his true nature when he

disobeyed God and succumbed to temptation? This power-motivated concept has been perpetrated upon man down through the ages; few sermons take I Romans 5 for text. This is very easy to understand: it's too dangerously exciting, too positive and hopeful for poor man, and too likely to give him an advantage over the religious power structure.

The question arises still: What was God's purpose for man, and What does it all mean, anyway—these interpretations and judgments? Dr. Paul Lehmann earlier expressed the belief that God's purpose for man was in "making and keeping human life human," and in his opinion, that was to be achieved by bringing about human maturity through the *new humanity*—the same *new humanity* described in the doctrine of the Second Adam. Dr. Lehmann also writes in his book *Ethics in a Christian Context* that: "The 'second Adam' is 'second', not so much because a 'first Adam' had preceded him in time, but specifically because the real Adam, having come in Christ, is the one with reference to whom it is important to speak about the other 'Adam' at all. Thus a '*christological*' rather than a '*temporal*' relation exists between the 'second Adam' (Christ) and the 'first Adam' (the primal Adam)." (18)

Dr. Lehmann calls attention to Karl Barth's *Christ and Adam* for further explanation: " 'Here the new point is', says Barth, that the *special* anthropology of Jesus Christ—the one man for all men, all men in the one man, constitutes the secret of 'Adam,' also, and so is the *norm* of *all* anthropology. . . . Man's essential and original nature is to be found, therefore, not in Adam but in Christ. In Adam we can only find it prefigured. Adam can therefore be interpreted only in the light of Christ and not the other way around." (19) Dr. Lehmann then goes on to discuss further the significance of the *doctrine* in our lives:

The doctrine of the Second Adam thus fortifies the christological focus and foundation of behavior in a twofold way.

In the first place, the doctrine of the Second Adam means that it is the new humanity which is at once the subject and the aim or goal of ethical action. The new humanity is a present, not a mere future, reality. It has already become a fact with the reality of the life, death, and resurrection of Jesus Christ. Christian behavior is behavior with a *forward,* not a backward, look. And the actions which make up this behavior are significant not in themselves but as pointers to or bearers of the new humanity which in Christ has become a fact in the world and in which, in consequence of what Christ is doing in the world, we participate. (20)

The revolutionary significance of the doctrine of the Second Adam affects, however, not only the doctrinal basis of ethics but also the ethical concern and claim of Christianity. It has already been remarked that Christian ethics is primarily concerned not with the good but with the will of God; it aims at maturity, not at morality. (21)

Having reviewed varied, and sometimes contradictory, passages of significant scripture and found them either inapplicable to contemporary life and morality, or representing a situational or interim ethic at best; having listened to theories of linguistics, semantics, and original intent; and having explored the exciting reality of the Second Adam, one begins to see that one can not rely upon the Bible. Nor can one rely upon the church's interpretations in general without allowing for the working of prejudices, and certainly not insofar as the homosexual is concerned. Therefore, pronouncements on morality that are based upon certain obscure passages from the Bible, or church law, must be seriously questioned, if not discarded altogether. If one must rely upon a historical guide to morality, it would seem more constructive—certainly from a humanistic point of view—to consider the new humanity of the doctrine of the Second Adam; for we have a great need of maturity in all areas of contemporary life, but nowhere is maturity so desperately needed as in matters of morality and ethics.

We also need more humanity in terms of Christian love—or any other kind of loving kindness for that matter—rather than judgmental and condemnatory prejudice; for only Christian love of one's neighbor is consistent with the message of Christ and the Gospels. Emil B. Brunner has said that "love of God, His surrender of Himself to man, comes to meet us in the Man Jesus. To love man means to be united to Him in love. This alone is the good." (22) In his book *Situation Ethics*, Joseph Fletcher discusses the principle of love in Christian ethics:

> Apart from the helping or hurting of people, ethical judgments or evaluations are meaningless. Having as its supreme norm the neighbor love commanded of Christians, Christian situation ethics asserts firmly and definitely: *Value, worth, ethical quality, goodness and badness, right or wrong—these things are only predicates, they are not properties.* They are not "given" or objectively "real" or self-existent. There is only one thing that is always good and right, intrinsically good regardless of context, and that one thing is love.

Later he tells us exactly what he means by his theory and its application:

> When we say that love is always good, what we mean is that whatever is loving in any *particular* situation is good! Love is a way of relating to persons, and of using things. As H. R. Niebuhr once said: "God nowhere commands love for its own sake." It is for the sake of people and it is not a good-in-itself. Neither, of course, is it merely one "virtue" among others, as some pious moral manuals and Sunday school tracts make it out to be. It is not a virtue at all; it is the one and only *regulative principle* of Christian ethics. (23)

Like Dr. Fletcher, Martin Luther, long before, understood love as the super *good,* and saw the conflict that could arise between love and law when he wrote:

> Therefore, when the law impells one against love, it ceases and should *no longer be a law;* but where no obstacle is in the way, the keeping of the law is proof of love, which lies hidden in the heart. Therefore you have need of the law, that love may be manifested; but if it cannot be kept without injury to the neighbor, God wants us to suspend and ignore the law. (24)

We have many laws that conflict with love, and the keeping of those laws causes immeasurable damage to the neighbor. The deprivation of civil rights to many of our citizens; the persecution of minorities: blacks, Indians, homosexuals, conscientious objectors, unwed mothers, women who choose not to bear a child they've conceived and women in general, to name a few. Laws concerning these people often inflict injury, and according to Luther, "God wants us to suspend and ignore the law." But just try it . . . the church will be the last institution to rise to the defense of such loving action.

St. Augustine advised a course of action in determining a man's goodness: "One does not ask what he believes or what he hopes, but what he loves." (25) There is much talk of love; certainly the church talks a great deal about love, but exhibits very little of it in its real and practical application. As has been stated earlier, on issues where the church's demonstration of Christian love would have made a great difference in effecting change in social attitudes and laws, in making them consistent with Christian love, the church has been consistently silent, and especially silent where the homosexual has been concerned. The church misses a great chance to become more relevant and meaningful in contemporary life by remaining silent on highly important social and legal reform. Whereas if the church supported reform within the Christian context, it might very well bring people back into the churches. Perhaps someone should make a *law* compelling us to behave toward one another in a loving fashion, and it might indeed get vigorous action.

To conclude, perhaps the most meaningful Biblical reference one could apply to the homosexual is Jesus' own statement, which St. Paul also supported: "If you don't love God, you can't love your neighbor as yourself, and if you don't love your neighbor as yourself, you don't love God." According to the statistics each of us has a lot of homosexual neighbors these days . . . and how are Christians and Jews who profess to love God going to interpret that passage of scripture?

Chapter 3

Contemporary Church Reform and Homosexuality

The phrase "contemporary church" is misleading, for the church as an institution is contemporary only in that it exists in our time. Taking into consideration all of the elements of church law—basic theology, canon law, major church hierarchy, and the Pope—not one has produced any meaningful advances in attitudes and laws concerning the homosexual to make it contemporary.

The reform—and there is reform—is coming from individual clergy who perceive their responsibility as ministers of God toward the homosexual. These men and women are for the most part acting individually in accordance with their consciences and with realistic understanding of the need that exists. They seem to take seriously their *call* to shepherd the flock—all the flock—and they are tired of waiting for the institutional church to catch up with the times. Because the position of the church, as has been said previously, does not only affect the homosexual in a religious and social sense, it affects civic law which is based on the historic attitude of the church.

The church bears heavy responsibility for our present attitude toward sex deviates and their problems, and for the severe penalties with which the law has requited them for their offenses. "If the church does not bear this responsibility alone, it must certainly share it," said John V. P. Lassoe, Jr., director of Christian social relations, Episcopal Diocese of New York, speaking before the Temporary State Commission of Revision of the Penal and Criminal Code, New York City, November 25, 1964, in direct reference to the revision of the law which cites homosexuality as a criminal offense. The recommendation of the commission was the change of that law to state: "Deviate sexual acts privately and discreetly engaged in between competent and consenting adults should no longer constitute a crime."

The bill was defeated by a top-heavy majority in both houses of the New York State Legislature, but it is not surprising that it was. In a personal interview, Mr. Lassoe said, "We lost on this issue for a number of reasons, but I think the most significant was the absence of substantial support from religious bodies in New York State. To the best of my knowledge, only my department and the Department of Christian Social Relations of the Protestant Council of the City of New York endorsed the change proposed by the Commission; other religious groups either opposed it or, more commonly, remained silent." (It might be noted that Mr. Lassoe's counterpart in the Catholic Diocese of New York spoke against the revision. However, that was in 1964, and according to Mr. Lassoe, the Catholic representative says that he would not oppose that revision today.)

It was the opinion of Mr. Lassoe, and that of others involved in the attempt to revise the law, that the legislators "ran scared" in the face of the opposition. It was felt that many of the legislators had been guided by their own prejudices, but many more were simply fearful of adverse public reaction and perhaps punishment at the polls. Said Mr. Lassoe:

"They needed to be able to say that the guardians of morality—the community's religious bodies—endorsed the change in the law, but the endorsement was not there."

On March 18, 1971, the Council of the Episcopal Diocese of New York adopted its own resolution on homosexuality and the law, putting itself on record and leading the way. The resolution read:

> In matters of private morality, the State rightly seeks to give the protection of the law to the young, the innocent, the unwilling, and the incompetent. However, while adultery, fornication, homosexual acts, and certain deviant sexual practices among competent and consenting adults may violate Judeo-Christian standards of moral conduct, we think that the Penal Law is not the instrument for the control of such practices when privately engaged in, where only adults are involved, and where there is no coercion. We favor repeal of those statutes that make such practices among competent and consenting adults criminal acts.

At this writing similar resolutions have been proposed by the Lutheran Church in America, Unitarian–Universalist Association, The Council for Christian Social Action, the United Church of Christ; recently there have been stirrings in Methodist, Presbyterian and even Baptist ranks. England, however, has made much greater advances. Backers of a bill introduced in Parliament to change Britain's laws concerning homosexuality included the Church of England, the Church Assembly, the Methodist Conference, and leading spokesmen of nearly every other denomination; the Archbishops of Canterbury and York and their colleagues on the Episcopal benches in the House of Lords. The law was changed.

Quakers in England were strongly enjoined to take a practical and Christian view of homosexuality in an essay entitled "Towards a Quaker View of Sex," excerpted in an article by Anthony Grey entitled "Christian Society and the Homosexual."

The excerpt stated: "The kind of morality that includes a vehement and categorical condemnation of the homosexual is not Christian. For it lacks compassion for the individual person and lacks understanding of the human problem." They further pointed out that "homosexual affection can be as selfless as heterosexual affection, and therefore we cannot see that it is in some way morally worse." They continued:

> Neither are we happy with the thought that all homosexual behavior is sinful: motive and circumstances degrade or ennoble any act . . . [and] we see no reason why the physical nature of a sexual act should be the criterion by which the question whether or not it is moral should be decided . . . The authors of this essay have been depressed quite as much by the utter abandon of many homosexuals, especially those who live in homosexual circles as such, as by the absurdity of the condemnation rained down upon the well-behaved. One must disapprove of the promiscuity and selfishness, that lack of any real affection, which is the stamp of so many adult relationships, heterosexual as well as homosexual. We see nothing in them often but thinly disguised lust, unredeemed by the real concern which has always been the essential Christian requirement in a human relationship.
>
> But it is also obvious that the really promiscuous and degraded homosexual has not been helped by the total rejection he has had to face. Society has not said, "If you do that, that is all right, but as to the other, we cannot approve of that." It has said, "Whatever you do must be wrong: indeed, you *are* wrong." Only if society is prepared to revise this judgment and to accept even degraded homosexuals as human beings, can they be helped to face the moral implications of their selfish relationships. (1)

The same article also included the views of a Catholic priest, Father William Dempsey, taken from an article in the *Dublin Review*.

He too regards blanket condemnations of all those who share the homosexual condition as un-Christian:

"A pagan society shrinks from human weakness. In many cases it will tailor ideas to its own pattern of behavior. What it cannot encompass it will harshly ostracize. This is very much the case with homosexuality today, excepting that the harsh rejection has been reinforced by a sterile puritanism found among Christian ranks but far removed from Gospel mandate."

"The attitude here," says Father Dempsey, "is to put the problems of the homosexual alongside the deviance of the heterosexual and ask society why it despises one, accepts the other." And he concludes by asking,

"Will society accept the duty of doing something about sexual deviance which puts the homosexual and the heterosexual in the same clinical department? If not, it faces the unredeemable situation in which sexual ghettos are formed. . . ." (2)

At this time it was generally accepted that there were at least half a million—and probably more than twice that number—male homosexuals in Britain, according to Mr. Grey, and this did not take into account Lesbians. In the United States there is a far greater number. In March 1971 the Reverend Robert W. Wood, pastor of Zion United Church of Christ, Newark, New Jersey, speaking at the Interchurch Center, New York, before the First National Conference on Religion and the Homosexual, stated:

We are here because the church, historically and hysterically, has been *the* greatest antihomosexual force in the history of Western man.

Lest there be any who does not realize the magnitude of the situation, we are talking about a minimum of 8,500,000 adult homosexuals in America today. Whatever can be said about why heterosexuals need or want a relationship with religion can be paralleled for homosexuals. Both are children of God for whom Christ died, both need to know forgiveness and hope. Both will be anxious over the welfare of loved ones, both can be sinner or saint.

With such impressive figures, how can the U.S. church and state retain such unrealistic laws? Only five states out of the fifty have eased their laws (Illinois, Connecticut, Colorado, North Carolina and Idaho), while England, France, Germany and the Netherlands permit homosexuality under the national law. The United States has, therefore, made minimal progress. The same can be said of the church, although some clergymen believe that inroads are being made.

"Churches are showing increasing sensitivity to the harm done by intolerance toward sexual deviance," writes Dr. Roger L. Shinn in his essay "Homosexuality: Christian Conviction and Inquiry." "In Great Britain, after the Wolfenden Report advocated that homosexual relations between consenting adults no longer be considered a crime, the Church of England moved more quickly than Parliament to take up the cause. But the churches are still perplexed and embarrassed by the many issues related to homosexuality." (3)

Commenting on the contents of his essay, Dr. Shinn goes on to say:

> What I have said thus far presupposes no ethical evaluation of homosexuality itself. It assumes only that, whatever judgment may be made on homosexuality, church and society owe to human beings a concern for justice and respect for dignity and privacy. Morality is not a valid pretext for cruelty...
>
> "Christians have prescribed crosses for others while exalting themselves. They have deceived themselves by cultivating trivial forms of self-denial while indulging in frantic self-aggrandizement. They have elaborated heresies that denied the joyful recognition of the good life, forget-

ting that their Lord came that men might "have life, and have it abundantly." (John 10:10)

Christian judgments of human conduct are subject to change. The hastiest glance at history will show such change in judgments of behavior—whether sexual, economic, military, racial, political, or almost anything else. The Christian community, living in history, modifies its judgments—both for better and for worse—in the light of new experiences, new temptations, new insights. But it always—insofar as it is true to its faith—brings to experience the awareness of Christ and of the biblical history that tells it of Christ.

All this means that Christian ethics approaches a problematic situation within a context of inquiry that in some important way is given. There is a discipline of Christian inquiry. The Christian community does not ask simply how men may have most fun or use up most consumer goods or lead the most untroubled lives. It does not even ask how they may achieve the fullest self-expression or happiness. It is concerned for the good of man, not for abstract causes. But in searching for the good of man it sees cruciform patterns in life. "If any would come after me, let him deny himself and take up his cross and follow me. For whoever would save his life will lose it, and whoever loses his life for my sake will find it." (Matt. 16:24–25) But the recognition of a cruciform quality in life, despite its history of distortions, is inherent in Christian ethics. It distinguishes the Christian ethic from the most prevalent alternative in Western culture, the ethic of self-realization that extends from Aristotle to contemporary philosophy.

This ineradicably theological factor in Christian ethics does not of itself provide many precise ethical judgments. Certainly it does not prescribe a code of behavior for contemporary man. If anybody thinks that it does, he might try to answer the simple question "Where?" He can hardly locate the authoritative code in the teachings of Augustine, Thomas Aquinas, or Calvin. If he proposes the Bible, again the question is "Where?" Does any contemporary person take the book of Leviticus as an adequate guide for the ethical perplexities of contemporary urban life? Or, to use a more embarrassing example, does anyone so take the Sermon on the Mount? Certainly there is no automatic process by which a believer can lift out of biblical or historical tradition a moral commandment to meet a contemporary perplexity. (4)

Dr. Shinn sums up with the following: "As Christians seek better understanding on this issue, they have a responsibility to remain open to any new source of information and insight. They have a similar responsibility to remain faithful to the moral apprehensions of the Christian gospel. Among those apprehensions those that have been most neglected in the past practice of the church in this sphere are the sensitivities that warn against condemnation and that evoke compassion." (5)

Many individual practical clergy working at the parish and community level have freed themselves from the religious legalistics of the past, and have formed a realistic situational theology. The widespread use of readily available contraceptives, which we have for the first time in the history of Western man, precludes procreation as the only motivation for sex, and therefore requires that any thinking individual evaluate all sexuality according to the same criterion—that being whether it is good or evil, kind or cruel in its motivation. In the words of Dr. Joseph Fletcher: "Whether any form of sex (hetero, homo, or auto) is good or evil depends on whether love is fully served."

Ronald Mazur, a Unitarian minister, carried his acceptance of the homosexual a step further when he remarked in a telephone interview in fall of 1971: "I think homosexual life styles are an option for us. We do not have to accept the negative judgment of our society that has seen this subject in the light of other criteria. We can realize that we can be whole human persons and still reach out to members of our own sex in a loving, sexually intimate way. This relationship is as humanly valid as a heterosexual relationship. It seems to me, that as we increasingly seek new forms of human relationships, we will value these relationships wherever lovingness, loving-kindness, gentleness or sensitivity is found—whether with the same sex, or the other sex."

Some clergymen are realistic about acceptance of the homosexual, as in the case of Father Herbert Rodgers at Fordham University (personal interview, spring of 1972). "The most important question on this subject is a practical one. If you get somebody who is objecting to homosexual practices, you say very well, what do you do? Here is a homosexual. What are you going to do? Execute him? Imprison him? Transform him into a heterosexual? Very unlikely. Transformation is a long and expensive psychological process, and the chances are he is too old to change anyway. Or are you going to suggest complete abstinence from sexual activity? Or just let him alone? It seems to me the only thing to do is the latter."

When asked about the possibility of a church theology on homosexuality, Father Rodgers answered: "Of course you don't prescribe for anybody—you try to find out what the person himself thinks, what he feels, what he needs. It's the question of identity and freedom of choice. This is the really important thing. This issue, it seems to me, is parallel to something a Mother Superior from Brazil said to me at a meeting in Mexico City about eight years ago. She said: 'Do you realize that the rules for nuns were written by priests?' I hadn't realized it up to that point, and it was staggering to me. What does a priest know about being a nun?

"It is the same as a heterosexual writing for a homosexual, or a man writing for a woman. This is bad thinking. If you're going to have a morality for homosexuals, then have the homosexuals write it. Listen to them and find out what is possible. If you write the whole thing off as immoral to start, you can't evaluate things. Under those rules, a very beautiful relationship of twenty years standing between two people is considered as evil as a one-night stand.

"If you condemn all homosexuals, you simply can't evaluate. You're putting a homosexual male hustler on the street, who is illegal being homosexual, in the same category as a man or woman who has been very useful, has a good profession, has been a contributing member of the community. You're lumping them altogether, if you go by the present rules. This is wrong, it really doesn't make sense."

Father Rodgers then spoke about that inevitable subject of procreation: "Once you get away from sex having its purpose procreational, then the most moral way of thinking of it is in the perfecting and developing of the personality in terms of love. You can't apply this attitude only to the heterosexuals. Are you going to say to the homosexual, you can't love? That is a terrible thing to say to anyone. Who are we to dictate? If you try to put him or her into a situation of heterosexuality, this is not right for this person. This is not natural for this person. And when you think the alternative is nonloving, then I think the choice becomes pretty clear."

Did Father Rodgers accept homosexuality as a life style? He answered: "We can't think of homosexuality without thinking of it as a life style. That involves not simply what two people do physically, but the whole way of life. Unless we're prepared to accept that, then we're going to ask people to camouflage, to be insincere, to be hypocritical about some of the most important facts of their existence. My comment on this, now, in the midst of it all, is that if you force a homosexual to lie about himself, he breaks the commandment 'thou shalt not lie.' You force him to become a dishonest person. There's no commandment that says thou shalt not love, there's no commandment of the entire ten that we use today that says thou shalt not love thy kind—the Laws of Sinai say that, but the

Ten Commandments don't. So if the homosexual has to hide, then he breaks commandments that we supposedly take our moral precepts from."

At Fordham, Father Rodgers has been conducting seminars for young priests and seminarians to prepare them to deal with homosexuality as they will meet it. Participating in these seminars are eminent psychologists, psychiatrists, social workers, members of counseling organizations, and organized homosexual movement leaders, professors of religion and philosophy. The subject is openly and freely explored in a spirit of learning and understanding. A new morality that includes the homosexual has been discussed, and the possibility of the need for a theology on homosexuality.

There are between eight and ten million *known* homosexuals in the United States at this writing; that many people can hardly be overlooked, especially when we know that they are scattered throughout all walks of life. They live next door; are members of our own families; attend our clubs, churches, and schools; conduct our business; treat our ailments; participate beside us in life, most often unrecognized. We have to acknowledge that we unknowingly accept and like them as fellow human beings. They don't seem any different to us. But should the fact of an individual's homosexuality become generally known, many people would turn on or try to ostracize the person—that very same individual they had known and liked and accepted as an equal—because he or she suddenly, in their imagination, has become different from them and therefore threatening, even evil, but certainly no longer acceptable. Yet our knowing his or her sexual proclivity does not change the individual we have known and liked and accepted; only our feelings about him or her have changed.

For some people, being confronted with the fact of homosexuality in another person is frightening because it hits too close to home. Somewhere along the way they too might have had homosexual experiences or secret fears of inclinations in themselves. According to Dr. Wardell B. Pomeroy: "About 37 per cent of the males above the age of puberty have had at least one overt homosexual experience to the point of orgasm . . . about 13 per cent of the females above the age of puberty have had at least one overt homosexual experience to the point of orgasm. Another 7 per cent have had homosexual experiences without orgasm." (6) Facts like that suggest that he who protests loudest or oppresses hardest is himelf quite possibly suspect. It also suggests that it is very wise not to make derogatory remarks about homosexuals because you never know who may in fact be one.

The next protest one hears against the revision of the civil law concerning homosexuals, and church reformation, is not based solely upon Biblical text but gets into the area of social anthropology. This argument against reform is that it might tend to encourage *proselytizing* among the young by homosexuals. This contention is sure to rally the rigorist to harsher resolve against any reformation; in fact, it is even a real concern for the liberal. Persons faced with a sound Biblical refutation of the condemnation of homosexuality will possibly concede a few religious points, but then they will fire their parting shot: reformation might tend to encourage proselytizing. At this point, reason usually gives way to irrational emotion.

No less an authority than Dr. Judd Marmor, clinical professor of psychiatry at U.C.L.A. and past president of the Academy of Psychoanalysis, and vice president of the American Psychiatric Association, strongly refutes the proselytizing argument in his book *Sexual Inversion:*

> One reflection of this stereotyping [of the homosexual] is the almost universal belief that homosexuals are not to be trusted with young people of the same sex. The assumption that they are somehow less in control of their impulses than are heterosexuals is the same kind of assumption that underlies white prejudice against Negros or native-born

prejudice against foreigners. In all these instances, the feeling is a reflection of fear based on lack of intimate knowledge of the people involved. A homosexual individual is neither more nor less trustworthy necessarily with young people of the same sex than a heterosexual is trustworthy with young people of the opposite sex. (7)

Many, many eminent psychologists and psychiatrists concur with Dr. Marmor's statement, yet the erroneous stigma remains. There is yet another argument against reform that goes hand in hand with the proselytizing one and makes just about as much sense. That is the contention that if the church eases up on the classic stand against homosexuality, it will seem to be condoning the practice, and will thereby weaken its statement that before he can be accepted by the church, the homosexual must confess, repent, make restitution by sincerely trying to change into a heterosexual, or at least abstain from genital involvement. Dr. C. A. Tripp replied to this issue both in his paper, and in his participation in one of Father Rodgers' Fordham University conferences:

I hope, with all these various observations on the frequency and variety of homosexuality, that I have succeeded in suggesting some of its similarities to heterosexuality. Not the least of these are its origins in the learning process, and the tenacity with which it is capable of staying put against the moralistic opposition that has been brought against it from time to time. Perhaps you have wondered why I have so strongly implied that the homosexual component is easier to come to terms with, than to eradicate. There are really two reasons. One has to do with practical necessity, and the other with the essential nature of human adjustment. As for necessity, let me point out that I am well aware of numerous claims of the successful treatment of the homosexual patient. Where success is marked in terms of greater personal efficiency and smoother social integration, the evidence is plentiful. But where basic change in adult sexual responses are claimed as a result of therapy, we have to be very careful in what we believe. Mere change in overt practice does not constitute an adequate criterion. The Trappist monk who takes an oath of silence and abstinence has certainly changed neither his voice, nor his basic sexual responsitivity.

As for psychotherapy, I know of not one single validated instance of any basic sexual change ever having been accomplished. Nor was the Kinsey Research ever able to find a single instance of any such change. Nor does the issue seem to be of the least importance. Even if there were treatment procedures for successfully revising an individual's whole personal value system, would we be ready to apply those procedures to a third of American males—or even to those millions of persons who are primarily homosexual for their entire lives?

From the point of view of personal adjustment, it is highly questionable whether any sexual behavior exercised between consenting adults is of any real social importance. From a psychiatric point of view, the thing that counts seems to be the efficiency with which an individual functions in life—his usefulness, his enjoyment, and the success of his human interactions. If society has an interest here, it is certainly in the maintenance of high personal efficiency, and low neurotic effects. In terms of this ideal, the particular sexual responses of an individual hardly seem to be of any major concern.   (8)

Again, many well-known psychologists and psychiatrists have substantiated Dr. Tripp's contention. But quite apart from psychological and anthropological findings, history and literature attest to the fact that homosexuality has been with us since the beginning of time; a proclivity that has been around for thousands of years will not be apt to succumb now.

Dr. Martin Hoffman is the author of *The Gay World* and a

practicing psychiatrist in San Francisco; his practice is almost entirely limited to homosexuals. In a discussion with the author at the American Psychiatric Convention in Dallas, Texas in May 1972, he said: "We psychiatrists suddenly seem to be the modern-day prophets. The church is asking us about the homosexual, but how much they're listening, I'm not sure. By temperament I tend to be pessimistic on that score, but lately I have seen many constructive changes, and I dare to be somewhat optimistic."

Thus far we have explored only the attitudes of the present-day Christian church on homosexuality and not those of contemporary Judaism. In an attempt to gain some intelligence on their attitudes I talked with some prominent rabbis. Most seemed somewhat reluctant to discuss homosexuality. Their general contention was that it is not a subject which comes up in Jewish life. I don't think any rabbi meant to imply that there are no Jewish homosexuals, but rather that homosexuals would not be as likely to go to a rabbi with the problem. By definition, a rabbi is a teacher and an arbiter, not a minister to a congregation in the sense of a Christian minister. Nor is there an episcopacy or hierarchy, as there is in the Christian church. Learned rabbis may be consulted for interpretations of elements of Jewish law about which they are experts. Said Rabbi Charles Sheer, "In the Protestant and Catholic communities there are groups asking the church to take a liberal position on homosexuality. In the organized Jewish community, however, there is no similar request being made. Although there certainly are Jews who are homosexuals, they have not turned in any significant manner to the Jewish community to assist them in defining their sexuality, nor have they pressed rabbinic leadership for any relaxation of the traditional position. If you are asking me how I approach homosexuality on campus—well, I don't see them, they simply do not come up. Although I see a large number of students for counseling, I have had only few instances where students will turn to me to discuss homosexuality.

"This factor—which I imagine is duplicated in the experience of other clergymen and counselors—is likewise reflected in Biblical and classical Jewish sources. There are only occasional references to homosexuality in the Bible, and even there, the prohibition, according to many scholars, is strongly colored by anti-pagan attitudes. Some rabbinic statements on homosexuality were in response to the practice and attitude of the Roman, Greek and Arab societies in which these men lived. Thus, there is relatively little in the medieval and Responsa literature on this topic."

When pressed for his personal attitude, the rabbi said: "The dominant Jewish attitude towards sex views this act as a source of gratification and pleasure, enhancing a bond between two individuals. Most authorities, establishing their positions on Midrashic and Talmudic sources, confirm the legitimacy of sexual pleasure as a means of establishing a love relationship between husband and wife. We do not find in Jewish sources a dualism which sees abstinence as a higher form of religious life. For example, the ideal and preferred cantor for synagogue services is a married man.

"Here comes the problem. Given the generally positive attitude towards sex in Jewish sources, it is possible that this activity, which God himself blesses in Genesis, can become a selfish, abusive one. Since the act itself basically involves only two individuals, it is possible for one to gratify his needs at the expense of the other, totally abusing and belittling the feelings and person of 'the other.' There is no other act which is so private and intimate as sexual intercourse. How does one define the difference between using and sharing with another individual in this act? Here is where the theme of reproduction enters.

"The two presentations of the creation of man that we spoke about earlier are generally played back to back in rabbinic sources. Insofar, as the legal literature is concerned, the divine imperative, the *mitzvah,* is not to perform sexually, but to reproduce, to have children. Although the second presentation of creation emphasizes companionship—shall we call it, in our contemporary terms, love—the rabbis modified that relationship by the implication of the first presentation of the creation of mankind. In order to avoid the danger of selfishness and abuse, the tradition felt that intercourse which is potentially reproductive involved a commitment which goes beyond the individuals, thereby elevating it and giving it special meaning. Through relations with another sex, man and woman affirm their faith in each other and in life. After all, it is with this individual whom I desire to create life and demonstrate my commitment to humanity. The implications of sexuality are significant; sex is not merely a means of satisfying my own biological or psychological needs, it expresses my faith in mankind and the world, since I thereby contribute part of myself by giving life to another. To be a parent in the twentieth century takes a lot of chutzpa. How dare I bring a child into a world with such tragedy, turmoil and hatred? This is precisely the meaning of God's blessing—'Be fruitful and multiply.' In spite of tragedy, sickness and perversity in the world, we must have faith in mankind and the ultimate triumph of justice, righteousness and moral values. Sexuality can be a source of blessing. It can be an act of love and commitment not merely to myself, not merely to my partner and spouse, but to all mankind as well.

"Since homosexuality cannot fulfill this function, the Jewish tradition has consistently opposed it. When an individual comes to me for counseling, I am personally sympathetic, although I am ideologically critical. Homosexuals should not be discriminated against, and their right should be affirmed and protected. Although Judaism, as a teaching system, is opposed to this life style, I would argue that individuals do have the option to work out their own life pattern. Despite the above-described position, I cannot accept legal or coercive actions against the homosexual."

Rabbi Eugene Borowitz had somewhat more specific views. "Since there is the positive emphasis on the family and children in Judaism, for carrying on to the Messiah, there has to be negative emphasis on homosexuality. Homosexuality makes it impossible to carry on the Jewish project. The Jewish project is future-oriented. Therefore, a person not involved in begetting children under Jewish law is not fulfilling the pact made between God and God's people."

Rabbi Borowitz was asked how he would describe the status open to the homosexual within Judaism. He said: "Can the Jewish tradition grant homosexuals a status equal to heterosexuals? I think the Jewish tradition, if it maintains its messianic orientation, its future-interestedness, cannot grant homosexuals quite the same status. It is the status equivalent to, but obviously different from, the status of someone who doesn't want to get married. In the eyes of the Jewish community—as you can find out from any Jew who has tried to remain single for very long—someone who doesn't get married is a problem. Everybody is immediately trying to make a match for him, or her, and get them married and get them set up.

"In all practicality, what should we do about the people who are homosexuals? We have something of a problem here. The problem is first, is anything natural [automatically] good? Simply because [homosexuality] occurs, does that mean that it needs to be viewed because it is there, and that it has to be good and okay? The answer to that, from the Jewish point of view, on the whole is no."

Rabbi Borowitz hinges his argument on volition . . . or the extent to which a person has a choice. And in that context he refers to psychology. Simply put, his point of view is that the Jewish community would have to consider the "born" homosexual differently from the "environmental-input" homosexual. He focused further on the problem. "Just for the moment, let's be technical. There is no law against homosexuals being together or living together and loving one another very dearly and tenderly in the Bible, but the law is against genital homosexual activity.

"The commandment not to have homosexual activity in a genital way is a *negative* commandment. To have children is a *positive* commandment. Now, in the Jewish tradition it is always said that for certain worthy purposes such as study, it is permissible not to get married and have children. The point the commandment is trying to make is this: one could kind of find an opening in Jewish law, even somewhat technically interpreted now, for homosexuals having the love and companionship and close association which would come with loving another human being. Trying to read the tradition somewhat more liberally, it's certainly far more acceptable in the tradition than the people who are involved in genital homosexuality, which is what the law specifically forbids."

Did the rabbi consider that the prohibition against homosexuality had originally been simply an anti-Canaanite law? He did not. "The law has another foundation," he said. "It's not an anti-Canaanite law, it's a pro-Messiah law. One has to feel the emotion that Jews still put into marriage and children in order to appreciate that this is a pro-marriage, pro-children, pro-Messiah law. There may have been some anti-Canaanite input in it originally, but that sounds like the typical reasoning which somebody uses because they want to change something. You invent a reason for a rule that is now past so that if the reason is past the rule is over. Very, very clever; very useful. And it's one of the reasons why the rabbinical tradition is against inventing reasons. You don't change a law because some reason of yours is changed."

What would be his response to a homosexual coming to him seeking help in reconciling his or her homosexuality with Jewish law? He answered: "I'm sure I haven't the slightest idea. But several things need to be said. In the first place, in terms of the sexual problems or the suffering of another human being—I, as a rabbi, would respond, I hope, with a good deal of understanding and compassion and personal acceptance and warmth. I have my own conscience to live with and I think I have some idea of what's going on. Of course, I can't be certain; I might respond to different people in different ways. I'd like to be of as much help to [homosexuals] as I can, and try to see to it that society makes it as possible for them to get along as anybody else.

"But I cannot say—believing as I do in what the human race is involved in, in what the Jewish people is involved in—that I can consider [homosexuality] an equivalent state, or that I think it should be allowed to become an equivalent model. I don't think it is from my point of view an equivalent model. I can understand it is another way, but in my system of values, and certainly at least within the Jewish community, it has to be considered a secondary level of choice. So far as it is not a matter of choice, then— Well, I know the homosexuals will be deeply disturbed about it, but I considered it within the level of 'sickness or illness'—of a psychiatric variety, or a neurotic variety—and I would want to deal with it on that level. Which is to say that a good many of us have neuroses, and we either have to cure them or live with them. When I say 'sickness or illness,' I am looking for some special language to describe it. By 'neurotic' I don't mean being in some sense nonfunctioning, or not as happy, et cetera. It is so difficult to try and find a language for this from the perspective of what the Jewish community values . . . Not to be able to grow into a heterosexual relationship by that fact is to be in—how shall I put it?—a less desirable state."

Suppose a couple were married and had produced children, fulfilling the commandment to marry and have children, and one of them discovered latent homosexual tendencies which they had acted upon—would they still be looked upon as in a *less desirable* state, or sinful?

"They should refrain from genital homosexual activity; they would still be breaking the commandment against genital homosexual activity. It is one thing to fulfill the positive commandment to have children, and another to break the negative commandment against genital activity." The rabbi explained that it is more sinful to break a negative commandment than to break a positive commandment.

"You see, I still would be concerned with setting models for the Jewish community—for people who are growing up. I think it's quite critical what in a general community is accepted and not accepted. Now, why do I say this? Not because I want to condemn or make life more difficult for people, but insofar as it comes within the element of choice or volition for people to be able to say what kind of life they will lead, I would prefer that they had models of heterosexual fulfillment, and that is what is critical to me."

If the New York criminal code came up again for revision of the so-called sodomy issue, what would the Jewish community's position be? Would he be for or against revision?

"My cynical comment is that as soon as the overall majority of the Jewish community spoke out on this subject, the minority of the Jewish community would appear the next day to oppose it."

What did he think the response would be if the Jewish religious leaders supported the change?

"On the whole, the overall majority of Jews are not interested in what their religious leaders think. Historically the Jewish community has generally been considered to be liberal on social policies, and I suspect that they would be in favor of the liberalization of the laws regarding homosexuality. With regard to the religious leaders, I haven't the slightest idea of where they would stand. It is entirely conceivable that they might say that matters of sexual behavior between consenting adults are not a concern of the state. They would certainly say they know what Jewish law has to say on the matter, as we have discussed, but that they didn't think the state ought to get involved in it. My guess is that many of them probably would prefer not to get involved in the whole issue because it is a somewhat delicate one. I could only add that with regard to this issue, in my own case, I would have no hesitation whatsoever in saying that the civic law should be repealed."

The rabbi qualified his statements to encompass his personal feelings. "So far we have been talking about the questions of Jewish law and tradition, of the Bible, et cetera; what I would take to be my fundamental interest in human beings has hardly had a chance to have equal weight. If I have anything to say in addition to what I have said, please understand that I am speaking as a Jew who is deeply affected by the teachings of the Jew Martin Buber, and therefore, I must say that wherever it is possible to help a person be a person, I want, if at all possible, not to stand in the way of that. Now, that is not always easy. Indeed, one comes into conflict with some of the things that Jewish tradition is about. Just simply to be a person is not enough for a Jew. Therefore, I want to make sure that my response to human situations as a whole is not confused with what I think is the specialty, the special responsibility, the special discipline, that is involved with being a Jew. So, how I might respond as a human being is secondary to what I think God wants of me.

Did he think that the Jewish religion, like other organized Western religions, was becoming rather irrelevant to the times, and that perhaps that was why the churches and Synagogues were losing people?

"You have to remember that Reformed Jews have specialized in relevance for fifty years or more. And it hasn't helped terribly much. It comforts the Orthodox and the Conservative to believe that we are becoming more Orthodox. I would say from the other point of view now that orthodoxy has probably showed that it is reformed, and that we are now all moving in a rather similar direction."

On the question of homosexuality, it is pretty clear from the statements of Rabbi Sheer, representing Orthodox Judaism, and Rabbi Borowitz, presenting the Reformed view, that they are essentially in accord. From the point of view of Judaism, therefore, homosexuality strikes at its very core in that homosexuality runs headlong into the messianic foundation of the Jewish purpose on earth. One fails to see any ray of hope for a

Jewish homosexual being able to reconcile his Jewishness with his homosexuality. If he is troubled by guilt for failing to fulfill his Jewishness, he is not apt to get a break from a rabbi or Judaism. His only recourse is psychotherapy.

One of the homosexual counseling services in New York City ran into difficulty getting a rabbi to serve on their board and to contribute help for the Jewish homosexuals. They approached a highly respected rabbi and found him in favor of offering his services, but before consenting he had to consult with his congregation. They refused him permission to serve on the counseling board. Like many another clergyman with a personal conscience, he finally elected to do it unofficially. He is a refreshing exception, but what he counsels the Jewish homosexuals is not known.

What is interesting about the positions taken by both Rabbi Sheer and Rabbi Borowitz in regard to homosexuality and the messianic pact is that it seems to further weaken the rationale of the Christian Church's stand against homosexuality. The Christian Church's theology includes a Messiah who has already appeared. Christianity therefore has no messianic pact; there are no commandments which say: Thou shalt bring forth children in order to fulfill your Christianess. You can be just as good a Christian with or without children. Therefore, in that sense the homosexual is not breaking a commandment in failing to bring forth children. One has to wonder, then, why Christians initially embraced this mania for procreation, and continue to hold onto laws concerning homosexuality which initially were developed because of the unique position of the Jews as exiles in a pagan land. The messianic pact and the command to bring forth children (or exist in a state of sinfulness and non-Jewishness), may help to explain St. Paul's strong statements against homosexuality—if that was indeed what he was speaking about—for Paul was a rabbi before his conversion to Christianity.

In view of the fact that a great deal of the innovative theory

—indeed, much of the basic foundation of psychiatry—was developed by Jews, one cannot help wondering to what extent the messianic pact between God and the Jewish people influenced early psychiatrists' thinking on the question of homosexuality, and on the establishment of a basic norm. It is inconceivable that some degree of personal prejudice does not enter into even the attitudes and theories of psychiatrists; after all, they are only human beings. Certainly elements so basic as the Judaic messianic concept and the commandment to marry and raise children could not be totally absent, even if subconsciously, in the psychological make-up of someone brought up in the Jewish tradition. It would not even be a question of objectivity, which I am certain any serious psychiatrist/psychologist or scholar would strive for, but a question of a well-learned orientation to a concept of life and a specific way of relating to the creator. As the rabbis have pointed out, to be Jewish is a total way of life, requiring a certain unquestioning and automatic acceptance of man's essential purpose for being. One might also question how much this same messianic concept influences some present-day psychiatrists and psychologists.

The obvious need the homosexual feels for a spiritual relationship to God is evidenced by the growing number of churches for homosexuals all across the country. Since homosexuals have been driven out of the formal established churches, they have founded their own. Although, as we saw before, many individual members of the clergy within the institutional church have attempted to make the homosexual welcome within its structure—a tiny light shining in the wilderness, but an important one—to some homosexuals the attempts of these clergymen seem like too little too late. Thus, the churches for homosexuals were established. "It seems to me," said Father Robert Clement (who was a straight priest for twenty-two years and is now pastor of the Church of the Beloved Disciple, New York, a church for homosexuals), "that Christianity has made its most serious error in becoming too legalistic, too caught up in condemnatory attitudes based on the slimmest evidence. There is so little in the New Testament to give any so-called solid basis to these preconceived notions and ideas and attitudes—and it goes beyond sex. Christianity has been distorted out of meaning, and the concept of love is too often given lip service and not real meaning, and if this is true, it will explain why churches are rapidly emptying."

Father Clement's church was founded on the concept of love. It is a sacramental church that celebrates the Mass with communion, and is, in his words, "the fastest-growing church in New York." It has been in existence a little over a year, and the congregation includes a worshiping group of three hundred on Sunday, a church membership of approximately seven hundred, and affiliated friends or interested persons numbering about a thousand. According to Father Clement, this number is growing all the time. "It grows," he says, "from relating to our own people, relating positively to the sexual identity and life style of gay people—just good, solid, positive people in a religious sphere."

Has the church helped gay people to bring about positive changes in their lives? "Oh, tremendously, and profoundly. I know because we now have a religious order—people who have come to us. We didn't start out to have a religious order. But people came to us who had separated themselves from other church affiliations to seek a stronger spiritual and personal relation to the church. It has created a change in their lives that restored them to a sense of faith. Other people have come to me and said, 'I haven't been in church for twenty years, and haven't received communion in as many years.' Literally hundreds of people have come to me with this kind of story. They have been moved by our service, by the fact of being able to accept themselves and God, and to once again be in God's church. It is quite a moving experience."

Did Father Clement feel there was a particular need among gay people for God, a sort of inborn sensitivity to the religious impulse? "I really don't know," he replied. "All I know is, there is a tremendous response, and we are witness to it. Whether this is universally true, or not, I don't know. I believe that amongst mankind in general there is a reaching out toward God and toward what we might call the religious impulse."

Did his ministry among gays differ from his ministry as a straight priest? "I don't have to hide my nature; I don't have to live a partial life. What I had as a straight priest was good, but this is much, much better. I could speak of love before, but I often thought my people didn't understand what I was talking about, and I couldn't relate it to the core of my being. I can do that now. There might have been a certain amount of need in the parishes I served in in the past, but the need is so much greater for these people who have been rejected and seriously hurt. Hopefully we are healing some of those wounds. This is a much more demanding, but in the long run, a much more satisfying, ministry because one can see where a great wrong has been done and one can see where one is helping to right it. You are called to God's work where you are. This work has been badly neglected and is long overdue."

Did he feel he was *called* to do it? "We believe in a vocation in the priesthood, and that vocation leads you to what God wants of you. I don't want to give the impression that I feel I had some supreme calling, that I have been set aside or something like that. My calling grew quietly from my own evolution. It became obvious that this work had to be done, and so it was, like, here I am, send me."

Were the problems of his present parishioners very different from those of his parishioners as a straight priest? "Universally, they are not different; specifically, they are different. Universally, people have problems of religion that the church has to attend to—and there are so many. But when we get to, or beyond, the universal need for seeking God, whatever needs there are in a person's life—to find joy and get rid of unhappiness—then we come to the specific. Specifically, the homosexual has been brutally shut out of the confessional, has been denied the sacrament, and has been made to feel a second-class citizen in the church. He or she is welcome in the formal, organized church only if he's a 'good queer' who doesn't admit it, minds his or her *p*'s and *q*'s, and doesn't make waves; if he or she is less than a human being. If the churches won't do their jobs, then this church had to come into existence to do it."

What future did he see for his church? He said: "We don't exist to exist forever. We exist to go out of business, when a true sense of humanity overcomes everyone—when a person's sexual identification won't be of any great consequence. Sexuality will possibly be more important for everybody, but its expression will be less important if all mankind realizes the positive values of sexual identity for each person."

Did he feel that the time was coming when this kind of humanity would be possible? "Yes. We often feel setbacks, and that we are not progressing at times, but we are. This church could not have existed a few years ago without great hostility, and that hostility is not there now. My mail indicates this. About 95 per cent of the mail I get is favorable. What little negative mail I get—in a sense, opposition mail—is usually, I discovered after a while, written by what must be the illiterate type of person. It is instantly recognizable; usually scrawled on the most basic level. They say things like: 'You are evil and terrible in the sight of God. You are a terrible sinner and God will destroy you.' That's the type of thing we get, when we get negative mail. We occasionally get a reasoned paper from a divinity student on the legalistic aspects of religion, but that's about it."

Father Clement and the members of his congregation also try to help people in practical ways as well, doing things such as getting jobs for homosexuals who are discriminated against, getting counseling service for persons having problems, and finding them places to live. However, Father Clement feels that there is so much more to do. And like almost every other group trying to help those who need help, Father Clement's church has to deal with the question of funds. "We have applied for funds through foundations, but we would also hope that other churches would start to be a little bit Christian and realize that here is an area they've neglected and that it's up to them to move to rectify what they have created in the past. I don't want to put a burden of guilt on them, but common sense says the church has been responsible for injustice and they should help to correct it."

How did Father Clement's congregation break down as to men and women, and of what religious backgrounds? "About 75 per cent of our congregation is made up of men, about 25 per cent of women. As for religious background, the congregation is composed of persons of Protestant, Catholic and Jewish backgrounds. And interestingly enough, we have quite a few straight members. They feel that something vital and real is going on in our church. They feel more at home at our services than they do in the institutional church."

This was also borne out by the Reverend Howard Wells, pastor of the New York Metropolitan Community Church, a branch of the Metropolitan Community Churches Movement, now in all major cities and the pioneers of a homosexual church movement. The M.C.C. was founded by the Reverend Troy Perry in Los Angeles in 1968, and now has an offshoot church in New York; Rev. Perry gave the general philosophy behind the organization when he said: "We like to say that we are not a gay church, but a church for gay people." Said the Reverend Wells: "And there is a difference. Everybody is welcome—black, white, male, female, straight or gay, whatever. In fact, as the church grows older the percentage of straight individuals coming to our services increases. We are now about 10 per cent to 15 per cent straight people. The church acts as a great agent of reconciliation for the straight and gay community." The New York church is still quite young and does not as yet have its own building; but Holy Apostles Episcopal

Church has granted them use of their church, and they meet after the regular Episcopal services.

Reverend Wells explained the concept of the Metropolitan Community Church. "We now have thirty-one congregations across the country, and we are first and foremost a Christian church in the Congregational tradition. Reverend Perry, who founded the Metropolitan Community Church Movement, was an ordained minister in the Church of God. We are incorporated as a denomination called the Universal Fellowship, and we now have a seminary for training ministers. We operate on a basically middle-of-the-road Protestant formula, but we vary it widely, in order not to become doctrinaire and restrictive. We are rather informal in worship format in that we sing a lot of gospel hymns and there is clapping and laughter, sometimes even dancing."

He told of the service he had held the previous Sunday which was called a *Godspell* Sunday. They used music from the folk opera *Godspell,* with costumes patterned from the musical. There was no speaking during the communion; instead, they used the *Godspell* songs, which concern the bleeding of Christ and his death. They danced to the music and then took communion. "This brings fellowship and the celebration of the joy of the reality of Christ into religion," he said.

"Most people who have become interested in our church have been turned off church in general, especially gay people—because they feel that the church has been their great oppressor. As a result they have disdained church, even become anti-church. But when they come to our church and we are able to show them a different approach to God and church, they overcome those feelings and are able to become involved in church once again. They feel something exciting is going on. The organized church doesn't always speak for Christ's spirit; in fact, oftentimes it is the antithesis of it, especially for gay people. Now they realize that Christ can be real to them, and that the spirit of Christ is applicable to them. It is perhaps an even more poignant way for gay people than for straight people. Perhaps they appreciate it more because they suffer more."

Had they formulated any kind of formal church doctrine? He replied: "We are careful about that, because *doctrine* has been the pitfall of the Christian denominations. We don't build our doctrinal basis around the very few references to homosexuality in the Bible. We do have an evening in which we all get together and talk about these references and what they mean. Our bylaws require that we set up a committee to study ways in which Christ's spirit can be applied in a pragmatic way to the particular life style of gay men and women. We make a report to the congregation quarterly, and we see a lot of interesting things growing out of this committee because they do investigate the areas of human involvement that probably have never been considered before . . . excepting, perhaps, by gay people; gay people themselves in their involvement in the church."

Did they have counseling services for members? Did they try to help them to solve their problems? "Not yet in New York because we are just beginning—we can't afford it—but it is something we very much want and consider necessary. We want to do a great many more things, but we haven't the funds. At present none of us is even on salary. Each church is self-supporting. In San Francisco and Los Angeles we have extensive community service projects. For example, a social services project where members can come who are homeless, hungry, jobless, in need of clothing, friends and counseling. We take care of them. There is a great need. Out there it took us nearly two years to get to that position. About 90 per cent of the persons who came to us for help were gay, and most of them were young, just out of military service, and needing something to help them take hold of their lives and get them in order. Here in New York, being new, we will review the services being rendered now by various agencies and service groups and try not to be redundant. We will try to complement their efforts."

What realistic hopes did Rev. Wells have for the institutional church bringing about reform in the area of condemnation of the homosexual? "Homosexuals are children of God and they should be brought into the mainstream of congregational life but the opposition is great. Last summer in San Francisco we needed a larger building, and we approached a minister of a church there to rent space when they weren't using it. The pastor and his advisory board, his lay board, all were for it, but when the pastor brought it before the congregation, *they* voted it down. It was unfortunate, especially when the church wasn't in use. Obviously those people have a long way to go before they can actualize their liberal-hearted intentions. I would say that most ministers, a great percentage of individual ministers, are in favor of civil and religious equality for gay people—more so than their congregations. But the ministers are afraid they are going to lose their jobs if they take a stand. It doesn't speak well for their conviction, but privately many of them are very much in favor of it. If we can just get the ball rolling in some way with some denominations making a stand, it will snowball. That will give ministers of other denominations courage to come out and make a stand. We need somebody to set a precedent."

Sincere efforts *are* being made in this direction, as we have seen in the beginning of this chapter, and they undoubtedly will continue. Let us say it is in the wind. One of the forerunners of reform was a conference held in 1967 at the Cathedral of St. John the Divine in New York under the sponsorship of the Episcopal Diocese of New York, Connecticut, Long Island, and Newark, New Jersey. The results of a daylong symposium on the church's approach to homosexuality were summarized in an article by Edward B. Fiske on the front page of *The New York Times* (November 29, 1967). The headline read: *Episcopal Clergymen Here Call Homosexuality Morally Neutral.*

While the majority appeared to take the position that homosexual acts were wrong per se, the clergymen at the conference succeeded in reaching a consensus that such acts should be judged in each individual instance by other criteria, such as whether the participants were expressing genuine love or simply "using" each other for selfish purposes. (One is at a loss to know how the church plans to determine this.) However, the ninety clergymen generally agreed that the church should classify homosexual acts between consenting adults as "morally neutral" and acknowledge that such acts may even be a good thing.

The Reverend Walter D. Dennis, canon of the cathedral, who organized the symposium, said, for instance, that Christians must "rethink the usual position that has turned homosexuals into modern-day lepers. A homosexual relationship between two consenting adults should be judged by the same criteria as a heterosexual marriage—that is, whether it is intended to foster a permanent relationship of love." He added, however, that "homosexuality should not be encouraged and that homosexual acts, like other extramarital sexual relations, can also be *promiscuous*."

There were those who agreed with this view but expressed difficulty in formulating the standards by which to distinguish "healthy" from "promiscuous" homosexual acts. Others disagreed completely, such as the Reverend L. Robert Foutz, pastor of Trinity Episcopal Church in Astoria, Queens, who declared homosexual acts "must always be regarded as perversions because they are not part of the natural process of rearing children."

The article went on to remind us that traditional Episcopalian doctrine, grounded in Roman Catholic moral law, states that the condition of homosexuality is not in itself sinful but that homosexual acts, like other sexual acts outside marriage, are wrong. "Most churches also teach that homosexuality is more sinful than other extramarital sexual acts, but theologians state that these attitudes reflect the mores of society rather than official doctrines."

However, leaders of the symposium felt that the conference reflected the increasing interest among churchmen in the problems of homosexuality. The National Council of Churches has sponsored conferences on the subject, and the Episcopal Diocese of San Francisco has openly supported an organization of homosexuals.

The article also stated that "there is much new interest in a widespread liberalizing of the traditional 'judgmental' attitude. 'Increasing numbers of Christians are coming to judge relationships on what they do to people involved, and to society as a whole,' said Rev. Neale Secor, pastor of St. Mary's Church in Manhattan. 'Many are open to the possibility that homosexual relationships can be as fulfilling or as destructive as heterosexual ones.'" The article concluded, as did the conference, with the recognition of the fact that "churchmen need more factual information on the causes of homosexuality and on such questions as whether it is possible for homosexual relationships to provide enduring 'fulfillment' and 'happiness.'"

In 1971 the Council of the Episcopal Diocese of New York passed a formal resolution on the issue of homosexuality, as have other church bodies. In the spring of 1972, during a private interview with Canon Dennis, he spoke about that first conference. He said: "I believed then, and I believe now, that homosexuality per se is morally neutral. But in any case, we were very much in the forefront then. It is the job of the Cathedral to be a voice for the voiceless, to raise issues in a public way so that people have to deal with them who would not otherwise do so. By raising the issue, we are not speaking *for* the church, we are speaking *to* the church, and to many people who would prefer to avoid it otherwise."

Although progress is slow, this is an exciting time; many attitudes now held by the church may soon be modified in such a way as to help make possible a healthier, more constructive society. Dialogues and symposiums that air issues hitherto swept out of sight and ignored may very well bring reform that will rescue the church; useful and worthwhile people will then be able to return to the churches and can build more useful and constructive lives.

Chapter 4

Animal Behavior, Anthropology, Genetics and Homosexuality

I think human beings are bisexual. And extreme homosexuals and extreme heterosexuals are both deviates.

—Dr. Margaret Mead

In the mammalian species it is considered normal for the male to mount the female during sexual activity, the male being the aggressor and the female being the passive recipient; anything else is considered unnatural. Yet, among mammals other than man, whose behavior is free of cultural taboos, social and psychological pressures, we find some interesting variations of this assumed *natural* pattern. In fact, just as in humans, we find an inclination to bisexual or so-called homosexual behavior.

"Homosexuality, that is, sexual activity among members of the same sex, and bisexuality, that is, behaving at one moment in the typical fashion of one sex and later shifting to the behavior of the opposite sex, are very prevalent among animals," said Dr. Lester Aronson, chairman of the Department of Animal Behavior, the American Museum of Natural History. "Observations of rats, cats, dogs, bovines, horses, monkeys and many other animals show, for example, males mounting males, females mounting males or females, and males behaving as females. Many of these observations were made in captivity where access to the opposite sex was not always available, but the same behavior is seen among free-ranging animals having access to both sexes. These forms of sexual behavior among animals are certainly not unusual."

While a good deal seems to be known about male sexual behavior, not much is known about female sexual behavior. Dr. Carol Diakow of The Rockefeller University, New York, who is currently engaged in research on the sexual behavior of female rats, remarked: "I have not seen a case where a female rat was homosexual, but I have not specifically researched this particular area of female animal sexual behavior." As for general mounting behavior exhibited by female rats, Dr. Diakow indicated that she is not altogether certain that mounting behavior indicates homosexuality. She feels rather that it may be a social function or message transmission.

Dr. Bernard F. Riess, a psychologist who has done extensive studies on human female homosexuality (previously an animal behaviorist), suggests that the animal behaviorists have given too much attention to male homosexuality in animals, both in captivity and in the wild, and have neglected studies of female homosexuality. Where there is attention given to female homosexuality, or mounting behavior, it is seen as male behavior; the female is ostensibly imitating the male position and mating characteristics. Dr. Riess feels that no one has really recorded two female animals relating to each other in a general sexual way to the point of orgasm; he thinks such studies would be enlightening.

Examination of some of the animal behavior studies of females does seem to indicate that everyone is fixed on the study of *masculine* copulatory behavior. For example, writing on "Masculine Copulatory Behavior in Intact and Castrated

Female Rats," Frank A. Beach and Priscilla Rasquin have said:

> Certain female animals are known to display mating reactions characteristic of the male of their species. Behavior of this type has been observed in the case of female pigeons, night herons, monkeys, and chimpanzees. Despite the widespread character of such "reversals" of sexual behavior, exhibition of masculine mating behavior by experimentally altered females is frequently offered as evidence to substantiate claims of induced sex reversals.
>
> In the case of the female rat, masculine copulatory behavior has always been regarded as either nonexistent or quite rare. Previously the senior author described 7 virgin female rats which mounted sexually sluggish males. More recently two experienced females have been observed to exhibit the complete masculine copulatory pattern exclusive of the ejaculatory response. In all of these instances the females were in estrus and readily accepted the male in typical feminine fashion.

Dr. Beach's research would seem to indicate that the rats were not exclusively homosexual. It might be of interest, however, to describe some of the behavior of the female rats which is termed masculine. Of the twenty adult female rats which were tested, three types of masculine copulatory behavior were observed: "the sexual clasp, clasping with palpation and pelvic thrusts, and the 'complete pattern' which includes all the foregoing plus dismounting after a final, vigorous pelvic thrust and frequently involves licking of the genitals."

It should be pointed out that the study was conducted "to determine the proportion of female rats showing masculine copulatory behavior, the frequency of such reaction in each individual, and the relationship of masculine responses to the female estrous cycle." The results showed that the rats displayed feminine sexual patterns—or "receptivity," as Beach and

Rasquin termed it—during periods of vaginal estrus, but this behavior could not be elicited at other times; the masculine copulatory behavior was "performed with equal frequency at all stages of the estrous cycle." When Beach and Rasquin castrated five of the study females it eliminated receptivity but had no effect upon the masculine behavior. The injection of estrogen and progesterone into these castrated females "revived receptivity and did not alter masculine behavior." When a group of the female rats were ovariectomized at twenty-one to twenty-seven days of age and tested over a period of about three months they showed various degrees of the previously described masculine copulatory behavior. When these prepubertal castrates and a group of other female castrates were tested with "a receptive female the prepubertal castrates showed a greater amount of masculine behavior" in response to the receptive female. These factors caused Drs. Beach and Rasquin to conclude "that the majority of female rats from the colony studied possess a neuromotor organization capable of mediating the masculine copulatory pattern. It is further concluded that in the female this motor pattern appears most readily in response to the same stimulus pattern by which it is evoked in the male, namely a multi-sensory pattern of stimulation presented by the receptive female. Finally, it is concluded that the masculine sexual reactions of the female rat are not dependent upon ovarian hormones." (1)

Investigations into human genetics have demonstrated that hormones are not a contributory cause of female homosexuality; this will be discussed later in this chapter. But as Dr. Riess pointed out earlier, the assumption is continually being made that the above-described sexual behavior in animals is masculine, and this seems a premature, perhaps even an incorrect, assumption—particularly in view of the prevalence of such behavior in a large number of mammalian species and the frequency with which it occurs. In *Perspectives in Reproduction and Sexual Behavior*, Dr. Beach states that published reports indicate that such behavior occurs in at least some females of thirteen species representing five different orders, comprising the rodents, lagomorphs, insectivores, ungulates, carnivores and primates. He further states that though "some of the accounts refer to single instances, a representativeness of which it is impossible to estimate, . . . in many cases evidence is sufficient to demonstrate that for some mammals female mounting activity is not 'abnormal' or 'atypical,' but instead represents a predictable and characteristic feature of the species repertoire." (2)

Their studies also found that in some instances this behavior signals the onset of estrus in the mounter; during the period of heat the female will mount other receptive females. In other situations this behavior seems in response to estrus in the mounted female. Such behavior was also observed in sows, cows and female lions. It tells us, however, little more than common sense might suppose: neither animals nor humans go around in a perpetual state of heightened sexuality. Naturally, there are times when both animals and humans are biologically more interested in sexual contact than at other times, and more responsive to stimuli. But that these periods motivate a masculine or so-called homosexual type of behavior is not to be supposed from Beach's earlier statement: "It is concluded that the masculine sexual reactions of the female rat are not dependent upon ovarian hormones." Furthermore, it would seem that the so-called masculine behavior cannot really be classified homosexual when one reviews another of Beach's statements: "In many cases evidence is sufficient to demonstrate that for some mammals female mounting activity is not 'abnormal' or 'atypical,' but instead represents a predictable and characteristic feature of the species repertoire." (3) In other words, it would seem from the above observations that females of many of the mammalian species participate quite naturally and "normally" in sexual play of variant degrees from that of male to female and female to male. One suspects the same would probably be true of humans without the overlay of social and moral complexities and the structure of male dominance and power. The real significance of these various studies would not seem to lie in the physical behavior or acting out of a ritual, but in the initial ability of one female to *attract* another sexually—of which the mounting or pelvic thrust or whatever is a manifestation.

Other pertinent studies of this behavioral phenomenon reported by Beach in *Perspectives in Reproduction and Sexual Behavior* should be briefly reviewed. For example, Beach reports that in field studies in 1914 Hamilton observed adult female monkeys displaying mounting behavior. In 1942 C. R. Carpenter studied free-living rhesus monkeys and observed females displaying mounting behavior under natural conditions. According to Beach, Carpenter, "observed frequent mounting of one female by another over a period of several days, and concluded that the continuing 'interaction' resembled in many respects a male-female consort relation." (4) It also "showed that the female mounted was usually more strongly motivated for sexual behavior than the mounter . . . This may be relevant to the tentative conclusion based on several other species that the most effective stimulus partner, the type of individual most likely to be mounted, is a second female in heat." (5)

According to the 1965 observations of Harry Harlo, this kind of behavior in the rhesus monkeys can occur quite young. He found such interaction taking place between animals as young as one to two months. He stated that the interaction "sometimes involves rubbing the bodies together and executing thrusting movements of the pelvic region. Beginning in approximately the third month after birth the frequency of this kind of behavior becomes greater in male infants than in females." (6)

In a 1928 study of sexual development in chimpanzees, Bingham observed several instances of two immature females "covering" one another. (1) In 1939 Robert Yerkes found that some adult female chimpanzees, when confronted with another female "in a state of genital swelling, may assume the masculine copulatory position, mounting the estrous individual and displaying thrusting motions. In this case again, as in several mentioned earlier, the most effective stimulus animal seems to be a second female in a state of sexual receptivity." (8)

In experiments with rats, possible hormonal influences or imbalances were considered as possible causes for the mounting behavior, as stated earlier; for example, a deficiency of estrogen was considered. The Diamond book cites several studies of experimentation in this area. Experiments included the injection of hormones into females displaying mounting behavior, but injections of estrogen, for example, failed to decrease the tendency to mount. In fact, it had the opposite effect: it increased the tendency to mount, and showed no evidence of decreasing the tendency. This reported evidence seems to rule out a hormonal imbalance as a contributing factor to the so-called masculine mounting behavior.

Beach reported in his symposium:

> The spontaneous occurrence of mounting behavior in females of many mammalian species is sufficient evidence to establish the fact that the feminine genotype provides for the development of neuromuscular mechanisms adequate for mediation of some of the elements of the "masculine" pattern of coital behavior. This genetic endowment must include sensory motor integrative elements which are shared by both sexes. Although their precise location and the functional characteristics of most of the elements remain to be established, some pertinent information is available. Thus in both male and female rats the pursuit and mounting of a stimulus female seems to depend upon some as yet undefined contribution by the cerebral cortex, for extensive injury to this portion of the brain eliminates mounting behavior in both sexes while

leaving the female capable of displaying such sexually receptive reactions as lordosis, ear wiggling, and darting or hopping. (9)

In his concluding remarks Beach states: "Descriptive and experimental reports reviewed in the foregoing pages make it clear that mounting behavior by female mammals is a fairly widespread phenomenon occurring in at least some species of several different orders within the class. It is evident that the behavior demands systematic analysis." (10)

In plain language, one can conclude that what these studies seem to be indicating is that mounting behavior is not the exclusive pattern of the male; that perhaps such behavior is more *sexual* than masculine. As we have seen, a female animal is quite able to become attracted, stimulated and sexually aroused by another female—aroused, in fact, quite naturally to the point of physical response and the acting out of the only sexual ritual known to them. Perhaps Dr. Diakow is correct in suggesting that female mounting behavior in animals may be a social function or message transmission, but a message to whom about what? Perhaps the female animal is simply signaling to another female that she feels sexy. Yet in studies of rhesus monkeys, we saw that the "female mounted was usually more strongly motivated sexually than the mounter." And we heard the conclusion that "this may be relevant to the tentative conclusion based on several other species that the most effective stimulus partner, the type of individual most likely to be mounted, is a second female in heat." Apparently the female being mounted is sending out a message, but she is not doing the mounting, so one wonders again if one can rely too strongly on the speculation that the mounting behavior is simply a method of message transmission. It would be interesting to know if there were many instances of one female rejecting the advances of the other. We are not told that, but it would seem a very important indication of what this action means to the animals themselves.

What we have been told, however, clearly indicates that under certain circumstances and at given times, many species of animals can and do respond to stimuli from members of their own sex—which is also what Kinsey told us about human beings.

Perhaps animals do quite naturally what we have to go through a trauma to arrive at. Aggressive sexual behavior or pelvic thrusts by females participating in heterosexual copulative activity are not unusual, nor are they considered particularly unnatural or abnormal. In fact, studies have told us that quite a few men are especially *turned on* by a sexually aggressive female in bed. Publically, socially, these same men might be likely to brand such behavior unfeminine, masculine, and probably unladylike; it would appear to threaten their prowess and supremacy. That love between two women or two men which is expressed physically will bring down a shower of righteous moral and social disapproval we have countless examples. It is unnatural, abnormal, sick, they cry. The animal behaviorists have shown us that there is considerable variability in the sexual behavior patterns of female animals, both in response to one another and to males, and this variability is not considered to be unnatural or abnormal by scientists studying these animals. It should be pointed out also that mounting behavior is not limited to female animals, it has been equally observed in male animals. Therefore, to say that homosexual behavior, or *sexual* behavior toward one's own sex, by members of the human species is unnatural seems the height of naïveté. The very naturalness of animal sexual behavior, their uncomplicated ability to be attracted, to respond, and to become sexually aroused and participate in a sexual ritual, suggests that perhaps there is really no such thing as heterosexual or homosexual behavior at all. There is simply *sexual* behavior, on which we impose our cultural bias in order to maintain a procreative and male-dominated social structure.

Anthropology also seems to dispute the claim that homosexuality is "unnatural." It tells us that homosexuality has existed since the beginning of time and has flourished to a greater or lesser degree in both primitive and complex, sophisticated societies, depending upon the presence or absence of applicable taboos. Most of us are familiar with the fact that homosexuality was practiced and was for the most part accepted in ancient Greece and Rome. It was recognized and institutionalized as an integral part of the Spartan social structure. Certainly there were homosexuals during Biblical times, as clearly illustrated by the laws against homosexuality which have come down to us. Homosexuals are found in many of the primitive tribes of other lands, as well as among the Plains Indians of North America—the Cheyenne, the Sioux, the Blackfoot and the Navajo allowed men of the tribe to practice it. According to the renowned anthropologist Dr. Margaret Mead, if lesbianism also existed, the Plains Indian tribes didn't seem to worry about it—with the exception of the Dakotas, who heartily objected. On the whole, homosexuality was the prerogative of the men. However, the Navajo did recognize the "manly-hearted woman."

Not only was there homosexuality among the Plains tribes, but there was transvestism. Such a man would be called a *berdoch* or *hemanah,* and among the Navajo such a man was the most admired person. He could do everything a man could do and also everything a woman could do, except bear children (according to Dr. Mead, even that could be pretended in the Mojave Tribe!). She cites the study of this tribe by George Devereaux as the best study of homosexuality among the Indians. "They did all sorts of things in that tribe," she said. "It was a wild situation, and it was accepted."

Dr. Mead's reference to the Plains Indians will remind many of us of the popular movie *Little Big Man.* It played to enthusiastic audiences a few years ago and was set among the North American Plains Indians. It also helps to identify the character "Little Horse" as a homosexual or transvestite, one was not quite certain which. He was, however, an amusing character and the source of great hilarity for the viewing public, who undoubtedly thought he was invented for purposes of comedy by the writers. That was not the case; the movie was historically authentic and presented an accurate picture of a Plains Indian society. On careful observation, one could see that the tribe did not consider Little Horse a figure for ridicule. His behavior was simply considered to be "his nature," and he was thus accepted as a rightful member of his society. The members of the tribe fittingly referred to themselves with pride as *human beings*.

In elaborating further about Indian customs, Dr. Mead went on to speculate that the presence of homosexuality among the Indians might well be due to the overemphasis on bravery. "They overdid it to such an extent," she said, "that they had to let some males out. One way of going out was to become a transvestite. This did not necessarily mean that they were homosexual, but it did mean that they took the roles of women publicly. They did not participate in fighting with the war parties, although they did go out with them. Their roles on such occasions were to tell stories and act as go-betweens in love affairs—things like that."

Other anthropologists have told us that among certain New Guinea tribes and the Australian aborigines, it was considered part of a young man's initiation into manhood to become the homosexual partner of an older man for several years of his youth. It is also said that a little over thirty years ago the famous anthropologist E. E. Evans-Pritchard, working among the Azande tribe of West Africa, found homosexuality being practiced by both men and women. However, for some reason or other, his reports were suppressed by the Anthropological Society until a few years ago when they came to light again. His findings evidently are to be published at last, and one can read exactly what did go on among Azande men and women.

Dr. Mead also called attention to the speculation over the

Maridindanims of New Guinea. This tribe institutionalized homosexuality and regarded heterosexuality as very difficult to initiate. Ceremonies were reported wherein a copulating boy and girl would be thrown into a pit and killed. These reports have been challenged by those who believe that the ceremonies were mock rather than actual. Nevertheless, according to Dr. Mead, whether actual or mock, the ceremonies indicate that they had the idea that people would be naturally homosexual, and could only be turned into heterosexuals through great effort. Obviously, there must have been some sex between males and females in order to maintain population levels.

Dr. Mead further theorized that in sexual relations between men and women (where women resist the approach of men), differences in female receptivity may be due to the structural differences in hymen and clitoris, which may vary enormously from individual to individual, with therefore tremendous variation in receptivity. She also suggested that the great differences in temperament among the women being institutionalized in society would have bearing on acceptance or resistance.

"I personally think," she said, "that human beings are bisexual. And extreme homosexuals and extreme heterosexuals are both deviates."

Dr. Mead called attention to the practice of homosexuality in traditional Japanese, Korean and Balinese societies, where a male may practice homosexuality for a period during his youth and then marry. "In Balinese society casual homosexuality was not difficult to accept because of the notion that sex can only exist with the penis, and the more penises, the better. Male homosexuality therefore was acceptable, but not transvestism. Actually they don't care what sex is with as long as the penis is honored," said Dr. Mead. "Lesbianism exists in these societies but it is not looked upon with any importance; it would be considered the lowest form of sexual activity because there is no penis involved—and the society was based upon the importance of the penis to sexuality."

In many societies where harems are prevalent, lesbianism seems to flourish. What the women do in private matters not at all, so long as they are available for the man who desires them, when he desires them.

Dr. Mead spoke of the attitude toward sodomy among one of the primitive peoples with whom she has worked. "Sodomy is spoken of pejoratively in everyday conversation. There are eleven words for sodomy among these people and they are used by everybody all the time, including the women to each other. One woman will say to another, 'I'll sodomize you,' and the other may reply, 'With what?' Naturally the children hear all this, and often the little boys will go around attacking each other sexually. Their elders would pull them apart and give them a spear, or stick, counseling them 'to fight instead.' " Dr. Mead's relation of these incidents of her experience among primitive peoples leads one to digress momentarily from the subject, and to speculate on the significance of the incident of the spear to the behavior of mankind in general.

The substitution of the spear for sexual play, the counseling "to fight instead," suggests that war very well may be a sublimely homosexual act. We have had a further suggestion of the idea, at least in a free association, although expressing the opposite, in demonstrations against the Vietnam war where placards appeared bearing the legend "Make love, not war!" Soldiering, which has historically been an exclusive activity of men—living and fighting together, having no responsibilities, sharing a camaraderie—has been extremely attractive to many men, and this very attractiveness may account for the continuation of wars from the beginning of time. Many men—especially after World War II, a major conflict with which all of this nation was in sympathy—have found it extremely difficult to adjust to civilian life and responsibility.

About homosexuality in our own American Judeo-Christian society, Dr. Mead is of the opinion that we do not have the proper taboos regarding it. "You either have to taboo homosexuality or institutionalize it, that's all there is to it. Otherwise, it will wreck public life." She explained the reasoning for her statement: "By institutionalizing homosexuality, I mean setting it up so everybody can name it, and recognize it. Where one can safely say, 'She is her girl friend,' or 'He's his boy friend.' Perfectly public. Sparta is the best example of institutionalized homosexuality. They had pairs in the army—homosexual pairs—who would die for each other, and it made for a strong army."

Institutionalization of homosexuality in America could work toward the betterment of society. "I don't mean that it should just be tolerated, I mean where it is accepted as an integral part of the society, in the same way that marriage is. I'm not advocating homosexual marriages, but I would advocate legal arrangements by which people could share property in common, tax benefits, rights to protect each other legally . . . rights of consent in cases of incapacity such as mental disturbance, or permission to perform autopsies in case of death, which presently is allowed only to a blood relative or a spouse. Provisions should be made beforehand to protect each partner, before a partnership is entered into. A homosexual partnership should be just as much a part of our society as marriage or as heterosexual partnership. We need to protect friendships by institutionalizing them. Only by institutionalizing homosexuality can we control it."

By "control" Dr. Mead was suggesting that we regulate homosexual relations in the same way we regulate heterosexual relations: they are legal between consenting *adults*. "The Dutch placed the age of consent for homosexuality at twenty-one, eighteen for heterosexuality. That's a reasonable point to start," Dr. Mead said. "We could have institutionalized homosexuality now by abolishing existing laws concerning it, making it legal between consenting adults—recognizing legal partnerships." Dr. Mead felt that the move is definitely toward legality of homosexuality as long as it is practiced among consenting adults in private. However, she felt that one of the problems has been that many homosexuals don't want it limited to "in private;" some want to flaunt, or to cruise. This upsets the hierarchical organizational lines, and opens people up to all sorts of destructive pressures.

Dr. Mead also felt that the gay activists and gay liberation movements will advance acceptance, but "running around wearing a button that says *I'm a Lesbian* whether a person is or not will not bring about the change in public attitude. Turning homosexuality into a violent attack on society may do a great deal of harm to their cause. The thing to do is to get rid of the laws that interfere with the behavior of consenting adults. Consenting adults in private should run their own lives, and that goes just as much for heterosexual couples who don't wish to get married but still wish to legalize or sanctify a partnership."

Discussing the issue of sex in public life, Dr. Mead's contention was that it is damaging. "Illegal homosexuality in the army, in the government, or anywhere else where it crosses organizational levels in public life, wrecks it. That's something we're going to have to learn in this country. Either it must be institutionalized or forbidden, and it hasn't anything on God's earth to do with morals—in the religious sense. It isn't about morals, it's about running an army, or running a government, or society. And it isn't just limited to homosexuality. For example, to run a family you have to have an incest taboo, and you have to have heterosexual as well as homosexual taboos. We have heterosexual institutionalization in the form of marriage, we need the same thing for homosexuals in the form of legalized partnerships."

Dr. Mead spoke of heterosexual behavior which crosses organizational levels as also being a destructive force. "If women are going to be successful in public life they have to stay out of bed with their bosses. Bosses are going to have to stay out of bed with their female employees, too. This crosses organizational levels and breeds a destructive element that can wreck business as well as society."

Dr. Mead observed that a strong and capable woman was often accused of lesbianism. Usually she had to either go to bed with the boss or be one of the boys in order to be accepted and to succeed. "In the past when a woman wanted to break into public life, she had to play at being a man. For seventy-five years we demanded that a woman lawyer or a woman doctor go around dressed like a man, with a collar and shirt and all that rubbish. This didn't necessarily demand lesbianism, or produce it, of course. But now women have decided that they don't want to just imitate men and so you get new developments."

On the social acceptance level Lesbians have not come in for quite the same discrimination as the male homosexual. For one thing, we as a society are not as disturbed by two women living together as we are about two men living together. This is not surprising, for, as Dr. Mead pointed out, "no society has ever been happy about women living alone. They're an open temptation, and they get into the men's fantasies, and men can't bear it. By and large, women would rather live with another woman than live alone. One of the major methods of interfering with male homosexuality has been to not let them set up households together. But we let women do it all the time; it keeps two women together and that doesn't give the men nightmares. Therefore lesbianism has been better accepted. To date, Lesbians have also been less promiscuous than the male homosexual. Where you have open lesbian promiscuousness, it is simply a cheap imitation of men. Women are homemakers by profession, if not by nature, so one of them cooks and the other does something else in the household for an equal division of labor. This in fact protects society. As I said, according to society, women should not be living alone, so lesbianism causes no problem unless, of course, the Lesbians are out on a rampage seducing. Women living together are establishing a home, and that's what society wants in the first place. So Lesbians, whether overt or covert, are not defying the woman's role, they are just doubling it. And besides, when you have ten million extra women in the country, what are you going to do with them if you don't let them live together?

"In a good part of the Western world there is less of a taboo on affection between women, there's less of a taboo on intimacy. Women can be close friends without raised eyebrows. A woman doesn't have a nervous breakdown if she's asked to room with another woman at a conference. They don't have the same fear of lavatories. We lock women's lavatories up for fear men will get in them, but we don't lock up lavatories because we fear that one woman is going to attack another. All of these things are important and significant, and make an easier climate for women. I believe that what attack there has been on lesbianism is an overflow from the attack on homosexuality in males."

Quite aside from Dr. Mead's positive observations, the population control people have in fact publically stated that we should look upon the homosexual with more understanding. After all, they are not propagative, therefore not contributing to the problem of overpopulation. Of course, this is often said somewhat tongue in cheek, but the point is well taken. Dr. Judith Blake, chairman of the Department of Demography, College of Letters and Science, University of California at Berkeley, in a study entitled, "Population Policy For Americans: Is The Government Being Misled?" has written:

> With regard to sex roles, it is generally recognized that potential human variability is greater than is normally permitted *within* each sex category. Existing societies have tended to suppress and extinguish such variability and to standardize sexual roles in ways that imply that all "normal" persons will attain the status of parents. This coercion takes many forms, including one-sided indoctrina-

tion in schools, legal barriers and penalties for deviation, and the threats of loneliness, ostracism, and ridicule that are implied in the unavailability of alternatives. Individuals who—by temperament, health, or constitution—do not fit the ideal sex-role pattern are nonetheless coerced into attempting to achieve it, and many of them do achieve it, at least to the extent of having demographic impact by becoming parents.

Therefore, a policy that sought out the ways in which coercion regarding sex roles is at present manifesting itself could find numerous avenues for relieving the coercion and for allowing life styles different from marriage and parenthood to find free and legitimized expression. Such a policy would have an effect on the content of expectations regarding sex roles as presented and enforced in schools, on laws concerning sexual activity between consenting adults, on taxation with respect to marital status and number of children, on residential building policies, and on just about every facet of existence that is now organized as exclusively to favor and reward a pattern of sex roles based on marriage and parenthood. (11)

Dr. Blake is not suggesting that we adopt homosexuality as a solution to overpopulation. She is saying that every coupling does not have to culminate in marriage and parenthood. She is concerned with demographics, numbers in terms of population growth. In the light of that, she is suggesting that our society allow different life styles to coexist. These can include unmarried heterosexual couples, couples who do not wish to have children, and homosexual couples. She is also suggesting that we as a society cease elevating parenthood as the pinnacle of personal achievement, and the purpose of every union. The homosexual is only incidentally a part of the group choosing alternative life styles. After all, our fixation on procreation has got us into the population *fix,* and Dr. Blake is suggesting that we look at other life styles and respect them as well.

Dr. Mead tended to agree with Dr. Blake: "Monosexual households are an alternative to everlastingly remarrying, which is one of the stupid things we do. We keep making people marry, even if they don't want children—and remarry, and remarry when they've had all the children they want. Of course, when the church's belief is so much in heaven, you have to have some procreation to populate heaven!"

An exhaustive exploration of anthropological studies, although interesting, would not particularly advance the purpose of this book any more than would an exhaustive presentation of animal behavior studies. Hopefully some familiarity with findings in both fields will raise the question of the validity of claims that homosexuality is "unnatural" or, "against nature." If one accepts this Judeo-Christian moral concept, then how is one to reconcile findings which clearly show such behavior to be natural in certain mammalian species and in other cultures? This is not to suggest that our elective cultural attitudes are totally invalid, but to open the questions of relevance, validity and justification.

Of course, any culture or any individual within a culture can elect to reject homosexuality as an acceptable life style, but this rejection should be considered an individual choice independent of justification by quasi-scientific claims. Such claims only thinly veil moralistic judgments.

The question of "natural" or "against nature" cannot be laid to rest without a discussion of genetics; for zealots in the field of homosexual repressiveness do not stop with those charges. The most deadly and generally unfounded claims come from the field of genetics. "Homosexuals are freaks"; "something is missing in them"; "they are made wrong"; "they're not like other people." From such pronouncements one envisions the homosexual as a kind of hermaphrodite, a eunuch—a freak that ought to be exhibited in the circus. A Lesbian is seen as a kind of surrogate male, consumed with penis envy to the extent of stuffing her crotch, and a male homosexual as a surrogate female behaving as a woman and probably wearing lace panties under his trousers. Some even go so far as to lay it to chromosomal and hormonal anomalies.

Listen to one of the foremost experts in the field of genetics and the homosexual: "There is no difference between the so-called 'normal' human being and the homosexual as far as the chromosome count is concerned. Once in a while I will have someone come to me who has a gender problem, or a homosexual problem, and he will turn out to have an extra X or Y chromosome. If I did a study all over the world, epidemiologically instead of casually, I might find that there is a higher rate than I have been able to find in my studies at the present. But when you take a physically normal homosexual whose life style is practicing homosexuality, it absolutely does not follow that he has the additional X or Y chromosome. It is extremely rare."* So said John Money, Ph.D., of the Department of Psychiatry and Behavioral Science, The Johns Hopkins School of Medicine and Hospital in Baltimore, who has done extensive work and written widely on the subject of chromosomes, hormones, and gender identity.

Dr. Money was even more specific when he said: "If you took a random selection of five hundred people from the gay liberation group—and I'm specifically citing that group because I don't want a sample out of an institution or jail; they're already biased—if you took people who are making it out in the hurly-burly of life, then you might find a very few, but generally you would find none of them with a chromosome count that was different. And I have to point out that I am very specifically saying chromosome count. There is no other evidence from any other source of genetic study which suggests that the genes would contribute to homosexual circumstances."

As for hormonal influences, Dr. Money cited the same kind of sample evidence. If the hormones of five hundred people

* Personal interview, Baltimore, Maryland, March 1972.

from gay liberation were tested, Dr. Money believes he would have only a very small chance of picking up one with abnormal hormone production. He pointed out that he was speaking only about males, because no one has extensively studied females. He speculated that there might be the possibility of some men with atypical hormone levels, including some who might be sterile. "But exactly what the connection might be between that and their development as a homosexual, we do not know. But the best interpretation would be the same one that is made for people with the extra X chromosome who have a homosexual gender identity —they have a relatively vulnerable or unstable psychosexual system in the beginning."

Dr. Money went on to explain the very complex circumstances under which such a condition might occur: "This occurs in the very important postnatal period, say between eighteen months and three and a half to four years, when almost all of a person's gender identity is being differentiated. Some people, you might say, have a strong affinity for an unstable differentiation of their gender identity. But they will not automatically differentiate a homosexual identity. There has got to be some other factor that meets the child from the environment to help it differentiate in a homosexual way. It may show itself up, it almost certainly will show itself up, in some of the behavior of the childhood period, but it doesn't show itself up clearly and definitely until you get the extra impetus to sex from the sexual feeling of the libido at puberty when the sex hormones come into play. That's when the whole behavioral pattern comes into play."

From Dr. Money's statements one understands that an unstable system can produce a vulnerability to homosexuality, and it may be influenced by the hormonal output of the mother during the prenatal period; however, this thesis cannot at present be proved, because there is no way of proving it after the fact. There is speculation that the hormonal activity within the mother may be produced by some medication she takes during the pregnancy: certain sleeping pills maybe, or some psychoactive drugs. But again there is no way of knowing. Yet even given that hormones can have an influence on the fetus, they still do not irrevocably determine his sexual orientation. Dr. Money puts it specifically: "A child's gender identification is not thus one hundred per cent determined at birth. His prenatal environment may make him a vulnerable creature, but what happens next is a result of environment outside the womb." Whereas social input postnatally can effect a homosexual identity, Dr. Money has stated that cases of a known prenatal hormonal influence are quite rare.

Dr. Money also calls attention to the fact that there are documented cases of girls born with the clitoris so overdeveloped as to be mistaken for a penis, and of boys born with such underdeveloped penises as to be considered female. Sometimes similar rare cases are not discovered until puberty, when the one begins to develop breasts, and the other fails to menstruate. However, these rare cases are not a question of genetics, and illustrate very well the power of social input in the development of gender identity. Although the type of girl mentioned above is genetically a girl, she has been raised to think of herself as a boy, and so differentiates; the same is true of the genetic boy who has been raised as a girl. This fact alone lends credit to the educated contention that homosexuality is not genetic. It should also be pointed out here that hermaphroditism should not be confused with homosexuality either. Homosexuality is no more a case of physiology than it is a chromosomal or hormonal matter. Nor should transvestism or transsexualism be confused with homosexuality.

After studying the literature on constitutional or physiological causes of homosexuality, S. E. Willis wrote: "After reviewing all the reports, the only conclusion possible was that positive evidence of a physical nature that might serve sine qua non as an indicator of homosexuality was absolutely nonexistent." (12)

As for the hormonal argument, Dr. Money has thoroughly

established the fact that sex hormones do not influence sexual direction. In the *Journal of Nervous and Mental Diseases* in 1961 he said: "The direction or content of erotic inclination in the human species is not controlled by the sex hormones. Hormonally speaking, the sex drive *is neither male nor female but undifferentiated*—an urge for warmth and sensation of close body contact and genital proximity." (13) This conclusion about findings in humans does not seem incompatible with the data from animal behavior studies mentioned earlier and further supports the postulate that sexuality is essentially neutrally gender-directed—neither heterosexual nor homosexual. The *natural* impulse is to respond to the *given* stimuli.

At the end of a study entitled "Factors in the Genesis of Homosexuality," Dr. Money further concluded:

> Chromosomes, gonads, hormones, genital morphology and body image, sex assignment, gender identity, psychosexual neutrality and differentiation, imprinting, family and cultural pattern—these and more factors in the genesis of homosexuality have been passed in review. One arrives at the conclusion that the final common pathway for the establishment of a person's gender identity and, hence, his erotic arousal pattern, whatever the secondary and antecedent determinants, is in the brain. There it is established as a neuro-cognitional function. The process takes place primarily after birth, and the basic fundamentals are completed before puberty. The principles whereby all this happens await elucidation. (14)

Dr. Money is supported by Alfred Auerback when he states: "No biological basis for homosexuality has been found. Hormonal studies, even of extremely effeminate men, have shown no variation from normal. There are no measurable physical characteristics to differentiate the homosexual from the heterosexual." (15)

M. B. Clinard adds additional support when he states in *Sociology of Deviant Behavior:*

> Biology is of little relevance, however, to the social or symbolic behavior of man. There are no physical functions or structures, no combination of genes, and no glandular secretions which contain within themselves the power to direct, guide, or determine the type, form, and course of the social behavior of human beings. Physical structures or properties set physical limits on the activities of persons, but whether such structures will set social limits depends on the way in which cultures or subcultures symbolize or interpret these physical properties (16)

Dr. Money reaffirms his conclusions in his article entitled "Matched Pairs of Hermaphrodites: Behavioral Biology of Sexual Differentiation from Chromosomes to Gender Identity": "Gender-identity differentiation is programmed to take place largely after birth, and also to be dependent to a large degree on stimulation from, and interaction with, the social environment." (17) In an article by Faubion Bowers in the *Saturday Review* Dr. Money chooses to use the words of a friend of his to put it plainly and simply: "Homosexuals are just like everybody else—excepting more so." (18)

Notwithstanding all of the aforementioned scientists' statements, there is yet another dimension to the term *nature,* and to what is *natural,* which is separate and apart from animal behavior, anthropology or genetics. To use nature as a definition of what is natural behavior for man or woman is to presuppose that nature is an end in itself, apart from man, above man, transcending human reason and will, a force determining morality and reason by a sort of osmosis. To unquestioningly accept the idea that nature is synonymous with good and right, and therefore moral, is to subjugate reason.

Nature may produce rain, which in turn produces flooding; it is a law of nature that when an overabundance of rain falls, a river will overflow and result in flooding. Is it also natural, therefore, that a flood will cost homes and lives—and is that good? It may be nature that makes man fight for his property and his young, but is it good if that fighting costs the lives of other men? It may be nature that makes human beings engage in sexual intercourse, and it will be considered quite natural that they do; but if intercourse is used as a form of power, if it results in mental injury, physical pain, unwanted parenthood or serious overpopulation, is it still good?

Dr. Robert Johann, professor of philosophy at Fordham University, New York, in a personal interview in New York in March 1972, put it this way: "It is not nature as such that has moral relevance. It is reason. The morally good is not simply what is in accord with nature, but what presents itself as reason in a particular circumstance." Dr. Johann called attention to his essay entitled "Nature, Reason and Morality," in which he quotes the French Jesuit Père de Finance: "It is not because reason is natural that we should follow reason. On the contrary, it is only because our nature shares in reason that it is good to act in accord with nature. The emminent dignity of human nature springs from its aptitude to follow reason to determine itself reasonably. Only in terms of this capacity does it have moral value." (19)

Dr. Johann stated his own position on the question of nature as it relates to homosexuality thusly: "I would say, one can't argue against homosexuality simply on the basis of the traditional understanding of sexuality, or on the position of *natural* law. The only law you have there is that it is a perversion of a natural faculty, and that's going back to the concept of nature as itself a norm apart from reason, apart from what is accomplished in a concrete situation. One could take a pragmatic stand towards it on the basis of consequence, but that would have to be based on investigation of psychology in terms of what homosexuality might lead to. But insofar as you have a genuinely mutal and personal relationship which happens to find expression this way, one can't, I say, simply argue in terms of *nature,* apart from consequence, or anything else. My own ethical thought is that man's task is the creation of community, genuine communication, mutuality, reciprocity, whatever. I am talking about community in terms of communication, you might say in reciprocal relationships in which those who are the participants are able to act autonomously in the light of insight and judgment and on their own terms—in other words, be themselves within the relationship. I can't foreclose any sort of relationship if that's the goal, except insofar as a certain relationship might be limitable, and I just can't see how that could necessarily be presupposed beforehand."

Dr. Johann's learned and civilized reasoning reminds us that we need to *keep* reminding ourselves to examine attitudes; question where our attitudes came from; question their relevance; examine our inner selves for a sound basis of personal philosophy. If we must begin from the basis of nature, then perhaps we need to define nature more specifically and understand it more rationally in the light of scientific findings, such as have been expressed by the scholars herein.

What seems to be both natural and reasonable is first to acknowledge that sexuality is a natural fact of life, and that it is not unnatural to respond with love, warmth, affection, and physical expression to another human being, regardless of sex. The foregoing data seems to support the validity of discarding such labels as "heterosexual," "bisexual," or "homosexual." There is sexuality in all mammalian species, and it may be expressed in a number of different ways, according to attraction, stimulus, and response. Beyond that, it is a matter of choice as to what one derives the greatest satisfaction from, and in what way one can evolve the most comfortable life style in a world where it is becoming increasingly more difficult to be comfortable on almost any level of life. One might conclude that life is becoming exactly the opposite of Dr. Paul Lehmann's definition of God's intention for man's purpose on earth—"to make human life more human"—human beings more mature . . . and maturity being a comfortable coexistence with reason. It is not reasonable, as we have learned from the animal behaviorists, anthropologists and geneticists, to continue to label homosexuality "unnatural" or "against nature," and it certainly is not mature to continue to do so.

Chapter 5

Psychiatry, Homosexuality and Bisexuality

The homosexual today is kind of like the invisible man. But what most people don't realize is that homosexuals are all around. They're not just somewhere "out there." They are in one's own family—they could be one's doctor, one's minister, one's friend, husband, wife, whatever. People don't like to think about this, but it is so. There are a lot of homosexuals, a group of people, in fact, numbering into the millions, and they're not going to stay invisible forever.

—Dr. Martin Hoffman*

Many homosexuals believe that psychiatry/psychology has often been their biggest enemy, and has done them the greatest harm. Some even believe that therapists have exploited them economically, increased guilt and self-devaluation, and tried to coerce them into accepting a way of life that has produced more anxiety and unhappiness. Naturally this does not apply across the board to all therapists and analysts, but many homo-

* Personal Interview, Dallas, Texas, May 1972.

sexuals are angry at the analytical profession and are expressing this anger. The charge, therefore, bears examination.

This smoldering anger surfaced at the 1970 American Psychiatric Association meeting in San Francisco when a panel of psychiatrists attempted to discuss "The Difference Between Transsexualism and Homosexuality." The seminar was crashed by the Berkeley Gay Liberation Front, a very angry group, who shouted down the participating psychiatrists and took over the meeting. Among the doctors on the panel were wise men, who sympathized with the homosexual viewpoint, but there were others who were not so understanding—Dr. Irving Bieber in particular, who has been negatively outspoken for some years, and is considered scientifically controversial by many of his colleagues. Dr. Bieber contends that homosexuality is in and of itself pathological. He bases his theory on samples of homosexual men only, and men in therapy. The data for his study was not taken from the homosexuals directly, but was supplied by therapists. For this reason, some doctors think that his study reflects a very limited point of view. (Dr. Bieber claims to have gathered data from observation of homosexuals while he was serving as a medical officer in the service during World War II. Aside from the fact that whatever information he gathered would now be almost thirty years old, it is fascinating intelligence in view of the facts that homosexuals are not accepted in the armed forces and that discovery of the fact of homosexuality earns a dishonorable discharge. Dr. Bieber's powers of persuasion must have been almost miraculous to induce a soldier to confess to him what he lied about to the induction officer, and Dr. Bieber must have inspired great faith as well for the soldier to trust him not to inform the army . . . which would presumably have been his duty in view of army policy. Did Dr. Bieber conduct his study unbeknownst to the army, or maybe unbeknownst to the soldiers? It is all a little confusing.) If the truth be known, however, Dr. Bieber probably was the main target in the invasion of the A.P.A. meeting, but by being on the panel, he may have paradoxically served to start a significant reappraisal of A.P.A. attitudes toward the homosexual.

"They were a very angry group," said Dr. Martin Hoffman, one of the panel members, "and while their methods were not mine—I am still committed to rational dialogues—their attempt had an impact on the association, the kind of effect that nothing else seems to have had. It was the thing, I think, that made possible a loosening up of the A.P.A. and brought about the panels we've had the last couple of years on homosexuality, with homosexuals participating in discussions. I don't think the association would have come around to doing that if it hadn't been for that disruption in 1970."

Two years later, at the 125th Annual Meeting of the American Psychiatric Association in Dallas, Texas, a constructive and spirited panel dialogue was scheduled which brought both homosexuals and psychiatrists together in open and free discussion. The subject this time was "Psychiatry: Friend or Foe of the Homosexual?" It was conceded at that meeting that many psychiatrists and psychologists had conducted studies and advanced theories on homosexuality based on small samples of homosexuals in therapy, and all too often reflecting the personal bias of the analyst. It was felt that this kind of so-called research was dangerous because of the influence of its conclusions upon an already prejudiced public, and invalid because it does not represent the nonpatient, nonneurotic homosexual who is making it out in the world, living a constructive, useful life without the need of psychotherapy. Additionally, it was conceded that to a large degree homosexuals seeking therapy did not do so because of their homosexuality, but for other reasons—reasons that would have existed regardless of their homosexuality.

This is not to say that homosexuality cannot place more pressures upon an individual who is already disturbed by a deeper cause, but that homosexuality was most often not the primary reason which caused the person to seek therapy, nor the cause of the deeper disturbance. Family difficulties, job tensions, relationship problems, anxieties—any number of pressures could impinge on either homosexual or heterosexual, motivating the person to seek therapy.

It was interesting to note that Dr. Bieber had been asked to participate in the discussion at Dallas, but had declined, as did some other more strident exponents of the orthodox attitude toward homosexuality.

Psychiatrists, then, are put in the awkward position of having to reassess their previous theories because homosexuals are refusing to allow therapists to advance theories which the homosexuals themselves consider invalid without protest. Additionally, the more advanced theoreticians with wide experience in treating homosexuals, as well as the newer generation of psychiatrists, are not buying the older, more orthodox theories. It was Dr. Hoffman's opinion that the A.P.A. could not return to the rigid orthodox concepts of the past. He said: "I teach at the University of California at San Francisco, and our medical students are simply not willing to buy this model any more. They are going to be the future members of the A.P.A., and they are going to have an important impact on the entire subject. It is important, too, because more and more the public and the church are looking to psychiatry to define social reality. In a sense we are the new priests. It is difficult for the church, and the public who look to them, to break with the old traditions. The antihomosexual bias in Western civilization is originally of religious origin, out of Judeo-Christianity, and it is just no longer relevant."*

Whenever and wherever homosexuality is discussed, one soon learns that two questions invariably surface as the core of the discussion: 1) What are the causes? 2) Can it be cured? These two questions elicit a rash of theories and claims, and

---

* Dr. Hoffman's practice is primarily among homosexuals, and he is the author of *The Gay World: Male Homosexuality and the Social Creation of Evil* (New York: Basic Books, 1968).

neither deals very realistically with the fact that it is the existence of the homosexual living from day to day in a hostile society as a human being entitled to equal rights which is really the pressing and important issue. In this respect the two questions are almost irrelevant. Yet, if *cause* and *cure* are the major concern of the general public, then they should be explored, but not exclusively fixed upon.

If, as estimated, there are some ten million existing homosexuals in the United States today, the cause and cure, the before and after, are hardly the major issues—particularly when most homosexuals will state that the cause is not of particular interest to them, and a cure of even less interest. They are interested in how to survive in a hostile society, and they flatly state that they do not feel the problem lies in their homosexuality, but in society as it relates to the homosexual.

There are many theories about causes and cures, but no definite answers. Answers ventured by the more strident old-line analysts are instantly attacked by younger, more liberal colleagues. Some basic assumptions, however, do emerge to be challenged by some and hailed by others of like beliefs. Few, however, do not equivocate to a lesser or greater degree, and whether or not their theories can be accepted as scientifically valid depends on how well their data stacks up against opposing data presented by other analysts. The arguments rage on, because homosexuality is obviously a highly speculative subject, as is any subject involving unknown factors. It is the nature of man and scientist to want to know what is not known, and what sometimes, in fact, seems unknowable. The fascination with the question was well stated by Dr. Hoffman: "The reason why people choose one particular kind of sexual object, and I hate to use the word 'object' because it comes out of a psychoanalytic context, but I still think that it is a fascinating question. I wouldn't want to close the door on that. I wouldn't want to close the door on why A chooses a heterosexual form of expression, B chooses a homosexual form, and

C chooses an ambisexual form of expression—while D may not be very interested in sexual expression at all. That is, and will remain, a fascinating question until much more is known."

Perhaps two of the best-known orthodox theorists are Dr. Samuel B. Hadden, who proclaims homosexuality a sickness in loud and almost violent terms, suggesting that the homosexual should be compelled to submit to treatment for cure, and Dr. Irving Bieber, who along with nine other colleagues authored *Homosexuality: A Psychoanalytic Study of Male Homosexuals* (New York: Basic Books, 1962). According to one of his colleagues Dr. Bieber dominated the study, and wrote the conclusion without the aid of his colleagues, some of whom do not entirely agree with his conclusions. The core of the Bieber theory is that homosexuality is in and of itself pathology. Exactly what this means is somewhat difficult to get at, but one of the participants in the study, Dr. Ralph H. Gundlach, summed up the Bieber theory this way (personal interview, September 1972): "Heterosexuality and homosexuality are distinct; they do not form a continuum. Man, like other animal species, is born with a sexual orientation which guarantees heterosexuality, a heterosexual response. In most mammals it is conveyed by smell, and there is evidence of this in man as well.

"Male homosexuality is always a result of a disordered sexual development. It is similar to frigidity and impotence in that first there are established certain unrealistic fears which get aroused by the attempt or thought of having a sexually fulfilling relation with a woman; fears that the behavior will invite or provoke attack by powerful dangers, such as a powerful father.

"The central fact is the inability to combine a close interpersonal relationship with a sexual one, as evidenced by the compulsive screwing, seeking the largest penis, or promiscuity, all carried out with no concern for the actual person involved. Rather, the aim is repressed in the endless attempt to compensate for feelings of masculine inadequacy, to top, placate and/or absorb the potency of the partner.

"Heterosexual inadequacies and seriously impaired masculine identities are a result of hidden, but incapacitating, fears of violent competition with males, with a consequent fear of showing heterosexual interests. Homosexuality is pathological adaptation, being an accommodation to unrealistic fears. We find no homosexual who has a reasonably warm and constructive relationship to both parents. Such a person is not demanding psychiatry."

Dr. Gundlach states that he finds the description true for a portion of male homosexuals in his experience, but he finds almost *none of this applies to the female homosexual, on which he has done extensive studies* in association with Dr. Bernard F. Riess.

It is one of the last paragraphs of the conclusion of the Bieber book which raises cries of protest from analysts as well as homosexuals:

> We assume that heterosexuality is the *biologic* norm, and that unless interfered with, all individuals are heterosexual. Homosexuals do not bypass heterosexual development phases and all remain potentially heterosexual.
>
> Our findings are optimistic guideposts not only for homosexuals but for the psychoanalysts who treat them. We are firmly convinced that psychoanalysts may well orient themselves to a heterosexual objective in treating homosexual patients rather than *adjust* even the more recalcitrant patient to a homosexual destiny. A conviction based on scientific fact that a heterosexual goal is achievable helps both patient and psychoanalyst to take in stride the inevitable setbacks during psychoanalysis. (1)

Theories such as those of Hadden and Bieber have been widely aired and referred to—perhaps because their theories are comfortable for those who prefer to dismiss the homosexual as a sick, neurotic plague upon society. Let us, however, explore the more realistic opposing points of view.

Of the Bieber theory, Dr. Hoffman commented: "While I

don't think I ever agree with Bieber, I will agree that perhaps there is more pathology in the 'gay' world than in the straight world. But where Bieber and I fundamentally disagree is in his belief that homosexuality is in and of itself a pathology. I deny that position. I maintain that the pathology is the result of a hostile society. I would say, for example, that there is more pathology among the American Indians because the American Indian is the subject of a lot of persecution, a lot of discrimination."

Many prominent analysts share Dr. Hoffman's belief, and abhor Dr. Bieber's theory. Dr. John Money says: "I do not agree with Bieber's theory of etiology. It is too incomplete for me." But it would be unfair to attack Dr. Bieber exclusively, for he is not alone in his theories. The school that believes homosexuality to be a sickness has many followers; many who have themselves done little or no serious work in the area readily agree, as does a large portion of the lay public, having taken assurance from these men that their own prejudices about homosexuality were *right* all along. It is interesting that these men cling rigidly to outdated theories while fifty years ago Freud himself wrote: "Homosexuality is nothing to be ashamed of; no vice, no degradation, it can not be classified as illness." Kinsey too, stated that "biologically there is no sexual outlet which I will admit as abnormal." Dr. Laura Perls (who with her late husband co-founded the Gestalt approach to therapy) says: "I see homosexuality not as a sickness, but rather as a *creative* adjustment to a given set of genetic and social circumstances. The 'successful' homosexual who accepts his homosexuality and can integrate it into his life style actually by-passes the more common possibilities for neurotic adjustment. The homosexual *patient* is usually dissatisfied with and unaccepting of his homosexuality and comes with anxiety, depression, family and other social problems—difficulties anyone can and does have." *

* Personal interview, New York, February 1971.

It would serve no particular purpose here to enumerate the doctors who subscribe to the theories of homosexuality as a sickness or an abnormality. The antihomosexual theoreticians have had a forum for the presentation of their ideas for many, many years, and most people are familiar with them—if not in a specific, at least in a general way. What is needed is some exposure of the new thinking and findings of more objective scientists. And because so many of the studies have involved only the male homosexual, this chapter will try, when possible, to present information on the female homosexual.

Firstly, it should be stated that almost no one is 100 per cent anything—heterosexual or homosexual. In the case of the homosexual woman, the few studies done indicate that not many have been exclusively homosexual from the very beginning. Many have had heterosexual relationships; many have been married and had children. Some are still married, some are bisexual, and some, of course, are exclusively homosexual.

It is generally acknowledged that all of us have the potential for ambisexuality, and that we all have both the male and female components in our make-up from the beginning. The potentiality for development weighted more heavily in either direction depends very much on environmental input. Several scientists have shaken guardians of the social structure with statements such as the one Dr. Money made in *Time* magazine (March 20, 1972): "Nature's first intention is to create a female. You have to add something to get a male." This idea gives much food for thought, and when widely known, what effect may it have on social structure and attitudes? Dr. Money is not suggesting that the female is inferior. He is stating that nature intends to create a female; that is the significant point. Nor is Dr. Money saying that the male is a kind of *improved* hybrid when he states that something must be added to get a male.

In a paper delivered at a symposium on "A New Psychology of Women or A Psychology for the New Woman Active or

Passive" at the Forty-second Annual Convention of the Eastern Psychological Association, Dr. Bernard Riess talked directly to this point when he began by quoting Dr. Mary Jane Sherfey from the *Journal of the American Psychoanalytic Association*. He said:

> Mary Jane Sherfey amply documents the neurology, embryology and anatomy of the developing sex structures and shows the essential femininity of the embryonic sexual apparatus. From conception to the fifth week of life, all embryos are feminine. Removal of fetal gonads proves this since all such operated organisms become structurally female. Masculinity arises from testicular inductors operating on the female substructures. The male is a deviant from the basic female pattern. Embryologically, the penis is but an enlargement of the clitoris; the scrotum is derived from the labia majora, etc. Truly Adam out of Eve.

This is not exactly the way the religious scholars put it to us. In the beginning was Adam/Eve, neither male nor female, but a creature combining both. Only when God perceived that the creature was lonely did he create two separate creatures which we identify as Adam and Eve, and not until later when he perceived that the land he had created needed to be populated did God make Eve and therefore women child-bearing. Now medical science tells us that the fetus is female, and everything seems to be coming together neatly to establish the fact that a lot of the accepted ideas upon which our social and sexual concepts have been founded are more myth than fact.

What is the significance of this intelligence upon a discussion of psychiatry and homosexuality? Homosexuality is *defined* by the so-called *sexual norm,* and this sexual norm is based upon the original order of creation, anatomical differences between man and woman, and the assumption that behavioral patterns should be dictated by that order of creation and those anatomical differences. Psychology then bases its concept of *behavioral norms* upon these basic assumptions. If those basic assumptions are erroneous in the light of what we now know about the order of creation and nature's intention, we must modify our concept of behavioral norms. Let's examine psychology's classic, or orthodox, theory of male-female behavior. Dr. Riess stated the classic theory quite succinctly in his paper:

> Sexuality in both male and female starts on a bisexual basis. Until puberty, sexual monism holds sway. However, this implies the primacy of the penis since it is so obvious an organ. The clitoris is only a small penis. The little girl is a little man until the castration complex when she discovers her "missing" part. Until puberty, maleness is phallic and femaleness is non-phallic or castrated. Since there is no penis, castration *fear* is absent, but castration *feelings* make for penis envy in the girl. This envy, in turn, forces her attention and libido to her father, whose child by her represents her possession of his penis. This is the female oedipus complex.
>
> What follows is a gradual withdrawal from the father. Lack of castration fear in girls makes for a slower, less traumatic resolution of the oedipus conflict than for boys. Hence the girl has a weaker superego. Since the clitoris is the analog of the penis, clitoral masturbation is essentially masculine or childish. With the recognition of castration, maturation must substitute the vagina for the clitoris as a satisfier of sexual drives and as a proof of femininity. Emptiness takes the place of an actual object and receptivity-passivity become the signs of the woman.

Dr. Riess then points out the basic conflict between the orthodox belief of the analytic world and the more recent and advanced theory.

> If the penis analog theory is fallacious, then much of the thinking about differences in behavior and conflicts must

be revised. What then of the Freudian concept of transference or maturation of clitoral into vaginal orgasm? Here the research of Masters and Johnson is crucial despite our attitudinal biases against its mechanical, photographic technology. In their work there was no such phenomenon as a purely vaginal orgasm nor can there be in the light of the neuronal innervation of both clitoris and vagina. Only the lower part of the latter organ has any innervation and much of the behavioral reaction during so-called vaginal orgasm has been shown to be the result of clitoral stimulation and labial and vaginal pressure on the clitoris. So much for the mythical superiority of vaginal orgasm.

Many women have known these facts for a long time, as can be seen by the discussions recorded in the second half of this book. However, they only now feel free to admit to their knowledge since many scientists have now offered scientific evidence for and have accepted as fact what once was merely "women's beliefs." Women no longer have to feel guilt and shame because they are unable to have "vaginal orgasm." Small wonder they felt that way—it was previously considered infantile sexuality, probably caused by too much masturbation.

Dr. Riess points out the significance of this new theory:

> I would like now to turn from the anatomic-biologic to the psychological arena and consider some alternatives to our male- and tradition-dominated theories.
>
> First, the clitoris, since it is not a penis analog, has qualities unique to it and it alone. Its sole function is to provide enjoyment. Unlike the penis, it is an organ of pleasure without the dynamic complications of urinary and reproductive use. This allows the woman to be narcissistic without guilt and confusion. The clitoris thus gives sanction to self-love and self-pleasure. It is my contention that this *uncomplicated* pleasure leads to many conse-

quences. Thus it has been said that the woman loves in order to be loved whereas the man *makes* love in order to gratify himself. In another sense, the clitoral satisfaction generalized into an expectation of pleasure from contact. The body as a whole comes to represent the pleasure derived by extension from the clitoris. It has been established by Gundlach and myself that homosexual women like the tenderness, the physical contact of skin on skin as much or more than specific genitality. Furthermore, in this respect, homosexual women are found to be indistinguishable from heterosexual comparison female subjects. In my work with women patients, there is often also said to be a need to be held, touched and contacted. Genital sex seems to be a secondary process which is more social and more enforced by societal and male expectations. The genital sexualization of narcissism is thus a later stage of interpersonal relationships. Further elaboration of this is given in an exciting book by Janine Chasseguet-Smirgel called *Female Sexuality: New Psychoanalytic Views.* Suffice it to say that, as analysts give up reliance on the equation of penis envy with submissiveness, they will discover what Masters and Johnson have stated: namely, that women have a capacity for sexual satisfaction not true of males. This threat to the male has required of him a repressive mechanism. Historically, this has been the institution of the family. Caring for the young and all the taboos concerning sexual activity during gestation protect the man from the demands of the female. Furthermore, by keeping his woman active at home, he has bought the time and freedom in which to exercise his own aggression and masculinity. Man's feeling of competence, his ability to demonstrate it in work and sexual prowess has been historically possible only by forcing his woman to take care of his domestic needs.

To a great extent, what I have outlined here is very skeletal since most writers on feminine psychology have been male or male-dominated. Melanie Klein, Helen

Deutsch and the others had to exist in the analytic associations dominated by their masters. Perhaps this is one reason why so few writers have dealt with the question of why women want children. To challenge this desire as a natural, organ-created "instinct" is to challenge the whole area of male dominance. And yet, it is the essential question in the battle for equality. Children lead to family life, family life has been oriented to free the man to do his thing and to prevent the women from having the same freedom. True liberation, therefore, means challenging the concept of the primacy of the family. (2)

Studies have shown that motherhood is not an inborn desire in all women. They have also shown that many women who have children resent them; some go so far as to reject them; some even mistreat them. Nor is it the ambition of all women to be married. Social and family pressures have driven many women into marriage, as has the absence of opportunity for equal employment and the need for economic security. Erroneous, male-instigated ideas about women are perpetuated by society, family structure, and even women themselves, most of whom have been brainwashed from infancy. In fact, the classic role of women as conceived by men and perpetuated by society is so masochistic it almost invites sadism. Yet women continue to tolerate a situation which can be the source of many of the ills they experience: hypochondria, alcoholism, insomnia, migraine headaches, and nervousness, to name a few. In many instances, these illnesses can be attributed to the frustrations inherent in being women under the suppression of the structure.

A surprising number of women, however, realize the source of their troubles, and this realization breeds resentments and sometimes outright rebellion. A surprising number of women actually desert husbands and children each year. But it is not the purpose of this chapter to plead a case for woman's liberation, although the author totally supports it in principle and believes it is the only way men and women will ever be able to coexist in harmony, develop the individuality and potential that can make them fulfilled and content, preserve the family as a constructive unit, rear healthy individuals, and build a society with realistic expectations. Unhappiness is the product of unrealistic expectations, and we have a lot of unhappiness in our society.

History has taught us that every form of slavery has bred rebellion, and we are witnessing a kind of rebellion in the woman's liberation movement. We are also witnessing rebellion in the young people, both male and female, who refuse to accept the old structure. The perpetuation of unrealistic concepts of men and women and of the family structure has many ramifications. Both unconscious and conscious resentments, disappointment, dreams, and angers, in both mothers and fathers, born out of the structural situation are sometimes projected onto the children. These same structural concepts motivate another unfortunate occurrence in the family. Studies have documented the difference in the treatment of boys and girls within the same family. Tradition demands that boys act as boys and girls as girls, and not all parents are equipped to handle these matters in wise and loving ways—particularly when unaccountable differences occur, and we see resistance to prescribed classic behavior. We have not been able to reconcile or accept that so-called *normal* may not be the same for every child. In fact, *normal* may not be *normal* at all. Rather, accepted convention has become a definition for normal, having nothing to do with scientific behavioral characteristics. A tree forcibly bent against the way it seems to naturally incline results in a deformed-looking and scarred tree; a square peg forced into a round hole often results in either a partially crumbled peg, or a split hole. It is not unreasonable to suggest that if we could allow for differences, adjust our concept of *normal,* accept a more realistic definition of maleness and femaleness, and keep our expectations within educated reality, our worst fears would be minimized, and a child would find its own way to his or her particular normality.

If women in general have difficulty with the structure, think of the difficulty a Lesbian must have—experiencing both the suppression of being a woman and the oppression of being lesbian. And if children in general have difficulty trying to maintain any individuality and identity, think of what the child experiencing feelings of homosexuality and difference must feel.

First, let's think about general differences. Consider, for example, a girl who shows more independence and aggressiveness than is deemed feminine by her parents. She may well be a girl of exceptional intellectual and creative ability; she may also be a girl who feels resentment at the inequity of a sibling situation in which she may be superior to her brother, yet her achievements and ability are not equally rewarded—in fact, may even be criticized. Meanwhile, her brother is praised and deferred to because he is male. The girl may also be unable to accept the example of the so-called feminine passive role, as exemplified by her mother within the family structure. The father often may represent a symbol of oppressive male power. Not wishing to imitate the unattractive and submissive role of the mother, she may elect to imitate the father and enter into competition with him or with her brothers, in order to retain her identity and develop her strongly defined abilities.

In contrast, another girl subject to the same family situation might be so put down as to become withdrawn and feel strange, even inferior. Having had her exceptional abilities criticized, she may pretend to conform to the classic structure, to the detriment of her own identity and personality. She may also nurture a deep hatred for her father and for the role of woman —and may, in later life, avoid contact with men and reject marriage. Such a woman might have a good potential for turning to another woman for affection and love, although studies have shown that many do not become Lesbians. What makes two women coming from the same situation develop differently is another of those unknown factors. Why does one woman develop heterosexually, and another out of the same set of given circumstances develop homosexually? It can also happen that a woman turns in neither direction, but remains withdrawn, unable to form any kind of close personal relationship. On the other hand, many women coming from so-called happy family backgrounds—families in which parents appear to have had a good relationship, and in which the children were allowed to express their positive and aggressive instincts—also turn to homosexuality.

Another situation that can sometimes lead to a rejection of the heterosexual way of life occurs when a family who very much wanted a boy has a girl. Often this fact is made known to the little girl in one way or another. She feels unwanted and unloved because she is a girl, and often tries to become the boy the family wanted in order to obtain approval, attention and love. Very often the family goes along with this, probably more unconsciously than consciously, and in doing so conveys to the girl the idea that girls are inferior to boys. By trying to become a boy, the girl unconsciously accepts the devaluation of her womanhood. The same thing can happen with a boy whose family wanted a girl.

A parent, out of disappointment with the other parent; a lack of love, overdomination, or whatever, can unconsciously replace the unsatisfactory mate with the child. They can also fix on the child resentments toward the mate. Any number of similar situations with slight variations turn up in case histories of homosexuals, and certain family situations can clearly have an influence on the sexual identity and sexual differentiation of a child, but this is never a certainty. Once again the question is left open to speculation.

Drs. Ralph H. Gundlach and Bernard Riess, in their study entitled "Self and Sexual Identity in the Female: A Study of Female Homosexuality," observed: "The growth and development of the human being from infancy to maturity is largely a socializing process accomplished by parents and others who are themselves products of a specific culture. They use both conscious and unconscious pressures to mold the child and do so in varying effective ways. Development is a phased process, moving from one stage to another and, at each stage, dependent on the preceding one." (3) And from another study: "It is clear, however, that the factor of differential atmospheres toward boys and girls is found almost everywhere in our culture and is present from the moment the child first appears in the family. That these attitudes persist and produce differences is attested to by several recent articles." (4)

In the instance of lesbianism the overall parent-child picture, the marked difference in parental behavior, was most important and significant. In their studies of Lesbians and non-Lesbians, Drs. Gundlach and Riess observed that the Lesbian was more frequently neglected, even ignored by the mother. She was treated impersonally and in many instances without love. Fathers of Lesbians tended to regard them as their least favored child, withholding warmth and affection, and regarding them with indifference. The Lesbian more often felt that the father regarded her as a stranger, which in turn caused her to regard him as such.

In terms of behavior between the Lesbians and the non-Lesbians, and the ways in which they described their childhoods, the doctors found some marked differences. "As a social consequence in distress at the female role, many Lesbians found it difficult to find real girls friends. Three-quarters of them were tomboys (but so were nearly one-half of the comparison women), and their difference set them apart. The Lesbians more often tried to excel in athletic competition and in tomboyishness. More frequently they were sexually attracted to or idealized older women, often teachers. This observation may indicate the increased frequency of reported neglect and lack of attention from either parent."

One would like to know some more detailed facts. For example, how did the girls feel about being girls? How did they feel about other little girls? How did they feel about their mother's position in the family? How did they feel about boys, men, brothers and other siblings? Were the girls more scholastically excellent, more inclined toward individuality and independence? Were they generally different from some of their contemporaries, and if so, how did they feel they were different? That difference could be very significant. If a girl was more intelligent, more serious-minded and independent, she might very well find boring and silly some of the little girls who had been encouraged into the classic ultra-feminine, little-mother roles. This of course would present a problem in forming real and meaningful friendships. If one could assess such specific facts it might help to substantiate the argument of prejudicial parental treatment of boys and girls. It might also indicate that very few parents are equipped to be parents, and that our culture does not attempt to raise individuals but rather cut-out models, forced into cultural molds that have little or nothing to do with the reality of individual difference and human potential. The results of this process are often confusing, disturbing, and even tragic for both parents and children. Parents, however, must assume the responsibility for both their own mistakes and for their participation in the perpetuation of the myth of boy/girl, man/woman social and sexual roles.

Lately there has been a tendency to minimize parental damage, but any family therapist will quickly dispel that theory. The distinguished family therapist Dr. Theodora M. Abel, chief of the Family Therapy Program, Albuquerque, New Mexico, Child Guidance Center, and Clinical Associate, Department of Psychiatry, Medical Center, University of New Mexico, states categorically: "Whenever there is any disturbed child, or disturbed children, in a family there is a disturbance in the whole family, and there is always a disturbance between the parents in those cases. If you have healthy parents you generally never have disturbed children, but if you have disturbed children, you always have disturbed parents. You may have some healthy children from disturbed parents, but if you have a disturbed child you're absolutely sure to have a family disturbance and basically centered between the parents. If you have healthy parents, you generally do not have disturbed children." (Personal interview, Family Therapy Conference, Puerto Vallarta, Mexico, January 1973)

For some reason, however, when one discusses the role that parents and the environment play in the causes of homosexuality, one invariably finds that sooner or later the discussion will get shifted to the argument that genetics are responsible—hormonal and chromosomal imbalances. People still cling to this argument, even though such authorities as Dr. John Money at Johns Hopkins has proved to the contrary in his studies. Not only does he disclaim the hormonal/chromosomal argument, he gives examples of cases where hormonal phenomenon have existed and still the child did not turn out to be homosexual. For example, he cites the case of a young girl born with a clitoris so extended as to be considered a penis. When the girl was surgically altered to be feminized, and was raised then as a girl, she developed a healthy female gender identity. Dr. Money also points out that one could take the same little girl and leave her with the extended clitoris/penis and raise her as a boy and she would develop a male gender identity, even though she is physically still a girl with an extended clitoris.

Dr. Money also points out that in cases where there are hormonal phenomenon such as females with no ovaries, and boys with empty scrotums, the absence of these essentials will not determine the development of gender identity. In fact, Dr. Money says, "These prenatal influences may create certain traits or dispositions that will be incorporated into the gender identity. The total gender identity, however, can not be differentiated until after the social influence in the very early years—after the social input takes place. I'm saying that these traits may be incorporated into the gender identity but they don't determine it. There is nothing that happens prenatally that actually determines gender identity. It feeds into it. I am saying that there may be a hormonal phenomenon which flavors, will flavor, the gender identity, but it doesn't determine it." (Personal interview, March 1972)

Dr. Money is supported by Dr. Judd Marmor, among others. Dr. Marmor writes: "Psychological and behavioral patterns of masculinity or femininity constitute what is meant by gender role, and are not necessarily synonymous with an individual's biological sex." (5)

Dr. Money describes some possible behavioral characteristics of girls who might have prenatal hormonal influences: "Such little girls may tend to be tomboyish; they may give preference to career rather than marriage, but they don't rule out marriage. They do tend to develop romantic interest much later in life than the teen-agers they go to school with. Some tend to like vigorous outdoor energy expenditure and getting into competition with boys. They actually have a tendency to dominate and they have to be careful so that the boys don't recognize it." (Personal interview, March 1972)

"But," says Dr. Money, "these little girls can and do marry and have a pregnancy and raise children, and maintain a female gender identity and differentiation. By the same token, if there were influences within the family or outside the family, social input which might weigh toward a homosexual differentiation, she might just as easily and happily fit into that. However, these are *rare* and specific cases, and this is *by no means to suggest* that any woman who is tomboyish, or who develops a homosexual differentiation has been subject to the prenatal hormonal phenomenon mentioned above. All little girls displaying tomboyishness are not victims of this phenomenon. The only ones that we can identify are those who have some kind of a physical marker that you can recognize at birth. What it does say, however, is that postnatal social environmental input is an extremely powerful force in gender identity and sexual differentiation."

It should be pointed out at this juncture, however, that confused gender identity and homosexuality, male or female, are not synonymous. The majority of Lesbians see themselves as women: some have had heterosexual relationships, some have been married, some have had children; those that have not do not necessarily see themselves as men. It is possible for a woman to love another woman without assuming a male role or denying her womanhood. And the same thing holds true for the male homosexual. The majority of homosexuals, male and female, are undetectable. They seem no different from anyone else, and the fact is, they aren't different—except that they may happen to relate better in a close personal relationship with another female, and find sex more fulfilling with another woman, in the privacy of the bedroom. That preference is not visible in the street, at the office, at the dinner table or a cocktail party, any more than what the heterosexual does in the privacy of the bedroom.

Returning to the Gundlach-Riess study, we find an observation relating to cases of lesbianism and to "sex-role identity." "The unique events in the history of each female that led to homosexuality were far more scattered than with the males. It also seems that these items, for instance, may not be as strongly related to 'sex-role identity' in women as in men."

L. K. Frank reports a study which calls attention to female confusion and conflict in patterns of sexual relations in general: "Girls in our society are caught in the confusion of changing patterns of sexual relations. For them there is a conflict between the older definition of feminine life centered around marriage and child-bearing, and masculinity as being strong, successful in intellectual activities, and decision-making. This conflict is in contrast to the propaganda about equality, the right to vote, the new ideas of sexual freedom, and equal opportunities for personal fulfillment in a career. For many adolescent girls, acceptance of a feminine role seems to mean defeat and submission rather than entrance into the life of an adult woman." (6)

Dr. Lewis Wolberg, chairman of the Board of Trustees of the Postgraduate Center for Mental Health, New York, and clinical professor, New York University School of Medicine, commented on the effects of the male-dominated society as it related to the female homosexual. "It can expedite a certain type of homosexuality," he said. "In our culture independence is equated with masculinity, and as girls grow up, they often acquire a sense of inferiority at being female. One homosexual pattern strives for independence through the magic of penis acquisition. Here a woman tries to function like a male. An asexual aspect of this takes the form of competitiveness with males. Another type is trying to beat down males. A tactic here is called 'caponizing the male,' the idea being to challenge and minimize a man's sexual performance in an effort to make him impotent. A whole variety of behavioral patterns emerge out of the feeling of relative inferiority for being female." (Personal interview, spring 1972)

While the conclusions seem somewhat too pat, simplistic and outdated in terms of advanced psychosexual studies, and in terms of present Lesbian attitudes, as can be seen in the portion of this book in which Lesbians speak for themselves, Dr. Wolberg's statement seems more applicable to the heterosexual woman who needs a weapon, while the Lesbian simply prefers women, but his statement does recognize the possible effect of woman's negated position in society upon her development.

More to the point perhaps is the Gundlach-Riess study. From their sample it was determined that few Lesbians considered themselves masculine; interestingly enough, more Lesbians than non-Lesbians felt that they achieved orgasm easily. The doctors conjectured about the overall female make-up as follows:

Factors other than sex may be of primary importance to many women in any close relationship, and many heterosexual women may simply accede to the more imperious demands of their male companions. Such an alternative is supported by the most frequent choices given by the heterosexuals as to why they married; "to find great happiness and shared love" and "to live with a man who loved me." These resemble the answers by the Lesbians on the primary importance of their Lesbian relationship: "her interest in me" and "her kindness and warmth." The majority of both female groups say they seek warmth, security and validation of worth through being loved. Sensual sexuality was not high on the list. In fact, 15 to 25 per cent of the married women answered "yes" to each of the following reasons for marrying: "to get away from her family," "to have a home of her own," "not to be alone," "to be protected in life," and "to have children."

Most significant in the Gundlach-Riess findings, however, was the fact that: "Homosexuality among women in our society seems unrelated to the establishment of feminine identity." (7)

In her book *The Second Sex,* the French author Simone de Beauvoir wrote:

One can say that all women are naturally homosexual . . . every adolescent female fears penetration and masculine domination, and she feels a certain repulsion for the male body; on the other hand the female body is for her, as for the male, an object of desires. . . .

The feminine body does not frighten her; with her sisters or her mother she has often known intimacy in which affection was subtly imbued with sensual feeling. Between women there is a complicity that disarms modesty; the excitement that one arouses in the other is generally without violence; homosexual caresses imply neither defloration nor penetration; they satisfy the clitoral eroticism of childhood without demanding new and disquieting changes.

Between women love is contemplative; caresses are intended less to gain possession of the other than gradually to re-create the self through her; separateness is abolished; there is no struggle, no victory, no defeat; in exact reciprocity each is at once subject and object, sovereign and slave; duality becomes mutuality. (8)

Dr. Wolberg would term this kind of relationship a form of narcissism, even symbiosis. "In some cases a narcissistic defense seems to prevail," he said. "Narcissism may figure in homosexuality, and I think that in such cases the individual is pretty much arrested in her sexual growth. She may perhaps have had a difficult experience with one or both parents. The normal process of transferring over to another person intensive involvement with herself may be inhibited, and she may focus her feelings, interests and energies on herself almost totally. Other persons merely function as an aspect of herself. Consequently, when she does choose a partner, that partner becomes a reflection of her own narcissism, of her own self. She tries to find an idealized individual that she can project herself into and identify with. Sometimes we witness a psychological symbiosis—an actual fusion with a person. Why would she want to fuse with this object? Probably because she has contempt for herself, feelings of nothingness within herself. But it is very hard to generalize about all women who are homosexually directed. Patterns are as different as every fingerprint is different. So the specific patterns that produce a life style of one homosexual woman will be different from that of another."

It seems fair to point out here that a symbiosis can exist heterosexually as well; homosexuals, if one credited Dr. Wolberg's statement, do not have the corner on the market for symbiosis. We've all seen the passive, rather effeminate man married to the strong, aggressive woman; the strong, seemingly virile man married to a little, fragile woman—even a seemingly strong, aggressive, virile man will be married to a strong, aggressive woman. In each case they are supplying some specific need in the other—some underdeveloped side of themselves that needs reinforcing, and is being reinforced by the other, or lived out through the other. Sometimes this can be a good and balancing combination, and sometimes it can be the cause of great conflict.

For example, take the case of a rather masculine woman who gravitates toward the fragile, ultra-feminine woman. This does not necessarily mean that the masculine woman is attempting to play a male role, although she may be. Instead she may well be looking to have the missing femininity in herself reinforced by the other. This may work, and both of them may get the reinforcement they need. If, however, the feminine woman demands a so-called ultra-masculine role from the already masculine woman, they may come into conflict after the fascination of role-playing wears off. These, of course, are extreme cases, and are very well illustrated in the group sessions amongst Lesbians in the second part of the book. As was stated before, "butch"-"femme" role-playing is not in fashion among the more aware, modern Lesbians. For the most part today's Lesbian is quite willing to fight for her right to be a woman and to be a sexual being in whatever direction she desires. Many of the women state that the woman's liberation movement has been instrumental in giving them a forum and an instrument to fight for their rights as women, and this in turn has given them more pride in being women. They are able to see that being a woman does not have to be a negative thing.

Gundlach and Riess also pointed out that the Lesbian population (at least from their sample) did not have strong prohibitions toward heterosexuality. They stated that three fourths of their sample had had intercourse with a male. Some 30 per cent had tried marriage, even for so long as ten years or more, and one fifth had had children. Gundlach and Riess concluded from their findings that "homosexuality among women in our society seems not closely related to the establishment of feminine identity. More frequently, women utilize sexuality to ward off loneliness or to supply a feeling of being wanted and needed or of being verified." They do point out, however, the influence the oppressive attitude toward women in general has had:

> Our business culture, with its eye on cost accounting and *"making a buck,"* sets a pattern for character and morality such that most men achieve the maturity level of opportunism or conventionality, covered over with a liberal touch of moralistic verbalization. Growing males are under stress to achieve conventional success and display lots of manliness. Few can or care to apprentice themselves to their fathers, and the most frequent models available may be seen in movies and on TV. Male sexual impulses are usually local, and sexual performance is often taken as a sign of assertive virility. Male sexual satisfactions may relate only with difficulty to the establishment of a couple relationship, with love, or with profound personal meaning.
>
> Being a woman is not usually an achievement such as being a man. Woman are still boxed between old patterns of settling for the homebody role or a career, but many cannot see that both are possible. Despite talk about equality, women have no equal part in government, business, professions, or the military. They are welcomed to home-building and shopping, and to subservient "helper" and service occupations. Even so, the patterns of femininity center more around interpersonal relationships than do men; they are less concerned with autonomy, more with harmony. ("Self and Sexual Identity in the Female") (9)

What Gundlach and Riess are saying is that women tend to be more mature and more integrated than men. They tend to care more about respect, consideration and understanding of the human being; to expect tenderness, mutuality, consideration, individuality and a pleasure in cooperativeness and close association within the marriage. Women tend to look for the more "spiritual or soulful" content of emotional relationships.

Pursuing the subject of cause and behavior, it seems fitting to examine further the importance of social and environmental input. What part does learned response play—pleasant and unpleasant association and conditioning? Dr. C. A. Tripp has pointed out (in his paper, portions of which are to be included in his forthcoming book on male and female homosexuality to be published by Atheneum) that the cerebral cortex, so necessary to the learning and conditioning process, occupies over 90 per cent of the volume of the human brain. He states: "From this point of view, it is not surprising that man not only can learn as much as he does, but that lacking the tight physiologic controls that are so apparent in his lower relatives, he *must* learn all of his behavioral techniques in that huge period of time that his maturity requires. Under a variety of circumstances, he can learn homosexual preferences quite as easily as heterosexual." He elaborates further on this point:

> The particular culture in which every man lives takes over the major job of directing and suggesting his behavior. No doubt it is the essential nature of man's flexibility that permits his cultures to take the unending variety they have assumed. And yet there are certain near universals: sexual activity between members of the opposite sex is generally, but not always, preferred to other sexual expressions. Heterosexuality certainly seems the most workable, considering the physical structures involved. Furthermore, some of the loudest psychological characteristics of each sex tend to be best tolerated at close range by individuals who are different in their behavioral emphasis. For instance, in man, as in other animals, the particular kind of aggressiveness displayed by males is generally easier for females than for other males to tolerate. And when females reject a sexual approach, their ways of doing so tend to be less hostile and retaliatory than the kinds of rebuffs that males tend to use. All of this, and much more, seems to have led to a preference for heterosexuality by the majority of persons in each culture.

Since a culture like our own clearly expects, advertises and approves only of sexual practices between members of the opposite sex, where does all that homosexuality come from? Why doesn't the cultural conditioning work better than it does? And when the heterosexual conditioning does work, why is the lure of homosexuality still often very robust? I assure you that you will not find satisfactory answers to these questions in theories of psychosexual mix-up, nor in theories that describe homosexuality as some sickness. Such theories assume that human heterosexuality is under a specific direction control. In reality, such controls simply do not exist in the human species. (10)

Dr. Tripp enumerated factors which very frequently appear in the histories of persons whose sexual conditioning is not in perfect alignment with heterosexual expectations. For example, he calls attention to prepubertal sex play, which according to him, is widespread and includes sexual play with the same sex. Such play "involves elements of excitement or even of affection which may give such experiences a lasting appeal in the sexual repertoire of some individuals." (11)

Dr. Tripp pointed out that early heterosexual experiments sometimes proved unsatisfactory, disappointing, even embarrassing and unattractive. Such experiences often lessen the appeal of the opposite sex, and open the way for homosexual practice which may be more satisfactory and rewarding. He further called attention to the fact that there can be other early fears and aversions to heterosexuality which "increase the appeal of members of the same sex," but cautioned against overemphasizing the fear element, which he felt the Freudians had done. He also pointed out that there can be positive inducements to homosexuality. "Glorification of the values of maleness, and exceedingly high expectations of masculine prowess, which a boy may come to expect of himself—quite without any neurosis being present, by the way—can lead to an idealization of male characteristics, a disparagement of female virtues, or both. Erotic feelings can certainly develop around what is idealized."

Acknowledging that any primarily heterosexual person would be inclined to see physical disadvantages in homosexual matchings, Dr. Tripp talked about the less often realized distinct advantages as well. "Some of these," he said, "are highly facilitating in the early sexual histories of people. For instance, the same sex intuitively knows what feels good and what doesn't. And on a psychological level, the shared interests and easy rapport of members of the same sex can facilitate compatibility. Furthermore, the association of opposite sexes tend to be chaperoned at early ages, or curtailed by a variety of other factors—while the most intimate contacts between members of the same sex are easily made and are naïvely thought to be sexually bland.

"As a matter of fact, overt homosexual contacts are so frequent before and shortly after puberty that the question is not how the homosexual conditioning develops, but why it doesn't develop even more often than it does. The general answer, of course, is that various social pressures and expectations work toward the development of heterosexual standards and tastes, and toward the eradication of any and all behavior which appears contrary to this mainstream."

Dr. Tripp goes on to describe the significance of a learned value system in successful sexual experience and emotional adjustment:

For any sexual experience to become sharply meaningful to an individual, it must have the support of a personal value system. Such a value system can develop in essentially two ways: Early sexual experiences can lead to a set of values built around various characteristics of persons who have proved highly rewarding sexually. Or, without any early sexual experience, a personal value system can be built up from the value structure suggested by the culture, and by the individual's personal needs. In that case, the expected heterosexual behavior will quite smoothly and reliably develop—and will be additionally reinforced and validated by gratifying sexual experiences. But inconsistencies and delays in the ultimate establishment of heterosexual values, or protests against them, can lead to the development of individually discovered alternatives such as homosexuality. Specifically, then, the best evidence indicates that the partial or even total conditioning for homosexuality proceeds along essentially the same lines as heterosexuality—that is, with the development of a set of values that either precede or follow gratifying sexual experience.

Dr. Tripp believes that people may respond to various sexual stimuli under certain circumstances. Given the right stimuli many heterosexual individuals might respond casually and briefly to a homosexual circumstance, or vice versa. He states:

It may be said that the human sexual response can be stimulated by the most superficial opportunities, or it may await the most profound and personally meaningful associations of which the individual is capable. In terms of anything basic in the organism, the physical and psychological differences in kinds of sexual behavior seem strictly trivial. People simply respond sexually in ways in which they have learned to respond and toward objects which, for the moment, for a longer time, or for a lifetime, have taken on sexual meaning for them. Conversely, people fail to respond sexually when, and only when, they have arrived at an aversion. Every sexually responsive person could respond to every other sexually responsive individual if it weren't for aversion reactions. Sometimes an individual will arrive at a particular aversion through powerful direct conditioning, such as a bitter experience with a kind of person, or a kind of situation. But otherwise, aversions seem to arise quite automatically toward charac-

teristics that stand in contrast to ones that are highly
valued. (12)

Turning now to the specific exploration of facts concerning
Lesbians, perhaps it is significant at this point to examine findings which compare the homosexual woman and the heterosexual woman for differences and similarities. Are Lesbian
women so different from their heterosexual sisters? Drs. Gundlach and Riess conducted a study of 225 lesbian women from
all across the nation, and 233 heterosexual women were used
for purposes of comparison. They found that among Lesbians
the place in the family and the sexes of the other siblings were
significant. For example they found that a first-born girl or an
only child was often put under pressure to excel and achieve,
which is sometimes considered masculine. In families of five
or more siblings the first-born girl was apt to be heterosexual
and the later born more frequently Lesbian. Explaining this
phenomenon, Gundlach and Riess suggest that the first-born
girl in a large family often winds up being mother's helper and
is thrown into the role of mothering very early. Whereas the
girl who is perhaps fourth or fifth in a large family may find
that being a girl is not very special, and the conditions for providing her with self-esteem and acceptance of herself as a person may be lacking. Gundlach and Riess felt that this could
provide a basis for lesbian choice not so much out of rivalry
for the favorite but out of a lack of warmth and nurturing.
There often isn't the time in a large family to give some children the necessary love and affection they require. Furthermore, the amount of need can not be generalized; some children
need more than others.

Dr. Gundlach stated that the semantic differential test given
in the study yielded the following results: "We found hardly
any difference between Lesbians and the comparisons, on the
32 pairs of adjectives used to describe mother, father, or
woman. But 28 of the pairs describing *man* were *markedly*

different, with the Lesbians selecting more frequently the derogatory adjective." (13)

Among the predominantly homosexual group in the study, very few of the women had a good experiences with males, although many had tried early. Over 30 per cent of the Lesbians had been married, with two thirds of the marriages ending in separation or divorce. Nearly three fourths of the Lesbians and non-Lesbians alike had tried intercourse with males but 60 per cent had never reached a climax with a male, while 42 per cent of the Lesbians had not been able to reach climax with a male. The women who had not been able to achieve orgasm with their male partners had been able to reach climax with their female partners.

They also found that 31 per cent of the Lesbians and 21 per cent of the heterosexual women had been objects of rape or attempted rape, with the Lesbians having been objects of rape before the age of sixteen. Again, they found that women, homosexual and heterosexual, were more interested in warmth, friendship, loyalty and love than men, and that sex was more secondary.

According to Dr. Gundlach, another interesting finding was that "in high school nearly half of the comparison girls (non-Lesbian) saw themselves as good, living up to strict ideals of conduct. About one fourth of each group felt lost, isolated, fearful. More Lesbians than Comparisons, however, saw themselves as either rugged, self-sufficient, or as idealistic, aiming for a life of service." (14)

A study of "The Lesbian Personality" by June H. Hopkins, a clinical psychologist, United Cambridge and Fulborn Hospitals, reported in the *British Journal of Psychiatry,* presents evidence quite compatible with some of the Gundlach-Riess findings. In data gathered from a group of twenty-four Lesbians and twenty-four heterosexual women, matched individually for age, intelligence and professional background, she found very little personality difference and no support for any claim of neurosis. If anything, she found the homosexual women exhibiting somewhat more positive qualities. She writes:

> This paper presents the hypothesis that there are no personality factors, either primary or second order factors observed on Catell's 16 P.F. Test, which will be statistically, significantly different between the lesbian and heterosexual groups. This hypothesis is consistent with Simon and Gagnon's (1967) contention that 'in most cases the female homosexual follows conventional female patterns,' although they were not discussing personality factors when making this statement. (15)

> "In the light of presenting findings, it is suggested that the traditionally applied "neurotic" label is not necessarily applicable. The following terms are suggested as appropriately descriptive of the lesbian personality in comparison to her heterosexual female counterpart:
> 1. More independent. 2. More resilient. 3. More reserved. 4. More bohemian. 5. More self-sufficient. 6. More composed. (16)

What seems to emerge from the various studies and from evidence gathered by practicing and clinical psychologists and psychiatrists is the fact that there is very little if any evidence to support an assumption that Lesbians are any more neurotic than heterosexual women, that they are any less sexually active or realized in terms of pleasurable sexual relations as such, that they are any less stable in their relationships, or any less effective as human beings. In terms of personality development and professional achievement, they tend, in fact, to weigh slightly more over on the plus side.

As to cause, certain samenesses in individual histories seem to occur, but they can not be taken as firmly decisive across the board. Family atmosphere and relationships to parents, social input, bad early expriences in heterosexual relationships or attempts at them, learned responses in pleasurable and non-pleasurable sexual experimentation—all appear in clinical documentation. However, if one might make bold to postulate—and it must be acknowledged that very little is yet known about female homosexuality—the deep-seated core of the matter may very well lie in the position of woman in our culture: her oppression, her devalued image, her longstanding frustration as an individual unable to select and direct her own destiny—not because she is incapable, but because from the time of her inception that destiny is inhibited by the culture into which she has been born. Prejudices, attitudes, restrictions and limitations will be imposed on her from the moment she utters that first cry signifying life. The doctor's announcement that "It's a girl!" can be a sentence—depending on how fortunate or unfortunate she is in the accident of her parentage. But even if she is supremely fortunate in her parentage, there is still the power of thousands of years of male-dominated culture to be reckoned with.

This fact will not only influence her potential for equality of opportunity and direction of destiny, it may influence her emotional development, her relationships with the opposite sex, her potential for successful sexual relations, and her ultimate happiness. Might not it also contribute, given certain sets of circumstances and experiences, toward a potential for homosexuality, for the repercussions of these attitudes must ripple through all elements of a woman's life.

Not to be overlooked either, if we are to credit some of the experts, is the seeming difference in the desires and expectations of men and women. Some of the foregoing evidence and some of the material concerning bisexuality presented later in this chapter—cases of married women turning to other women for love and tenderness while still being married—indicate that often men and women want different things of a relationship, and approach sexual relations with different motivations.

The rupture of man-woman relations certainly does not ensure the onset of homosexuality, but it seems reasonable to speculate that it could create an atmosphere for the excercising of *alternatives,* should they present themselves. If a woman's ability, her aspirations, hopes, and needs are continually put down then she must either succumb or rebel. Actually, in either case, the result may be rebellion in one form or another. She may rebel quietly, secretly in some form or other, or she may rebel openly, politically, militantly, as evidenced by the women's liberation movement. At any rate, due to the influence of a male-dominated culture, women are often forced into unrealistic and unjust positions; this seems very worth taking a look at when investigating the causes of female homosexuality. This is not to say that men are totally to blame, for men are just as often victimized by the unreality of our culture—forced by the pressure of the culture into roles unwanted and unsuitable to them individually.

It may be that our cultural structure, aside from being grossly unrealistic, has become a monster controlling the individual instead of the individual controlling it. It may be the source of most of the ills of our society; in fact, our culture may be destroying not only man-woman relations, but ultimately the culture itself. We may live to see in our lifetime either the total destruction of our society, or the total restructuring of it. The general unrest abroad in the land would seem to be telling us that something is very wrong. Maybe it is that we are ignorant of what human beings are really like, what their intellectual and visceral needs actually are. We study the behavior of animals to learn things about humans; perhaps our efforts could be put to more productive use by studying more intently the behavior of our own species.

Having discussed "cause," perhaps we should now investigate the second most voiced question in the discussion of homosexuality: "Can it be cured?" Of course, the question automatically presupposes that homosexuality is a sickness, and seems to fall more into the category of wishful thinking than educated reality. It has been clearly stated in the foregoing by Dr. John Money and others that genetics are not the determining factor. Prenatal hormonal influence or chromosomal imbalance may exert some potential influence, but even then— and these cases are extremely rare—gender identity development postnatally will be the determining factor. The chromosome phenomenon, also quite rare, cannot be substantiated in the determination of homosexuality. Therefore, while a physical phenomenon can be corrected surgically and hormonally, it would still only be decisive with gender identity correction coming from parental influences and environment. That would not be strictly a case of classical homosexuality, anyway.

So the answer to the question is: There are no pills, no magic cures despite the debate over hormones of the estrogenic and androgenic type. "Estrogenic substances administered to homosexual females do not alter either the sexual drive or sex object. Large doses of estrogens administered to male homosexuals occasionally reduce their sexual drive, but do not influence the sex object," writes Dr. W. H. Perloff. And he adds: "These observations lead one to believe that steroid hormones of the estrogenic and androgenic types have nothing to do with the choice of sex object and therefore with the determination of homosexuality." (17)

It boils down then, if one is to deal with the "sickness" charge, to the implication that it is a matter for psychotherapy, and that too has to seem questionable when men of the caliber of Dr. C. A. Tripp state: "As for psychotherapy, I know of not one single validated instance of any basic sexual change ever having been accomplished. Nor was the Kinsey research ever able to find a single instance of any such change. Nor does the issue seem to be of the least importance. Even if there were treatment procedures for successfully revising an individual's whole personal value system, would we be ready to apply those procedures to a third of American males—or even to those millions of persons who are primarily homosexual for their entire lives." (18)

Naturally, there are doctors who claim to have effected change through psychotherapy, and there are those who claim that it *can* be done. Dr. Tripp himself says:

> Notions that homosexuality is unnatural and sick—and that its so-called cure would always be desirable—are still held by some professionals, and the lay public in general. Issues of sickness are made seemingly more valid in the eyes of clinicians by the fact that they consistently see a sample of the population for whom homosexual tendencies are associated with severe guilt, conflict, or other neurotic disturbances. It seems fair to say that sexual conflicts are far more frequent in the person who sees himself as part of a disapproved minority, than in the person who believes himself to be quite ordinary. In fact, neuroses of various kinds have so often been observed in persons showing degrees of homosexual responses as to suggest to early observers that neurosis leads to homosexuality, or vice versa. Today, it is more generally realized—at least by sophisticated clinicians—that no action which a person takes and enjoys can ever lead to neurosis unless he or she feels guilty about it. (19)

The question of cure, with the thoughtful, knowledgeable doctor, lies in the realm of electives. Does the homosexual wish to change? Some do, most don't. But the matter of desire for change seems to lie not so much in homosexuality per se, but in society's attitude toward the homosexual. For this reason doctors of great wisdom and experience in the field feel it is most important to ascertain the person's reason for desiring change, and the expectations he or she holds for his or her life should he or she achieve it. Sometimes the reason for desiring change is not sufficient or realistic enough to attempt a long and involved process, even if a change could be guaranteed. No ethical, knowledgeable doctor embarks on an attempt to effect some degree of cure from homosexuality, or promises a person such a magical transformation, without very thorough investigation into inner reasons and surface factors being brought to bear. Great damage, even tragic results, have occurred from doctors actually trying to force the homosexual to change. Many come to the analyst with problems that may not in fact stem from homosexuality at all. Greater guilt, self-hate and desperation have been thrust onto many homosexuals by doctors seizing upon the obvious—homosexuality—while ignoring perhaps a more basic disturbance. This often develops out of the analyst's own personal prejudices and urge to play God. Many of these analysts have their own personal axe to grind, while many others are more objective and realistic, more interested in turning out individuals able to respect and live with themselves than in trying to turn out heterosexuals. Heterosexuality is not always the desired answer for either patient or doctor. People have been known to succumb to an analyst's coercion, and to make a determined and valiant effort at heterosexuality, only to find out that they're just as mixed up as they were before: the basic problem had not been solved. In fact, some case histories show that they're more than a little worse off: they've spent a lot of time and money, failed at homosexuality, failed at heterosexuality, are still unhappy and anxious, and feel more guilt and confusion than they had before they tried for the magic panacea of heterosexuality.

Let us examine the attitudes and methods of some of the more objective and realistic analysts. Dr. Bernard Riess states that he has had very few patients who have come to him for cure, or change, from their homosexuality. And perhaps it would be well to substitute the word "change" for the word "cure" at this point, for "change" is more to the point, and eliminates the stigma of sickness; "cure" presupposes sickness.

"I try to find out why a patient wants to change from homosexuality to heterosexuality," says Dr. Riess. "I want to know the cause of dissatisfaction. If it is the public myth that homosexuality is neurotic, then I guess in that case I would be against arguing for change. I don't feel that homosexuality is neurotic any more than anything compulsive is neurotic. If someone can show me that compulsive is neurotic then I would say that the compulsive heterosexual and the compulsive homosexual are equally alike." (Personal interview, spring 1972)

In fact, Dr. Riess cited a reverse case history where a woman who had always related heterosexually, through treatment, discovered her homosexuality and swung more over in that direction. "She has just developed her first relationship with a woman," he said. "She has had a lot of experience with men and I think she is fundamentally bisexual. She is a professional woman, very productive, and from late adolescence on she had affairs with men. She's attractive, well-built. She's always admired the female figure, and felt that aesthetically, women give a softer, more touchable feeling, but she had never had an affair with a woman. In the course of treatment she began to talk about these things and finally admitted, through examination of her dreams, that she wanted to experience what it was like with a woman. She went a little overboard at first— going out to a lot of gay bars, places of that sort: she didn't know how to meet women otherwise, and she was unable to pick up or be picked up by a woman—she didn't like that kind of marketplace atmosphere.

"However, very recently she met another professional woman who was an admitted Lesbian, and they had an affair. She found the affair with the woman more exciting than the affairs she had had with men. Although when I asked her about her sexual satisfaction she stated that it had been about the same as with a man, but with the woman it had been more emotionally rewarding. The experience was a good one, and she is no longer tempted to hide her homosexuality because she now sees nothing to be ashamed of. She feels better about herself now that she can express those feelings and be honest. Fortunately, she operates within a culture where it is acceptable."

Dr. John Money states that "it is extremely difficult to change gender identity in which the pendulum has swung all the way over into the lesbian direction in exactly the same way that it is extremely difficult to take a woman whose gender identity has swung all the way over to the extreme cliché stereotype of feminine identification and say, 'I'm going to give you psychotherapy and make you into a Lesbian.' The ones that are frequently recorded as successes of psychotherapy are in fact the bisexual people whose pendulum is still in swing. Understand that they are not consolidated at one extreme or the other extreme."*

Some doctors feel it is essential that the homosexual try heterosexual encounters. They contend that it is essential for a homosexual to have heterosexual experiences as well in order to live a whole and complete life. Dr. Judd Marmor responded to that idea thusly: "That is a value judgment. Would they say equally that in order to live a whole and complete life every heterosexual ought to have a homosexual experience? They wouldn't. Nor do I believe that. The wonderful thing about human beings is that they can find their own way of living full and complete lives. Some do it as bachelors, and unmarried women; others do it as married people without children; others do it with families, and others do it with homosexual relationships. The important thing is whether the individual is capable of achieving some sense of fulfillment within himself or herself. And many of them do. One of the revelations to me in recent investigations I have been doing with successful homosexuals has been how much they enjoy their lives —how happy many of them are and how completely fulfilled they feel. They have no desire for children, and in that regard

* Personal interview.

they are no different from some very happily married hetero-sexual couples I know. In fact, they find many advantages in their way of life. They are perfectly happy, and they are entitled to it. It is another of those pseudoscientific value judg-ments, that really disguises a moral judgment, that says two homosexuals can not live a full and complete life within a homosexual relationship. The trouble is, not enough people come into close contact with well-adjusted and happy homosex-uals. They don't include them within the spheres of their lives, and that is their disadvantage. If they knew them better, got to know them as human beings, they would see them quite differ-ently. People tend to be afraid of what they don't know. I'm reminded of a definition I read somewhere, that 'Prejudice is being down on something you're not up on.' "*

In regard to persons who had had both heterosexual and homosexual relationships, and found themselves in conflict about the direction of their lives, Dr. Marmor replied: "I don't try to push such persons one way or another. I try to help them understand what the nature of the conflict is, what the options are that are available, and then make their own decisions about the way they want to go. I do try to remove any underlying guilt and anxiety in order to give them a chance to think rationally about it . . . rather than in an atmosphere of self-condemnation. Some decide one way, some another; I can't prejudge that. Differ-ent people have different options open to them."

Dr. Lewis Wolberg, however, commenting on whether psycho-therapy can be effective in altering sexual direction, states that while he does not really consider the particular choice of a sexual partner too significant, he believes that it is essential to explore the motivational aspects of why a person might want to change. He very definitely believes that change can be effected. "But," he says, "there has to be a strong expressed desire for change. There has to be strong motivation. I have homosexual patients

* Personal interview.

who come for other problems; they don't consider their homosexuality a problem. In that case, I don't go into it. In most cases where a desire for change is expressed, it is due to unhappy relationships, society's pressures, difficulty in getting along in a society that discriminates against the homosexual, guilt, shame, self-devaluation. Since the homosexual is almost put into the same class as the criminal, naturally a person will feel very deeply about this. Many of the neurotic manifestations among homosexuals are the product of the attitudes of society, and his rebellion against society."

But for the homosexual who has a strong desire to change, Dr. Wolberg believes in reverse conditioning, and says there are many variations of it. He concedes that the homosexual is more difficult to treat than the average psychiatric patient, primarily because of sexual anxieties which must be worked through. However, from other evidence stated herein, it would seem that such a patient's problem would be more sexual than homosexual. Most homosexuals seem to have active sexual relations, a high degree of enjoyment and successful orgasms.

According to Dr. Wolberg: "Anxieties related to heterosexuality are not often felt as much. They motivate a variety of defenses, like unfeelingness toward and detachment from the opposite sex, which shield the individual from anxiety. Because these defenses work so well, she is reluctant to give them up. This is one of the biggest reasons why psychotherapy is a failure."

Dr. Wolberg believes that the analyst must bring the patient to an awareness of her basic anxiety, which relates to her sexual role. "When she realizes her basic anxieties and admits that they do exist, one may help her recognize her patterns of behavior. A reconditioning process is then in order. What one has to do then is to approach homosexuality quite gradually, attempting to help the patient gain rewards of pleasure for each successful heterosexual step. In other words, she obviously cannot, even if she so desires, just plunge into full heterosexuality at the beginning. It doesn't work that way. She has to begin to alter her responses to men, both in terms of communication and in terms of physical contact, to experiment with feelingness towards men, to work out any aversion that she has developed towards touching contact with men. And then she has to approach slowly some sexual behavior with men. And if she develops certain withdrawal responses like frigidity, pain on penetration (dyspareunia), one has to continue to deal with such responses." (Personal interview)

That seems as if it could be a lifetime project without any real guarantee of success. Average homosexuals would throw in the towel about the time they reached the point of trying a heterosexual relationship only to find themselves experiencing withdrawal, revulsion or impotence. Of course, we have already heard that some eminent doctors disagree with Dr. Wolberg—doctors who believe that changing an adult, practicing homosexual is unrealistic and sometimes not the ideal solution. There are those who do not share his theories of anxieties either—not only doctors, but homosexuals themselves who are familiar with his area of thought as well as other theories, and have been subjected to both.

Some degree of success may have been achieved with this method in the sense of getting homosexual men to include women in their sexual repertory, and Lesbians to include men, but not exclusively. In most cases, according to research, the homosexuals have already engaged in heterosexual relations and have opted for the choice of homosexuality as a life style. Others have gone so far as to enter into a heterosexual relationship, even to marry, to satisfy whatever their social hang-up may have been, while at the same time continuing homosexual practices outside the heterosexual relationship. Perhaps Dr. Wolberg's theory of fears and anxieties, Freudian in content, and his conditioning process might be more applicable to homosexuals who have never engaged in any heterosexual activity at all. From the verbatim tapes of discussions with Lesbians on their life styles, and discussion with other mature, sophisticated, well-adjusted homosexuals, one would have to question whether or not the doctor's ideas are not somewhat unrealistic, possibly even dated. They seem to suggest a somewhat elementary understanding of the subject, one more within the realm of theory than actual practice.

Dr. Wolberg does concede that males seem easier to swing over than females, and he speculates that the reason for this is due to anxieties about sexual contact being much greater in women than in men. "Some women equate female sexual functioning with the role of humiliation, subjugation, being torn by a large penis, being subjected to a bloody attack." One wonders what generation the doctor is talking about. Study after study— not to mention the group discussions among Lesbians—has told us that a very large percentage of Lesbians have not only had sexual relations with men, but have been married, and have had children. However, Dr. Wolberg qualifies his statement by saying that he was speaking about a particular type of homosexual woman. One still wonders why the doctor has chosen to speak about that type of woman, since she seems to be very much in the minority in this day and age.

Dr. Wolberg went on to comment further on this large tearing penis and bloody attacks. "In many of the Lesbians I've treated, one does run into a tremendous disgust of the penis and fear of the penis as an attacking instrument. This of course produces a lot of resistance. In some cases there is no outward disgust or fear, just indifference and nonfeelingness in sexual relations with men." Again, one has to wonder what generation the doctor has been treating. One is reminded of a Radclyffe Hall type of the twenties and thirties, which is very much out of style today. But more than that, one wonders if the doctor has treated many homosexuals—for no real feeling of understanding of the subject seems to emerge from his discussion. It is all classic, elementary, clinical and simplistic, and he seems to assume that all homosexuals, male and female, have never had any sexual contact with the opposite sex. In the cases of women we have been hearing about from studies made, and will hear from in group discussions, while the sexual contacts with men have not always been satisfying, the indication seems to be that women make a choice for homosexuality more because of the difference in the quality of a relationship with a woman, which they have found more compatible and rewarding. The sexual aspects have been secondary, and this has not only been true of the lesbian women, but of the non-lesbian women who were comparisons.

In recent years, there have been attempts to recondition the homosexual through behavioral approaches. This involves the tactic of showing the person slides or pictures of homosexual behavior concurrent with an electric shock or some other unpleasant stimulation. In the absence of the unpleasant stimulation, the patient is then shown pictures of heterosexual behavior; in the case of a man, the shock is discontinued and pictures of a progressively more naked woman are shown. This is supposed to produce a pleasant association. This unpleasant shock technique is supposed to make homosexuality less desirable, and the heterosexual exposure, minus the unpleasant physical stimulation, more attractive and pleasurable. According to Dr. Wolberg, this technique has not been too successful in terms of numbers because the resistance elements are so strong. Obviously there is a reason for this resistance, and if it is so strong, what is the purpose of trying to force it?

Perhaps if homosexuality only involved sexual acts, and the psyche was totally absent from the consciousness of the human being, this method might be creditable. However, the human being has not become a robot yet, although one begins to wonder when one hears a discussion of homosexuality by analysts of the orthodox persuasion if the homosexual is not looked upon as something of a subhuman by the people he or she often turns to for help, not necessarily to change his or her sexual orientation, but to work out personality and relationship problems.

At a conference of analysts in New York in November of 1972, it was brought out that some analysts refuse to accept any homosexual for treatment (whatever his or her complaint) unless he or she will agree at the outset to work toward change. This amounts to emotional blackmail, and well substantiates the homosexual community's contention that analysts have often been greater foes than friends. When one hears some analysts discuss homosexuality, it becomes increasingly clear that they know very little about it, and are unwilling to learn. They refuse to accept the possibility that any advancements or revisions of orthodox theory have been made; they are amazingly unaware of new findings and writings in this area by highly respected and highly qualified analysts.

As for changing an adult homosexual's sexual life style, the complexities and dangers involved in any attempt to effect change are well illustrated in Dr. Tripp's lecture to future analysts delivered at the University of California Medical School. In this lecture he offers a hypothetical approach to treating a homosexual who comes for help because of extreme feelings of guilt over his homosexuality. He asks them to suppose "that a patient comes to you in a state of disturbance or conflict over his homosexual responsivity. Regardless of the nature of the presenting complaint—that is, whether he suffers from guilt feelings, or whether he is in local trouble in a particular situation, or whether he has already analyzed his own case as hopeless without a basic change in his sex life— all these possible attitudes of the patient tend to share the same underlying idea: Namely, that there is an intimate connection between one's sex life and the problems which one feels. Here the therapist must do what the patient is not doing. He must distinguish between the sexual and social nature of the patient's complaints. No patient is *really* complaining about his sex interest per se, which is, after all, usually quite rewarding. Rather, he is complaining about the possible social problems he sees, or some inner conflict. Confronted with such complaints, you will have a choice of at least two basic postures toward the patient's position. Either you can side with the religious and social mores, or you can side with the patient's right to be himself. If you agree with society and the part of him which says he should not do what he wants to do sexually, you will be siding with the surface claims of the culture and treating him as though homosexuality itself is extraordinary, or as though its practice is in some way injurious. Unfortunately, you will be locked in a struggle with the patient's whole value system. Whatever sense of isolation he may already have is likely to be increased by such treatment. He is apt to suffer renewed anxiety or depression, and you will find yourself in no position to be at all critical of other things, such as various parts of his social behavior. The motivation he has for therapy is likely to decline drastically. And he is now prone to get worse instead of better, if, indeed, he stays with you long enough to effect any change at all.

"If, on the other hand, you choose to uphold the patient's right to be himself, you can inform him that although he is outside the cultural recommendation, he is in fact within that considerable portion of the population which shares his homosexual practices. Such information may tend to ease or reduce the patient's guilt or anxiety in this area. In any case, you will be recognized as a friend of the most powerful part of him. And with this leverage, you need not tread softly; on the contrary, you will be free to be sharply critical of any part of his social behavior that seems to bring him into direct conflict with society, or with himself. A variety of techniques of this general kind are in use. They all try to help the patient toward a social adjustment which is acceptable, and which is in line with his already well-adjusted pattern of sexual rewards. It is in the primary interest of the individual to find his particular sexual gratification with a minimum of social conflict. It is not in the primary interest of the individual to significantly alter his sexual choices."

Dr. Tripp concludes his talk to the young analysts-to-be with some practical and realistic advice on the nature of homosexuality and its similarity to heterosexuality. He also defines what he considers realistic goals for treatment of the homosexual: "I hope, with all these various observations on the frequency and variety of homosexuality, that I have succeeded in suggesting some of its similarities to heterosexuality. Not the least of these are its origins in learning processes, and the tenacity with which it is capable of staying put against the moralistic opposition that has been brought against it from time to time. Perhaps you have wondered why I have so strongly implied that the homosexual component is easier to come to terms with than to eradicate. There are really two reasons. One has to do with practical necessity, and the other with the essential nature of human adjustment. As for necessity, let me point out that I am well aware of numerous claims of the successful treatment of the homosexual patient. Where success is marked in terms of greater personal efficiency and smoother social integration, the evidence is plentiful. But where basic change in adult sexual responses are claimed as a result of therapy, we have to be very careful in what we believe. Mere change in overt practice does not constitute an adequate criterion. The Trappist monk who takes an oath of silence and abstinence has certainly changed neither his voice, nor his basic sexual responsivity." (20)

Suffice it to say that from the foregoing opinions on the subject of change, it does not seem a very realistic, or perhaps even desirable goal. Thus it would seem obvious that society will have to alter its attitudes. It cannot be more *morally right* for society to inflict unhappiness and oppression on persons who are simply doing what comes naturally to them, particularly when the reversal of their nature is not realistic or desired.

While we don't, as a society, understand the homosexual, we possibly fail to understand the bisexual even less. After all, if one is quite able to accept and enjoy heterosexual relationships, why would one want to participate in a homosexual relationship, with all its complexities and social problems? Perhaps, however, it would be well to try to arrive at an actual definition of bisexuality. A bisexual, we learn, is someone who finds both the opposite sex and the same sex attractive and sexually desirable, someone who can and does participate in sexual relations with both.

Within that context, a discussion of bisexuality will often involve the question as to where bisexuality leaves off and homosexuality takes over. It seems a very difficult question to answer, particularly when we find that most homosexuals have had heterosexual relations at some time or other. One might assume that if one has had heterosexual relations at some time, one might very will do so again at some other time, even though one might have swung more over onto the homosexual side, and may have found his or her most rewarding relationships to have been homosexual. During the time a person is involved in homosexual acts, he or she is relating homosexually, and would technically be termed "homosexual." If the same thing were true heterosexually, he or she would be relating heterosexually at the time of the heterosexual involvement. Therefore, the question seems to be not who is a homosexual or a heterosexual, but who is a bisexual; for the bisexual is relating either homosexually or heterosexually at any given time. Technically, there is no such thing as a bisexual act at a given time of performance. In both instances, however—heterosexual and homosexual—the participants are relating *sexually,* and that is the essential thing: the acts themselves share some similarities. Perhaps, then, it might be more accurate to define a bisexual as someone who cannot, or does not, feel a need to make a choice, and is able to praticipate in both kinds of relationships alternately, whereas the homosexual may relate only homosexually and participates in homosexual acts exclusively, and the heterosexual likewise.

It is interesting to find, however, that the bisexual is possibly more discriminated against than the homosexual. Heterosexuals find them almost as difficult to understand and accept as the homosexual, and some homosexuals find them intolerable in some instances. To the heterosexual anyone who has homosexual relations is homosexual. To the homosexual, the bisexual seems something of a maverick who is trying to be just a little bit better than a homosexual. He or she wants the best of both worlds, and hasn't got the *guts* to make a choice. The latter, of course, seems unfair; for it may not be a true assessment of the psychology of the bisexual individual. He or she may not, in fact, be able to make a decision for some very good reason. A bisexual might have difficulty in forming close, exclusive, lasting relationships; he or she may fear acceptance of the responsibility for another person's love. A bisexual might just happen to be a truly earthy person whose appetites are such that he or she can not be totally categorized; sex may very well be vital, and he or she may have difficulties with any relationship more complex; in fact, he or she may not wish to become any more involved than sexual encounter. Suffice it to say that the bisexual's needs are obviously different from the heterosexual or the homosexual. At any rate, as bisexuals see it, bisexuality is the halfway house between heterosexuality and homosexuality, somehow a little bit better than the homosexual, while the homosexual sees the bisexual a little bit less admirable than the heterosexual or another homosexual.

Bisexuality, then, remains something of an enigma. Dr. Judd Marmor discussed the phenomenon in 1972, but notes in his statements that when he refers to ostensibly heterosexual women who have turned to other women he does not say they've become bisexual but rather homosexual. He said: "I think we had better realize that in adult human beings sexuality plays a highly important role in the pattern of relationships. It isn't just a simple biological thing. When we are talking about women who have been primarily heterosexual, we've got to realize what is happening in these women when they turn to homosexuality. Often they turn to it because they are caught in an unsatisfactory heterosexual relationship. Their husband, or lover, makes no effort to really satisfy them, or he uses them and gives them no real affection. Or he has stopped having sex with them entirely and neglects them. These women are looking for affection, warmth and love. Sometimes they find that warmth, affection and love in the context of a homosexual relationship. Sometimes they discover that they can also find sexual gratification within that context, sex that is more gratifying than their unsatisfactory heterosexual relationship. First of all, this illustrates the multipotential quality of human sexuality. We know this from other sources. We know, for example, that prisoners and sailors or women or men in jails sometimes turn to each other in the absence of other outlets. And I think the married woman who in her middle age, or after ten to fifteen years of marriage, turns to a homosexual experience is going through a similar kind of pattern. We mustn't reduce it, however, simply to the urge for biological experience. If they had had really satisfying heterosexual relations with husband or lover within the context of tenderness and affection, they wouldn't have a need to turn elsewhere. Many more women turn to other men than turn to lesbianism because that is the obvious thing to do. On the other hand, many of them are caught in a Judeo-Christian ethic which says that adultery is bad, and yet there is nothing in the Judeo-Christian ethic which says that being loved by another woman tenderly is bad, and so they move into that avenue more easily. They don't go into it seeking a lesbian relationship. They turn to another woman for affection and tenderness and find themselves eventually in a sexual relationship. To go out with another man is always in a sexual context. They know if they go out with another man he is going to want to sleep with them. For many married women that is taboo." (Personal interview)

There are, however, women who become involved in homosexual relationships who contend they've had completely satisfying sexual relationships with their husbands or male lovers, and in fact are able to continue having what they contend is completely satisfying sex with the male and with the female. In contrast, sometimes women who have been exclusively homosexual in their contacts for a long period of time will turn around and enter into a heterosexual relationship if some appealing male appears. It might be added that the latter case is somewhat like that of the women described above, those who have turned to other women to compensate for unhappy and unsatisfying relationships. If there has been an unhappy and disappointing relationship with one sex, the tendency is for the hurt person to hate all members of that sex for a time.

As regards the women who claim to have had completely satisfying relations with husbands or lovers before turning to homosexual encounters, Dr. John Money expressed skepticism: "I don't think these women did completely identify heterosexually. There was a little swing still left in the pendulum. I think we make a mistake if we accept the statement that a woman was completely satisfied within the context of her heterosexual relationship. If you look into her life you will find that there was something about it that didn't quite fit right, but she couldn't pin down exactly what it was that she was looking for. As people grow older and get more and more accommodated to having sexual experiences as part of something that is about as acceptable and ordinary as eating and urinating, they are in a very different position than when they were young—as, for example, a young girl having her first sexual experiences. Preparing herself for that first experience, she is influenced by all the mores and ethics of society. People do ease up a lot on the rigidity of the demands they put on themselves when they're younger, and particularly when they pass the active childbearing period."

Dr. Money went on to pose a hypothetical case of a woman's discovery of her homosexuality. "Perhaps by some coincidence, or accident, some woman comes along and a friendship is formed, one that turns into a close and rewarding relationship. Given the right circumstances, this friendship gradually gets over into the body contact area and becomes a homosexual relationship . . . and the experience is pleasurable and rewarding. The person says to herself, 'Well, this really isn't so terrible after all. It seems natural, I'm happy.' Or maybe the person has had a very close relationship with another woman, and they read in *The New York Times,* or in *Time* magazine that a lot of people are into homosexuality, and some psychologist says, 'A little homosexuality never hurt anybody all that much.' And a gradual reordering of values takes place. So by one path or another a person who has always been having some little unsatisfied urge decides maybe to try it. Now, if you really talk intimately with that person who has gone through the change, I think you'll find out she did have a different sort of biography-of-feeling back when age twenty, twenty-five, or thirty. I think the secret of the question, then, lies in the fact that the person was *nearly* completely identified heterosexually, but there was some kind of a little window there she (or he) could look through and wonder about other possibilities."

Despite Dr. Money's comments, one is still left with the question as to why a woman would accept a homosexual liaison if she had been perfectly well satisfied within her heterosexual relationship, as some women claim to have been. About this, Dr. Money suggests that a clue may lie in the definition of the word "satisfied." "How does one know that his or her degree of satisfaction is the same as somebody else's? A woman may say she was totally satisfied with her sexual relationship within the marriage, but one doesn't have any absolute criterion to say how strong is total satisfaction. One person's own experience of it subjectively is unacceptable to anybody else. You can only listen to words—how perfect is perfect?" Dr. Money elaborated on this point: "If you study a woman who has become bisexual or who has become homosexual after being heterosexual, and compare her biography to the stereotypic heterosexual woman of conventional femininity—if you compare biographies, you might find there is a difference. For example, if you take the biography of a woman who has her first actual in-bed lesbian relationship with another woman when she's, say, forty, you might very likely find that as a teen-ager she was able to get a great deal of relationship satisfaction in a friendship with a girl, but it never became body contact, or if it did, it was only kissing and hugging in a more conventional sense, never in-bed sexuality. Whereas if you take the other kind of woman who doesn't turn on in the slightest degree to another woman, then you might very well find, and I think you will find, that she was never very big on girl friends. She was always boy-oriented, and all her confidence sharing was with her boyfriends. So you actually have the antecedent. After all, simply going to bed is nothing. As I often say, somewhat irreverently, you can use a vacuum cleaner if that is what you prefer. The whole thing is the *relationship*. Even for the people who've got the most awkward relationships with sex itself, which I sometimes define as about the same for some people as picking their nose, even for those people it is a relationship that somehow or other is important, and for them it happens to be the very casualness of the relationship that's important. But for all of us human beings it's the relationship that counts in sex. So, if you want to know what has happened to a woman who finds that she suddenly can release herself in a lesbian affair in bed, you have to understand the history of her relationships with both sexes. I think that is where the key lies."

As for the woman who was not terribly unhappy with her husband, but still was attracted to another woman, Dr. Money said: "She may not have been all that unhappy in her bed relationship with husband or lover, but she did recognize that something was not happening just right either, and this may have been because she didn't have access to knowledge of what it was like to her sister, or to the woman next door, to be in bed. She can never have the opportunity to compare what she was getting with what another woman was getting. She might have been getting seventy-five per cent satisfaction while another woman was getting a hundred per cent. There is no absolute measure, and I keep reminding myself that it is very important not to try to imagine, not to assume too much about the other person's sexual feelings inside of him or her. So, a woman may very well say that she had nothing to complain about sexually with her husband or boyfriends, but when she had a relationship with a woman, she found that she did have something to complain about, because she could then compare. And she is being perfectly honest. How could she ever find out how much she was getting if she didn't have any other relationship to compare it with?"

Dr. Money also pointed out that some women who are able to swing both ways may have their pendulum a little more heavily weighted one way or the other—that is, the woman may get something more out of her relationship with another woman, but may decide to weigh the scales in favor of marriage for social reasons or because of the pressures of society. She may also wish to have children.

As to the difference in emotional health between the bisexual and the homosexual women, Dr. Money said: "I think that you get all degrees of health and ill health regardless of psychosexual inclinations or activity. The circumstances of the life style of the two can have an effect on adjustment. While the woman who decides to swing over to the homosexual life style exclusively may feel some pressures from society, the woman who carries on a relationship on the side with another woman may feel the pressures of secrecy, if she hasn't got her husband to agree to it and if she is not very good at deception. There might be a slight bit more distress attached to the necessity for deception and fear of being found out." Dr. Money pointed out that some women consciously and unconsciously calculate that if they get married they will then have the opportunity to carry on an affair with a woman-on-the-side. "This woman may in fact chose a man whose business takes him away from home a lot. For example, if a woman is married to a traveling salesman, or an airline pilot, she would find plenty of time to carry on her affair with a woman in his absence."

Alternatives are perhaps more open to women today who have unsatisfactory married relationships. The other man in a woman's life, or the other woman in a man's life, has always been there; affairs have always been carried on, some openly, some secretly, and some have been conducted with arrangements accepted by both parties. The psychologists tell us now that many, many more women exercise the alternative of the homosexual relationship on the side than was hitherto suspected. Many seemingly conservative, middle-aged housewives and mothers have been quietly carrying on a relationship with a best woman-friend for years. In some cases this can keep a family together, by serving not only as an emotional outlet for the woman but also as a constructive alternative.

There is much fine literature available to help us better understand what goes on inside our fellow human beings, how they manage to hold their lives together in their search for love and in the expression of love. Many fine studies and much extensive work has been done clinically and theoretically by scientists of the highest qualifications and standards, in an effort to have psychology expand its scope to become more realistic and relevant. Men and women such as Dr. C. A. Tripp, Dr. Judd Marmor, Dr. Evelyn Hooker, Dr. John Money, Dr. Bernard Riess and Dr. Ralph Gundlach, Dr. Martin Hoffman, Dr. W. B. Pomeroy, Dr. A. C. Kinsey, Drs. Masters and Johnson, and many others offer invaluable materials toward the understanding and acceptance of the homosexual—materials that revise and expand earlier work. Yet their newer findings are ignored by many of their profession, doctors who stubbornly cling to outdated and rigid concepts—concepts which scientists of more educated insight abhor and consider both harmful and reprehensible; concepts which justify the homosexuals' feeling that psychiatry has, and does, continue to victimize them.

Dr. Money, for instance, feels that both female and male homosexuals often lead constructive lives and experience relationships of wholeness and satisfaction. "There are male homosexuals and Lesbians who lead responsible and stable lives. I do not feel that their homosexuality makes them more unstable . . . Nobody has the epidemiological statistics to say otherwise. Too often the psychiatrist or psychologist sees only the unstable ones. That's whom they ask to see. But what percentage of people come to them for their homosexuality? How many come for anxieties that are perhaps founded elsewhere, anxieties they would have even if they weren't homosexuals? We don't have good studies on these issues, so people can only express their prejudices. Until the day comes that it isn't so dangerous to publically and politically identify themselves as homosexuals, we will always have difficulty in finding those who are making the grade perfectly happily. They are the important ones who will give us the answers we don't have yet."

Dr. Tripp seems to be agreeing with Dr. Money, but takes the issue a few steps further when he suggests that "from the point of view of personal adjustment, it is highly questionable whether any sexual behavior exercised between consenting adults is of any real social importance. From a psychiatric point of view, the thing that counts seems to be the efficiency with which an individual functions in life—his usefulness, his enjoyment and the success of his human interactions. If society has an interest here, it is certainly in the maintenance of high personal efficiency, and low neurotic effects. In terms of this ideal, the particular sexual responses of an individual hardly seem to be of any major concern." (21)

Writing on normal and deviant sexual behavior Dr. Marmor remarks:

There is no way in which the concepts of normal and deviant sexual behavior can be divorced from the value systems of our society; and since such value systems are always in process of evolution and change, we must be prepared to face the possibility that some patterns currently considered deviant may not always be so regarded. The fact that we now refer to sexual "deviations" rather than "perversions" already represents an evolutionary change within our culture toward a more objective and scientific approach to these problems than the pejorative approach of the previous generation.

We are the products of our culture, and within the context of our current Western culture value system there are indeed certain patterns that can be regarded as psychologically optimal and healthy. Although there is a wide spectrum of variations in human sexual motivation and behavior—most human beings, in the privacy of their bedrooms, in one way or another, and at one time or another, violate the rigid conventional standards of "proper" sexual behavior—there are nevertheless certain more widely deviant patterns of sexual behavior that in all likelihood would be considered abnormal in every society, i.e., practices that involve serious injury to one of the participants in the sexual relationship. . . .

The choice of deviant pattern is dependent on complex determinants which have to be ferreted out by a painstaking history and psychodynamic evaluation in each individual case. Disturbances in core family relationships, impairment in gender identity development, poor ego development, and specific conditioning experiences are all involved. Human sexual relationships are often complicated by unconscious motivations of fear, hate, or guilt, which leave their stamps on the quality of the sexual transactions between partners. In our culture a key distinguishing factor between what is regarded as healthy or unhealthy sexual behavior is whether such behavior is motivated by feelings of love or whether it becomes a vehicle for the discharge of anxiety, hostility, or guilt.

A sharp line of distinction, however, cannot always be drawn between healthy and neurotic sexuality. Since patterns of sexual behavior always reflect personality patterns and problems, and since no one in our complex society is totally exempt from individual idiosyncrasies, tensions, and anxieties, they will be manifested in sexual patterns no less than in other areas of interpersonal transactions. No human being is perfect, and nowhere is the humanity of man more important than in the varied patterns of his sexual relationships. (22)

As regards attitudes and practices of the psychological community toward the homosexual, the following statements have been made by members of their own profession:

DeSavitsch: "These people [well-adjusted homosexuals] should, in my opinion, keep as far as possible from the medical profession, except when suffering from appendicitis, pneumonia, or some organic ailment, the treatment of which will not upset their psychological balance." (23)

Ernest Van Den Haag: "I find no reasons and no evidence to assume that homosexuals have a 'psychopathological' personality." (24)

Judd Marmor: "If the judgments of psychoanalysts about heterosexuals were based only on those they see as patients, would they not have the same skewed impression of heterosexuals as a group?" (25) In his book *Sexual Inversion: The Multiple Roots of Homosexuality,* Marmor wrote: "The ordinary adult homosexual who does not wish or seek psychiatric help does not, simply because he is homosexual, belong within the purview of the psychiatrist." (26)

D. Curran and D. Parr: In their study of one hundred male homosexuals seen in psychiatric practice they discovered that on the whole they were "successful and valuable members of society, quite unlike the popular conception of such persons as vicious, criminal, effete or depraved." About the majority who came for treatment for reasons other than their homosexuality Curran and Parr said these people "were considered to be free from gross personality disorder, neurosis, or psychosis during their adult lives." (27)

D. W. Hastings: "The homosexual patients whom I have seen in practice . . . were living productive lives. Few of their friends, and in some instances not even their husbands or wives, were aware of the problem." (28)

S. E. Willis: "We are naïve if we ignore the fact that many mature people with predominantly homosexual proclivities have excellent ego strength and fine character structures which permit them to respond to their life situations with an appropriate mobilization of their intellectual, social, and creative resources. They often constitute an accomplished and highly informed group within their particular subculture." (29)

One is sorely tempted to quote from many splendid sources facts and theories which advance our understanding and illustrate the tremendous advances from earlier, more orthodox psychological findings and theories, but we will sum up the chapter with the following quotations:

> *A. C. Kinsey, et al:* The data indicate that the factors leading to homosexual behavior are: (1) the basic physiological capacity of every mammal to respond to any sufficient stimulus; (2) the accident which leads an individual into his or her first sexual experience with a person of the same sex; (3) the conditioning effects of such experience; and (4) the indirect but powerful conditioning which the opinions of other persons and the social codes may have on an individual's decision to accept or reject this type of sexual contact. (30)
>
> *John Money:* Chromosomes, gonads, hormones, genital morphology and body image, sex assignment, gender identity, psychosexual neutrality and differentiation, imprinting, family and cultural pattern—these and more factors in the genesis of homosexuality have been passed

in review. One arrives at the conclusion that the final common pathway for the establishment of a person's gender identity and, hence, his erotic arousal pattern, whatever the secondary and antecedent determinants, is in the brain. There it is established as a neurocognitional function. The process takes place primarily after birth, and the basic fundamentals are completed before puberty. The principles whereby all this happens await elucidation. (31)

In view of those therapists who cling to Freud as the Bible, interpreting him as suits their own particular bias, it is interesting to read the following from the writings of Freud: "Inversion is found in people whose efficiency is unimpaired, and who are indeed distinguished by specially high intellectual development and ethical culture." (32) The following is an excerpt from a letter he wrote to an anonymous American mother on April 9, 1935, about her homosexual son:

> Homosexuality is assuredly no advantage, but it is nothing to be ashamed of, no vice, no degradation, it cannot be classified as an illness; we consider it to be a variation of the sexual function produced by certain arrest of sexual development. Many highly respectable individuals of ancient and modern times have been homosexuals, several of the greatest men among them (Plato, Michelangelo, Leonardo da Vinci, etc.). It is a great injustice to persecute homosexuality as a crime, and cruelty too. If you do not believe me, read the books of Havelock Ellis. (33)

Nearly forty years ago Freud wrote:

> By asking if I can help, you mean, I suppose, if I can abolish homosexuality, and make normal heterosexuality take its place. The answer is, in a general way, we cannot

promise to achieve it . . . What analysis can do for your son runs in a different line. If he is unhappy, neurotic, torn by conflicts, inhibited in his social life, analysis may bring him harmony, peace of mind, full efficiency, whether he remains a homosexual or gets changed. (34)

In a study of 480 homosexuals in Chicago, P. Gebbhard found that when presented with the hypothetical option of change to heterosexuality if they could achieve it by simply taking a magic pill, the majority stated that they would refuse. (35) *Modern Medicine* reported in 1969 the results of a study which stated that only one in four female homosexuals interviewed wanted to become heterosexuals. (36)

Obviously there is a great deal more to homosexuality than meets the eye of the layman, or is disclosed on the analyst's couch—enough, in fact, to act as a warning to therapist and society to deal with it with greater wisdom and deeper compassion. No one has the right to harm another individual by depriving him or her of civil rights, of love, of sexual expression, and of peace of mind. Writing in 1972, G. Weinberg wisely warns:

From what I have seen, the harm to a homosexual man or woman done by persons trying to convert is multifold. Homosexuals should be warned. First of all, the venture is almost certain to fail, and you will lose time and money. But this is the least of it. In trying to convert, you will deepen your belief that you are one of nature's misfortunes. . . . and by the time you stop trying to change, time will be lost, and it may take you years to believe in individuality once more. Your attempt to convert is an assault on your right to do what you want so long as it harms no one, your right to give and to receive love, or sensual pleasure without love, in the manner you wish to. . . . It ought to be considered too that there are no

> specialists able to restore opportunities to an aged person
> who has foregone his chances for erotic experience, to-
> gether with its enrichments, and is now dying. (37)

There are many deaths worse than the cessation of breath,
and none worse than the death of self. That in effect is what
society has been demanding of the homosexual, and what the
homosexual is rebelling against. The foregoing theories, studies
and case histories seem to support the postulate that heterosexuality and homosexuality are erroneous terms, terms for
things which do not actually exist biologically. There is basic
human sexuality, which is activated by varied stimuli and is
expressible in many and varied ways. In the case of expression
in a so-called homosexual way, we have learned that charges
of sickness, pathology, neurosis and so forth are not support-
able; in fact, quite to the contrary, there is considerable evidence that there are many healthy homosexuals living useful,
constructive and happy lives. We have learned, too, that the
percentage of successful change to a heterosexual orientation is very small indeed, with many doctors claiming it
unrealistic and impossible. And at last we return to the question we began with: has psychology/psychiatry been a friend or
a foe of the homosexual? It would appear that it has been both.
In the case of the foes, one suspects that considerable personal
prejudice has been at work. The alternative to that is to assume
that the doctors have been ignorant of advanced theory and
studies which invalidate many orthodox assumptions; in other
words, they haven't *kept up*. But prejudice or ignorance in a
therapist is reprehensible—as reprehensible as the ignorance of
an internist who in failing to keep up with new advances in
medicine allows a patient to suffer disability, illness, perhaps
even death, simply because of his lack of knowledge of new
drugs and other scientific advances that could have made the
patient more comfortable, speeded recovery, or saved the life.
The frequency of malpractice suits and the high rates of mal-

practice insurance carried by medical doctors attest to the fact that many people have finally learned that the doctor is not God; nor is the analyst, and perhaps it is high time even more people realized that. Arrogance, the companion of prejudice and ignorance, has no place in the practice of medicine, psychiatry or psychology.

Chapter 6

Lesbianism in Literature

Come hither to-night I pray, my rosebud Gongyla, and with your Lydian lute; surely a desire of my heart ever hovers about your lovely self; for the sight of your very robe thrills me, and I rejoice that it is so.

Excerpt from "To Gongyla,"
The Songs of Sappho
J. M. Edmonds.

Probably every reasonably aware person who has at least a passing acquaintance with the liberal arts knows of Sappho, the lyric poetess of ancient Greece, who celebrated the love of woman for woman in superb verse—mainly, and most particularly, her love for certain maidens with whom she experienced love that would be termed "lesbian." But aside from the works of Sappho, most people are not particularly aware that there is such a thing as a literature of lesbianism. Yet there are some 2,041 listings of books in which lesbian episodes occur on one level or another in a bibliography compiled by Gene Damon and Lee Stuart for *The Ladder,* a publication circulated by the Daughters of Bilitis.*

One of the reasons we are not more aware of such literature is because lesbian characters, or sexually variant women, are often cleverly worked into plots and seldom identified. To openly spell out such a proclivity or relationship—to depict a direct and overt lesbian relationship or scene—could until recently possibly have gotten the book banned or withdrawn from the market. But if the material was handled with subtlety, and presented obscurely in an unsympathetic or negative light, it might very well enjoy some degree of acceptance. In fact, it would quite probably intrigue moralists, who delight in reading "naughty" things so long as they are not so labeled.

Until quite recently, books involving lesbianism followed a pattern of astonishing sameness. Almost without fail, one or both of the partners had to reform to heterosexuality, usually overwhelmed by the irresistible charm and force of a strong and positive male bent on rescue. Oddly enough, books involving male homosexuality do not emphasize reform, which might be due to the fact that while male homosexuality comes under more severe scrutiny by civil law, it is not considered as insidious an evil as lesbianism. It is still extremely unsettling to a great many people to admit that lesbianism exists at all. Men may dally with men—not a great deal is lost; men are expected to dally sexually in some form or another—but for women to dally with women is a dangerously subversive activity that strikes a deadly blow at the moral structure supporting male dominance. In this respect one is reminded of Dr. Mead's recounting of the lack of concern of Balinese society with male homosexuality because, after all, the penis is involved, and the penis is celebrated above all else in Bali. Is it out-

* This publication may be obtained by writing to *The Ladder,* P.O. Box 5025, Washington Station, Reno, Nevada 89503.

rageous to wonder if our own Judeo-Christian society does not unconsciously share a kinship with the Balinese attitude?

However, to return to the formula for lesbian-related literature: it was expected that one or both of the lesbian partners would see the light and reform to heterosexuality, but if that did not happen, one of the women would quite likely commit suicide or decline and expire as a result of sexual excesses, drug addiction, alcoholism and other vices accompanying lesbian practices. Not to be dismissed either were the possibilities of insanity or demise by other violent means. Certainly everyone knew without doubt that lesbianism, like masturbation, would result in all kinds of physical ills such as tuberculosis, dangerous depressions, brain tumor and eventual unhingement of the mind.

It was also quite necessary for one of the partners to be grotesquely hermaphroditic, transvestite, or so absurdly butch and pathetic as to be the object of great hilarity, ridicule or instant revulsion. She would also need to be sadistic, outrageously promiscuous, and totally male-imitative. She might very well be an eccentric member of the aristocracy; her nationality was probably British, as British ladies were considered more headstrong, independent, intellectual and subject to absurd notions about equality of the sexes. She would also be tweedy, a superb horsewoman, and more often than not, a fencer.

Another stock lesbian character was the courtesan (courtesans figured quite prominently in lesbian literature from the beginning), who was also quite apt to be an actress. Courtesan/actress/Lesbian seemed to be the pattern of the day, at least in France—if one is to credit early French literature. She very often would have a salon frequented by those of her persuasion, where a few innocent young maidens would be held captive. And that brings us to the young innocent fresh from the provinces, endowed with flawless facial beauty, breasts to inspire poetry, and a figure ravishingly beautiful enough to cause the goddess Aphrodite herself to swoon. Such a girl would usually be destitute and near starvation when she would either enter a house of prostitution or would be taken up by an older lesbian woman who would corrupt her entirely. It is sometimes difficult to feel much concern for the young maiden, for she was usually dim-witted and probably fared a lot better with the woman than she would have in a house of prostitution. However, morality being a curious thing, and vices often taking on the face of near virtue when compared to other taboos, prostitution in many of the novels appears to be more desirable than lesbianism. In prostitution the penis is also celebrated, and therefore more acceptable than a total rejection of it, as in lesbian relationships.

This type of young innocent from the province was a favorite of seventeenth-, eighteenth-, and nineteenth-century writers, and was nearly always rescued and reformed by a male, or became a calculating and accomplished seductress about town. More often, however, the former happened. Sometimes she would flee to a convent, torn between her female and male lover, but that happened less often. Suffice it to say that relationships between Lesbians had most always to be fraught with unrelieved cruelty, pain, hardship, struggles of domination and jealousy, and scenes of hysterical possessiveness and despair so extreme and burlesque as to be about as believable as the Three Stooges or Mighty Mouse. Under no circumstances, however, should the relationship seem to have any positive aspects, and gentleness and tenderness between the partners had to be kept to the barest minimum—for to suggest gentleness and tenderness between two women would give women and children ideas, perhaps suggest alternatives to women trapped in loveless marriages. The world would surely go straight to hell if the idea of such an alternative got about.

If a writer stuck pretty close to the negative condemnatory formula, the chances were the book would meet with some success. Even in the twentieth century this formula would get the book off any moral hook, prevent it from being damned by the church and banned in Boston, Philadelphia and other capitals of World Morals Watchers. From where we sit today, with some degree of psychological awareness, the formula was perfectly understandable, if ridiculous, because it reassured everybody, particularly the children, that the expression of such dark and evil emotions could only lead to destruction and death, and that sacred heterosexuality was the only right and true form of emotional expression, the salvation of every single soul on earth. In effect, it said that God was in his heaven, men and women were in bed with each other propagating, and all was right with the world, Amen.

When one first begins to investigate literature for evidence of lesbianism or variant behavior, it is not so easy to find. Few libraries index the subject as such, and when armed with some foreknowledge of authors and books containing such material, it is frustrating to find that many of the books are out of print, unavailable, missing, or available for perusal only in the library reading room. Having the good fortune to locate the material, one begins to read, and the first half-dozen or so stories astonish with their horror and unrelieved bleakness—a kind of lesbian snake pit. After a large dose of this kind of literature, one begins to be mildly amused at the unimaginativeness, the naïve and obvious prejudice. Finally as one conscientiously reads on, one gains a total emotional immunity, but at the same time, becomes aware of the fact that these rigid formulistic attitudes have been responsible for some of the most melodramatic, repetitive, cliched and boring literature anybody ever had the misfortune to wade through. That in itself might perhaps be forgiven; after all, it isn't necessarily reprehensible to be boring. One can elect to reject or endure. What is both reprehensible and unforgivable is the damage such exploitive writing has done.

If the church is to be blamed for prejudice, repression, oppression, suppression and great suffering, then literature must also share the role of villain, for succumbing to moral and religious pressures. In many cases, however, it is blatantly exploitive, and cannot be dignified by the term "literature"— it is simply trash. While all writing certainly is not literature, some of the writing on this subject has been produced by writers of august reputation under pseudonyms—and small wonder! It is clearly exploitive, royalties being the primary motivation.

Much of the negative and scathingly condemnatory writing involving lesbianism, or female sexual variance, has been written by male writers, often acting out personal vendettas against wives or mistresses who have preferred lesbianism, and in some cases rejected them in favor of women. Such a happening could present a difficult problem for the male ego, and if one's weapon is the pen, it can be a lethal one indeed. The danger in such literary indulgence lies in the fact that ordinary readers have no knowledge of what the author's motive might have been, and they, having no acquaintance with the subject themselves, form their opinions and attitudes from the books and stories of these writers.

One is struck by the predominance of male writers on the subject. Of course, men have largely dominated the world of letters. There was a time, not so very long ago, when a manuscript of female authorship would be rejected without even a consideration of its substance. This circumstance, of course, led some women to write under male pseudonyms. But there is quite another factor involved in the male writer's preoccupation with lesbianism as a theme. It is a scientific fact that men are fascinated by Lesbians—even to the point of becoming sexually "turned on" by someone of known lesbian tendencies or overt life style. The subject of the psychological phenomenon of male fascination with the Lesbian would be too complicated to explore here. One might conjecture briefly that for the male uncertain about his own virility, and easily threatened by women in general, the Lesbian could easily become an object for sadistic conquest and heated competition.

Given the historical pattern of inbred self-devaluation of women in general, and society's prejudicial attitude toward the Lesbian, she would seem to be an easy victim, if not a willing compliant. For this kind of inadequate male the temptation to create scapegoats would seem almost irresistible.

But there is another kind of sexual perversity which often encompasses the Lesbian. It certainly is no secret to the psychologically aware that lovers and married couples, for various reasons, participate in sexual rituals which would outrage the moralists. There are women who find that their male partner can not excite them sexually, and vice versa, yet the woman can be excited by another woman to the point of accepting the male and achieving an orgasm. There also are men who can not be excited to erection by their chosen partner, yet when another woman is introduced into the triangle, and she makes love to his partner, he becomes turned on enough to satisfy his wife or mistress.

There are situations where a husband or a lover will accept the extra partner as long as he is allowed to watch, then make love to one or both of the women, having been sufficiently excited to produce extraordinary prowess. As will be seen later in verbatim interviews with Lesbians, sometimes under the guise of acknowledging a Lesbian's superior ability in sexual love, a man will attempt seduction by claiming that he only wishes to be taught by her how to satisfy his wife or mistress. Once persuaded into such a compromising situation, the Lesbian finds that she is the target, and the unhappy, frustrated wife is either nonexistent or not cause for concern. However, if one is to believe reports, that "line" is so old that very few Lesbians fall for it. Then, of course, there are voyeurs, peeping Toms who enjoy themselves by watching others; and too, the jaded experimenters looking for a new and different thrill.

A tiny book "published for the trade," entitled *The Romance of Violette* and published in Paris in 1902, accommodates both formula and perversity. Told from the point of view of Christian, a suave man about town, it concerns little Violette, an innocent from the provinces, who late one evening seeks his emergency protection from the unwelcomed attentions of a clumsy type—in the house where they both lodge. Our suave man about town instantly recognizes his advantage and wastes no time in setting our young innocent up in rooms, and gently tutoring her in the joys of sexual play. To his delight, he learns that his little Pygmalion is also admired by a wealthy widow known as the Countess Odette. Recognizing the true nature of the countess' affections, he instructs his little captive to encourage the countess' attentions. Out of obedience, gratitude, and love for him, she complies.

Christian instructs Violette on how to incite passion in the countess, and together they plot to entice the countess into a compromising situation from which he will benefit. A love sequence then takes place: Violette and the countess engage in love play while Christian, concealed in a cupboard, watches. When the countess is deep in ecstasy at Violette's love-making, Christian, as planned, slips from his hiding place and takes Violette's place, unbeknown to the countess.

> I applied my mouth to the spot and had no trouble in finding the thing which Violette pretended not to have found. It was all the easier, because I noticed that in the case of the Countess it was longer than usual. It seemed to be the nipple of a virgin's breast excited by a lover's lips. I seized it in my mouth, and rolled it gently between my lips.
>
> The Countess heaved a voluptuous sigh.
>
> "Oh!" said she, "that is just the thing; and I think that if you keep on like that . . . I think . . . I think you, you will no longer be in my debt."
>
> I went on as she bid Violette, but drew the latter to me and pointed out to her the part she was to take in the trio.
>
> But with me Violette was not clumsy as with Odette.

Divining the thousand caprices of love's pleasure, she placed her mouth where I had put her hand, and I found that she was doing to me the very counterpart of what I did to the Countess, save that there was a difference in the shape of the objects performed upon.

The Countess seemed to experience the most voluptuous pleasures.

"Oh! really," said she, "it is just as I like it. Ah! you little storyteller, you said I must teach you; but you are the clever. . . . not so fast! . . . I wish it lasted forever . . . forever! Oh! your tongue . . ."

Had I been able to speak I would have paid just the same compliment to Violette. The passionate child had certainly the instinct of all the artifices of love.

I own I derived considerable pleasure from the caresses which I lavished upon the Countess. Never had I pressed my lips upon a sweeter peach. In this woman of twenty-eight all was firm and youthful as in a girl of sixteen. It was easy to perceive that the brutality of man had exercised itself there only to open a way for more delicate caresses.

The Countess gave expression to her wonder and admiration.

"Oh!" said she, "how strange, I never had such pleasure before. OH! I will not let you go on unless you promise to commence again. The impression of your lips and your tongue is so sweet; I cannot keep it back any longer! It is coming! I feel it! I feel it! No! It cannot be Violette who gives me so much pleasure; it is impossible!"

Violette did not at all feel inclined to reply.

"Violette, tell me, is it you! Oh, no! That is impossible. You are too clever for a woman. A woman could never do this!"

The Countess tried to raise herself up, but with my hands firmly pressed to her breasts I kept her down. Besides the supreme sensation was nigh; I was quite aware of that. So I redoubled my efforts, and my moustache began to play its part in tickling. The Countess writhed and almost shrieked; then I felt the climax come; my lips gave the finishing touch, and the amorous spasm shook the whole frame of the Countess.

My excitement had also reached the highest pitch, and I gave way to it at the very same moment.

Violette was lying half dead at my feet.

I had not sufficient strength left to prevent the Countess from rising from the bed.

At a single glance she realized how matters stood, and springing up, she cried with anger.

"Well, dear Violette," said I. "I have done my best to quarrel with the Countess. You must now be the peace-maker."

Thereupon I retreated to the dressing room.

Although peace was made between the parties of this 1902 drama, and an agreement was drawn up which shared Violette with the countess only in his presence, and he often played the part of oral lover to the countess in the threesome arrange-ment above described, the countess was never reformed and never accepted him as a male lover. At his bidding, Violette continued her relationship with the countess, in his presence, and apparently enjoyed her sexual attentions, at the same time remaining the devoted mistress of Christian. The countess, for her part, remained devoted to Violette until the poor little creature expired at an early age. The countess was, however, united in an ideal relationship with a popular woman actress of the day, a relationship which is described in highly graphic language, and is typical of many of the privately published, or what we would today term *underground,* works of the period.

Most of the literature, however, concerning lesbian relation-ships seems to fall into about four categories: personal axe-grinding; sensational exploitation motivated by royalities; sincere autobiography; and psychologically inquiring. The latter two tend to qualify more nearly as literature.

Ideally literature should represent life, like a film slowed down to emphasize the intricacy and subtlety of action. Literature should command us to examine, to comprehend, to experience vicariously, to act. History tells us of the deeds of men and nations; archaeology reveals the visual art, architecture, commerce and tangible evidence of culture or the mode of life; but it is literature that helps us to understand what the people were feeling and thinking, and allows us to relate to them meaningfully.

"Literature," says Dr. Barry Ulanov, professor of literature at Barnard College, "when it is literature, and not just journalistic narrative, deals with the oblique, with the covert— deals with meanings. It is, I think, in a sense allegorical, metaphorical by definition. Therefore, it takes up whatever man hides, represses, suppresses; what society attacks or wants concealed. It is the place to find the hidden revealed."

The foregoing critical comment on lesbian literature is not meant to suggest that neurotic and destructive relationships do not exist; one only objects to the repetitiveness of such themes, the leaving out of the positive and constructive elements, and the lack of objectivity and scientific awareness as a basis for story and character development.

It should also be mentioned that not every book or story which contains an intense and unusual relationship between two women automatically implies lesbianism. Relationships do exist without overt physical expression, without either party recognizing the implications. However, the fact remains that the extent of the intensity, the quality of the feeling, the variance from prescribed or accepted concepts of friendship or relationship between women, constitutes what would be considered in psychological context potentially lesbian. This literature does, however, serve to illustrate that from the beginning of recorded human interaction, neither morality nor social structure has been able to program the human capacity for love and relationships.

The Book of Ruth in the Old Testament gives us our earliest example of love and devotion so strong as to qualify as variant. The relationship between Ruth and Naomi subtly and delicately suggests it to the psychologically sophisticated. Some may possibly take offense at the suggestion, but this does not mean that Ruth and Naomi were necessarily lovers in the physical sense. The intensity of their emotional attachment, however, suggests feelings which can only be defined as variant. "Entreat me not to leave thee, or to return from following after thee; for whither thou goest, I will go; and where thou lodgest, I will lodge; thy people shall be my people, and thy God my God: Where thou diest, will I die, and there will I be buried: The Lord do so to me, and more also, if aught but death part thee and me." These very beautiful and tender lines spoken by Ruth convinces us of Ruth's great love and devotion for the mother of her dead husband. Ruth's declaration is as passionately loving as any one will find in literature. But her statement is not just a verbal declaration, for actions suited the words.

It is a matter of Biblical narrative that Ruth did, in fact, leave her people, did forsake her God, did follow after Naomi, doing her bidding in all respects, to the point of later marrying Boaz at Naomi's request, and bearing a son whom she dedicates to Naomi thusly: "He shall be unto thee a restorer of life and nourisher of thine old age; for thy daughter-in-law, which loveth thee, which is better to thee than seven sons, hath borne him."

Mythology, too, furnishes us with examples of extraordinary relationships amongst women, goddesses who demanded virginity and aversion to sex with males from their devotees. Legend is ripe with stories of female cults with masculine attributes and interests. The two most familiar of these are the Valkyries and the Amazons. The Amazons were warring maidens dedicated to the goddess Artemis. They were said to have been bound in love to each other, choosing for life. According to some scholars they accepted no males; according to others they suffered men sexually only periodically and purely for the purposes of procreation. An interesting episode involving this cult and describing certain of the religious rites appears in the chapter on Pontos in Mary Renault's novel *The Bull From The Sea.*

Virgil's *Aeneid* (Book XI) tells of Camilla, who was leader of a cavalry troop made up mostly of women. The goddess Diana was much enamored of her—so much so, in fact, that she avenged her death. The goddess Artemis was much devoted to the nymphs Callisto and Iphigenia. Among other maidens of mythology, Diana, Atlanta, and Daphne showed little interest in men—in fact, in some cases, a direct hostility toward them. Mix-ups of sexual gender are also recounted in Ovid.

Happily, poetry gives us more free expression of love between women, and more insight into their deep and passionate love. Of these it is Sappho from Lesbos who in her exquisitely passionate verse first reveals the love of women for women as early as the sixth century B.C. In her "Ode to Brocheo," a poem which scholars have called the most economical description of passion to be found in literature, she leaves little doubt to her own preference.

> It is to be a God, methinks, to sit before you and listen close by to the sweet accents and winning laughter which have made the heart in my breast beat fast, I warrant you. When I look on you, Brocheo, my speech comes short or fails me quite, I am tongue-tied; in a moment a delicate fire has overrun my flesh, my eyes grow dim and my ears sing, the sweat runs down me and a trembling takes me altogether, till I am as green and pale as the grass, and death itself seems not very far away. (1)

Nor are we left in doubt in two other poems addressed to maidens of her favor.

XXVI. *To Anactoria In Lydia*

The fairest thing in all the world some say is a host of foot, and some again a navy of ships, but to me 'tis the heart's beloved. And 'tis easy to make this understood by any. Helen, who far surpassed all mankind in beauty, chose for the best of men the destroyer of all the honor of Troy, and thought not so much either of child or parent dear, but was led astray by love to bestow her heart afar; for woman is very easy to be bent when she thinks lightly of what is near and dear. See to it then that you remember us, Anactoria, now that we are aparted from one of whom I would rather have the sweet sound of her footfall and the sight of the brightness of her beaming face than all the chariots and armored footmen of Lydia. I know that in this world man cannot have the best; yet to wish that one had a share in what was once shared is better than to forget it. (2)

XXXII. *To Gongyla*

Come hither to-night I pray, my rosebud Gongyla, and with your Lydian lute; surely a desire of my heart ever hovers about your lovely self; for the sight of your very robe thrills me, and I rejoice that it is so. Once on a day, I too found fault with the Cyprus-born—whose favor I pray these words may lose me not, but rather bring me back again the maiden whom of all womankind I desire the most to see. (3)

To Atthis, a maiden to whom she addresses several verses, she writes at her parting. Here Sappho is presented in literal translation rather than interpretive prose translation.

LVII. *To Atthis Leaving*

I ne'er shall see my Atthis more,
And sure 'tis dead that I well might be;
And yet as she went she wept full sore
And cried "Alack and woe is me!

God knows 'tis not that I would."
And I said "Good speed, and forget me never,
I wot you know how I loved you ever.
But if so be that you know it not,
I'll e'en tell all that you've forgot
   Of those days so dear and good
And how many wreaths of the violet
And the sweet, sweet rose together met
   You've bound about your hair,
And round your pretty throat how plenty
Chains of a hundred flowers and twenty,
And phials how often from my chest
Of balm the best and costliest
   You've poured on your bosom fair.
And cushioned soft, from cup and dish,
Of all Ionian taste could wish
   Or handmaids trim supply
You've had your fill; mount, sacred spot,
Brookside, there's none we haunted not;
No grove was loud at break of Spring
With nightingale's sweet jargoning
   But we went there, you and I . . ." (4)

In parting from friends, she writes of the sweet times they had together:

xxx. *Parting From Friends*

"Sweet dames," I answered, "O,
But you'll remember till you're gray
How we lived in Youth's heyday,
And all that we three used once to do,
And how 'twas good and how 'twas true;
And now that I must part from you
   My lovesick heart's all woe." (5)

It has been estimated that Sappho wrote over twelve thousand lines of verse, most of which were lost. What we know of her work today is contained in works of other writers and some fragments on papyri discovered during modern excavations in Egypt. The high quality of her verse commanded the attention of scholars and kept her work alive despite attempts to destroy it due to its obvious celebration of the sensuous and sexual. Yet critics have described her poetry as some of the greatest love lyrics ever written.

Sappho's work somehow survived the exceptional effectiveness of the Christian Church, and despite the order of Gregory of Nyssa that it be burned in 380 A.D. Earlier church fathers had pronounced her a *gynaion pornikon erotomanes*—a lewd nymphomaniac. We are told by Scalinger that in 1073 A.D. her books were burned at both Rome and Constantinople. When charges of lesbianism were leveled against her we do not know, but that arguments as to their validity have raged over the centuries is known. Many scholars have preferred to believe that her verses were addressed to young men. There is, of course, the fact that she was married briefly, and gave birth to a daughter Kleis, whom Sappho remained devoted to throughout her life. Additionally, there is the legend of her unrequited love for the young ferryman Phaon, for want of which she plunged to her death from the cliffs of Leucadia. In her book *Sex Variant Women in Literature,* Jeannette H. Foster tells us that "certain references in Sappho's work and that of others, however, indicate that she died peacefully at home at a relatively advanced age. In fact, modern scholars are inclined to pronounce the whole Phaon anecdote legendary."   (6)

The Oxyrinchus papyri found centuries later contributed greater evidence of the poet's preferences and proclivities. Says Dr. Foster: "In many poems and fragments addressed to girls her ardor is evoked oftenest by maidenhood, its moving aspect not virginity so much as physical grace and delicacy and a certain light freedom of spirit. In one fragment, indeed she describes herself as 'eternally maiden' at heart. . . . There is no comparable evidence with regard to her feeling for men." (7)

There still remains the matter of her having been a courtesan, as was charged in the later part of the classical period. Some scholars think that in those times the word "courtesan" may have implied lesbian activity. During this period homosexuality in both men and women no longer was tolerated as it had been during an earlier period in Greek history: Dr. Foster states that "in Rome its practice among women was associated only with courtesans; thus it may equally well have been rumors of lesbian irregularities which gave rise to the conviction that she must have been a courtesan." (8)

It has also been suggested that since homosexuality was under fire at that time, the rumor of her being a courtesan may have been created to detract from the suspicion of lesbianism. Whatever the case, the fact remains that her passionate love poetry was written to women. Whether she was bisexual, homosexual, or whatever is of very little importance and hardly worth further debate. The poems are extraordinary for their beauty, and the woman is extraordinary for having written them.

It does seem significant that both her name and her native Island of Lesbos have given our vocabulary the terms *sapphism* and *lesbianism,* both meaning "female homosexuality"; she will undoubtedly be considered lesbian by future generations. No serious modern scholar would argue that she was not.

Classical Latin literature preceding the Christian era offers some examples of lesbianism. In his satires Juvenal describes the orgiastic rites in honor of the Bona Dea—rites in which well-born women of rank compare erotic skills and endurance with the courtesans, performing upon each other. The work is a rather devastating attack, and is said to be directed at the Empress Messalina, who appears in Juvenal's text as the character Saufeia.

Most material on the subject of lesbianism written during

this period concerns courtesans—who, unlike prostitutes of the twentieth century, were women of good families, great intelligence and refinement. They excelled in the art of love, the most important part of which was not necessarily the sexual act. Whether they were Lesbians or not, no one can prove how exclusive their proclivities were; one doesn't know.

In his epigrams Martial describes hermaphrodites. The erotic writer Philaenis is claimed by some to have been the author of a work describing her prowess with women, as well as sodomy with boys. Others deny that she wrote the book. For our purposes it makes very little difference whether she did or not; it existed at that time.

Among the works of the minor Greek writers, mention of love between women can be found in Aliphron's *Letters from Town and Country*. He writes of a picnic given by a courtesan in which men and women and women and women pair off to enjoy sexual activities amongst the pastoral beauty. In his *Dialogues of Hetaerae* Lucian relates the story of a flute girl's night with two wealthy Lesbians who had engaged her for musical entertainment but kept her on for a swinging sexual threesome.

Much of the literature that may have existed during this period probably met with destruction or drastic expurgation at the hands of the members of the growing Christian sect. Classical belles-lettres were withheld from the public by churchmen for centuries, and who can guess how much the churchmen may have altered them during that time. At any rate, one can only imagine what gems may have been destroyed by the heavy hand of the church, and one is a little staggered that that same heavy hand is still felt today.

Not until the eleventh and twelfth centuries A.D. do we find literature again flourishing. What happened to the written word during those long centuries of the Dark Ages can only be imagined, for it is difficult to believe that nobody was doing anything interesting and nobody was writing about it. We do, however, know that it was a time of heresies and witchcraft; a time of cults of many kinds, and practices wild and strange. Homosexual practices fell into the witchcraft category, the worst of all heresies, and so far as anybody knows may have been considered another pagan cult. If that were so, it is not surprising that no one was writing about it; to do so could have been a very risky business.

From the twelfth century onward we find so much pertinent literature that it would be impossible to list, let alone review; therefore representative selections will be made for discussion. (A selected bibliography of Lesbian literature is included in the back of the book.)

In 1531 the Italian writer Ariosto introduced *Orlando Furioso* which told the story of the Amazon Bradamante, a fierce and colorful warrior affecting full armor and exploits to match. Stricken with a head wound and shorn of her hair, she is seen to resemble her twin brother. This resemblance causes her to be surprised while sleeping in the forest one day by Flordespine of Spain, who is so enamored of the sight that she awakens the innocent Bradamante with passionate kisses. Nor is the young princess to be put off when she is acquainted with Bradamante's actual sexual gender. In fact, the princess is really "turned on"; she takes Bradamante home to the castle, where she presents her with rich gifts befitting a loved woman. All this, however, is a bit disconcerting to Bradamante, who finds it impossible to muster mutual attraction, and flees.

It is the twin brother who benefits from the happening, for when it is related to him by his sister, he becomes so intrigued with the princess that he goes off to impersonate his sister. The princess is delighted with the return and once again supplies women's apparel. All seems well until night when the princess discovers some physical differences, which the clever twin brother explains as magic. Because he is so feminine in appearance, they get away with the deception for some time.

It is interesting that Flordespine, who adored the sister,

accepts the twin brother, believing in fact that it is still the sister magically altered. Not to be overlooked either is the fact that the ultra-feminine Flordespine is from the beginning the aggressor, with Bradamante the Amazon and with the twin brother, while Bradamante remains passive and unmoved.

In England, Sir Philip Sidney circulated his pastoral *Arcadia* among his friends in 1580, thereby introducing the first lesbian love into English literature, according to Iwan Block in his bok *Sex Life in England*. Sir Philip's book *Arcadia* was not brought out for public distribution until nearly a decade later, and bore a resemblance to Ariosto's *Orlando Furioso* in that it too concerned the hero masquerading as an Amazon to approach the princess. In the case of *Arcadia,* not only the princess is smitten by the masquerader, but likewise her father and her mother. After much sighing, jealousy and struggles with overwhelming passion, the princess finally learns the masquerader's secret, preventing the exchange of what would have been a lesbian kiss. The morals of Elizabethan England remained intact, but not before our princess, languishing for the supposed Amazon, bemoans their impossible circumstance:

> No, no, you cannot help me: Sinne must be the mother, and shame the daughter of my affection. And yet these be but childish objections . . . it is the impossibilitie that doth torment me: for, unlawful desires are punished after the effect of enjoying, but impossible desires are punished by desire itself . . . And yet . . . what I do, sillie wench, knowe that Love hath prepared for me? Do I not see my mother, as well, at least as furiouslie as my selfe, love Zelmane? And should I be wiser than my mother? Either she sees a possibilitie in that which I think impossible, or else impossible loves neede not misbecome me. And do I not see Zelmane (who dothe not thinke a thought which is not first wayed by wisdom and virtue) doth she not vouchsafe to love me with like ardor? I see it, her eyes

depose it to be true; what then? And if she love poore me, shall I thinke scorne to love such a woman as Zelmane? Away then all vaine examinations of why and how. Thou lovest me, excellent Zelmane, and I love thee: And with that, embrasing the very grounde whereon she lay, she said to her selfe (for even to her selfe she was ashamed to speake it out in words) O my Zelmane, govern and direct me: for I am wholy given over to thee. (9)

The passion of the princess for what she believes to be a woman is surely expressed in terms that leave no doubt; her primary concern being that she can imagine no way in which the love can be expressed and satisfied. It may be that the reader, knowing Zelmane's sex, understands that despite the Amazon masquerade the princess' femaleness is intuitively attracted to Zelmane's disguised maleness, and the strength and honor of heterosexuality remain intact. But how one gets around the fact that the princess, believing Zelmane to be woman, admits her love for her and regrets only what seems the impossibility of its proper consummation—that is hardly explained away.

There seems to have been a great fondness for gender masquerading during the Elizabethan era. Viola in Shakespeare's *Twelfth Night* and Rosalind in *As You Like It* come to mind at once, although there is no evidence of real lesbian inclination. Still, one wonders what real significance the wide preoccupation with gender masquerading had for people of that period.

Two dramas of the seventeenth century depict woman transvestites, the characters based on real women. In 1611 Middleton and Dekker's *Roaring Girl* concerned Mary Frith, a transvestite of the London underworld who is never identified as Lesbian, but who vows that she will never marry and has a passion for righting wrongs done to women. Juan Perez de Montalban's *La Monja Alferez* gives a picture in 1626 of the life of Catalina de Erauso, a real live Basque woman who posed as a military man. In real life, Erauso, as described by Fitz-Maurice Kelly in *The Nun Ensign* was lesbian. The play was sympathetic but did a good job of glossing over escapades. After the play was published, Erauso was granted permission by Pope Urban VIII to continue wearing men's clothes, provided she did not also continue deception about her true sex. Erauso herself was apparently a colorful character, but the play was a wordy apologia. Those interested in her escapades would do better to read the Kelly work.

Brantôme implies in his *Lives of Gallant Ladies* (1655) that lesbian activity was taken for granted, and Anthony Hamilton in *Memoirs of the Comte de Grammont* (1913) lightly depicts a rivalry between the Earl of Rochester and a maid of honor to the Duchess of York, a Miss Hobart, for a young beauty at court. Unfortunately, things ended rather badly for Miss Hobart, who wound up disgraced at court and minus her reputation in London.

Montaigne in 1581 relates the case of a young woman transvestite who was hanged for effecting a marriage with a young woman. Casanova's memoirs relate tales of lesbianism, even among nuns. Various pamphlets and other writings issued toward the end of the sixteenth century suggest that Henry III was homosexual, and later Louis XIII. The house of Orleans was reputed to have leanings in the homosexual direction in both the male and female lines. If true, then certainly such practices would not have been frowned on at court. If the court set the moral tone of the country, it would explain why French literature gives us so much material in this area. It would also explain why people with homosexual leanings fled to Paris. Later Napoleon failed to include a law regarding it in his Napoleonic Code, so France has not been burdened with a civic law—but a Catholic country could not ignore the church's condemnation.

One such royal personage who fled to Paris after her abdication and remained there between 1670 and 1680 was the fascinating Queen Christina of Sweden. Her dramatically stylish and somewhat eccentric dress must have caught attention even in Paris, and her lesbian habits were hardly disputable. A century later another royal refugee came to Paris—Marie of Austria, later known as Marie Antoinette. However, her removal to Paris was far more dismal and ultimately fatal. She became the bride of the hopeless Dauphin (later to become Louis XVI), a happening which undoubtedly contributed fuel for her rumored affairs with Lamballe, Polignac, and other ladies of the court, and which afforded material for sensational pamphlets about her. Biographers, however, have not been able to dispel these rumors; rather, they seem to make the potentiality of such relationships quite likely.

The eighteenth century under the Bourbons brought an extravagance in sexual freedom. Popular actresses and courtesans were said to enjoy lesbian activity, and gossipy memoirs described it. Private societies were formed, at least one being made up of lesbian women. At times, in fact, it appeared that variant practices were more popular than heterosexual ones. Two works attest to the thinking of the time. In 1777 and 1778 eleven volumes under the title *L' Espion Anglais* appeared; they featured contributions from several authors, among which were a series of letters from "Milord All'eve" in Paris to "Milord All'eve" in London, said to have been written by Mayeur de Saint Paul. They described a young girl from the provinces who enters an elite *maison* in Paris and is trained for the services of a prominent lesbian actress. Things do not turn out very well for the actress, however, because true to formula, a young man in disguise gains entrance to the actress' temple of pleasure and converts the young girl.

Felicite de Choiseul-Meuse, an author of rather racy novels, presented *Julie, ou J'ai Sauve me Rose* in 1807. She tells of a woman who sets out on something of a sexual odyssey. Her aim is to be seduced by every type of man in every type of setting, but she is said to also entertain a strong attraction to lovely women. However, it is only when the man she actually loves becomes fascinated by a boyish lesbian that our great experimentor, thirsting for revenge, herself turns seducer and seduces the lesbian. To her surprise she finds the lesbian encounter more pleasant than what she has enjoyed with men up until that time. Nevertheless she winds up marrying her original lover.

Toward the turn of the century writing began to be more psychologically oriented. Denis Diderot's *La Religieuse,* begun in 1760 but not published until 1796, appeared on the surface to be anticlerical, and in all probability it was; however, its real significance lies in its examination of the effects of celibacy on women in convents. Celibacy was imposed upon girls who often had been forced into convents by family or church. Specifically, it concerns itself with an illegitimate girl forced into a convent by her guilt-ridden mother and stepfather. During her convent experience she encounters sadism and homosexuality, and a great part of the action deals with the Mother Superior, who entertains no religious feelings and is an overt Lesbian. The action deals particularly with the Mother Superior's attempts to seduce the young girl, but includes scenes with the Mother Superior's *favorites*—their attention to her, and her favors bestowed upon them. Dr. Jeannette H. Foster in her book *Sex Variant Women in Literature* states that Diderot's "picture of fevered intrigue, jealousy, skilled seduction, and finally of the frustrated Superior's decline into acute neurosis, is unparalleled in fiction before the present century. Indeed, for clinical accuracy of detail it had no equal until Westphal's scientific case study of a homosexual woman was published in 1870. Thus it stands as a landmark in the literature of female sex variance." (10)

Of equal importance is *Mary, a Fiction,* written by Mary Wollstonecraft, which appeared in 1788. It is of great importance because it was the first known book on female variance written by a woman, and an Englishwoman at that. Dr. Foster tells us that only a handful of copies are still in existence. Additionally, in 1798 Mary Wollstonecraft published *Vindication of the Rights of Women,* and Dr. Foster cites the comments of Lundberg and Farnham in *Modern Woman, The Lost Sex* (11), who contend that "*Vindication* is the germ of all subsequent rebellion of women against their normal social and biological roles." Dr. Foster does not incline to credit it that seriously.

According to authorities on Wollstonecraft, *Mary* was based on the author's consuming attachment to Fanny Blood, an attachment which Wollstonecraft's husband William Godwin in his *Memoirs* describes as "fervent . . . to have constituted the ruling passion of her mind." (12) At any rate, the story of *Mary* follows very closely the pattern of Wollstonecraft's own life, and actually is a rather dreary story of early childhood with a drunken father and a passive mother, and an ineffectual and irrelevant husband whom she marries to fulfill her mother's fondest wish, and who mercifully goes off on an extended continental tour. The rest of the story is equally dreary as it relates Mary's struggle to support herself and the tubercular Ann (as she is called in the book) and to have Ann come and live with Mary and return her affections in kind. The scene moves to Lisbon, where Mary takes Ann for her health, but Ann, thoughtless to the end, dies anyway.

Mary returns to England where she faints at the sight of her husband, gains her freedom, and retires to the country to do good works and await death, when she will be reunited with Ann. *Mary* is a novel of highly idealized romantic love, in which, according to Dr. Foster, "Numerous variations on both these themes appear in the succeeding century and a half." (13)

The nineteenth century gave birth to a wealth of novels containing instances of female sexual variance, with French literature still predominant in this area—Balzac, Gautier, Flaubert, Lamartine, Zola, Henri de Latouche and others. One of the

more interesting is de Latouche's *Fragoletta,* which was originally published in 1829 and gave a wider scope of plot as it
was set among the color and intrigue of the Napoleonic wars.
It concerns Fragoletta, again a boyish girl not yet sexually
awakened by man or woman. And again we find the masquerade caper—the girl posing as her twin brother Adriani. After
seducing the sister of her long-discouraged suitor d'Haute-
ville, she is challenged to a duel by the outraged brother-suitor;
during the duel she falls over a cliff, uttering a feminine cry
which reveals that Fragoletta and Adriani were one and the
same.

The novel moves through Austria, France and Italy, and
concerns international diplomatic circles, which adds interest. Additionally, there is a spicy scene between Queen Caroline and Lady Emma Hamilton which takes place in a sunken
marble bath and involves considerable erotic play before the
two drowse off lovingly entwined in the warm pool.

Although Honoré de Balzac states in *Cousin Bette* (1846)
that "the strongest emotion known [is] that of a woman for a
woman," his basic concern, one feels, is not with lesbianism or
sexual variance. One is somewhat mystified, however, about his
use of variance in three novels: *Seraphitus-Seraphita, The Girl
with the Golden Eyes,* and *Cousin Bette.* Writing of *The Girl
with the Golden Eyes,* Dr. Foster suggests that "the extravagance of the plot and the description of the hero, which occupies a good quarter of the tale, might cause one to suspect
satire upon the Byronism which was sweeping Europe, except
for the romantic seriousness of the whole. Another long inter-
polated essay is an arraignment, mordant in brilliance, of the
cruelty, stupidity, and license of Parisian life, in which one de-
tects echoes from Rousseau; in such an 'unnatural' milieu excesses of evil are only to be expected. Such romantic social
philosophy concerned Balzac here more than the psychology of
either woman. (14) Still, one wonders why he fixed upon
female variance to demonstrate an unnatural milieu and excesses

of evil. Surely there must have been other unnatural and evil excesses to choose from.

Each of the three above-mentioned novels deals with a different kind of variance, so that one is led to feel that variance is perhaps after all his preoccupation. Dr. Foster remarks:

> Thus, the faithful observer of the Human Comedy presented three contrasting types of emotional variance and offered three distinct explanations of it. In the first, intellectual conditioning was the causal factor; in the second, a possible inheritance of temperament plus the certain freedom of self-indulgence provided by limitless wealth; and in the third, poverty of both circumstances and emotional opportunity. The resulting experiences also show the writer's imaginative range. The first seraphic heroine is as innocent and passionless as the biblical Ruth. The Spanish Marquise is violent to the point of melodrama. The warped spinster is confused and groping in expression as well as feeling. (15)

Théophile Gautier, more psychologically sophisticated and humanly tolerant of bisexuality, published *Mademoiselle de Maupin* in 1835. According to Dr. Foster this book is "the most generally popular of all variant 'classics.'" The description of its leading character, Maupin, became the classic model for what many people still identify as the homosexual woman: a tall, broad-shouldered, flat-chested, slim-hipped woman, usually an accomplished athlete, almost always a horsewoman, and sometimes a fencer. She is certainly the physical type of Radclyffe Hall's twentieth-century Stephen Gordon, but Maupin has none of the feminine tenderness, idealism, honor or pathos of Miss Hall's heroine. One does not find Maupin a sympathetic character. She is nevertheless bizarre, uniquely male-imitative and interesting from a psychological standpoint. She describes herself as "of a third sex, one that has as yet no name above or below." (16)   Her escapades, however, are not without a certain humor, and at times horror.

The story begins with her setting out upon a bizarre mission, dressed in men's clothes, to discover how men live and think when not in the presence of the female of the species. One of her first adventures is with a young man who has found women only physically satisfying; he falls in love with Maupin, only to be distressed with what he feels is an abnormal passion, believing Maupin to be a man. Upon discovering her true sex, he falls even more in love, realizing for the first time he has found complete love because he enjoys much in common with her. Maupin, however, has a well-developed masculine attitude toward love. She also has in tow a young woman disguised as her page, whom she had rescued from the exploitation of an aging rake. Maupin lavishes the most ardent erotic attentions upon her. The girl finds Maupin's attention exciting, and continues to do so even after she discovers that she is actually a woman. When Maupin is ready to take her leave of the young man and the young woman she spends half of her last night with each, then takes her leave of them without the slightest concern—thus categorizing her emotional attitude as definitely masculine. Dr. Foster suggests that the portrait of Maupin was drawn from "personal or at least close secondhand acquaintance with George Sand, so newly come to Paris in her male costume and so prominent in literary circles at that moment." (17)

Having reviewed some of the early and lesser-known material it becomes necessary simply to list others of this period and move on. Important were Lamartine's *Nouvelles Confidences* (1851), "La Sapho" by Céleste Venard, Comtesse de Chabrillan (1858), Flaubert's *Salammbo* (1862). Adolphe Belot's *Mademoiselle Giraud, Ma Femme* began in 1870 as a serial in the newspaper *Le Figaro*. Zola's *Nana* appeared in 1880 followed by *Pot-bouille* in 1883. *Monsieur Vénus* was published in Brussels in 1884 under the authorship of Rachilde, who was actually Marguerite Eymery Vallette. In an article entitled "Rachilde, Homme de Lettres" appearing in *Nouvelle Revue Critique* in 1924, André David states that the book was condemned, copies confiscated, and the author fined. Fortunately for her, she was in Paris and not subject to Belgian jurisdiction. A year later the book was brought out in Paris.

Works in English on the subject during the latter part of the nineteenth century are notable: Henry James' *The Bostonians* appeared in 1885, serialized in *Century Magazine*. His publisher informed the author that he had "never published anything so unpopular." It was brought out in book form a year later and did not receive any better reception. It is interesting to read that it did not appear again until 1945, and was omitted from the collection of his work brought out by Scribner in 1923.

In 1898 James presented *The Turn of the Screw,* a horrifying story which can be termed a unique ghost story, and is one of the earliest examples of lesbian child corruption. Considered by literary scholars to be a masterpiece of creative genius, it seems only fair to point out that in so far as it concerns the subject of lesbianism or female variance, like James' earlier work it is condemnatory in the extreme—which is not surprising considering his background as the son of an American clergyman, and the fact that he rejected Paris as a permanent residence on the grounds of its "immoral atmosphere." He found England more to his liking, and settled there.

His fellow countryman Oliver Wendell Holmes was more of a psychological prober. Dr. Foster tells us that throughout his life he was preoccupied with intersexual personality in women and explored it at least tentatively in each of his three novels: *Elsie Venner* (1859), *The Guardian Angel* (1867) and *A Moral Antipathy* (1885).

Of the three novels *Elsie Venner* is perhaps the most unusual and interesting. Elsie's mother is bitten by a rattlesnake during pregnancy and dies shortly after little Elsie comes into the world. The young child grows up unafraid of snakes. Rattlers abound near her home, and she wanders among the hills, spending nights on the rocky slopes where they are known to be. She is apparently immune to their venom. From the beginning she shows a strangeness which alienates people. Her strangeness later develops into a sort of reptilian hypnotism which she uses to gain power over others less powerful. When applied to someone, her steady gaze is described as not unlike that of the fearsome snake itself.

A teacher in the academy Elsie attends becomes the subject of Elsie's affection, an emotion so intense it frightens the poor woman into a hysterical revulsion, which is hurtful to Elsie. However, she later attaches her affections to a young male instructor, who partially understands her strangeness and tries to display a sympathetic feeling toward her. When she offers herself to him, however, he is unable to respond. Finally, Elsie dies of an illness as strange as her personality, attended by the woman teacher whom she calls for care and companionship. It is a strange and fascinating novel.

Thomas Hardy's novel *Desperate Remedies* (1871) also contains rather detailed variance. Olive Schreiner of South Africa published her novel *The Story of an African Farm* in London in 1883; it is also said to be somewhat autobiographical. It was a strong and touching outcry against woman's lot in life. It also contains perhaps the most obvious example of narcissism in a variant-inclined woman up to that time. In contrast, Strindberg's *Confessions of a Fool,* written in 1887 and 1888, is a violent condemnation of women's rights and female sexual variance. Its leading character is said to have been a thinly veiled portrait of his first wife, Seri von Essen, Baroness Wrangel, to whom he was briefly married and from whom he was bitterly divorced, and who has been described by Dr. Foster as masculine, an ex-soldier, archeologist, and progressive educator. Later his play *Miss Julie* suggests lesbianism while it never directly identifies it. For a better insight into Strindberg himself, and possibly a better understanding of his work, Elizabeth Sprigge's *The Strange Life of August Strindberg* is suggested. The fact that his wife was a Lesbian obviously explains the harshness of his attitudes.

Catulle Mendès' *Mephistophéla,* published in 1890, pulls out all the stops of stock lesbian stereotype, and is a marvelous example of the *formula.* In scenes of lurid detail, it depicts drug addiction, implied syphilis, hysterical convulsions, fevers, somnambulism, attempted suicide, child desertion, husband abandonment, orgiastic lesbianism, and final debauchery. It also credits heredity with cause, and takes a high moral tone, which undoubtedly got it past the censor of the day. Its importance in literature, however, lies in the attempt to trace a complete lesbian history. In the case of Sophie, the Lesbian whose history is being traced, modern psychologists would recognize lesbianism as a symptom of a deep and all-encompassing neurosis, but not as the cause of the neurosis. Given her heredity and history she would have been disturbed whether homosexual or heterosexual. This would be the case of much of the material written during that and the preceding periods, even up to the present time. Writers without psychological insight have created a horrifying picture of the Lesbian and the homosexual male, which has served to reinforce prejudice and oppression. Of course, the fact that writers and publishers, influenced by prevailing social and moral attitudes toward homosexuality, have seldom dared to present constructive, successful homosexual relationships has led to the condemnatory, lurid and more sensational approaches.

Oddly enough, a woman, Josephine Peladan, author of *La Gynandre* (published in 1891) expressed the same Catholic attitudes as Mendès and declined to believe in the possibility of any real feeling or love existing between Lesbians, calling it instead only sexual bias. Through the character Tammuz, in a long series entitled *La Décadence Latin,* Peladan writes a rambling saga to expose such vices, for according to her, to let them rage unchecked would destroy French civilization.

For some light-hearted relief after the inundation of lurid debauchery and tragedy, *The Florida Enchantment* (1892) by two Americans, Archibald Gunter and Fergus Redmond, is recommended. Dr. Foster identifies it as "an unmistakable burlesque of such novels as Rachilde's and Peladan's." (18)

In 1896 Remy de Gourmont wrote *Le Songe d'une Femme* for the *Mercure de France* as a serial. He explores the anatomy of a successful sexual relationship and concludes, like Baudelaire, that the pursuit of romantic perfection dooms all love to failure. Such an ideal as romantic perfection is a feminine dream.

As if to cap off the century, Pierre Louÿs arrived on the lesbian literature scene with *Chansons de Bilitis* (1894), "Aphrodite" (1896) and "Adventures of King Pausole." While Louÿs's writing is a delicious and refreshing breath of air after the cloud of dark doom and reprehensible sin one has suffocated under until his appearance, one regrets that his knowledge was limited to the courtesan class and does not shed any more insight upon other classes of women. Because he wrote in a quasi-classical vein, and claimed his works were based upon research and translations of ancient works, classicists discredit his claims and cry "exaggeration," and their learned pedantry is justifiable in the strict sense, but in the popular sense, no one really cares, their appearance is such welcome relief.

The Songs of Bilitis, published privately in 1894, recounts three periods of the maiden Bilitis' life, from her childhood in Pamphilia, her young womanhood on Lesbos, and her later life as a prosperous courtesan on Cyprus. Dr. Foster states that "the emotional highlight of her roving existence is the period in Mitylene (Lesbos), during which she loves and marries another girl with whom she lives happily and faithfully for a decade." (19)

In the second part of the book, "Elegies in Mytilene," we

hear the beginning of the romance that was to result in marriage to Mnasidika, a girl whose beauty Sappho herself praised.

LII *Desire*

She entered, and passionately, the eyes half closed, she fixed her lips to mine, and our tongues touched each other . . . Never in my life have I had a kiss like that one.

She stood erect before (against) me, full of love and consentment. One of my knees, little by little, mounted between her hot thighs, which gave way as though to a lover.

My wandering hand upon her tunic sought to divine the naked body, which softly bent like waves, or arching, stiffened itself with shiverings of the skin.

With her eyes in delirium she signs toward the bed: but we have not the right to indulge our love before the ceremony of the wedding, and brusquely we separate.   (20)

Next she writes of the wedding:

LIII *The Wedding*

The next day they laid the wedding feast in the house of Acalanthis, whom she had adopted as her mother. Mnasidika wore the white veil and I the man's tunic.

And then, in the presence of twenty women, she put on her robes of fête. Perfumed with Bakkaris (elecampane), powdered with powder of gold, her cool and delicate skin attracted furtive hands.

In her chamber filled with greenery, she has awaited me like a spouse. And I have set her on a car between me and the (nymphagogue) guardian of the bride. One of her little breasts burned in my hand.

They have sung the nuptial song, and the flutes have played it also. I have carried Mnasidika under the shoulders and under the knees, and we have crossed the threshold covered with roses.   (21)

Thinking back on her early romances Bilitis sings of her Metamorphosis with Mnasidika:

LV *The Metamorphosis*

Once I was amorous of the beauty of young men, and the memory of their words once kept me from sleep.

I remember to have carved a name in the bark of a plane-tree. I remember to have left a bit of my tunic in a path where a certain one might pass.

I remember once to have loved . . . Oh, Pannychis, my babe, in what hands have I left thee? How, oh unhappy one, have I abandoned thee?

To-day, and forever, Mnasidika alone possesses me. Let her receive as a sacrifice the happiness of them I have deserted for her. (22)

In two poems, "Endearments" and "In the Shadows," she sings of their tender passion.

LXI *Endearments*

Close softly thine arms about me like a girdle. Oh, touch, touch my skin thus! Neither water, nor the breath of the south wind are softer than thy hand.

To-day endear me, little sister, it is thy turn. Remember thou the endearments that I taught thee last night, and kneel thou near to me who am fatigued; kneel thou in silence.

Thy lips descend upon my lips. All thine undone hair follows them, as a caress follows a kiss. Thy locks glide upon my left breast; they hide thine eyes.

Give me thy hand, it is hot! Press mine and leave it not. Hands better than lips unite, and their passion is equalled by nothing. (23)

LXIII *In the Shadows*

Under the coverlid of transparent linen we have slipped, she and I. Even our heads were hidden, and the lamp shone through the fabric above us.

Thus I viewed her dear body under a mysterious light. We were nearer the one to the other, more free, more loving, more naked . . . "In the same chemise," she said.

We had left our hair arranged in order to be more un-covered, and in the close air of the bed there rose up the odors of two women; of two natural cassolets.

Nothing in the world, not even the lamp has seen us that night. Which one of us was loved, she alone and I can ever tell. But the men, they knew nothing of it.   (24)

LXV   *The Kiss*

I would kiss the whole length of the rich black locks that grace thy neck like wings; oh! sweet bird, Oh! cap-tured dove, whose passion-filled heart beats under my hand.

I would take thy lips between mine own, as a babe takes the breast of its mother. Tremble!—Thrill! Sweet one—my kisses reach far, and should satisfy thy love.

Lightly will I touch thy breasts and arms with my tongue and lips and behind thine ears, and upon thy neck I will leave the marks of my kisses; and while I kiss thee my hands shall stray in mad delight over the ivory naked-ness of thy sensitive body, trembling under the touch of my nails.

Listen, Mnasidika! Hear the murmuring of my love in thine ears, like the wild humming of the sea. Mnasidika, thy look drives me mad; I will close thy burning eyes with a kiss, as if they were thy lips.   (25)

Louÿs's work met with such popularity that it drove him into seclusion, and he never again wrote anything of note, with the exception of the unfinished work *Psyche,* which was pub-lished after his death, and which some feel was his greatest work. Writing in the Foreword to *The Collected Works of Pierre Louÿs,* Mitchell S. Buck says of *Psyche:* "It is probable that *Psyche,* being an unfinished work, will never be a famous book; and this is unfortunate because it is, perhaps, the most delicate and most significant production of his genius. But its fabric is far too frail to be generally appreciated in today's world; and this he knew very well. It has an atmosphere as intangible as the soul. 'It is too intimate.' " (26) Buck says of Pierre Louÿs's retirement:

> The widespread distribution of his books displeased him. Men and women wrote to him to ask for a fuller description of Queen Berenic's "costume, shamelessly pierced." Eugene Ledrain had criticized him for representing Chrysis as a Jewess, claiming that Lesbianism did not exist among the Daughters of Israel. He felt that the true spirit of his work escaped readers intent on unimportant details. His seclusion was endangered; he was too conscious of a public he did not particularly like. He decided it was time for him to follow the dictum he himself had put into the mouth of Phrasilas. He stopped writing. (27)

There is a category of literature that is difficult to identify in this vein—literature which does not present either overt examples of variance or suggestions of it. This literature is the work of women who led eccentric lives, often manifesting rather masculine qualities, yet their work appears heterosexual. Other facts of their lives have led scholars and speculators to suggest that gender names in their works may have been deliberately misleading in order not to come under critical fire and moral condemnation.

Dr. Foster suggests in her book certain writers that should be considered in that light. She defines her chapter concerning them thus: "The purpose of the following chapter is to consider those few whose lives most readily yield suggestive hints, and to correlate such hints with corresponding traces, however carefully masked, in their writing." (28) She reviews the lives and work of such authors as Louise Labé, Charlotte Charke, Karoline von Günderode, George Sand, Emily Brontë, George Eliot (Mary Ann Evans), Margaret Fuller, Adah Isaacs Menken, Michael Field (pseudonym of Katherine Bradley and Edith Cooper) and Emily Dickinson.

The coming of the twentieth century ushered in a slightly more liberal attitude toward homosexuality with growing psychological awareness. Dr. Foster tells us that "a first peak in variant literature was reached between 1925 and 1935. . . . . Thus, it is not surprising to discover that during the first third of the present century, literary titles dealing with variant women averaged more than one per year, that at least half were written by women, and that a majority were more favorable to variance than otherwise." (29)

Beginning the century with the poets, wherein we find some of the most passionate outward expressions of lesbian love, we find Renée Vivien, who was born Pauline Tarn, the daughter of a Michigan heiress and an English gentleman. Although born in Hawaii, she grew up in England, Germany and France, and finally made her home in Paris. She adopted the name Renée Vivien and wrote almost exclusively in French. Dr. Foster states that her "poetry has been pronounced most perfect in form of any French verse written in the first quarter of the century." (30)

Vivien was openly lesbian, and much has been written about her strange life and early death at the age of thirty-two. She is known to have been involved with another American poet living in Paris, Natalie Clifford Barney, among others. An essay giving a fascinating picture of the last year of Renée Vivien's life is contained in Colette's *The Pure and The Impure,* and a volume by André Germain gives a more comprehensive account of her personal life.

Although she died young, she produced a staggering number of poems, prose poems and an autobiographical novel, and collaborated with a friend on several works under the pseudonym Paule Riversdale. Her work breathes romantic sensuousness, imagery, an eagerness for life and later death, and an acute awareness of nature. Two examples are her poems entitled "La Fourrure" ("Fur") and "La Pourre" ("The Moat"), here translated by Richard Tedeschi, Department of Romance Languages, University of Massachusetts.

Fur

I breathe the animal warmness of this fur—
Silver blue, opal blue—and trembling,
Savor its rich scent more powerful than taste,
Vaster than a voice in rut, blaspheming.
And I inhale the fragrance of the Woman
Whom I fear and these breasts that I adore.

My hand in trembling moves along the fur—
Along the softness of the fur—and stops,
Made keen by the nearness of its prey.
My northern dream requires skies whose cold
Dispassion draws me, calls me—and the
Deep laid forest under sleeping snow.

For I am one enkindled by the cold.
A child, I gloried in the crystaled air,
The frozen light, exulted in the wind,
Adored to gaze full-face upon the storm.
True daughter of the North, and cold,
I sometimes dream of sleeping in a shroud of ice.

Ah, this vexing fur! It makes the pleasure
Of your nakedness, while chafing my desire!
But I can feel a warm betrayal rising
From your thawing flesh—desire's treason;
And my winter soul with its winter thoughts
Is wrapped in the faithless scent of your soft fur.

The Moat

The dawn has furtive, she-wolf steps
   And jackals' eyes. . . .
I with my hands (no vassal helped me)
   Have dug this moat,
   Built this tower,

These walls I destined for your cloister.
You in terror watch the swelling abscess
   Of my feudal love.

Your stricken look—sad, silken like a dove—
   Matters little;
The hunger of a bough that bears no roses
   Matters little
To the selfish torment of my need.

I am as craven as a man would be.
I summon you to languish in the narrow
   Dungeon of my kiss,
And on your sex I shall maintain
Prerogatives of masterdom.
Your fragile brow will break against
   The metal of my will;
And weary of the sickly fog
   Descending from the sky,
Hope will become despair, and you will die.

A strong, almost violent poem from a woman depicted as
sensitive, fragile, ethereal, almost mystical, and probably somewhat schizoid from descriptions of her behavior. It is her
friend Natalie Clifford Barney who is the more aggressive,
dominating, egotistical, merciless lover. Barney also wrote almost exclusively in French, but never with the power and skill
of Vivien. Two poems, "Equinox" and "Suffisanace" ("Self-
Sufficiency"), are perhaps reasonably representative of her work
(also translated by Richard Tedeschi).

Self-Sufficiency

Since with eyes half-closed and glistening
You can conjure up a formless, faceless love,
Have you longer any need of passing lovers?
What pleasure can they offer you that matches
Your disgust? Like wolves,
They prowl in search of prey, ineptly lusting

For your body that their lust will only sully.
Aloof from that, removed, your own desire—
(True master of your bed)—remains
The nightly author of your pleasure.
And when this master forces your surrender,
When it makes you warm and supple,
When your doubled self—become both lovers—
Takes you—then better than any couple
You bring yourself to flame.
(Your act is more harmonious.)
Loving only you, you pity any woman who is
Saddled with the risks of easy love.
Not proud you. Alone you serve your beauty—
In darkness.

Equinox

I feel autumn in my bones tonight—
Its grays, its drifting dead, its desolation,
And all the apprehension
Of thieves that lie in wait along a stormy road.
I, the disinherited of mankind—*your* race,
My haughty, headstrong friends!
I, its willing dispossessed (For I've left
Your celebrations) How your laughter galls me!
But don't be smug, I can pay you back in kind!
I am the errant Jew, the dispossessed,
Lord of my destiny—and sometimes of yours,
I too inconstant woman—my single loves.
But in me alone, it seems, the mark of it
Remains. Must you, in this gray declining
Season, remember it so faintly?
Now is autumn sifting down
Now's the hour to go home
To your snug familial love
In a pretty little house.
But we whose hands are warmed at passion's hearth,
Where's our roof? Our strong sustaining shoulder?

> Those of us who love the open road
> Must keep our wits about us, give ourselves completely
> To our love that's always old, and always new—
> Our faces scarred with barbs (the answers of those
> Bitches who call themselves our sisters!)
> But lifted high, ecstatic—
> And die with one last blow against the heart.

Both women had inherited money, and lived in rather grand style, part of a cult of literary figures of the day. In addition to her poetry Barney wrote several poetic dramas, but her output was meager in comparison with Vivien. Both were women of exceptionally free and pagan spirits. (Highly colorful material about them makes excellent reading—alas, space prevents going into it.) Barney herself inspired two volumes by Remy de Gourmont, *Lettres a l'Amazone* and *Lettres Intimes a l'Amazone*. And Dr. Foster says of Vivien: "All the critics who grant her this superlative poetic quality agree that she has received nothing approaching her due recognition because of the lesbian element in her work. In view of the small number of persons in any generation who are tolerant of such love, it may be that she will never receive it." (31)

Since the publication of Dr. Foster's book in 1956 the world seems to have moved a little closer to understanding and objectivity, and it may yet be that Renée Vivien will receive her just due. If her works were translated into English, it would not only advance appreciation of her great talent but it would also enrich the world of literature. In this period, other French poetry concerning variance can be found in the works of Marguerite Yourcenar, Paule Reuss and Henry Rigal. German poets writing in the same vein were Marianne Plehn, Marie Madeleine, Peter Hille, Toni Schwabe and Iris Ira.

English poets are not so frankly expressive as the French and Germans, and their work has not been examined as critically for evidence of sexual variance. This is probably again due to our Judeo-Christian rigidity on matters of sexual freedom. Amy Lowell, who lived and died in Massachusetts, was a refreshing exception. In "A Dome of Many-Colored Glass," we find these lines:

> Tis night and spring, Sweetheart, and spring!
> Starfire lights your heart's blossoming
> In the intimate dark there's never an ear . . .
> So give; ripe fruit must shrivel and fall.
> As you are mine, Sweetheart, give all!   (32)

In *Sword Blades and Poppy Seeds, Pictures of the Floating World,* and *What's O'Clock* one will find evidence of the passionate spirit and burning heart of this respectable New England spinster. In the poem "The Letter" one will find these lines:

> I am tired, Beloved, of chafing my heart against
> The want of you;
> Of squeezing it into little ink drops
> And posting it.
> And I scald alone here under the fire
> Of the great moon.   (33)

These lines can not fail to move the reader, and inspire admiration for Lowell's depth of feeling and skill of expression. Nor can one fail to feel the anguish that must have accompanied the obesity which she felt made her unattractive for persons to whom she found herself attracted.

Charlotte Mew and Rose O'Neill both wrote verse that to the trained mind give evidence of variant attitudes. However, it is the work of Edna St. Vincent Millay that is particularly intriguing, and the more so because of her poems celebrating heterosexual love and her reputation for heterosexual promiscuity. Dr. Foster cites "Interim," which was written in 1912, as her "first poem of variant significance." Specifically Dr. Foster calls attention to a passage in that poem which runs thusly:

That day you picked the first sweet pea—
I know, you held it up for me to see
And flushed because I looked not at the flower
But at your face; and when behind my look
You saw unmistakable intent
You laughed and brushed your flower against my lips
(You were the fairest thing God ever made
I think). And then your hands above my heart
Drew down its stem into a fastening
And while your head was bent I kissed your hair.
I wonder if you knew . . .
   . . . If only God
Had let us love—and show the world the way!
Strange cancellings must ink th'eternal books
When love-crossed-out will bring the answer right! (34)

Millay was twenty when she wrote those lines, and was already known to have a highly emotional temperament. Dr. Foster suggests:

> For a considerable time in her late teens Millay was completely absorbed in a passionate variant attachment, which then suffered some abrupt termination. Out of her grief grew "Interim" and a number of other laments which trickled into print throughout the next two or three years.
>
> During her years at Vassar (1913–1917, her twenty-first to twenty-fifth) she admitted an attachment to another fair delicate girl, at least to the extent of her own "Memorial to D.C. (Vassar College, 1918)," which appeared in the volume "Second April." Death actually terminated this friendship, but the group of "little elegies" assembled under the above title are merely slight and graceful by comparison with "Interim" and its aftermaths. It is probable that certain later laments, such as "Song of a Second April" and "To One Who Might Have Borne a Message," were truer expressions of this later loss. (35)

Dr. Foster feels that a third woman is pictured in "The Harp Weaver," as she calls attention to specific lines:

> Love is not blind. I see with single eye
> Your ugliness and other women's grace.
> I know the imperfections of your face—
> The eyes too wide apart, the brow too high
> For beauty. Learned from earliest youth am I
> In loveliness, and cannot so erase
> Its letters from my mind, that I may trace
> You faultless, I must love until I die.   (36)

Dr. Foster, who has compiled the only work of its kind known to this writer and therefore must be heavily relied upon, states:

> That variant emotion was at least an intermittent preoccupation with Millay until she was thirty is evident from examination of her total work before 1923, the year of her marriage. There are a number of sonnets and other verse in which the sex of the subject is uncertain, if not deliberately concealed, but which do not have the tone of those specifically written to men. Then there is her poetic drama, "The Lamp and the Bell," . . . written during a sojourn in Paris soon after graduation from Vassar, and presented at the college in 1921. Its theme is an undying devotion between two young women.
>
> By the time this drama was written, however, Millay also had published a number of lyrics of heterosexual inspiration. Indeed, among the conventionally minded she had gained a quite shocking reputation on the strength of them, for they antedated the now notorious Twenties. Many of them are flippant or bitter in comparison to those inspired by women, and they flaunt inconstancy and promiscuity. . . .
>
> After her marriage in 1923 all of Millay's published verse was marked by greater emotional reticence, and if

she wrote privately anything comparable to her earlier variant lyrics the chances are against its ever being made public. (There has been no providential Reinach to salvage her relics for posterity, and it is rumored that censorship is being exercised. Letters have been admitted to the published volume of her correspondence which imply some early heterosexual indiscretion, while all variant traces have been eradicated save a proper name or two in connection with which the published implications are unrevealing. To the student of variance, however, they are significant.) (37)

In the light of our more sophisticated age, it does not seem *unusual* that a poet of Millay's thirst for life, her sensitivity and refinement of feeling, could feel love for both sexes. Certainly any writer has the right to conceal or expose feelings according to their own requirements, and the works themselves should stand alone for their quality and substance. The literary student, however, deserves access to any insight which will better help him or her to understand and appreciate what the writer is attempting to convey, and it hardly seems in that interest for editor or critic to attempt to obscure that knowledge.

Other verse expressing variant sentiments are found in Edgar Lee Master's *Doomesday Book,* and George Stirling's *Strange Waters.* In England we find in Richard Aldington's *Loves of Myrrhine and Konallis,* Victoria Sackville-West's *King's Daughter,* and Katherine Mansfield's *Scrapbook.* Space prevents giving examples from these poets, but Dr. Foster sums up the century's variant poetry for us thusly:

The most notable feature of all these twentieth century lyrics is the women's relatively articulate confession of variant interests. Before 1900 only "Michael Field" and Matilda Bentham-Edwards admitted inclination toward their own sex. Now the Catholic O'Neill, the New England Lowell and Millay, the British Sackville-West reveal it without apology. Schwabe and Madeleine offer their testimony still more openly, and Barney and Vivien, with the independence of expatriates and women of fortune able to create their own milieu, proclaim it not only in writing but in their lives. Indeed, Vivien at least promises in any long view of Western literature to figure as a minor Sappho, the greater part of her work dedicated to this limited but seemingly imperishable theme. (38)

The twentieth century has thus far presented us with such a wealth of variant literature that one hardly knows where to begin or what to select. There is much of high quality, and much trash; much that is obvious and much that is so subtle as to be almost unrecognizable. For the most part, however, discussion here will be limited to English language fiction.

Perhaps the earliest twentieth-century fiction which gives us a forthright presentation of lesbianism is that of Colette in her Claudine series. In translation it consists of *Claudine at School, Young Lady of Paris, The Indulgent Husband,* and *The Innocent Wife.* The series traces the emotional history of Claudine from young schoolgirl through marriage and into widowhood.

Beginning with *Claudine at School,* we reencounter the "girl's school formula" of adolescent "crushes," passions, intrigues and jealousies, and domineering, seductive headmistresses with their favorites. The usual types are all there, but are handled with wit and skill; the sophistication of Colette gives the girl's school installment a freshness and charm that makes it less tiresome than most.

The series—tracing as it does the emotional history of one girl's lifetime, and probing the emotional psychology of women (being strongly autobiographical of Colette herself)—gives us insight into Colette's own sexual philosophy. Dr. Foster interprets that philosophy: "Lesbian attractions are legitimate, but they belong to youth. Mature love is neither uninhibited sophistication nor romantic idealism, but a mutual devotion in whose interest each sex must sacrifice something and must attempt to acquire some part of the other's outlook." (39)

It is a perfectly valid philosophy, and one could hardly argue with the concept of mature love. However, given over seventy years of psychological research and experimentation with life styles since that philosophy was formulated, there are those who would undoubtedly take exception to the blanket implication that lesbian relationships could not also be mature relationships. That would seem to exclude the possibility of even individual growth and insight. As we have seen from the chapter on psychology and lesbianism, many psychiatrists today feel that these relationships can and do mature and succeed. This may be due to the fact that the social and moral climate is somewhat more conducive to constructive evolution, which in turn contributes to reduction in the occurrence of neurosis and tragedy.

To return to the *girl's school formula,* fiction has been plagued with this everlastingly. It is a subject which continually attracts writers, probably because a good deal of homosexuality undoubtedly does exist in them, but this attraction is probably also due to the fact that homosexual tendencies are very much prevalent during adolescence. It would seem drolly naïve to imagine that it does not exist at the same age in other atmospheres not so isolated and noticeable. The question would seem to be whether or not it has a more convenient opportunity for expression and observation in the boarding school atmosphere.

Two works, also in the boarding school group, seem worth looking at briefly: *Olivia* by Olivia, a pseudonym for Dorothy Bussy, published in 1949, and *The Children's Hour,* a drama by Lillian Hellman, which opened on Broadway in 1934. Both recount the story of a boarding school and the women who run it. Both schools as well as the women who run them meet destruction by vindictive characters utilizing lesbianism as a weapon. In the case of *Olivia,* lesbianism did exist, but it is not lesbianism as such that destroys the school and the two women, but a jealous and scheming teacher who uses the relationship between the two women in order to gain control of the school. In *The Children's Hour* it is a twelve-year-old paranoiac student who destroys the school and the two women by spreading erroneous rumors of lesbianism between them—a circumstance which did not exist, but was imagined by the child upon overhearing a quarrel. The student's supposition was based upon her having read *Maupin,* the early French lesbian work.

In *Olivia,* the character of the title, a young student, falls in love with Mademoiselle Julie, one of the headmistresses, who is inclined to have favorites; unlike the stock sadistic headmistresses of other works, however, she handles the young girl's passionate crush with affection and tenderness, fully understanding Olivia's potential nature and avoiding situations which would provoke physical intimacy. However, Mademoiselle Julie is not so fortunate in preventing a scheming German teacher from fanning the jealous fires of Mademoiselle Julie's lover of fifteen years, Mademoiselle Cara, into hysteria, and presumable suicide by an overdose. Although a question still hangs in the air at the end of the tale as to whether Frauline did not herself administer the overdose or at least place it in an accessible place for the ailing and already sedated Mademoiselle Cara. The schemer had also seen to it that Mademoiselle Cara's will had been changed to benefit herself. Heartbroken, Mademoiselle Julie cries that Mademoiselle Cara was the only person she had ever loved, and departs for exile in Canada, the school having been snatched out from under her by the German. Soon thereafter she dies of grief, and whatever ailments grief can create, in exile.

In the Hellman play the two headmistresses are innocent of the exaggerated charge leveled by the disturbed child. However, the rumor is sufficient to motivate horrified parents to snatch their children from the school. Quickly the young women bring suit for slander, but lose the case owing to the disappearance of an aunt who had been witness to the scene from which the overly imaginative child fabricated her slander. They also lose the school. One of the women breaks off with her fiancé, believing that he will never be entirely convinced that there was not a seed of truth in the rumor. The other woman is tormented into introspection on her true feelings for her friend, and comes up with the realization that although subconsciously restrained in the past, she does have such feelings for the friend. Shocked at this realization, she shoots herself.

The play was taken up by Hollywood: the scandal was changed to the discovery of intimacy between the headmistress and her fiancé, the doctor; the lesbian issue was all but bypassed; and prejudicial hysteria replaces the lesbian persecution—a typical Hollywood translation which should surprise no one. Fortunately, the film industry has grown up some since then.

It would, of course, be impossible to discuss French lesbian fiction without acknowledging the importance of Marcel Proust's *Remembrance of Things Past*. Although the lesbian capers of Albertine and her playmates are generally acknowledged to be the transposition of male homosexual affairs (for Proust's personal protection), a technique which Proust was warned against by his literary colleagues (including Natalie Clifford Barney) as being invalid from a socio-anthropological standpoint, from a literary history standpoint the work is highly significant in that its psychological types are splendidly drawn.

Only two other works of French fiction will be mentioned as important, significant and well-done, although there are others. Romain Rolland's *Annette and Sylvie* and Jacques de Lacretelle's *Marie Bonifas*. Both books avoid the stereotypic exaggerations of earlier works, and the plots and characters are intricately and interestingly drawn. They avoid social and moral condemnation, although they do not teach homosexuality as a suggested way of life. The characters are participating members of society with interactions of kindness and devotion evidenced. The effects of social prejudice are particularly illustrated in *Marie Bonifas*. Rolland mercifully refrains from having his characters do a complete reform act. Refreshingly, no one takes to drink, drugs or suicide, although Claire in *Marie Bonifas* does contact tuberculosis and die while being devotedly attended by Marie. The characters of each book are believable today, as are their problems and struggles.

A French drama, *La Prisonniere* (*The Captive*) by Edouard Bourdet, produced in France in 1925 and the following year in New York, generally condemned lesbianism. However, the young heroine Irene, who is the not exactly unwilling captive of the older woman Madame d'Aiguines, does marry an earlier rejected suitor to escape the older woman, only to find that she cannot feel passion for him. She resumes the relationship with Madame d'Aiguines a year later when she and her husband return to Paris. He returns to his former mistress. One is left with a question about what Irene really does feel for Madame d'Aiguines.

The play enjoyed success in several capitals of the world, but in New York the ending was changed; American morals had to be protected. Irene did not return to Madame d'Aiguines, but rejected her appeal, and destroyed Madame d'Aiguines' bouquet of violets, which were always the romantic symbol of their relationship. In New York the play enjoyed success at first, but then closed after five months. That same year Thomas Hulbut's *Hymn to Venus*—on the same theme but with a suicidal ending—opened in Atlantic City in preparation for New York and Chicago, but was withdrawn after two performances. The same fate attended the opening in Boston in 1927 of a play entitled *The Drag,* by Jane Mast, which featured Mae West and concerned male homosexuality. It was greeted with such strong public condemnation that it is credited with effecting the close of *The Captive*.

In 1928 Radclyffe Hall's *The Well of Loneliness,* an eloquent plea in defense of lesbianism, broke on the scene and stirred up a holocaust. The novel became unique in the annals of the British court; for it was the book itself which stood accused, a circumstance which must have caused many a barrister to scratch his head in wonderment. Since the book had been out only six weeks when it was withdrawn, it had not had time to cover the costs of publication, and the publisher, Jonathan Cape, shortly became an unenviable man. He was equal to the case, however, because he was courageous and liberal-minded and stood his ground for both book and author. The British press had a field day with the book, and certain critics had apoplexy in print. Righteousness ascended to Olympian heights, as journalists called for the censorship and suppression of the book. James Douglas, editor of the *Sunday Express,* mounted the bastions for righteousness and decency when he wrote in his article:

> *The Well of Loneliness* (Jonathan Cape, 15s. net) by Radclyffe Hall, is a novel. The publishers state that it handles very skillfully a psychological problem which needs to be understood in view of its growing importance. "In England hitherto," they admit, "the subject has not been treated frankly outside the regions of scientific textbooks, but that its social consequences qualify a broader and more general treatment is likely to be the opinion of thoughtful and cultured people." They declare that they "have been deeply impressed by this study"; they have felt that such a book should not be lost to those who may be willing and able to understand and appreciate it. They believe that the author has treated the subject in such a way as to combine perfect frankness and sincerity with delicacy and deep psychological insight.

Uncompromising

In his prefatory "Commentary," Mr. Havelock Ellis says, "I have read *The Well of Loneliness* with great

interest because—apart from its fine qualities as a novel—
it possesses a notable psychological significance.

"So far as I know, it is the first English novel which
presents, in a completely faithful and uncompromising
form, one particular aspect of sexual life as it exists among
us today.

"The relation of certain people—who, while different
from their fellow human beings, are sometimes of the
highest character and the finest aptitudes—to the often
hostile society in which they move presents difficult and
still unsolved problems.

"The poignant situations which thus arise are here set
forth so vividly, and yet with such complete absence of
offence, that we must place Radclyffe Hall's book on a
high level of distinction."

That is the defence and justification of what I regard
as an intolerable outrage—the first outrage of that kind
in the annals of English fiction.

The defence is wholly unconvincing. The justification
absolutely fails.

In order to prevent the contamination and corruption
of English fiction it is the duty of the critic to make it
impossible for any other novelist to repeat this outrage. I
say deliberately that this novel is not fit to be sold by any
bookseller or to be borrowed from any library.

Bravado

Its theme is utterly inadmissable in the novel because
the novel is read by people of all ages, by young women
and young men as well as by older women and older men.
Therefore, many things that are discussed in scientific
text-books cannot decently be discussed in a work of fiction offered to the general reader.

I am well aware that sexual inversion and perversion
are horrors which exist among us today. They flaunt
themselves in public places with increasing effrontery and
more insolently provocative bravado. The decadent apostles

of the most hideous and most loathsome vices no longer conceal their degeneracy and degradation.

They seem to imagine that there is no limit to the patience of the English people. They appear to revel in their defiance of public opinion. They do not shun publicity. On the contrary, they seek it, and they take a delight in their flamboyant notoriety. The consequence is that this pestilence is devastating the younger generation. It is wrecking young lives. It is defiling young souls.

The Plague

I have seen the plague stalking shamelessly through great social assemblies. I have heard it whispered about by young men and young women who do not and cannot grasp its unutterable putrefaction. Both aspects of it are thrust upon healthy and innocent minds. The contagion cannot be escaped. It pervades our social life.

Perhaps it is a blessing in disguise or a curse in disguise that this novel forces upon our society a disagreeable task which it has hitherto shirked, the task of cleaning itself from the leprosy of these lepers, and making the air clean and wholesome once more.

I agree with Mr. Havelock Ellis that this novel is "uncompromising." That is why criticism cannot compromise it. The challenge is direct. It must be taken up courageously, and the fight must be fought to the finish. If our bookshops and our libraries are to be polluted by fiction dealing with this undiscussable subject, at least let us know where we are going.

I know that the battle has been lost in France and Germany, but it has not yet been lost in England, and I do not believe that it will be lost. The English people are slow to rise in their wrath and strike down the armies of evil, but when they are aroused they show no mercy, and they give no quarter to those who exploit their tolerance and their indulgence. (40)

Mr. Douglas' tantrum raged on for some twelve more hysterical paragraphs, a regular call to arms sounded to the tune of "God Save The King!" But when one compares his tantrum with the quiet dignity of Radclyffe Hall's own statement in defense of her book, Douglas does not fare well. She said: "I wrote the book from a deep sense of duty. I am proud indeed to have taken up my pen in defense of those who are utterly defenceless, who being from birth a people set apart in accordance with some hidden scheme of Nature, need all the help that society can give them." (41)

Home Secretary Sir William Johnson-Hicks recommended the withdrawal of the book, and the publisher complied, but secretly sent the molds of the book to a Paris firm. Pegasus Press in France reissued the book in September 1928, and copies were imported into England. On the orders of the same Home Secretary these copies were seized whenever found. Charges of government censorship rose, and the Director of Public Prosecutions applied for orders under the Obscene Publications Act of 1857, which gave local magistrates throughout the country power to order destruction of any publication judged obscene.

In late November of 1928 the Magistrate, Sir Chartres Biron, refusing to hear evidence in defense of the book by many of England's finest writers, handed down a decision branding *The Well of Loneliness* an obscene libel, and saying all copies were to be destroyed with the payment of twenty guineas in each case. The *Daily Express* carried the following notice on November 17th. "Two hundred and forty-seven copies of *The Well of Loneliness,* the novel which Mr. James Douglas condemned in the *Sunday Express,* will be flung into the furnace at Scotland Yard today." (42)

The *Daily Herald* carried a statement by George Bernard Shaw: "George Bernard Shaw in an interview with the *Daily Herald* said: 'I read it, and read it carefully, and I repeat that it ought not to have been withdrawn.' " (43) The climate was such at that time, everyone's hostility having been whipped up by the press, that nothing much could have helped the case. What is interesting, however, is the fact that no definition was ever given of obscenity by which the book could be judged. However, on December 14, the case came before an appeals court and again lost, the earlier charge of obscenity being upheld.

It fared a little better in New York. After a sale of more than 20,000 copies by the New York publishers P. Covici and D. S. Friede, the publishers were arraigned on a summons obtained by John S. Sumner, Secretary of the New York Society for the Suppression of Vice. Eight hundred and sixty-five copies of the book were seized from the publisher's offices. The case was tried in the Court of Special Sessions of the City of New York on April 8th, 1929. The publishers were defended by the New York firm of Greenbaum, Wolff and Ernst. A splendid brief was prepared by Mr. Morris Ernst, and unlike the English court, the American court allowed and studied the brief carefully. *The New York Times* announced the results of the trial April 20, 1929:

"Well of Loneliness" Cleared in Courts Here

Justices Solomon, Healy and McIneriney in Special Sessions declared yesterday the book, *The Well of Loneliness,* by Miss Radclyffe Hall, the English writer, although dealing with "a delicate social problem," was not published and sold in the city in violation of the law against objectionable literature.

The court therefore discharged Donald Friede, President of the Covici-Friede Corporation . . . and quashed the charge against the Corporation made by John S. Sumner, Secretary of the Society for the Suppression of Vice. (44)

It was not until years later that *The Well of Loneliness* was again published in England, but since the book could be had from either France or the United States, it made very little difference. In many ways *The Well of Loneliness* paved the way for literary freedom, giving the serious writer opportunity to examine emotional motivation and behavior and depict differing life styles. Try as we may, we cannot legislate emotions or morality, and to try to do this only drives everything underground.

In the case of *The Well of Loneliness* one wonders today at all the hysteria. To read about it, one would think that the book contains scenes of outrageous sexual orgy, moral debauchery and shocking language. Exactly the opposite is true. Miss Hall's book was one of the first to present the subject of relationships between women in a serious, dignified, adult fashion—presenting with deep feeling the pain suffered by honorable and responsible individuals of deviant inclination in their struggle for the right to live and love in the fashion right for them. It was also one of the first English language works in which childhood patterns and parental relationships were examined giving insight into what the child and the young woman were feeling. *The Well of Loneliness* was clearly autobiographical, and one can only guess at the pain, anger and frustration suffered by the sensitive Miss Hall when the book was dissected and battered by the newspapers and courts.

Prior to Miss Hall's experience with *The Well of Loneliness,* D. H. Lawrence's *The Rainbow* had met with the same fate. However, the book was not a sympathetic treatment of homosexuality (nor was his subsequent work which depicted overt lesbianism), and Lawrence did not contest the court order for withdrawal. Two years after the appearance of Lawrence's book, Clemence Dane brought out *Regiment of Women* which was no more sympathetic to homosexuality, and the plot of the book was wholly on variance. It was another of those girls' school books; Dane's leading character, Clara Hartill, a brilliant headmistress, is a domineering sadist, who feeds upon intellectual and emotional seduction of students and undermistresses. Hartill drives a young student to suicide, and her beloved Alwynne, a young mistress, to nervous collapse and final disillusion and escape. It is a bitter tale, suggesting at its conclusion that variance is due to frustration and a lack of sexuality because of spinsterhood.

Three years before the publication of Miss Hall's novel, three novels had appeared which dealt with variance: Virginia Woolf's *Mrs. Dalloway*, Sherwood Anderson's *Dark Laughter*, and Naomi Royde-Smith's *Tortoiseshell Cat*. Woolf, touching on it briefly, did so with sympathy; Anderson, just as briefly, did not present it favorably; and Royde-Smith, who dealt with it as the major theme, served as the voice of condemnation. Mrs. Woolf also dealt with the subject in *To the Lighthouse* in 1927 and the following year in *Orlando*.

Rosamund Lehmann's *Dusty Answers* appeared also in 1927, and was said to be autobiographical, tracing the growth from childhood of Judith, a lonely girl. At school she meets Jennifer, and of course they become inseparable until a rival appears, and then conflicts and agonies occur, which eventually strain the friendship. The relationship finally broken, Judith tries a heterosexual fling with a cousin, only to be disappointed and hurt; he prefers his friend Tony. The book leaves Judith as lonely as she was in childhood, but considerably wiser.

The year 1928 also saw the publication of Compton Mackenzie's *Extraordinary Women*, Elizabeth Bowen's *The Hotel*, and as mentioned before, Virginia Woolf's *Orlando*. Compton Mackenzie's *Extraordinary Women*, set on Capri, is a potpourri of lesbian types of all nationalities and their eccentricities and intrigues against a background of wealth and frivolity. It takes a rather detached yet witty position, but manages to make some of the characters appear somewhat ridiculous.

Bowen's *The Hotel* is an interesting study of a beautiful

cosmopolitan widow's power over a young girl and her own son. Variance is very subtly handled in this book, and it is rather quietly amusing despite the young girl's struggles for maturity and stability—a struggle which finally succeeds without an evangelistic heterosexual experience.

Orlando, a rich literary tapestry, is too lengthy and too deeply complex to be dealt with in the brief space available here. It qualifies as more basically bisexual, but the commentary on changing sex roles and artistic creation allows it to present a wider view than some other works.

Skipping ahead now to the 1930's, Graham Green's lesbian journalist in *Orient Express* is slightly sensational, but his portrait of her is not hostile. Struthers Burt's *Entertaining the Islanders* also has a lesbian journalist, but his treatment of her is less gentle. Sinclair Lewis was plainly unsympathetic in *Ann Vickers,* and George Jean Nathan was openly hostile in *Design for Loving.*

Henry Handel Richardson, Victoria Sackville-West, Isak Dinesen, Anthony Thorne, Dorothy Parker, Sheila Donisthorpe, Tiffany Thayer, Leyla George, Isabel Williams, Gerald Foster, Lilyan Brock, Gawen Brownrigg, David Dresser, Gale Wilhelm, Francis Brett, and Marcia Davenport all contributed works which dealt with the theme of variance on one level or other, and with varying degrees of sympathy or hostility.

In 1937 Djuna Barnes, another American expatriate living in Paris, published *Nightwood;* a work of high quality, it featured a preface by T. S. Eliot, and told the story of Nora Flood and Robin Vote. Although Robin had been married and suffered motherhood, the experience served only to convince her that neither marriage nor motherhood was for her. Instead she turns to a kind of compulsive lesbian promiscuity. When she meets Nora, life seems to change for her, and the two travel together very happily before settling down in Paris. Her compulsion for transient affairs returns; she seems to participate in them without any feeling, and is always happy to return to

Nora. It's almost as if she must destroy her happiness or constantly prove to herself that she is happy with Nora.

One of her affairs, however, proves fatal to the relationship. An older woman with an insatiable appetite and an intense possessiveness binds an almost helpless Robin to her, and brings about the rupture of the Nora-Robin relationship.

Painfully torn between Nora and the older woman, Robin, never too stable, cracks and flees Paris in search of Nora at her country place in the United States. Nora learns of Robin's flight and traces her there. The book ends with Nora finding Robin quite deranged—acting out a strange and terrifying ritual game with Nora's great dog. It is a tragic book, disturbing in its absence of hope and belief in the human and cultural capacity for understanding and tolerance of persons who do not conform—who, in fact, hear an altogether different drummer.

Like *The Well of Loneliness, Nightwood* is often included in college courses on fiction. They are both of good literary quality (*Nightwood* being the superior) and of important social significance. However, in light of the present younger generation's more liberated attitudes, both seem somewhat melodramatic and somewhat irrelevant. This is more true of *The Well of Loneliness* than of *Nightwood* because *Nightwood*, although lesbian in theme, is more applicable to all different states and encompasses psychoneurotic elements in the character of Robin which are not basically rooted in homosexuality.

Dr. Bertha Harris of the University of North Carolina says: "My students read *The Well of Loneliness* as kind of 'camp'; they don't read it with the intense seriousness of the preceding generation. They are more liberated and accepting of bisexuality and homosexuality—to the point of experimentation. In fact, to my astonishment, they consider it kind of chic, and the relatively secure ones talk about it quite openly. Some wear gay liberation buttons and are quite calmly open about their experimentation—at least those in the arts are." Asked if she believed that this was generally true on other campuses, she replied: "I think so; I seem to be picking that up. Some of them are very aggressive about it. Here, we are a kind of experimental university, and in many ways it makes the atmosphere of acceptance more conducive to this. Students are not brainwashed into any sort of radical chic, or right-wing attitudes."

Before we leave Djuna Barnes, it might also be mentioned that she produced a kind of satirical chronicle, illustrated and published anonymously in the twenties; it was entitled *Ladies Almanack*. It was reissued in 1972 by Harper & Row, this time under the author's own name. It carried a foreword written by Djuna Barnes, who is still alive and living in New York. The foreword read as follows:

> This slight satiric wiggin, this Ladies Almanack, anonymously written (in an idle hour), fearfully punctuated, and privately printed (in the twenties) by Darantière at Dijon; illustrated, with apologies to ancient chapbooks, broadsheets, and *Images Populaires;* sometimes coloured by mudlark of the bankside and *gamine* of the *quai;* hawked about the *foubourg* and the temple, and sold for a penny, to the people, cherished by de Gaulle as "the indolent and terrible." That chronicle is now set before the compound public eye.
>
> Neap-tide to the Proustian chronicle, gleanings from the stories of Mytilene, glimpses of its novitiates, its rising "saints" and "priestesses," and thereon to such appitude and insouciance that they took to gaming and to swapping that "other" of the mystery, the anomaly that calls the hidden name. That affronted, eats its shadow.
>
> It might be well to honour the creature slowly, that you may afford it.   (45)

The *Ladies Almanack,* written and illustrated in a somewhat bawdy and heavy Elizabethan Baroque style, certainly qualifies as "high camp," and should be read for the sheer galloping, hedonistic relief of people who have grown weary of the subject of lesbianism as one to be whispered in dark rooms and attacked by the Catholic League of Decency. *Ladies Almanack* is quite delightfully and outrageously indecent. For example:

> He had Words with her enough, saying: "Daughter, daughter, I perceive in you most fatherly Sentiments. What am I to do?" And she answered him High enough, "Thou, good Governor, wast expecting a Son when you lay atop your Choosing, why then be so mortal wounded when you perceive that you have your wish? Am I not doing after your very Desire, and is it not the more commendable, seeing that I do it without the Tools for the Trade, and yet nothing complain?" (46)

* * *

Among such Dames of which we write, were two British Women. One was called Lady Buck-and-Balk, and the other plain Tilly-Tweed-In-Blood. Lady Buck-and-Balk sported a Monocle and believed in Spirits. Tilly-Tweed-In-Blood sported a Stetson and believed in Marriage. They came to the Temple of the Good Dame Musset, and they sat to Tea, and this is what they said:

"Just because woman falls, in this Age, to Woman, What has England done to legalize these Passions? Nothing! Should she not be brought to Task, that never once through her gloomy Weather have two dear Doves been seen approaching in their bridal Laces, to pace, in stately Splendor up the Altar Aisle, there to be United in Similarity, under mutual Vows of Loving, Honouring, and Obeying, while the One and the Other fumble in that nice Temerity, for the equal gold Bands that shall make of one a Wife, and the other a Bride?" (47)

Skipping to the 1940's, and having to necessarily pass by many works by good authors, we come to Gertrude Stein. Although not written during this period, both "Fernhurst" and "Q.E.D." came into circulation. Among her very first works, they represent the beginning of her lifelong probing of human emotional psychology. They underwent many revisions, and the original manuscripts are in the Beinecke Rare Manuscript Collection at Yale University. "Fernhurst" had the girl's boarding school setting, and is the story of Philip Redfern, a doctor of philosophy, Miss Thornton, the dean of Fernhurst College, and Miss Bruce, head of the Department of English Literature. Presumably it is the story of Philip Redfern, for Miss Stein subtitles the story "The History of Philip Redfern, A Student of the Nature of Woman," but his characterization becomes slightly overshadowed by the relationship between Miss Thornton and Miss Bruce, whose close attachment is one of many year's standing.

Into this peaceful academic love nest comes Philip Redfern, who stirs an intellectual fire in Miss Bruce, despite the fact that he has a Mrs. Redfern with whom he shares his life. The relationship between Redfern and Miss Bruce grows into a deep emotional attachment which threatens the good, good friends and comes within an inch or two of giving Fernhurst a juicy scandal. Fortunately, through the manipulative genius of Headmistress Miss Thornton the scandal is avoided, and dear Dr. Redfern's departure and moral and academic downfall come about. As Miss Stein put it in the last paragraph:

> Patiently and quietly the dean worked it out and before many years she had regained all property rights in this shy learned creature [Miss Bruce]. It was sometimes disconcerting when Miss Bruce was moved abruptly to inquire concerning Redfern from people who had known him but this too gradually faded away and Fernhurst was itself again and the two very interesting personalities in the place were the dean Miss Thornton with her friend Miss Bruce in their very same place. (48)

"Q.E.D." illustrates Stein's painful and somewhat ponderous intellectual dissection of emotions. Autobiographical, it concerns her agonizing affair with her fellow student at Johns Hopkins, May Bookstaver. Leon Katz writes of this affair in his introduction to the collection of Stein's early writings:

> This affair with a fellow student at Johns Hopkins, May Bookstaver, had been following a complicated and desperate course not only because of a rival, but also because of the frustration of trying to fathom the woman she loved, and the impossibility of ever knowing whether May Bookstaver loved her in return, or was capable of loving at all. The affair was to end a year later with a moan and a whisper, but it was years before the effects of its torment wore off. These years with May marked the decline of Stein's assertive naïveté about herself and the beginning of her somber psychological wisdom. Through the long misery of the affair Stein suffered a series of insights concerning human conflict which lay at the bottom of all her subsequent psychologizing. (49)

Mr. Katz's statement is undoubtedly true, but in reading "Q.E.D." one can't help wishing that Miss Stein had agonized and intellectualized a little less, and been a little less heavy-handed about her feelings. But one needs to remember that she was trying to understand her own feelings, and that the whole affair took place seventy years ago.

In 1954 Mary Renault published *The Middle Mist,* an interesting tale about two women, Leo and Helen, living together on a houseboat in apparent harmony until they are invaded by Leo's seventeen-year-old sister Elsie, who has run away from home. Aside from inconveniencing the two lovers, Elsie strikes up a friendship with Dr. Peter Bracknell, and brings him into their circle. The good doctor has a healthy ego and a strong streak of meddling. He creates an emotional devastation that disturbs the delicate balance of the girls' relationship and finally destroys it.

Six years prior to *Middle Mist,* Miss Renault had written *Promise of Love,* again a story of two women: a laboratory pathologist and a nurse in a large English hospital. The two strike up a relationship, at first feeling great delight at being able to be together, to meet and talk and make love. Owing to bisexual leanings in the one and promiscuous inclinations in the other, however, the relationship becomes complicated and finally caves in under stress. One girl marries, and the other is abandoned by her newest flame in favor of a male suitor. This leaves the twice-deserted woman contemplating the advent of age on her life style: she will be less attractive and therefore her conquests shall be fewer.

Miss Renault has also written about the male homosexual in *The Last of the Wine,* a particularly fine and beautiful book, *The Charioteers, The Mask of Apollo,* and *The Persian Boy;* incidences of homosexuality figure in all her works. However, despite her sympathetic presentation of homosexual characters, it is regrettable that a novelist of her caliber is unable to resist the temptation to imply that *homosexuality does not pay.* Miss Renault also projects a distinct pessimism regarding permanance or lasting and loving devotion in such relationships. Whether this is her firm conviction or simply done in conformity to convention, one is never quite certain.

Margaret Landon's *Never Dies The Dream,* which appeared in 1949, is a somewhat puzzling, if not a downright schizophrenic work. It expresses both horror at variant passion and a constructive and delicate presentation of lesbian love. Perhaps Miss Landon had some conflict between her intellect and her emotions.

The 1950's teemed with variant literature, some good, some bad: Hugh Wheeler's *The Crippled Muse,* Sara Harris' *The Wayward Ones,* Simon Eisner's *Naked Storm,* Fletcher Flora's

Strange Sisters, Rhys Davies' *A Trip To London,* Tereska Torres' *Woman's Barracks,* Jack Woodford's *Strange Fires,* Vin Packer's *Spring Fire,* Fay Adam's *Appointment in Paris,* May Sarton's *A Shower of Summer Days* and Claire Morgan's *The Price of Salt* all appeared.

With the coming of the sixties variant literature hit the jackpot, and continued right on into the early seventies. Over forty-six authors qualified as writers of variant fiction with the briefest investigation, and that eliminated writers of sensational trash. Writers such as Simone de Beauvoir, Stephen Birmingham, Paul Blackburn, Maxwell Bodenheim, Brigid Brophy, Anthony Burgess, Marcia Davenport, Patrick Dennis, Peter De Vries, Lawrence Durrell, Violette Leduc, Mary McCarthy, Norman Mailer, Henry Miller, Iris Murdoch, Vladimir Nabokov, Anaïs Nin, John O'Hara, Jane Rule, Muriel Sparks, Leon M. Uris, Anthony West, Tennessee Williams, Edmund Wilson, Herman Wouk and others have written books that are readily available. The Bibliography will supply titles. (Two American authors who preceded this period should be mentioned, even if out of order: Ernest Hemingway dealt briefly with lesbianism in his story "The Sea Change" in *The Fifth Column and the First Forty-Nine Stories.* And F. Scott Fitzgerald suggests latent lesbianism in *Tender Is the Night.*)

Beginning in the late fifties and spanning into the beginning sixties was Lawrence Durrell's fascinating *Alexandria Quartet.* The theme of lesbianism is woven throughout the quartet—beginning in *Justine,* through *Balthazar* and *Mountolive,* finally coming out in the open in *Clea,* the most specific of the interrelated quartet—all of which must be read to fully understand and appreciate the splendid work. The *Alexandria Quartet* is a thoroughly pleasurable reading experience for anyone—the general reader as well as the student of variance.

In his later work John O'Hara appears preoccupied with the theme of lesbianism. One finds examples of it in "Clayton Bunter," "James Francis And The Star," "Jurge Dulrumple,"

The Lockwood Concern, "The Skeltons," "Yucca Knolls" and *Lovey Childs.* Early in 1963 Hermann Hesse's *Steppenwolf* was reissued by Holt, and met with very great success among college students and hippies.

Paperback stands in drugstores, stationery shops, discount stores—almost everywhere—offered a rash of trashy novels with lesbian themes, their covers depicting torrid scenes, and their texts quite forgettably graphic. Hacks saw the chance to turn a quick buck, taking advantage of the gay liberation movement and the public's secret fascination with the subject—the public having become suddenly aware of a new kind of sex to get a thrill from.

Very few novels dealing with the subject, however, attracted major attention because of the more relaxed attitudes and the ready availability of such books. Also the publishing business seemed to trend more toward nonfiction works in the late sixties and early seventies. Works appeared by admitted Lesbians, social anthropologists, biologists, psychologists, and clinicians with varying credentials. The subject began to be dissected from every possible angle.

However, novels did appear. Bertha Harris brought out *Catching Sarahdove* and *Confessions of Cherubino* based on the Mozart character in *The Marriage of Figaro.* Both books were blatantly lesbian in theme and well done.

Isabel Miller's *Patience and Sarah,* based on an actual story of two nineteenth-century ladies, appeared and was well received by the critics, and favorably reviewed. Opening in Pennsylvania in the late nineteenth century, it told of two women, somewhat out of step with time and place, who met and fell in love—one a primitive painter, the other a farm girl used to hard work. They decided to homestead and live together. They came to New York and took a packet boat up the Connecticut River. On this sojurn they found their ideal farm and bought it. They settled together, and amazingly stayed together. The book has a happy ending for them! The book is done with gentleness and fey humor. It is touching in its innocence, for the girls are just that—their love being physically exploratory and experimental. The book is handled with skillful craftsmanship and loving good taste; it is honest, refreshing and hopeful. Only the most prejudicial and calloused soul could judge *Patience and Sarah* harshly.

To conjecture about where fiction with lesbian themes will go in the continuing seventies would be futile and arrogant. It is an age in which anything can happen. Social opinion can contract into prejudicial rigidity as easily as it can expand into tolerance and compassion. The present climate is promising, and one suspects that things could never return to the ostrich-headedness of the Radclyffe Hall period. Persons of variant inclination, if one is to believe the progress of the liberation action, will not hide—and if that is so, we will quite likely see less fiction and more informative social studies, commentaries and personal autobiographies. When homosexuality does appear in fiction, it will not be a major, earth-shattering revelation, but rather a realistic presentation of another integrated fact of life and relationships—and that, after all, is what fiction should be.

PART TWO

The People:
Discussions
among Lesbians

WE HAVE HEARD from the scholars and clinicians, and one always hears from them, but what about the people living in the so-called homosexual life style? They are seldom heard from, seldom have the opportunity to speak out on the ideas and theories which affect their lives, and seldom have the chance to tell it like it really is out in everyday life, and in their intimate relationships. The second part, then, gives insight into what the clinicians can not explain to us, with flesh-and-blood feeling and daily incidents, in their studies and theories. We do not get to know the real people that way, we cannot empathize and relate; we cannot ask questions, hear answers, feel the pulse. The second part of this book lets us do that, and hopefully it tells the clinicians some helpful things as well.

In collecting these attitudes and feelings of lesbian women, group sessions were arranged, over a period of time, for free and open discussion. All sessions were taped and are presented herein verbatim. In some instances there will be repetition, but it has been left in to emphasize the validity of the shared feelings and experience, and the prevalence lest there be doubters.

It is interesting to note the move forward in openness and positiveness in the sessions conducted after the tape of spring 1971. It seems to illustrate the advancement of the movement, which later projects more optimism and more comfort with being women and Lesbians. Both the woman's liberation movement and the gay liberation movement seem to be responsible for the stride forward. Not least among the positive influences are the more aware and knowledgeable therapists who have taken a more humane and practical approach toward the subject and toward patients seeking help. Also not to be overlooked is the fact that many therapists have stated categorically that many homosexuals never seek therapy and lead well-adjusted and constructive lives. They have also acknowledged that it is a valid life style, and change is not necessarily the desired goal.

Chapter 7

The Lesbian
Life Style

General group discussion, all professional women of considerable accomplishment, all attractive, well-dressed, all with college degrees and several doctorates. Ages ranged between
twenty-five and fifty. The group discussion was conducted in
the late fall of 1971. All were volunteers and not part of any
organized group or movement.

What do you find the most difficult aspect of the lesbian life style?

ISABELLE: I happen to enjoy the company of men. I do not
enjoy a sexual relationship with men, but that does not mean
that I don't enjoy being with them. I had lived with a
woman for several years who did not like men, and she did
not even really care for homosexual gentlemen. And I found
myself at many times associating with people who I would
not have been associated with had they not been homosexual.

And I kept saying to her all the time, I mean, we're seeing these people just because they're homosexual—

NANCY: That's a very good point.

FLORENCE: I think a lot of us here come out where you do. We enjoy the company of men, we like to see men, we like to go out with men, or couples—and it is an extending thing, a good thing that this happens. You know, you just can't live in an entire world of women, for God's sake.

MARIA: But you can't double-date.

(General laughter)

ETHEL: I go to gay bars, I really enjoy it, and I think it's great the people you can meet there. In fact, I met a prostitute in one one night. So, ever after that, I cease to think of a prostitute as, oh, that girl over there! A prostitute has an identity to me. She was interesting; they're all people—everybody. She introduced me to a pimp who came in that she knew; now, I've never talked to a pimp before, but he wasn't so different than other people. One night I met somebody who'd killed her father—and I met twin girls who were homosexual—

JOAN: Were they together?

ETHEL: I don't know.

(General laughter)

NANCY: I had a dinner party one night at my home with six women—and all of them are well-mannered, nice people, but someone disagreed with somebody rather strongly, and the girl got really hostile, and the first thing you knew everybody got into it and we were all screaming at each other, and I couldn't believe it—all these nice, well-bred people who knew and liked each other were suddenly hostile. It disturbed me, and I thought about it a lot afterwards, and I was thinking that one of the things involved with being a Lesbian is the assertion of identity. You're more at stake in a lot of ways. Because you don't have the support from the social thing because you have made a choice, and it is sometimes an uncomfortable choice. And, I wonder about the stridency that might be involved; if this isn't a more acute problem in a homosexual relationship—just who is who? How does one assert oneself? I just found it interesting that six people sitting together couldn't speak in a calm way and let each person say something, and take turns. Instead we were shouting each other down.

JOAN: Well, I happen to have been at the party, too—and two of those people are perennially angry. They're almost pathologically angry almost all the time, they always have an axe to grind—

NANCY: That's not true—

JOAN: I think it is true, pretty much true. The third person had just come from a marathon and was still worked up about that and provided a lot of fuel for other people to make comments, so there were three people who were potentially explosive to start with—and those three drew the others into it. It was a very emotional evening, I quite agree.

LILLIAN: Well, don't you have occasional successful evenings? I mean, I'm sure every social evening with women is not like that, is it?

MARIA: Well, I'm married, and I've had evenings with heterosexuals, and believe you me, I've been at a great number of social evenings where bankers and industrialists behave just like that.

NANCY: It is the same thing, that people just need to assert themselves in such a desperate way that— Like at the beginning of our evening, I had the feeling that we weren't really talking to each other, we were doing monologuing.

MARIA: The point is, people don't know how to listen, and it's got nothing to do with Lesbians.

(General agreement)

ELLEN: I think it is an extremely widespread trait in our culture that people don't know how to listen, I agree, and I don't know if Lesbians are any worse. I think it tends to be a male-identified thing; that is, like going to a heterosexual party—the men tend to be into that, doing that thing you were talking about, and the women are kind of listening, or else they go off and talk about something else. But I think you learn, and maybe this goes back to the career thing, that if you are in a career, to some extent you learn how to stick your oar in and make your point. So, maybe it has more to do with the competitiveness of achieving and being a middle-class or upper-middle-class person. And, it generally happens in more Lesbians, at least in the upper classes, or in careers, or in the business world, or professional world, or something. And you learn then because you're a woman in that situation that you have to make more effort; otherwise, you won't be listened to.

NANCY: Well, you see I made that connection in thinking about it. But I thought, my God, what has been sacrificed? And what has been sacrificed is the ability to accept, and respect one another, and relax. But that night everyone felt so at stake . . . that no one could take the chance to let go of it.

ETHEL: But Nancy, couldn't it also have been that they felt so strongly— I mean it happens to me personally, I always do that. You get so excited about the subject and you can't wait to be polite for the ladies and gentlemen, and you can't just listen and wait your turn. You just have to talk—and what's wrong with that?

NANCY: Well, what's wrong with it is that if everyone does that it just doesn't work. This particular evening what happened was we stopped doing it, we stopped—and then the evening turned out quite wonderful. And somehow we just relaxed. I mean, I thought we got to a certain pitch and it was unsatisfactory. But when we calmed down and we got to talking about the marathon, and everyone got to say what they wanted to say—it was fine. At some point we just stopped being hysterical and we sat back and relaxed.

ETHEL: You don't seem to want to accept the explanation that there was something particular about that evening. You feel this was more of a problem on that particular evening?

NANCY: Yeah, I do. I'm not saying it was a unique evening, but—

ELLEN: Well, are you suggesting that the Lesbian or the homosexual person has more of a daily problem—you said something about your social isolation that makes them be more competitive and therefore makes it more difficult?

NANCY: Yes, I think it's more on the surface. Not that a homosexual has any more of an identity problem than anybody has—I don't buy that—but that the problems are more diminutive. For one thing, there are not defined social rules; it has not been recognized—

MARIA: But there are defined social rules.

DOROTHY: Won't you accept the fact that we could finally get to the stage where we are—as I'm sure most of us here would like—just human beings reacting to human beings, whether homosexual or heterosexual?

NANCY: I resent that statement. We'd like to say that, but it's not true.

DOROTHY: If we can't, no one else can. If we can't get to the stage where we can accept others as human beings, then we can't expect heterosexuals to accept us.

PATRICIA: What makes you think we don't?

DOROTHY: I didn't say we didn't.

PATRICIA: But it was implied—if we can't get to that stage—

DOROTHY: Well, Nancy said she didn't think so, and I said if we *can't* get to that stage then we can't expect anybody else to.

LILLIAN: Are you that involved with— I mean, aren't you mainly involved with being a person and functioning? I mean, knowing you, I don't think you're that involved with homosexuality, period!

DOROTHY: I am first of all and basically a human being—

PATRICIA: You were saying the heterosexual relationship is easier for you to maintain—or have privacy and to feel—

ETHEL: Not one hundred per cent, no. But in a way I can be more honest, more at ease.

PATRICIA: Well, looking back on it, what made it a different kind of problem for you?

ETHEL: What do you mean?

PATRICIA: Well, you're experiencing something very different in the heterosexual relationship than you've experienced in the homosexual.

ETHEL: I had some positive homosexual experiences—

PATRICIA: I'm not saying positive or negative. It's a *different* experience for you.

ETHEL: Yeah.

PATRICIA: And you have the preference?

ETHEL: Well, right now I have the preference—

DOROTHY: She has a preference for a person, not for a way of life.

LILLIAN: And are you more yourself now?

ETHEL: I'm allowed to, I have the freedom to be myself.

PATRICIA: Who allows you to be yourself?

ETHEL: I allow myself. I can be more— I don't—maybe I'm more secure, and society, too. I'm not a woman, I'm not a girl, I'm not anything—in terms of society. You know, in terms of society. And maybe I've been a long time in coming to it, and it may not last long, but I want it for a while. I want the approval for a while. Because maybe if I do this— and it is enjoyable—maybe the world will leave me alone for a while.

PATRICIA: Well, I'm impressed with this whole business of the world leaving you alone. Maybe the line of psychology in which I work carries fewer pressures than if you were in business. I work for myself, and the question is, Would my work change? Well, perhaps my teaching position may change if I declared myself as homosexual—with my colleagues—

NANCY: How about going through medical school? Wasn't it ever a problem?

PATRICIA: It could have been, because they only let so many blacks and Catholics and Jews and girls into medical school—and you are aware that you are a member of a minority group. It was the Middle West, which has a different attitude, I think, than the East has. You do become, as a woman, somewhat of a mascot in certain situations.

ETHEL: So you're not a sexual object, but a mascot. That's the worst of all!

PATRICIA: But it isn't necessarily disrespectful. The thing of it is, you're aware of it, so you work with it.

ETHEL: But why? Were any of the men a mascot?

PATRICIA: No—

NANCY: But they could have been.

PATRICIA: I didn't have the impulse to protest it; some of it was being banished already. Let's say I recognized it, but I could see the advantages of it, too—of being a woman, and being able to stand there—

BROOK: And look helpless—

PATRICIA: —look helpless. Let him change a tire, or something.

BROOK: I don't know what all this doing stuff is about. If you were with another woman, and you had a flat tire—if she wanted to change it, wouldn't you let *her* change it?

ETHEL: Sure.

PATRICIA: I would tend to think I could do it better than she could.

BROOK: If that were the only reason you would allow your tire to be changed—

PATRICIA: There is a difference. In that I would defer to the man.

BROOK: I thought you said you'd be perfectly glad to let him come along and take it off your hands, and if that were the reason, why wouldn't you be just as glad to have a woman do the same thing?

JOAN: Because, as she said, it is the way we've been trained.

PATRICIA: It's a different relationship; it's a very interesting—

NANCY: I'm hearing the strategy in which you place yourself in this hypothetical tire-changing situation, as you will take the role in changing the tire, unless a real tire changer comes along, in which case you will let him change your tire.

FLORENCE: Precisely.

PATRICIA: But no, it isn't the matter of *him* being able to do the tire better than I, but there is a social contract that we've agreed to. That's trained into you. There might be times when I might even object to it.

JOAN: I identify very much with what you are saying. When some of us tonight were talking about enjoying going out with men, for the silliest of reasons— I like having the door opened for me, a cigarette lit for me—all these little things that are common courtesies. Essentially it's the game-playing; it's playing a woman. What it is really, I think, is wanting to be taken care of. Society has taught us that it is man's role to take care of woman.

NANCY: I like being valued without having to do a thing. All I have to be is a woman. It's so easy—you expect it.

MARIA: The reason men put women up on a pedestal is that they can see up her skirt.

NANCY: Well, that's one way to look at it, but I would say the trouble is, you pay for it.

FLORENCE: How do you pay for it?

NANCY: You pay for it by the implication that you are valued, poor dear, because you really can't do this and that, and the rest of it as well.

PATRICIA: I use to object to it, because I was in the habit of opening doors, and I had to learn—

FLORENCE: Oh, it's all that role-playing stuff. Men basically have a better deal in the world—that is, if they don't have to go to war—so that basically there is still a strong desire by many women to be a man.

JOAN: There's another element here, too, and that's trust. If I felt this way, and I enjoyed these things that men do—these little common courtesies and so forth—then why haven't I chosen men? Well, it's because even though I like the courtesies, I don't trust it, I don't trust men. I really think that most men are not as capable as I am, whether it's changing a tire, or doing anything else.

BROOK: But Patricia just said it's almost the same thing, she doesn't want a woman to do it either.

PATRICIA: I wanted to bring up this. You're so antagonistic about this *game* men and women play—but if both parties are aware of it, and are enjoying the game, and it's not a negative game, why shouldn't both persons enjoy it?

ETHEL: Because for the most part it isn't an equal game. It works more in favor of the man, rather than the woman.

JOAN: Oh, I don't see that. It's political, I think, but if people enjoy having a little hypocritical fun—so what?

ETHEL: Yeah, well, maybe if it were just for an evening, okay, but it's not just for an evening, it's an endless way of life.

JOAN: Well, I don't recommend it as a life style.

BROOK: But it is a life style for many people—a constant, hypocritical game-playing.

NANCY: I can see a gay relationship—where by games you are using certain social roles—there are some pleasures that are attached to—and I can see where that could be fun, a pleasure. But I think what happens most often is that the role gets in the way. Not that it makes things easier, but more difficult.

PATRICIA: How?

NANCY: Because it keeps you *from*. I see roles as things that separate you *from* a person, in the feeling of who the person is, and what you're doing together—the roles are getting in the way.

PATRICIA: Well, if the whole thing were just roles, I would agree with you.

FLORENCE: I immediately see two women, each trying to saw a board—both saying, "I can saw that better than you can, you let me have the saw" . . . that sort of thing.

BROOK: I never did that to you!

(*Laughter*)

FLORENCE: I just got a double plank so we could both saw—

(*More laughter*)

NANCY: Well, I've been in those little groups in East Hampton where people sit around and talk about their prowess with the lawn machinery. They're the most absurd conversations I've ever heard. Who has the largest lawn mower, who is best at operating her lawn mower. Both Florence and I have tractors.

BROOK: That's a class up entirely.

(*Laughter*)

NANCY: Yeah, but the thing that goes on in the groups I'm talking about is the women are saying who can curve the most—in an essentially masculine way . . . in that the role that really counts is being able to control and manipulate the tractor.

BROOK: I don't see it that way at all.

ETHEL: I don't either.

BROOK: With help as hard as it is to get today, you have to learn how to do things, and if you own property, it has to be taken care of. It is of great concern to property owners, and when they get together they're apt to talk about it.

JOAN: Yeah, but society thinks—

(*General protest and putting down*)

BROOK: Oh, come on, Joan, get off that society fixation.

JOAN: But we've all been influenced by it.

BROOK: Well, you may, but I haven't. I really don't give a shit about them.

PATRICIA: I should have never brought up that tire-changing bit. I should just have changed it myself.

(*Laughter*)

ESTELLE: I'd like to speak about something that Florence said a couple of times . . . and that is the desire to be a man. I grew up with that desire. I realized very young that the little boys had much more freedom, and much more prestige. I went to progressive school, where supposedly everyone was to be equal, and yet it was as plain as the nose on your face that my father was a more important person than my mother. I mean, I think every woman is faced with this situation, and some of them react a certain way and some another way. My reactions to that situation was to want to be a boy—I definitely did—and I went through a whole phase in my life where I was one of those, you know, much-despised bar lesbians, and I wore almost drag. That is very painful, because then you are very obvious, and a lot more stuff comes down on you than if you can pass much more easily. A lot of people have said that they've been *shrinking,* or whatever, and I've had a lot of the shrink, but the thing that has been most helpful to me in getting over that desire to be a man— which I think is a reasonable desire given the situation of society—is really women's liberation more than anything. Much more than my analysis, because my shrink would come on with the business of "Oh, no, I just want you to be happy," but the trip I kept getting was that I would be happy if I'd just adjust and preferably get a man, but at least adjust and accept being passive and so on and so on. But the woman's movement has done more for me in that respect, much more than analysis has, because I wasn't being asked to change. In fact, the straight women were saying, "We should change"—and not be so passive, and not be playing this game, and so on—and that made space for me to consider which parts of myself I wanted to change, and which I did not. It changed the definition of what a woman was for me, enough that I could fit in. I found that range of variation where I don't have to think of myself as masculine in order to exist and do the things in the world that I want to do. That has been an enormous change for me and that's why I feel very loyal to the woman's movement.

BROOK: I asked a psychiatrist once why women dressed up like men, and she answered, Why do women dress up to attract men?

ESTELLE: Because you have to catch a man in this world, or you're in bad shape.

JOAN: That's what she was saying—women dress up like women to attract men, and women dress up like men to attract women.

ESTELLE: Well, I no longer feel as much as I used to that I have to come on in a dykey way in order to attract women.

BROOK: Do you *live* with someone?

ESTELLE: Yes.

BROOK: Well, maybe that's the reason.

ESTELLE: No.

PATRICIA: I think you were saying, Estelle, if I hear you right, that you were making a protest until you realized that you didn't have to protest.

ESTELLE: I had to reject woman's role as I saw it, and I felt a superior role as being a man. And I wanted to identify with that.

BROOK: And now that you see other possibilities—

ESTELLE: I see women as better models—worthy, with much more self-respect, doing more things—as the whole issue of woman's lib has come up and the thing has become public. Plus my experience in a consciousness group, which was because there were— Actually, in the beginning I was the only gay woman, and then two other straight women started having an affair with each other. (*Laughter*) That was very interesting.

ETHEL: What happened? Did they become homosexual?

ESTELLE: What happened was that one of the women decided that she was gay, and the other one decided that she wished she could be bisexual, but she had a boyfriend and he was, of course, very upset by the whole thing, and she finally had to make a choice between him and the woman, and she chose the woman. I don't know how she thinks of herself now. I guess she's kind of in limbo. It was a very shattering experience for both of them. Another interesting thing that happened was that in my group I was kind of Uncle Tom-ing—or Aunt Tomasina-ing or something—to straight women. I was gay, but I didn't let out my anger toward them. I was very happy that they were accepting me on some level. But when the other woman came out and decided she was gay, she was so threatened by being gay that she became super-militant about being gay. She confronted the straight women on every occasion. I mean, a word couldn't come out of their mouths unless she was saying, "Wait a minute, that oppresses homosexuals; that oppresses me." That kind of changed my head—and I thought well, I can be angry too, and I can say this stuff, and you are stepping on my toes. And you know, I got tired of listening to things that really did knock me. So after that I let it out. And they accepted me for what I really was. And we all got to know each other better, and I got to really like some of the straight women and to respect what they were trying to do for themselves.

BROOK: It was the courage of the anger, of the straight woman who discovered herself homosexual that gave you courage, and she had the courage because she had not been conditioned by society to hide. She came out at a time when things are beginning to open up more.

> **What do you think about the statement that homosexuality is a symptom of emotional background and make-up?**

BROOK: It's a lot of nonsense.

ETHEL: If you said homosexuality is a symptom, then you would have to say heterosexuality is a symptom, too. To behave sexually is a symptom also. You're born a sexual person. Speaking from my own experience, I was attracted to both little boys and little girls. It started a very long time ago, and there was no difference. It was only society that said you have to go in this direction.

MARIA: You've changed since you grew up, I take it?

ETHEL: I've changed several times, but it's not really changing. I'm still attracted to both.

> **Would you subscribe to the theory that the question is one of sexuality and not heterosexuality?**

> > (*General agreement*)

JOAN: I personally feel great rancor when people start talking about homosexuality being a sympton.

PATRICIA: The word, as I understand it, is being used as a sign. Clouds as a symptom of rain.

BROOK: The statement of homosexuality as a symptom is slightly better than the statement that it is a sickness—and that's what most of the world thinks. Sexuality is the goal—not homosexuality or heterosexuality—and I think they're all on a par with each other.

FLORENCE: Well, we as a nation have a lot of trouble with sexuality. We're just not comfortable with it, let alone homosexuality.

MARIA: Yeah, but some people say homosexuals are sexually

promiscuous, and others say they have infantile sex and for the most part, particularly with Lesbians, they're more interested in affection, and holding, and comforting, than in actual sexual activity.

ETHEL: Oh, we're all supposed to be infantile, like children masturbating—

(General laughter)

MARIA: Oh, yes, I've heard that one too. I've also heard that Lesbians have rejected their sexuality, and therefore turn to other women out of fear.

FLORENCE: Old *wives'* tales!

(General laughter)

BROOK: Well, since many heterosexual women, if one is to believe the studies, have problems with sex—I guess it would follow that they would think Lesbians would have them, too, and more so.

MARIA: I think sex is great. I guess I just must be a different Lesbian.

FLORENCE: Oh, for heaven's sake, nobody believes those things. They're written by people who know next to nothing about it.

What do you think of the theory that many women because of their hang-up on sex in general, turn to women rather than a heterosexual relationship because a homosexual relationship doesn't seem as threatening?

LILLIAN: I don't even know what you're talking about.

(General laughter)

JOAN: I guess you could say that it is one factor in some individuals.

MARIA: All that is so generalized—and each case is individual—but I don't think that is a widespread cause for women being homosexual.

ESTELLE: It's the lesbianism is a *sickness* one that gets me.

PATRICIA: Yeah, if you're going to talk about homosexuality as a symptom, then heterosexuality is a symptom, too. I think if we're going to talk about something being a symptom—which is the general run-of-the-mill brainwashing attitude about deviates—we have to differentiate between preference and inhibition. Because when you talk about a symptom you're talking about an inhibition. Very early learning experience in a pleasurable direction creates a positive preference and is reinforced by repetition. That's one thing, and the other is inhibition. For instance, I got the impression that on David Susskind's show the other night, when homosexuality was discussed, by men who had supposedly changed over to heterosexual behavior, this was not differentiated. If someone has inhibitions, you can convert them—I don't care whether it is sexual inhibition or any other kind. One can arrive very frequently at a rather rapid and remarkable and seemingly magical cure or conversion, or whatever other word you want to use for it. Because you lift the inhibition, and whatever is there potentially can come forward. But I think that the differentiation is important.

NANCY: I think that positive reinforcement works better than negative conditioning or punishment.

PATRICIA: Negative conditioning tends to disappear unless you reinforce it.

NANCY: That question about women become Lesbians out of the threat of sexuality and fear of men, and see women as acceptable sexual partners . . . there seems to be another side to it: that is, one of the pluses of homosexual life is a greater sexual freedom. In general, people change partners more; there is more sexual experience, and more invigorating sex, more liberated sex—which is a definite plus. There is, I think, a great deal more sexual activity among homosexuals—

PATRICIA: More among homosexual women than heterosexual women?

FLORENCE: Men and women, yes, I think that is true.

BROOK: From what we hear about the changing of partners and sleeping around among heterosexuals—the divorce rate notwithstanding, it seems to me it's pretty hard to draw a line of comparison.

NANCY: Gee, that sounds like the nymphomaniacal thing. I tend to think just the opposite: I think within the homosexual world there is more opportunity—for liaison, much more freedom.

LILLIAN: I think there is more desire, too.

NANCY: There may be; I just don't know.

BROOK: Why more desire?

LILLIAN: Because it's more available. It's there.

JOAN: Also, it's easier to get into—

LILLIAN: And easier to get out of.

FLORENCE: Since you're not operating with society's rules anyway— Therefore you have a kind of freedom which I think the young are only getting to now, which is really that you can do what you want. There isn't really anybody who is going to do anything to you; something isn't going to fall on your head.

JOAN: There isn't a marriage license, there isn't an alimony court.

BROOK: However, you do have the fact that you're illegal.

FLORENCE: Yes, but this is not something that, at least with Lesbians, has been coming before the court, unless in a custody suit or divorce proceeding. But, I think a lot of the society's anger and disgust at homosexuality is certainly tied in with the idea that these people are much freer, and that there is a certain kind of social freedom which homosexuals have, in a certain sense. I think there is a lot more of it among homosexual men than homosexual women. You have homosexuals who are making good salaries—and not having dependents, they have houses in the country, at the beach, and so forth, and they're having fun and so forth. And heterosexuals say, "Here I am having to put two children through college," and so forth. And I think there are a lot of advantages to being outside of the social laws—

BROOK: If the heterosexual who is stuck with cleaning house, putting kids to bed, putting kids through college, and so forth, and is very happy with that situation—the alternative life the homosexual is demonstrating is confusing and therefore frightening. "What is going on? What are they getting out of it? Why do they choose that rather than to be married and have children and be—"

FLORENCE: Yes, well, everyone likes their own way of life to be reflected by other people. That's why the same kind of people stick together; you want to see some kind of reflection of your own way of life, unfortunately. And it is unfortunate in a lot of ways, this kind of conformism. I think you see it in heterosexual groups also; it's perfectly obvious. And I think it's probably perfectly natural.

MARIA: You make it sound as though lesbianism is simply a constant changing of relationships and an inability to hold anything down mutually. It sounds to me sitting over here stuck in a relationship—I don't want to be married and I know what it's like to be tied down and wanting out of it—but you make lesbianism sound as though there are thousands of people lined up. Like Stanley Holloway said, "There are girls all over London, and how can I get to more tonight if I'm getting married in the morning?" (*General laughter*) And I'm not quite sure what you feel. You have to get from each one before you change to the next. (*More laughter*) I know that I am constantly looking for some kind of— I hesitate to use the word *permanent* because it petrifies me at this point in my life, but I'm certainly not looking for another bed partner—unless I'm in some kind of trouble with my girl friend—but I think what I am looking for initially is a relationship. Someone with whom I can spend most of my time for a lengthy period. I know that there are people I can go to bed with tonight and I don't want to see them tomorrow, or ever again perhaps, or maybe in a month. But in general, my feeling about a lesbian relationship is to have the sort of thing I would have gotten in a marriage actually—and didn't in my marriage—but knowing that if it doesn't work out, that I can turn to her and that I can talk to her and say, "Look, this really isn't working, and there is no point in staying together." I envy the fact that you people are free enough to do this, but at the same time I'm not looking for freedom to leap from one bed to the next.

FLORENCE: Well, that certainly wasn't what I was trying to imply. I think that having a certain kind of freedom doesn't necessarily mean that it's license to just move from anybody to— I mean, that it's just endless—

MARIA: But it is a license, as you put it, isn't it?

FLORENCE: It is a license, but it doesn't mean that that's the ideal. I'm saying that it accommodates whatever you want.

MARIA: It makes the whole thing sound rather profligate, in fact.

FLORENCE: Yes, but I don't think it is. All it means is that you're not stuck with the girl next door or the boy next door for the rest of your life. I think that it means that you just simply have a certain kind of social and sexual mobility. I think everyone would have it if you didn't have the kind of marriage we have.

MARIA: I agree, and this links up with what you said about the young today. I happen to be at graduate school, too, and I'm with people who are quite a lot younger than I am, and the difference between the sort of life they're leading and the sort of life I led when I was an undergraduate years and years ago—it is very enviable, the position that they're in. When we were in school we had been sort of tapped on the head and reminded: "Now, listen, you're twenty-one, you're going to have to be looking for somebody—you can't go on like this." And you begin to get frantic. And, my God, if no one called by Friday, what *are* you going to do on Saturday? Because if you're alone on Saturday, something is wrong with you: you're either ugly or you're not bright enough to interest a man—he's not interested in intelligence, really—but there is definitely something wrong with you.

BROOK: You may be too bright.

MARIA: Yes, well, I didn't want to bring that in yet. (*General laughter*) But inside that society, you have this awful feeling: My God, I'm a wallflower and on the shelf. You go home—and every time I went home it would be: "Have you not got anybody yet?" And you felt this terrific drive. You must get somebody; you must set up a permanent relationship; otherwise you're not normal. Consequently, I think lots of people who would be much, much happier not tied down, even though they are heterosexual, do go and throw themselves into marriage. And, I think, today in school the kids that I talk to and share classes with are not about to, because lots of them are not living at home—they're either in dorms or have pads in the East Village. In fact, some of them even live up here on the East Side. And they can switch around whenever they feel like it. And lots of kids I know today are quite happy, will tell you without even asking, that they are in a threesome relationship. They don't regard this as permanent, but my God, can you imagine twenty years ago being in this kind of society?

BROOK: I think—to comment on what you said—that the alternatives today are greater, the expectations are greater. They've only just become greater. Now people can think in these terms—that a girl today does not *have* to think that she must get married for social or economic reasons, that she cannot have a career. The expectations are larger; they're greater today than they were twenty years ago, so the pressure is not as great to do what seemed the *thing to do* then—because now there is the expectation, the possibility that you can have a career, that you do not have to marry for support, and so forth.

MARIA: And hopefully when these kids are old enough to have kids themselves, homosexuality may even decline because they will not be putting this kind of social pressure onto their own children—to grow up like a *girl,* or grow up like a *boy,* because a *girl* doesn't do this, and a boy doesn't do this—

(General uproar)

NANCY: Now wait a minute. Are you saying that to be homosexual is not desirable?

MARIA: I think for me personally, it is desirable, but for me in my social position it isn't desirable.

ETHEL: What social position?

LILLIAN: Well, it isn't granted on social position.

NANCY: Well, there's another issue, a very important issue. There are a couple of things that I picked up on that you said, Maria. Such as "Hopefully, homosexuality will decline." I kind of bristled at that, because my feeling is it is an acceptable sexual position—perfectly acceptable—but that brings up another thing which interests me very much: the fact that sexuality really can't be separated from a social role. And the very fact that one takes the attitude that to be homosexual is to be a deviate in some way—which isn't a good thing—and immediately one approaches it, as you began, from a negative point of view.

BROOK: Not necessarily, Nancy, because I think you have to say that not using the word "deviate" is negative, and not using—

NANCY: Categorically, "deviate" is negative.

ETHEL: A deviate can be a dirty old man playing with himself.

(General laughter)

BROOK: You can deviate if you do anything in a social sense which is not what everyone else is doing—and that is not necessarily a negative thing.

NANCY: But as a matter of fact, it is used that way.

PATRICIA: It is being used with a negative connotation.

BROOK: All right, in that you deviate from the accepted norm. No, people who are, let's say, the people you were referring to, Maria, who are in a threesome, you could say that that is a deviation from the accepted social norm.

PATRICIA: The accepted *public* norm.

BROOK: Yes.

MARIA: I was obviously showing up some of my colors before when I made some of those remarks, but I think what I was trying to say was that there would be less pressure put by parents onto their children. There was someone—one of my children, or one of my friend's children—that said: "When I grow up I'm going to marry some rich man so that I can have a horse." And it was my friend or myself—I no longer remember, we've gotten very like that—pointed out that you don't have to marry a rich man to have a horse. Then she said: "How can I ever get one?"

FLORENCE: Study hard, and get a good job, that's how!!

MARIA: So I had to think—have I put this idea into my own children without thinking about it? Where is it coming from if not just coming from the parents? It's coming from all over: people they meet in the playground, for example. It's coming from school, just every social contact. "You're a little girl and you have to work along this path and a boy has to work along that path."

BROOK: Oh, now wait a minute. You're a student attorney, and you've just been telling us that at school you find this idea is no longer true among the student generation. Yet you're saying that in the playground today, this is still true?

MARIA: No, I said that as of now, I felt that this kind of pressure would lessen. Of course, I don't think for one minute that the parents of these kids that are living in this *ménage* are delighted; they're probably in an absolute fury, but the kids are having a ball. And you know they're not eighteen, they're kids in their early twenties. And when I look back at myself in my early twenties, they're so much further on in their way of thinking than I was, and they're so much freer . . . and they don't see anything wrong with having sex with a man and with a woman.

FLORENCE: No guilt—isn't that lovely? You mean you can finally get rid of it.

MARIA: I never tried a *ménage*.

LILLIAN: Is there anything wrong with it?

MARIA: No, I think it's marvelous, and I'm furious that I didn't think of it!

JOAN: But you talk about society's opinion, and you talk about those people that you've come across who are flaunting it—and everybody at N.Y.U. knows about it—but what about the people who are still in closets?

MARIA: Well, down at N.Y.U. I've also been with the Women's Phi Beta Kappa Club of New York—up to Columbia University to see the woman's liberation group up there and talk with them. There they are not afraid to walk around under banners saying "Get your mitts off Lesbians, for Christ's sake!"—and I wouldn't have dared do that! But there are kids parading up and down every now and then in front of N.Y.U., you know, kids that you wouldn't— Well, in my day anybody that was homosexual you knew immediately, while these are kids that you wouldn't suspect, and they walk up and down in front of N.Y.U. demanding acceptance. I think this is fabulous.

BROOK: Do you think that is necessary?

ETHEL: Of course it is. How else will they get it?

MARIA: Well, let me put it this way. I don't know how necessary it is, or how much good it does—but it certainly warms my heart.

ETHEL: It's been a long time coming.

NANCY: But this is the point that I wanted to make before: that sexuality is woven into the social fabric; that to be a heterosexual implies a certain stance socially, while to be homosexual implies a certain stance. I was wondering very much—what if you had said to us, "I want to write an article and talk to people who are sexual moderates, and I would like to use your names." Now I certainly would have thought that it would have been an issue with myself: Did I want my name to appear in a magazine or a book as a Lesbian? And I don't know, but I'm glad it wasn't an issue.

BROOK: I don't think it is an issue. Articles shouldn't be forums for people to make a confession.

JOAN: Yes, but this is a reflection of how we feel about how society feels about us.

NANCY: Absolutely.

JOAN: In other words, I would think twice about publicly declaring myself in any kind of forum, or in the office, or anything like that.

ESTELLE: Who cares?

JOAN: I care. And it is because society has *made* me care. We were talking about deviance before, and deviance does have a negative connotation.

ESTELLE: To me it has a negative connotation.

JOAN: Well, to me it also means to be an outcast, up to a point. In any other society a deviant is an outcast.

Would you say that homosexuality is an imaginative, experimental and creative sexuality?

FLORENCE: Wow, that makes sexuality sound great!

ESTELLE: I don't find it experimental at all. To me it is a way of life.

You've all been involved in it for a long length of time, but how did you feel when you were fifteen?

PATRICIA: How about four?

BROOK: God, does anybody remember that far back?

PATRICIA: I remember women being very attractive to me when I was four. I had a lot of little boyfriends—four, five, six chums—but women were very attractive to me. And I had neurotic feelings which didn't get expressed completely sexually until later on. But if you look at them they were essentially homosexual relationships. They began that early—women were just more interesting to me than men.

Why were they more interesting?

PATRICIA: That's a difficult question.

MARIA: The men gave you a feeling of competition.

PATRICIA: I don't think we really know enough to be able to answer that. Perhaps because some of my more pleasurable experiences occurred at an early age. Perhaps also going along the line that people who are experimental sexually are more sexual. Perhaps my sexuality began later. There are so many variables—

MARIA: But I never heard the word homosexual until I was about twenty, I think, and I was very interested in boys. But when I look back I can also see these things—the women I was attracted to. But I was very keen on boyfriends; everybody had boyfriends, and I had to have one, and I had to have the nicest-looking boy in the village, or the class, interested in me. And there was a colossal amount of competition, but I was never really me. I always had to pretend about certain things . . . that I was more frivolous, that I couldn't do things to make them feel tough. I had to be terribly like this, whereas with girls— I could be very "straight" with them, and I could be me, and I could compete with them on the same level somehow. I could beat their brains out at hockey—but you weren't supposed to beat boys, if we played hockey.

NANCY: That's very interesting, your reaction to that. It's something I notice now that I do much less of, but I catch myself doing it. In fact, I did it this afternoon in a taxi with a taxi-cab driver; it is to play a game, and the game that I play is *woman*.

MARIA: Right.

NANCY: And it's a very difficult thing when one is put in the position of being an attractive person. Men approach you in a certain way, and it calls for a certain response—and I find myself playing right along with it. Of course I'll be charming, of course I'll be—

What's wrong with being a woman? You are a woman.

NANCY: Certainly I'm a woman, but I would like to relate to a person as myself who is a woman too, but not playing a role which is a *woman*.

When you come in contact with this situation where you feel some pressure to do that, do you ever realize that the man is perhaps participating? He is dealing within his limitation the best he knows how, and all he knows how to do is to react to a woman as a woman and he is reacting as a man in that way—both things are going on here. So if you wish to be understood, couldn't you say to yourself, I understand that he is doing what is

within the limitation and expectation of his life, what he has to do, this is his role as well. Who knows, he may just as well be saying, "Oh, hell, here's another woman, and shit, I have to perform."

NANCY: But that doesn't make it all right—

Could we just get rid of the words "right" and "wrong"? I think they're irrelevant.

PATRICIA: But you're bringing in the issue of right and wrong.

NANCY: Well, in a way, I feel sorrier for men—

PATRICIA: I do too. I think men live much more difficult lives than we do.

MARIA: Everybody pretending to be what they aren't—

NANCY: This whole *machismo* thing that they have to prove themselves—to be constantly competitive— I mean, poor men— When you get a group of men together who are strangers, if you watch them, what they do with one another, they have a list and they rate each other.

ETHEL: Heterosexual women are like that too. I would put heterosexual women in the same category with heterosexual men. I do not like heterosexual women at all. I'm heterosexual right now, but all my female friends are homosexual women. I don't understand heterosexual women.

Why?

ETHEL: I don't even know how to describe it; I mean, I never stopped to analyze it. I thought, well, why am I staying away from them? Well, I do find them boring, I do find them ridiculously feminine to the point of idiocy. They cannot turn off—they're learning to now—but it's not even that: they relax, but they don't relax. They cannot be themselves, they're so into this game-playing.

Do you accept the idea that femininity is a state of mind, and not an outward expression such as how they dress, look, speak, even make love—

ETHEL: If you're a woman, you're a woman. That's it, period.

FLORENCE: I think the difficulty is that femininity has been so clearly defined in our society . . . what is feminine and what is not feminine.

BROOK: And that by and large it is witless, frivolous—

FLORENCE: Whoever a woman is, I don't know— I think there are an enormous number of ways you can be and still be a woman. And I think that one thing that Lesbians do have to possibly offer in this sense is this whole business of the fact that there is a very wide variety. And I'm not talking about truckdriver type to little flibbertigibbet kind of thing—but the fact that you can be primarily and first a human being. I mean, I think you can be a woman without going through what Nancy is talking about. I think it is very easily misunderstood. It's not that you don't want to be feminine—whatever that is, for you—but it's the compulsion to feel that you must be feminine within society's definition of femininity, I think that's the problem.

BROOK: But then of course you don't *have* to do it.

FLORENCE: No, you don't, and I think this option is becoming increasingly open to a lot of women now.

LILLIAN: How many homosexuals have the same heterosexual set up in their lives? I mean the male-female roles, the men and woman roles?

FLORENCE: Oh, I think very many—but I think this is breaking down to some extent.

LILLIAN: Well, I think a lot of them are trying to play heterosexual living, when they shouldn't, you know.

BROOK: How about just people living?

ETHEL: Or human being living?

NANCY: When I was going out with men, having affairs primarily with men, something that I very often did if I wanted to have lunch or go to a play or a concert, I'd call up a friend—somebody who perhaps was my lover at the time—and I'd say, you know, let's go to the movies or out to lunch—and their reaction was delight and surprise. They would say, how great that you called me, how unusual. Women never call men, and I never thought anything of it—because the relationship was with friends and they never thought anything of it; it went both ways—but they were astounded that I did that. And I was checking out that it has changed. I was stepping out of a conventional role and doing something else. Five or six years ago that was unthinkable—"women don't do that"—I was being more aggressive. And that's a lot of nonsense, but that kind of stuff is still with us.

JOAN: I identify very strongly with you when you were talking about your taxicab thing. Because all of the years that I was in business I had the problem fighting off men; "fighting off" is probably the wrong word, but putting them off, nicely, gracefully. And I was always afraid to say to a guy when he would invite me out to dinner or what have you—no, I'm just not interested in you. My first thought was that he would think I was gay. Then I was thinking about this on the way up here—and I thought, well, I probably would have the same fear with a woman, too, but not with the same reason. But simply because I have the problem of telling people, look, I'm just not interested in you. I have the problem with acceptance and approbation to such a degree that I would be afraid of offending anybody. At least in the business world, where I was afraid of being an outcast or what have you, I felt that under no circumstances could I dare show my real feelings, because if I did this then every-body would know I was gay and then immediately my job might be in jeopardy. So I played the game, the same game that Nancy was playing—and sometimes I played too well, and then I had worse problems of not being able to follow through.

PATRICIA: Well, I had some of the same problems. I was trying to think whether this is still true, that most of my friends were men. Now, as I became older, it became more difficult: it tended to be cast into a sexual thing. So that now more and more of my male friends are homosexual men. But this thing about the ease of moving with women and being *straight* with them, as I think Maria said, I always thought I could be *straight* with men. Because I was homosexual I thought I could be more straightforward with men.

LILLIAN: Can I ask a question? Do you think in your various businesses— Do you think that if people knew you were homosexual, you would be accepted? Would you keep your job, do you think?

FLORENCE: Yes, I think I would.

LILLIAN: Do you think you'd have full acceptance of what you have now?

JOAN: I think probably I would have kept my job, but every-body, particularly the men, would have looked at me differ-ently.

LILLIAN: It would have been difficult?

JOAN: Yes. It might not have been a pleasant social situation going to the office every day.

MARIA: I have found that sometimes I have wanted to say to them, "For Christ's sake, I am gay, leave me alone." The constant hanging around and asking you to go out— It's not that they're simply interested in taking you to dinner, and it's not the old fashioned idea that they simply want to take you to bed—it's that they want to take you to dinner *and* to bed.

Would you be happier if they said to you, "Look, I sort of like you; let's make out?"

MARIÀ: Well, I now have, in fact, nonsexual relationships with men who are straight—one in particular, a professor who was interested in me sexually. I got so tired of taking him off me, but I didn't want to stop seeing him because I liked him as a person; he was bright and interesting. In the end, I said, "Look, for God's sake, I'm gay," and he said, "Why didn't you tell me? This is ridiculous, all I've been trying with you." So now we have a superb friendship, still. And he calls me up every so often and says how delighted he is to come around and take me out—it's really nice.

FLORENCE: He's not waiting to see you reform, in other words?

BROOK: It was probably a little bit of a relief. The pressure is off you both. He can relax now; he doesn't have to play the seductive man—which probably was a little bit of an effort for him too. Now everybody can relax.

FLORENCE: Yes, that's probably true.

MARIA: I think he would have been perfectly delighted . . . pardon me, honestly, to go to bed with me, but—

Why do most women who choose to have a homosexual life love to make the statement that they have had relationships with men, and that they were attracted to men and that men found them attractive? There always seems to be some point where a woman is bound to say this.

NANCY: You're absolutely right.

ETHEL: What's wrong with that?

FLORENCE: Gee, I've never said it; I must be out of touch.

MARIA: Well, I find that an awful lot of women find me attractive, too, and want to go to bed with me.

If we could return to the question, why do women hasten to reassure one of their option for choice?

NANCY: I think you've picked up on something that is real one hundred per cent on. I've noticed the same thing.

FLORENCE: Yes, so have I. I think it's the idea that women want to be accepted, and so forth. It's one thing to say that I've found men attractive, and another to say I don't want men, I like women as friends . . . and it's another to say—which is what people always imagine homosexual women are like—that they're perfectly horrible, unattractive, stringy-haired. Lesbians who couldn't get a man if they tried.

NANCY: I think it's a social thing. I've been with gay guys and exactly the same thing has come up—very attractive guys. There's a feeling of being a deviate that is uncomfortable—and I think when someone says well, I've had affairs with men, what the person is really saying is look, I'm not a creep. You know, I've chosen this way of life because it's more me.

BROOK: What they're really saying is look, I had a choice, and this is the choice I made and I'm happy with it—so fuck off the theories.

(*General agreement*)

NANCY: But the other thing is, *I'm not a creep.* I have had some other kinds of experience; I'm not some kind of bizarre person who doesn't know what it's all about.

BROOK: Frankly, I think bizarre people are rather interesting.

LILLIAN: Why is homosexuality so fashionable now?

FLORENCE: Oh, because the population explosion has gotten everybody worried.

(*General laughter*)

FLORENCE: Frankly, it's an enormous relief for them to talk

about something that has just very recently and chicly been something you could talk about not in a whisper. I think it's not so controversial any more. And we have all our agonies about Vietnam and the economy, and it has become a fashionable issue. After all, the blacks have had their period of militancy, and they haven't gotten what they wanted, and society is breaking down in that respect, so now we have a new group in the limelight.

LILLIAN: Do you think more homosexuals are finding that it's easier? You know, they're coming out.

MARIA: Yes.

FLORENCE: I think that an awful lot of women in the woman's liberation are finding that there is no alternative.

LILLIAN: I think one of the reasons it is so fashionable is because there is great interest among heterosexuals and curiosity now—

FLORENCE: And I think it's that suddenly people are now more free to follow some of their homosexual urges. That doesn't mean that they will forever after become practicing homosexuals, but that maybe they do have an affair with the woman next door—without the kind of guilt and the feeling that oh, my God, I'm queer and there's something terribly wrong with me. I mean, maybe we're coming to that, but I'm sure we're not there yet. Still, there's a little bit more leeway.

MARIA: Well, I have found in my little heterosexual society down there that there are so many bored wives who are absolutely delighted when they find out that you're gay—and are never off the phone.

FLORENCE: Attack you in the laundry room?

(*Laughter*)

MARIA: No, but they would probably quite likely like to have some kind of relationship simply to try it. And I think a few years ago it wouldn't have even dared come into their consciousness.

PATRICIA: Do you think that is as true of women as it is of men?

BROOK: I don't agree with you, Maria. I think it existed even then; it was just very quietly done with a *best* friend.

PATRICIA: Well, women have always been more free to experiment because they didn't have to carry that terrible burden of masculinity.

JOAN: Also, I think there is a great deal more protection within the heterosexually married circumstance. Talking about freedom of choice, a married Lesbian has, in a sense, more freedom to experiment because she won't begin with that awful label; she has the protection of her husband and her home and that marriage license, so, I don't know, it might give them more freedom in that laundry room.

LILLIAN: Well, you know, when you think about the threesome there's no third sex is there? It has to be two of one—

ETHEL: But if you have a foursome, there's not so much freedom—

(*Laughter*)

ETHEL: But at first there is. I once knew a man who I was going out with who said how about a threesome? I said okay, a few more men, it might be great. Then he said no, I was thinking of two girls.

(*Laughter*)

How did you feel about that?

ETHEL: Well, I liked it, but I would have preferred two guys. Because I would have been too jealous, that's all.

NANCY: Did you do it?

ETHEL: No.

Why?

ETHEL: There's still time. I'm slow.

BROOK: You didn't want to shoot the whole thing at once, huh?

ETHEL: Yeah.

MARIA: I tried that once actually, a long time ago. And I had difficulty in that I was interested in the girl and I knew the one that was going to be doing all the fawning was the man, and this sort of annoyed me somewhat. And we ended up, the two ladies clutching one another, trying to get rid of the man. It was just a complete flop!

PATRICIA: For him, anyway.

(*Laughter*)

BROOK: Well, it could have gone the other way. You could have been left out.

MARIA: Well, the next time I try it, if ever, it will be with two men.

FLORENCE: I wanted to pick up on something you said, Patricia. I think it ought to be emphasized again, and I probably will misquote you, but the whole idea of being homosexual has a negative connotation for so many people, which we began to discuss in terms of deviation. I think what you said about the reinforced very early pleasurable experiences—I think this is so important to emphasize, because I think for the most part, people see it as trauma, ghastly things happening . . . the dreadful father beating the little girl so that she rushes off to mother. Well, that may be somewhat true because she's obviously getting more pleasure from her mother than her father, who is beating her, but still it can be primarily a pleasurable thing, and it doesn't have to have the terribly negative connotation always. As I look into myself, I think I'm putting a much more positive face on it than I maybe actually think. But I also feel that I have been so brainwashed as to feel that it is the result of trauma. It is in a certain sense for me, and I think for many other people; there have been a lot of negative experiences which obviously have turned you away from a much easier path. But I wonder whether that's really straight thinking? I wonder whether or not if you follow the pleasure principle, that where you have gotten the most pleasure is where you will ultimately end up sexually . . . and that is the most creative thing, and we really should just forget the other? And when you look at it that way, without guilt, with just that feeling that you've followed where you've had pleasure, that's really a very healthy thing.

> **Would you accept the idea that most of you have had a desire to be loved, to feel warm? And the realization of that pleasurable thing was first of all in the desire—first of all, to be loved and to feel warm, which possibly you did not feel to a satisfactory extent from the family first of all, and siblings secondly, and so you were reaching out for that warmth and that love which was withheld in the family situation, and you happened to find it with a woman, and it therefore became a learned experience.**

PATRICIA: You're reading us the litany. (*Laughter*) That's one of the popular explanations. It was expressed fairly recently in one of those magazine articles they're always writing.

> **I'm speaking of when you were a very young child —as you said before, four years old.**

PATRICIA: I imagine a four-year-old would have an acute desire to be held and to receive affection, among other things—but how can you explain some homosexual four-year-olds and some heterosexual four-year-olds?

ETHEL: Well, where they got the most love from, first, and secondly, repeated experiences—

PATRICIA: Then hopefully the child will go on, and grow up and seek love and warmth, and come to give it also.

ETHEL: Right, but one tends to go back to where one got it originally. If you got it originally from the female, you'd probably go to another female rather than a male.

MARIA: Don't you think— I mean I do have this feeling about needing love and warmth, and I think that everybody is looking for it—even pet rabbits, you know how they huddle together. Except when you huddle up with a male from my huddling up at the age of fifteen on—always the huddling didn't last very long and it got around to let's screw, to use the vernacular. You either said, "Oh, my God, no, because I'll get pregnant, and I'm only sixteen" . . . or you know, you did, and he gets up and goes to the bathroom and cleans his teeth, or whatever they do in there. Whereas with a woman, it just doesn't end like that. I had heterosexual experiences until I was about twenty-three, and I did enjoy the warmth and loving feeling, and I could imagine myself to be madly in love a number of times, but always when it got around to the sex act, they would do it and it was over with, and they invariably got up fairly soon afterwards and said, "Let's go to see a football match, or let's go to a movie," or something else, when I was perfectly happy to spend the whole evening cuddling.

Was there something else that you expected to happen that did not happen?

MARIA: I wanted to stay racked up with somebody for a long period, because I enjoy the feeling. Now I would have thought it was a sort of protected feeling that I wanted, but I never felt protected somehow by men. I felt that whatever they were doing with me initially was so *they* could eventually jerk off. That's what they were aiming for right from the beginning; it was in their minds all the time. And it wasn't necessarily in mine. I was certainly interested in having sex with them, but that always seemed to be the thing that they were aiming for right from the first kiss—this is what it's going to be tonight. Whereas with women I found it not like that; very often I did end up in bed with them, but—

ETHEL: But you were just talking before about if you wanted a sex jag with some women, you could call— You knew several people you could call up. And sex with them, I think, would be the same as these men you were talking about . . .

MARIA: Yes, but I didn't say I did it.

ETHEL: Well, I know you don't, right, but obviously every sex relationship you've had hasn't been that perfect.

ESTELLE: But even if you don't see them again the next day, the sexuality with them could still be more like what she's looking for and less like the "get up right away and brush your teeth."

MARIA: There's much more caring, even so.

LILLIAN: There are men who do care—

ETHEL: Yes, there are—but I think I would agree with you, for the majority of experiences, yes, men are more like that than women. Well, we're getting into kinds of men, but some men are more frightened of showing some kind of sensitivity.

MARIA: But it gets back to what you said. It simply was a great deal more pleasurable with women—maybe because it lasted longer.

LILLIAN: But now you have the reverse of the woman role— young people who go to bed with guys, and get up and say goodbye. Young women today say goodbye just like the men did that you're talking about.

BROOK: Did you put the same thing into it that you expected to come out of it?

MARIA: What? The feeling of warmth and love? Yes, yes, I did, and I felt the women I went to bed with picked this up and gave me that back. Let me put it this way: after you've made love with a man you feel *used;* when you make love with a woman you feel *loved*. That's really where the difference lies.

NANCY: The thing that turned me off men as an adult, where it got down to the point of getting married—and it got to that point several times—and I woke up in terror at the idea. What put me off was . . . the guys without exception wanted me to take care of them. And what terrified me was the simple thought, My God! I've got to cook for this guy the rest of my life, or for *X* number of years; I've got to keep the house together for him, wash his clothes, put him to bed when he's drunk, and keep him together in some way—and I was terrified at the idea. I mean, this is without exception. Perhaps it was the men I picked on that needed that, but they certainly did.

JOAN: Well, most men in our society expect that of a woman.

LILLIAN: Well, it's the mother role—

NANCY: That is *definitely* what they wanted, and I knew I *definitely* didn't want to do it. As a young girl in my twenties, I knew I didn't want to get married. In some way this terrified me, and I wasn't too clear about it, just what was wrong, I just knew that whenever it got to that point, I got very uncomfortable and—

JOAN: What you were objecting to was the rest of the role that went with it—which was the mother role.

NANCY: Right.

MARIA: Maybe men want mothers and maybe Lesbians want mothers.

NANCY: I think there's a lot of truth to that, because it's certainly true of me. I know I need to feel a great deal of warmth and security and comfort, and I care very much to have a sort of stability. I think comfort has a great deal to do with it.

Where does our original premise of realized sexuality come into this? Our primary basis of thinking in terms of sexuality rather than homosexuality
or heterosexuality—where does this fit into the
comforting maternalism you're now discussing?

NANCY: I think there are many different kinds of sexuality. It's
possible to have sexuality among all different kinds of com-
binations. There's parent and child sexuality, sibling sexuality— And I think people work it out in their sexual life.
I think there are many variations.

Don't you think that is in very general terms?

NANCY: Yes, but it is the best I can do. A lot is said about
adult sexuality, and I think that—
BROOK: Define "adult."
NANCY: Yeah, I'd be very hard put to define it. I think sexuality is various—

Would anyone care to define adult sexuality?

PATRICIA: I think it would have to be defined socially. We all
start out with polymorphesis perverses, and if we weren't in-
terferred with, we'd all enjoy our polymorphesis preverses.
Adult sexuality is defined in terms of social prescription.
And some of the fallacies are in my field of psychiatry.
ESTELLE: Would you, as some kind of definition, say that
adult sexuality is male-female screwing—and that's exactly
what it is. But as opposed to that, would you accept the idea
that the difference between child sexuality and adult sexuality

is that childhood sexuality has to do more with interaction with another person?

PATRICIA: We may end up trying to define what maturity is, and that pan-sexuality* occurs within that.

ESTELLE: But in my definition I am not ruling out pan-sexuality, I'm not ruling out various kinds of sexual object choices.

PATRICIA: I would think that mature sexuality would be a lack of inhibition, but showing judgment and awareness of the other person.

JOAN: And a certain amount of pleasure in gratifying the other person—where as Estelle was saying, childhood is so egocentric—me, me, me.

PATRICIA: Awareness of the other person—

JOAN: First aware and then second gratified.

NANCY: Yet part of the nature of sexuality is so wild—because there is a loss of ego boundary in sexuality—in orgasm. So that certainly the climate of sexuality is very interesting. You can think of that as an infantile experience; to be surrounded, to be overwhelmed—

BROOK: Maybe sexuality, in its final moment, when you are not thinking about any of those spiritual things, is really the infant saying, I want to be pleasured?

MARIA: Yes, it has become egocentric.

BROOK: You've forgotten anyone else at that particular moment of where something is happening for you which is physical and biological. It stops being anything else but the climax of that pleasure you're about to experience.

PATRICIA: Arriving at sexual orgasm is the ability to be able to say I want to be pleasured and just to give all over. However, because there are two people involved one does have to

* The term "pan-sexuality" derives from the theory of pan-sexualism: All human behavior stems from, or is motivated by, sexuality—a theory no longer felt to be valid by modern psychiatrists.

learn how to keep the relationship going long enough to get the pleasure.

BROOK: Nobody is thinking about the relationship right at the moment when orgasm is about to occur.

PATRICIA: No, I agree.

NANCY: I think it's interesting that at the moment of orgasm it really has to do with letting go, and that can have to do with a sense of self.

BROOK: It has to do with accepting—

NANCY: Yes.

BROOK: A letting go and an accepting too, at the same time. It's a conscious thing, but that's what happens.

Why are there people that you feel aesthetically and intellectually close to, spiritually akin to, and yet it doesn't work sexually?

NANCY: I always go to bed with someone I feel that way about, I never miss a chance!

(*General laughter*)

BROOK: Yeah, and on the other hand, there can be somebody with whom you do not have that same meeting of the minds, that same spiritual closeness—and yet for some reason, the actual act of sex can be extremely gratifying, sometimes quite surprising to you.

PATRICIA: I think you could apply what Brook said: that it is the experience of pleasure, that maybe that is really where we are. The idea being that very possibly, maybe, we put up with trying to be adult and reasonably easy to live with, or at least somewhat pleasant to have a relationship with, simply for that moment when all the ego boundaries disappear and there is the marvelous pleasure. So then it maybe doesn't really matter whether the person is someone who you have a spiritual or intellectual kinship with.

BROOK: Aren't the two things separate? Don't you have to say that for a certain part of your relationship you have this thing going—the intellectuality, the spirituality—and it comes down to this thing of what you do in bed being incidental to the rest of your life?

PATRICIA: Not incidental—no, ideally sexuality is an integral part of personality and human wholeness.

BROOK: Okay, agreed—ideally—and a relationship that has the whole thing is marvelous and beautiful. Maybe what we all need to do is work more on developing our relationships to the point where there is respect and mutual trust and giving, and then the sexuality will come out of that love—and probably be better than we dreamed or hoped.

NANCY: I'll buy that.

(General agreement)

Chapter 8

The Gay Activists

Group discussion was held with women members of the Gay Activists at their clubhouse headquarters in New York's Greenwich Village. The women ranged in ages from about seventeen to fifty and represented a cross section of educational and socioeconomic levels. The group discussion was held on April 24, 1972, and the women made it clear that they spoke for themselves individually and not for the organization.

Some psychiatrists have stated that in their opinion, Lesbians suffer from penis envy. How do you respond to that charge?

(*General laughter indicates scorn of the question, and disbelief at the professional naïveté of those making the statement*)

DORIS: Well, yes, maybe for about two weeks it occurred to me to be jealous. The actual extent of my penis envy, however, was that I wanted to pee faster. It just seemed faster and easier for boys—that was the extent of my envy.

Since you don't credit the validity of some psychological conclusions, what do you think might give the impression of penis envy?

DORIS: There is another side of that. In my case, in addition to wanting to pee faster (*Laughter*), there was the matter of recognition. I never thought about it very much, I guess—not until recently, that is—but I grew up in a very isolated community. I fell into a role because that was the assumed manner in which lesbianism was displayed; you either had to affect being a man or a woman—this was the image of Lesbians. The ones that I saw, must have been probably in their forties or fifties—the old school. And I'm sure there were hundreds of Lesbians in my community that I never saw or recognized. At that point I thought it would be better to be mannish—because that's how I would be obviously gay. Once I realized that wasn't necessary [to be "butch" or "femme"], and that wasn't what I wanted, that was the end of it.

Some of those same psychiatrists we spoke of before are still saying that lesbian women are so because of penis fear—fear of being attacked, fear of the aggressive assult of the penis, or of being physically hurt by it. How do you respond to that theory?

POLLY: But that whole idea goes down the tubes as soon as you talk to a number of Lesbians who have had relationships with men. I myself have slept with a lot more men in my lifetime than I have with women. Men just do nothing for me; they don't interest me sexually. As people they interest me—

in a sexual sense, they don't. I find it difficult to relate to them on any deep emotional level, so why go through all those changes? But I'd like to speak about this whole subject of "butch" and "femme". When I first realized that I was gay—this was a lot of years ago—a friend of mine took me to a bar on the West Coast and it scared me out of being gay for three years. (*Laughter of appreciation and understanding from group*) I mean, it was a total bum trip! It really set me back—I mean those women were not women, they were either caricatures of men, or caricatures of women. (*She flexes muscles to imitate mannerism of "butch dyke" and minces to imitate "femme"; general appreciative laughter from group*)

CLAUDIA: Yeah, with the big pipe or cigar?

POLLY: Yeah, I mean really—you know, they were just not being themselves. They were very busy being something they weren't. I mean, who could turn on to them? So I spent three more years trying to do the whole straight bit. Then suddenly just a few years ago something changed—and all of a sudden this "butch-femme" nonsense began to disappear. Thank God!

CLAUDIA: About this penis envy: I always felt lucky I didn't have a penis—because my two brothers were always getting theirs caught in their zippers. (*General laughter*) No kidding! I have a younger brother, and when I was toilet training him, it was really a problem. He'd always have to run to me to get me to take him to pee so he wouldn't get caught in the zipper. I also find that true of two kids I baby-sit once in a while. They're two years old—a boy and a girl. And the problem is peeing in the toilet—they both want to go at the same time. Well, she can sit on the toilet, but then when she does, where is he going to go? So I solved it; I stand them both up in the bathtub and let them spread their legs and they can both go at the same time. She watches it dribble down his leg—because he hasn't yet learned that he can control the direction with his hand—but she pees straight down and she's proud of that; she doesn't get all messed up. Like I remember when I was a kid with my brothers— it was a question of who could pee farther. Well, I couldn't compete in that, so I used to pee in a bucket to make more noise than they did—and that made me special. (*General laughter*)

POLLY: How did you feel about the "butch-femme" thing?

CLAUDIA: Sure, I went through that confusion too. You see I fell in love with this girl, and it was like after six months that we were happily sleeping together that we began to talk about the fact that we were Lesbians. You see, she had been a Lesbian before, but I hadn't, and I didn't really consider myself one. I mean I had had some affairs, but it was just whoever I was in love with that day. But then we'd had this relationship that had lasted six months, and we began to think of whether or not it was going to be a forever thing. My girl friend asked me one day: "Are you going to always be a Lesbian?" A Lesbian, I asked? Well, I guess this does make me a Lesbian. So, then I said to myself, how do I be a Lesbian? You know, I thought I had to get out a rule book or something so I'd do it right—I always like to do everything right. (*General laughter*) So, we went to this gay bar and my girlfriend went to get me a drink—and when she'd gone this big "dyke" comes up to me, with a pipe in her mouth, yet! And I'll never forget it (*She imitates masculine voice*), she said: "Wanna dance, honey?" It nearly blew my mind! I mean it was just like being in a straight bar and having some man come up and ask me that—she was doing the same number! I said, Oh, my God! Is this what we have to do to be Lesbians? So, when my friend came back, I said, listen, we'd better forget it. Let's not tell anybody we're Lesbians—and we can just do our own thing. But then I felt guilty about keeping her away from her friends, the gay women, that I was coming to know also. Those were the people we saw because my straight friends felt uncomfortable with us. It was all right for them to dance together, and kiss together, but they felt uncomfortable if we kissed.

DORIS: And God forbid that you should dance!

CLAUDIA: Right. I mean, for us to dance the grinder—well! But they felt perfectly free to do it in front of us. So, I came to the conclusion— Well, you've got to be one or the other. So I decided we'd have to be Lesbians. Then I thought if you're going to be a Lesbian, that means you've got to "butch" or "femme." So, I decided I'd try being "butch." Well, I just couldn't do it; I couldn't handle it. The gestures were all wrong. I couldn't get comfortable in plain clothes and heavy shoes. I mean I was getting all calluses on my feet.

DORIS: Dyke boots, already?

CLAUDIA: Yeah. And my girl friend tried being "femme"—and did she really look funny as a "femme." So we decided I'd be the "femme." Okay, I tried it—but I didn't have any more luck with that. I just couldn't take the long eyelashes and the false nails. So I said well, I guess we're just going to have to be freaks and just go around looking like regular women, or at least like somebody's idea of it.

How did that work out?

CLAUDIA: Well, we didn't fit in at the gay bar still—or even with a lot of the older gay women who were into this "butch-femme" business. But it was interesting as I got to know them better. Like the older ones that had been together like ten or twenty years—they looked alike. They tended to look like twins rather than like "butch-femme" that they thought they were looking like.

DORIS: That's something I've always wondered about. Like a fifty-year-old "butch" woman will always be—not being able to be a man—a little boy. It seems that way to me, but I wonder if an ultra-"femme" at fifty will be a little girl?

CLAUDIA: (*Kidding her*) But didn't you see the movie *The Killing Of Sister George?* You should know these things—that's what you *have* to be. Remember Girlie, or Childie—What was her name?

DORIS: Childie.

CLAUDIA: Yeah, you have to be like a nympho—no, not a nympho, a nymphette!

(*General laughter*)

Are you talking about the passing of a generation that was not knowledgeable about such things on a wide sociological and psychological level—which was into role-playing because of society's concept of them? Are you saying that the "butch-femme" element is not going to exist any more?

POLLY: No, parts of it will survive for a long time yet.

CLAUDIA: Yeah, for a long time yet.

POLLY: The attitude still exists in the gay world. The only way it really is going to change—and I notice a lot of negative reaction among Lesbians to those that are into the "butch-femme" thing, some of whom are close to me. But as long as I recognize that's not for me, they can go ahead and do their own thing. If they're good people, they're good people, that's how I look at it. But there is definitely a strong undercurrent of negative reaction and resentment among gays; and I think the element is going to disappear only when they are welcome and made not to feel different. Their isolation, I think, makes them hide behind the super "butch-femme" roles—not only from society at large but other Lesbians—and this makes them defensive and just more so. It's even a kind of rebellion against established ideas of the men/women thing.

Do you think that younger people coming on now will be different—I mean will there be less delineation and role-playing? Will they feel more comfortable just being women who happen to, incidentally, be attracted to women and like to sleep with them?

CLAUDIA: Yes, I think so. If you remember back in the 1950's you either had to have a crew cut or a great big crinoline skirt to be masculine or feminine even in straight society. So, when it's that ridiculous and that separated, anything is likely to happen. You know, women couldn't wear pants, they couldn't do anything. If you wanted to wash your car you had to wear a dress or a skirt, or you were looked at as some kind of oddity. It was really freaky if you look back on the forties and fifties. There was such a difference between what the men and the women could do, could wear. I remember going to the first Daughters of Bilitis meeting and my girl friend and I dressed "butch" and "femme." I forget who was who that night. (*Laughter*) But there was this woman there who had a crew cut—and she really freaked my mind! (*Putting the group on*) I keep thinking I'll find her again some day. But somebody told me she probably let her hair grow, and that's wrecked my whole fantasy! (*Laughter*) But I think that when she was "coming out," she had to have a crew cut so people would know she was a Lesbian—in order to attract another Lesbian.

POLLY: Yeah, that's really a problem—

CLAUDIA: I know I had a hard time attracting other women, or knowing who to try with. You know, if you try to make it with a straight woman, you really got a hard time of it. Or if you try to make it with a gay woman and she's not sure you're gay—so they didn't want anything to do with me because I was too young. Or they didn't know, and they didn't want to be the one to bring me out. So I think it's less of a problem now. If you can just go to a Gay Activists Alliance meeting, you know, and somebody will say they're gay—or you assume they are because they're there—something like that, and you don't have to play footsies back and forth, and always be wondering and worrying. You don't have to have a crew cut or a crinoline skirt any more.

How do you feel about the totally aggressive woman—one that doesn't want to be made love to herself. Do you consider her more of a transsexual?

DORIS: She's just a "stone butch," or a "stone dyke." She's certainly a Lesbian in her own right. She hasn't had a sex change. She can't be a transsexual any other way, so far as I know. There's every reason in American society for any woman to be afraid of her own sexuality to the point that she would never want to be touched.

Why do you say that?

DORIS: Because there is no respect given to the sexuality of women—as far as I can see.

You mean there is no respect given to a woman aggressively enjoying sex?

DORIS: Yes, that, in terms of them developing their sexuality—and being seen as someone who should be granted respect for her sexuality.

You're saying that sex is something men do?

DORIS: Something they *enjoy!*

CLAUDIA: What she's saying is so important.

POLLY: Yeah, sex is something women suffer and men enjoy.

CLAUDIA: It is something done *to* a woman.

(All agree)

CLAUDIA: And so if you were a "butch" trying to be a man because you felt you had to be or the relationship would fall to pieces, then maybe you'd be afraid to enjoy it yourself; you'd always have to be doing something to them.

POLLY: I have a friend who is one of the "stone butches." I personally would not care to sleep with her—I mean, it just doesn't quite appeal to me—but I know that she definitely does not think of herself as a man. She thinks of herself as masculine, but as a woman. You know, there could be some women that might be considered transsexual because they think of themselves as a man, just as there are some men who think of themselves as a woman. And whether or not they've gone through an operation for sex change doesn't matter. The way they think of themselves is what matters. But the "stone butches" I've met—well, sneaking down there somewhere, hidden inside, is still the soul of a woman.

CAROL: I'd like to say something, but there's a man in the room, and I don't talk when there's a man present. (*At the far end of the room sat a boy with his head down on the table as though asleep*) The way I feel about a man being here is that I can't say what I want to say. I can't be me when he's within listening range of what I have to say. The reason behind that is because men do things to me; men have always done things to me. Men rape women, men rape Lesbians, men can beat me up on the street. I have no reason to trust this man. I don't know him; therefore that's why I'm not saying anything (*The man was a member of the Gay Activists also.*)

CLAUDIA: That's funny, because I've been raped and everything like that, and I can still have a man in the room, and I can be making love and enjoying a woman with a man in the room. I mean they don't infect my head—and that's what they're doing to you. Some men can, but not all men.

CAROL: What would be the difference between one man and another? Was one of them you're talking about put up in a vacuum bottle or something?

CLAUDIA: No, he just happens to be a person rather than a male chauvinist. He probably was a freak in his own family and in his own time, and he's still considered an oddball for not getting married, or not putting down women like other men, or not being the kind of male society says he should be.

CAROL: Well, that just makes your friend male, and the kind of male society has caused him to be—but that doesn't make him sensitive to women.

CLAUDIA: Oh, I feel he's sensitive. I don't feel put down by all men, or uncomfortable with all men.

POLLY: Some men are rather enjoyable people.

CLAUDIA: Yeah.

Do you feel easy or comfortable being friends with straight men? Is it even possible—without the subject of man-woman sexuality entering into the relationship and hindering the friendship?

CLAUDIA: I think it's harder to become friends with most men because they've been brought up to believe that they have to make a pass, or try to sleep with you. A date has to lead to going to bed, or it isn't a successful evening. But I think it's a lot of crap to say that's the way it has to be, or that it necessarily does end up that way. That would be like saying because I'm a Lesbian, I have to try and make it with every woman I know, that eventually I have to make an appeal for her body. That's not the way it is, and it doesn't have to be that way with a man.

You're saying it doesn't have to be that way, but I'm asking you if it usually is. Can you be friends with a man and be honest about not being interested in him sexually and still remain friends?

POLLY: Well, it's just the same as you pick your friends in any situation. I wouldn't find it difficult. Not all women are my friends, and not all men are my friends. I have spent a great deal of time around men—and without problems. This is the thing—for instance, there is a bar I used to hang out in a great deal when I first came to New York. It's a straight bar, and these people who hang out in there are my friends. We can go in and talk—whether they're male or female really doesn't matter if we're having an enjoyable conversation. Now, if somebody comes up to me and says: "Hey, you want to go home?" I just say no, that's my trip—and that's cool and that's the end of the discussion.

When you see that man again, is he uptight about the rejection?

POLLY: No, they're not uptight about it. Sometimes some of them are—but those are just—
DORIS: That's *their* problem.
POLLY: That's what I was going to say. That's all in their heads, and I can't be bothered with that. I have better things to do with my time.

What about lesbian couples who do want to go out, who feel having men friends is important to balance, and so forth, yet find it difficult. Women who want to be a part of the community—yet feel isolated from normal social behavior because of the man/woman sexual games.

POLLY: Yes, but I'm curious whether the basis of their wish for going out is that they'd like to go out and there's no place to go with a woman—or whether they'd just like to go out.

DORIS: But you see, here's the thing. If they can't deal with being known as gay people, then they have an immediate problem right there. Also, when women finally learn to say no to men it will be easier for all of us. I think that is possibly the problem.

CLAUDIA: Yes, I think that they've already expected that they're going to be expected to go to bed with the guy who takes them out.

DORIS: Well, men do expect an affirmative answer, because, of course, they have to be irresistible.

CLAUDIA: And that they're doing you a favor in taking you out—that kind of thing. The straight men I know—I treat sometimes and they treat sometimes, and it's not that they always buy for me. I refuse to be friends with a straight man who insists on always treating me. If it's for a dinner, or a soda, or if I need a nickel for the toilet, or a quarter for a Kotex, or whatever. It's like, you know, it has to be some kind of an equal thing. But if the men are always taking them out, most women have been conditioned to feel that they should be doing something to make it worth the man's while. Most women have inferiority complexes that way.

POLLY: It's the whole "I have to be taken out" attitude that's wrong. That business of "Somebody has to take care of me" rather than "I'm an adult and I can take care of myself." Women have to find their own identity.

What is your general attitude toward the movement you're involved in?

CLAUDIA: Mine is a humanistic attitude, I suppose: a brotherhood and sisterhood. I see my life as a total human being and this is just part of my life. I don't consider myself a gay liberationist. Some people say that's an occupation, but I don't. I consider it a part of my life—and I'm a part of the group, but I also consider myself a part of my four-year-old class too.

You're a teacher?

CLAUDIA: Yes. I'm in a college class where I'm under another teacher who is like above me, and I'm in the subordinate role; that's a part of my life. Or I'm marching in a parade, and that's a part of me at the time. It's all a part of my life, part of what I consider my reason for being.

DORIS: I'm very involved in gay liberation for many reasons. One, for very political reasons. I want to see the laws against homosexuals abolished. There's no point to repression, and nothing to be gained by it excepting to the detriment of our society, to the world society. I personally want to see these changes come about so that people growing up will not have to go through that kind of struggle. It's a struggle based on what I consider to be ridiculous standards that were only useful to a very small segment of the population. Whenever these laws and moral attitudes have been pressed for change, it is the church that has stood in the way. There's no time left; the changes have to come now.

You want to see these changes in your lifetime?

DORIS: Oh yes, and it will happen absolutely. The fourteen-year-old of today has all the media at his or her disposal, and they will know that there is no reason for hiding. Neither religious or educational reasons will be enough to hold them back from being the largest person they can be. And if that's as a gay person, then they're going to change it in order to be that person.

What is the major focus of your movement?

MAGGIE: Well, gay people say, for example—they've never had a picture of who they could be. There's been an occasional Gertrude Stein or Oscar Wilde or Marcel Proust whom they could be proud of, but they're going to have to create images of their own today here and now—not superstar images but human images. With that in their minds there's not going to be any reason to have to hide or fake. They will know that they don't have to accept brands like "sick" or "closet"— or that they don't have to repress their tendencies and hide. They're not going to have to go through what we've had to go through.

DORIS: It's not being gay that's the problem; it's what society puts on you for being gay. There will be a time when society will not put those problems on people.

CLAUDIA: I agree entirely with that. I see it all the time with my kindergarten children. I see children from the time of birth, practically, on up. Suddenly when they're around seven years old they come up against what society expects of them, and where they are. That's when all the guilt and things like that start coming in. Before that, they are very openly loving. Little kids have to be taught hate and guilt. There's no hate and guilt in them before that. They are totally loving.

MAGGIE: I'm nineteen, and I guess I realized that I was gay or had gay tendencies when I was around fifteen. I went the whole route: psychiatric treatment because I thought I was really sick. That's what people said about gay people—they were sick. Finally, I knew I couldn't take it any more. I couldn't change, it was impossible, and I didn't want to. So I said to myself: "Okay, if I'm gay, then I'm going to be gay and enjoy it. Forget society: Forget what they say about me and how I'm supposed to act!" So, I came to Gay Activists Alliance and I became more and more involved in the movement. Now I'm on the speakers bureau, and I go out and speak to groups because I can't stand bigotry. I feel like somebody.

How has the reception been?

MAGGIE: Pretty good on the whole. The last engagement I was on a woman said, "But you're only nineteen; how can you decide that you want to be gay? How can you make that decision? How can you decide you're gay? How can you know a thing like that at nineteen?" Well, I just looked at her and I said, "You told me you had a daughter who is nineteen. Do you say to her that she doesn't know that she wants to be straight? Do you say to her wait and see if you may not like women—because you can't possibly decide now if you like men." I told her she was being bigoted when she said to me that I should wait to see if I liked men, and not saying to her daughter to wait and see if she might like women.

POLLY: Oh, why don't you just tell them to stop that crap.

MAGGIE: What I told her was that she wasn't reaching me at

all. I am nineteen, and that is nearly a quarter of my life that I haven't been doing what I wanted to do. I'm not wasting any more time sitting in a closet.

What general age group do you have in the movement?

DORIS: There's total coverage. I was thirty when I joined just a few years ago. There are women who are thirty and just "coming out"—going to the Sunday afternoon Lesbian socials. And there are women who are fifty and sixty—and a lot of them have come up to me and thanked me for the opportunity to come there and be honest. I'm sure Maggie isn't the youngest at nineteen, either.

POLLY: No, in fact, I know one of the fellows who is only fourteen.

How do you feel about the charge that gays proselytize—and if gay was accepted openly, people would be concerned for their children; they wouldn't want their sons and daughters exposed to gays because of course the gays would try to convert them.

CLAUDIA: I like the answer that someone else gave to that question. She said, "Both my parents were straight—but look what happened to me. It didn't work on me."

(General laughter)

DORIS: People with gay tendencies will eventually be gay—no matter how long it takes them. By the same token gays will always be gay in their heads. As for the movement—how it influences them and influences them very much is that they "come out" proud instead of guilty. They are willing to accept their love feelings, and from that they are able to explore and develop themselves instead of becoming very warped from the pressure they find—society's pressure. I think at long last people can say, "I don't really give a damn! If I lose my job, I'll fight it out. If I lose a friend, that's too bad. In that sense there is a great deal of influence in terms of the movement. But no one can be influenced sexually.

> **Do you feel that anyone who isn't gay is to be distrusted? That the society of being gay is all that's important and the rest of the world is separate from you?**

CLAUDIA: I strongly feel that whatever one is, is their own business. Unless someone is in love with me, and I can't respond; then maybe I'll tell them to forget it, I'm not available. Or if I'm available, I encourage them to come on stronger.

POLLY: I think people should be honest with each other.

CLAUDIA: Being in the gay movement, I've found that because you're standing up as a Lesbian, you're more subjected to curiosity and insult. People feel that they can come up to you and say, "I'd like to know this or that." They come on as though they're sympathetic. In Albany when I was lobbying last year, a guy was just getting turned on to my life style. He was really getting a hard-on because I was telling him about things that I thought he was interested in because I thought he was gay, or trying to be gay and maybe still in the closet. When I realized he was not sincere, I really got angry. I was really violent, and if I'd had my judo lessons then, he'd have gotten an example of it. It's really disgusting when someone is getting a charge out of your love life ... and for the wrong reasons.

Do you find that you're more attractive to a hetero-sexual man because you are a Lesbian?

CLAUDIA: You mean that I became more attractive to him because I was gay?

Yes.

CLAUDIA: Yes, I think so. When I first realized that I was really in love with a gay woman, I was not aware of the guilt and everything like that, I was simply in love—and I told everybody. A lot of straight men I knew were very turned on who hadn't been before. They said they wanted to convert me: "All I needed was a good lay from a perfect stud to change." And even at the GAA deorientation meeting that I went to, there was a man who came over to my lover and I and said that he wanted to know Lesbians. I said that I thought that was nice. Then he went on to say that he wanted to *make it* with Lesbians. I said, "If somebody wants to make it with you, they're bisexual or something, and you'd better forget it and get out of here. We don't want to hear from you." He went over then and approached another Lesbian. I don't know what he said to her, or what she told him, but he left the meeting very fast. I could tell from her anger that he must have said the same thing to her.

POLLY: The most annoying are the ones that want to get into threesomes—

CLAUDIA: Well, that's what this man wanted. That's what I was trying to say.

MAGGIE: We got some very beautiful phone calls here at the Firehouse, too—(*General laughter*). There are some *sick* people in the world, and they're not gays. You'd pick up the phone and they'd say, "Is this the Gay Activists Alliance?"

We would say yes. Then they'd say, "Am I speaking to a gay person?" We'd say yes. Then they'd make some nasty obscene cracks—and sit back and enjoy themselves at our expense. It is very annoying.

DORIS: Homosexuals have been used in pornography for so long I guess we should assume it's going to happen. It's the whole myth of lesbianism: the myth that it's something out of this world, somehow much better than something else sexually; or so different or so exotic that we are continually getting straight men who put you through things like that. I assume they're straight anyway. There should be a whole little breed of them; I mean they're like *Peeping Toms*. There should be a name for them.

CLAUDIA: And, I mean it really hurts sometimes, it hurts deep. I was very upset in Albany when that guy came up to me— and he was very young. I felt he was trailing after us because he was gay, and maybe more in the closet than the rest of us there, who were being very public. He was asking questions, too, and they weren't the obvious sexual things— so I wasn't clued in to his motive right away. But then, I never am.

(General laughter)

POLLY: I think that's just as well.

CLAUDIA: (*In a light vein*) Yeah, I haven't become hardened by it—you know, like suspecting men. And I'm not worried that somebody is straight, or somebody is bisexual, or somebody is gay, or whatever. Some of my best friends are straight. (*General laughter*) If they talk honestly with me I can talk honestly with them.

Do you think the younger generation has a very much different attitude toward all sexual practices? They seem to accept people for whatever they are,

and don't separate their sexual life from their general acceptance as a nice person.

DORIS: I think so. I think that more younger people just accept that we all have a shared sexuality, and what anyone does with that is entirely their business. And I feel very sorry for say the teen-agers who for whatever reasons—whether it's for practical reasons, because of the way they were brought up, whatever—don't feel that way. If they don't there is going to be a terrible division within that age group. Total nonunderstanding. Hopefully there will be very few.

CLAUDIA: I'm twenty-five and I didn't feel the oppression, or anything like that. Maybe I wasn't brought up with it strongly enough stressed: the antihomosexual thing. Although I was Catholic and I went to parochial schools. I was raised a "good Catholic," you know, and for a while I think I was a "good Catholic." I considered myself to be. I knew I never wanted to be a nun, but I thought I was doing everything right until I hit my teens. Then it suddenly hit me that Catholicism was totally ridiculous and irrelevant. I had a lot of ideas that just didn't coincide with Catholicism.

Such as?

CLAUDIA: Well, for one thing, I felt attracted to women, and I didn't see anything wrong with that. It was a good feeling, and I just couldn't see anything wrong with loving. In the beginning, however, it was a bigger trip for me to live with a black woman than it was to be living with a woman rather than a man. Then there was my family. Finally I told them—and they know now that I'm living with a Lesbian. They totally accept her; of course, it helps a lot that she's a Catholic. We have a "good" Catholic home. (*General laughter*) Of course, if I was living with a black man or a Jewish man, oh wow! But a woman who was Catholic, that was all right!

Do you find any conflict between your Catholicism and your homosexuality?

CLAUDIA: Oh no! I don't believe in Catholicism any more. But as I said before, that's how I was brought up, but when I got old enough to think for myself, I found I didn't agree with it, and didn't believe what I'd been told.

Perhaps this question is not important to you all where you are now, but I think it is important to a lot of people who haven't yet reached where you are, and are still confused about themselves. I also think it important to heterosexuals who perhaps have a misconception of homosexuality. What do you feel contributed to your being homosexual; what brought about your development as a homosexual?

POLLY: Wow, you really hit a sore spot! (*General laughter*) I mean that's a heavy! We could just turn around and say what made a heterosexual turn into a heterosexual? We all develop into something, and we don't sit down and try to analyze how a person became heterosexual, and I'm very much against trying to analyze why I became homosexual. Everybody became something, and the fact that I'm homosexual is irrelevant.

DORIS: It is, sadly, part of the fact that because of society we all have to be *something*—

That's the point, that *something*—

POLLY: No, you've got the question in the wrong form.

Then what is the right form?

POLLY: Everybody *is* something—why did we choose to recognize ourselves?

(*Applause*)

CLAUDIA: Right on!

Then why did you make a choice?

POLLY: Because I love women.

CLAUDIA: I didn't choose it—

POLLY: No, it's a whole different perspective. What's this nonsense of saying everybody is heterosexual? It just isn't so. It has never been so, and the question is, Why did we recognize ourselves? This is the point of departure and what happens is you recognize yourself when you get sick of the bullshit!

DORIS: Some people will not accept lies at the age of twelve, and some will not accept lies at the age of fifty, and some will always accept lies. But it still gets back to this thing: there is more than one narrow way to be. I don't think there are very many people who could honestly say that they are easily what we call bisexual. But I'm really talking about more of a head thing—more what's in your head than the act of having sexual acts between men and women. I mean, you don't do what you like—but I think that just as there are homophobic heterosexuals, there are homophobic homosexuals, or homosexuals who cannot stand the thought of, say, a Lesbian having sex with a man. She doesn't have to bring it home to herself—and she could not accept another Lesbian who does. That's what I mean about sexuality in your head. I think the time will come where there will be freedom to allow each other to exist in our total sexuality. Claudia used the word "choose"—she said she didn't choose it, and I agree with her. There is no choice to be made; the impulses are overwhelming; the drive is overwhelming. Some people are overwhelmed and commit themselves to a way of life—and some people are overwhelmed and commit suicide. The point is, an adult should be able to set up his or her relationship the way she wants to, and deal with it adultly. The only thing that there's ever conflict in . . . is if you don't want to deal with a man sexually. Usually his initial reaction is to try and make you feel very apologetic. Well, what have you done? You've simply said no to the power structure that we have lived with since we were born. Now, when a woman can respect herself, and her own decisions, and her own strengths, then she will immediately recognize that she can say no—and then, as Polly said, if he gives her a hard time, it's his problem, not hers.

Are there questions which I haven't asked which you consider important?

DORIS: Women have really got to start loving each other—
CLAUDIA: I don't fight for that. I'll fight for *people* to start loving one another. In my class my little boys need just as much love as the little girls. And it's just as hateful and harmful to make them have to be bullies, and not cry when they're hurt, and all that, as it is to always be pampering little girls when they're hurt.
DORIS: But the one difference I see is really concerning that word *woman*. I don't think it is unusual to find a man who

comes to his sexuality, or comes into his manhood, with a certain amount of respect for himself—for his mind, his body, or his potential as an American male. I do find this lacking in women—and I do find that as they hate other women, it is to the extent that they hate themselves, and have been taught to hate themselves. Men's learned aggressiveness, I think, is very negative, and it hurts us all. Women's learned passivity hurts us all, but the difference is that women don't have the power to gain ground past the negatives that they've been taught whereas men do. All I wish is—as women are getting their consciousness raised, and working very hard at it—that they will eventually beat the struggle. Men aren't working on their consciousness. The way women react to the threats that they feel will be interesting—it will be interesting to see what those threats are . . . and how they will come out. It will be definite reactions, of that I am certain.

Chapter 9

Lesbian Mothers

A group session with Lesbian mothers ranging in ages from twenty to fifty, representing a cross section of educational and socioeconomical levels. The women were participants in group therapy for lesbian mothers which met weekly with therapist Bernice Goodman, who is also associated with the Institute for Human Identity in New York. Most were accompanied by their lovers, who felt that they had something to gain from group therapy inasmuch as they too were part of the *family* situation and directly related to the child, or children, in that sense—living in a family atmosphere. The session was conducted on June 19, 1972, in the therapist's office.

FRANCES: (*Mother of two*) I was homosexual back in the fifties, before all the movements started and everything, and I found that particular life style very difficult for me then. So I got married and had a child, then another. I was married for twelve or thirteen years before I got divorced. I had two children while I was married, and now I am again living as a homosexual with a lover and my two children.

My lover has one child also. And I have to deal with the fact that my children are going to come up against many prejudices. My oldest child, who is going to be ten years old, is fully aware that my friend and I are living together, and have a relationship, but he doesn't want anyone else outside of the house to know because of fear of reprisals.

What exactly does he fear?

FRANCES: I don't know what kind of fears or fantasies they have other than the general ones of being ostracized, being made fun of; being different and having the whole neighborhood come down on us. Anything in our house, however, goes; that's perfectly all right. My lover and I can kiss each other and hold each other. Everybody dances in the living room, and we can fight with each other, you know, and the kids take sides, and they don't take sides, and it's the same kind of thing—it's no different than any other relationship, I guess. But when we get outside, my son doesn't allow me to put my arm around my lover; he doesn't allow me to show her any particular attention, as I would at home. He even anticipates that I am going to do it. Like in a restaurant, or something, he says, "Not here, not here, *they* won't understand." *They* are those people around us that are not accepting of this relationship that he at ten already knows. It is something that he does not want to deal with and it is bigger than him.

What do you mean, he doesn't *allow* it?

FRANCES: Well, he has a double set of standards, it seems. I mean not he, but as a result of what he feels—like, in the house it's fine. For example, if my lover and I have a fight, he's apt to say, "Well, are you going to kiss and make up?" and things like that, the way any child might say to its parents. But, if we're out in public—no such thing.

I'm interested in the phrase "He doesn't allow." Who is the parent—you or your son?

FRANCES: Well, I'm the parent, but— Well, you see, what is not apparent is how I feel about what kind of trip I'm going to put him through if I push it.

ELEANOR: (*Her lover, mother of one*) What about the sign on the phone pole saying *This Way To Women's Lib?*

FRANCES: Well, you see, women's lib to him is something else. I mean my car is plastered with signs about abortion appeals things, and *Sisterhood Is Powerful,* and all kinds of things, and I have a woman's lib T-shirt I wear. I live in a suburban neighborhood, and of course they can't help but see that a lot of women are walking in and out of my house for one meeting or another, at any given time or another, and the house is always being visited by women—in and out. Woman's liberation doesn't go too big there—and so the kids got together and they put up a sign on a tree saying *This Way To Libby Land* or something. I think my son was very relieved that it didn't say anything else. You see, woman's lib is perfectly acceptable to him, and he can't understand how they can't even accept Woman's Lib. You see, *that* he can fight for, because he understands that women are supposed to get equal pay for equal work and all that, and he thinks to object to that is pretty foolish. But somehow the homosexuality part of it, he feels would be totally unacceptable around there. And he has a tremendous fear of it, but then he has tremendous fears anyway. The other child just says, "I don't understand this business—two women living together,

it doesn't make any sense! Period!" He just goes through life
that way—but then he's only seven. He verbalized that—two
women aren't supposed to live together—but I don't know
that that's *his* head. I'm sure it's not his head. Well, I have
a family, I'm very fortunate, and they are aware of the situation, and as a result we don't get to see each other too often.
But we do speak to one another, and they do have a lot to do
with my children. There have been situations and conditions
where they have had "the head"—I mean, my oldest had
"the head" with my aunt right in front of me one day. She
was saying that my relationship is "sick," and he's saying,
"What's so sick about two people loving each other?" and
she tells him that his psychologist is a quack, and he says
back to her, "I don't have to sit here and be insulted"—
and they went on. And this was a ten-year-old, and my aunt
is in her fifties, and I just didn't have anything to say because I thought the kid was doing pretty well by himself.
Anything I would have said would probably have loused it
up anyway. But, I was very surprised to hear some of the
things—and yet, I understand how difficult it is for him.
Intellectually, I think he understands because he has seen
that I have with my lover a better relationship than I had
with his father. But by the same token he knows that there
are certain pressures that are going to be brought to bear.
That's what he fears; I don't know how realistic his fears are,
but they are there, and I haven't found a way to push him
into it. I think I'm afraid, too; I mean, I'm going to be
honest. I think I'm afraid—but not for me, me I'll take the
whole world on—but when my kids are involved— Well,
you lose some control.

**Why did you choose to make it known to your
children—in a demonstrative sense—your relationship? Did you want to be honest with them? Could**

> you not have conducted the demonstrative part of
> your relationship in private with your lover?

FRANCES: I think being honest is the only way I could have done it.

DONNA: (*Mother of six*) My children have never known the meaning of a closed door.

FRANCES: Yeah. I had been going to a psychologist at the time I first met Eleanor, my lover, and I said to him, "I want to live with this woman, and I really don't know what to do about the children." And he said, "Well, children are like anyone else; they need certain things to have them grow—and one is love and consideration and good food and shelter. If you can provide this then what difference does it make who is in the house?" It made a lot of sense to me, and I said, "Yes, why not?" Then I began to think about the old days in terms of prejudice. Children aren't brought up to—I mean, they don't understand what a person is, or what a Jew is; they just see these people and somebody else has to get to them and tell them this. Maybe I have to get to my kids first, and that's the way I felt about it, and that's why I have been open with them.

ELEANOR: My son is five, and he has no feelings about it. He doesn't verbalize about two women together because, well—I left my husband when he was three, and I went into a relationship with a woman. I was very open; I never wanted to be dishonest with him. He just accepts it as another part of life. He's at an age where you can accept new things. So, when I moved with Frances here, it seemed fine. He has never verbalized anything about two women living together. That's just as cool to him as a man and a woman being together.

GEORGETTE: But he isn't old enough to understand sex yet.

FRANCES: Yeah, but my seven-year-old isn't old enough to understand prejudice either.

ELEANOR: Yeah, but I mean I don't hide—even with Frances' older one, the ten-year-old. I have a book which shows reproduction; it explains reproduction from beginning to end. It's a fantastic book, and my five-year-old also sees the book. Now, the older one understands that it takes a man and a woman to reproduce, but that two people of the same sex can love—and give love to each other, and affection, physical affection. I think that my son will grow up with that acceptance too.

HENRIETTA: I disagree fundamentally with the idea that a five-year-old is not old enough to understand sex; they get the vibes. And if they're good vibes, great.

ELEANOR: I don't think he'll ever have any bad feelings about it. It's as good as any other relationship.

You don't think when he really hits the street, he will come under the influence of his peers?

ELEANOR: I think he will be stronger—or strong enough to take it because he has known it since he was so young—not like Frances's ten-year-old. I don't think the fear will be there in him as it is in the ten-year-old. I think he might fight back first.

To what extent do you think Frances's ten-year-old will affect your five-year-old?

FRANCES: Very much so—they do already. The little five-year-old patterns himself after my two bigger ones. And he constantly follows my seven-year-old around—that's his hero. Once they get out there in the street, with their peers—and each child brings into the street the attitudes of their own homes—they're going to find an overwhelming attitude that is not in their own homes. How do they deal with it?

Do you feel you can fortify your son with enough love and security to sustain him? In other words, can he feel secure enough in his home life that when he hits the street and a kid picks on him about his mother and her lover—or however they put it—can he feel secure, even perhaps superior, and reply, like, "Hey, man, you just don't understand." Can he be helped to feel very special because of his home life?

FRANCES: Well, part of my feeling about what you just said is, yeah—you're not living in it and you don't have to take the knocks for it. And you're also not around when this kid is getting kicked around. It's a pretty rough feeling to know that your kids can go out in the street and get the shit kicked out of them because of what you are. And you know it's the bastards out there, and they're all fucked up, and it's not really you—and that's intellectually. But maybe there's a little bit of what you say—you feel like you're different and you know that you're different—and it's a tough damn grind anyway, and why are you putting this trip on this kid to go out and carry this kind of load for you?

Then why are you?

(*General group laughter and agreement with question*)
FRANCES: Well, it's a two-part thing. I feel, you know, I'm angry at them for being the pricks that they are, and they are

and I know it, and see it every day. But, man, I'm not perfect.

You deserve a life of your own?

FRANCES: Right, and I want it. And this relationship is what I want. Maybe I'm going to have to tell my kid to go out there and get the shit kicked out of him twice—one for being Jewish and one for being the kid of a Lesbian. For me it was the same. I grew up where I was the only Jew in a Negro neighborhood, and it wasn't too good. It was a little rough for me, but I never really felt it was so terrible that I was Jewish. I just didn't understand why I was getting hit because I was Jewish. It just didn't make sense to me. In a way, maybe I'm asking him to do the same—but I'm having a heavy guilt trip, you know, with the kid, and I have to admit that it's something I've got a problem with. That's why I'm here in this group.

ELEANOR: God! She said more about her feelings now than she's ever said in therapy sessions.

FRANCES: I don't see what— Oh, well, I don't know what I said.

ELEANOR: About your guilt over the kid.

FRANCES: I thought it was assumed that we all sitting in this room—we all certainly had all degrees of guilt about being gay.

ANNA: I don't feel that.

ELEANOR: I don't either.

Why are you so guilty about being gay?

FRANCES: Personally I don't feel it for myself—if it was just me it wouldn't make that much of a difference—but in conjunction with me the attitude of my children and what's going to happen to them . . . I do feel like I'm putting a bad trip on them—

BETH: I feel if you felt good about yourself then you wouldn't feel that you were putting any trip on your kids. I think if you really felt good about what you were doing, and you knew that it was good, then you wouldn't feel that you were putting anything bad on your kids.

THERAPIST: You don't feel the same about the fact that he's Jewish. You had nothing to say about that fact. But that you're a Lesbian—it is a different feeling. Part of that is your own projection.

FRANCES: Well, I don't know, I don't know. I live in a Jewish neighborhood, so you know, what's the problem? Maybe I'm different—but he's not different. Maybe I would worry as much about that if I was living in a neighborhood where I felt they might chase his ass because he was Jewish; I might still have the same feeling about that.

BETH: But you can't do anything more about his Jewishness than you can do about your homosexuality.

FRANCES: No. Well, when I see, when I talk to my son, I say look, that's the way it is. I can't push him to accept something he's not ready to accept either.

BETH: No, but if you accepted it and you were demonstrative outside in the street, and you accepted that, then he might accept that also.

ELEANOR: Yeah, I think he is picking up a lot of your own guilt about yourself.

BETH: You go along with him mostly, I feel, because you also agree with him.

FRANCES: But I also forget at times, and I'm in a restaurant and I go to Eleanor—

ELEANOR: Yeah, but he says stop and you stop.

ANNA: He's your conscience. He's not only your son but he's your conscience, as well.

ELEANOR: Yeah, but honey, when he says stop, you stop!

FRANCES: Yeah, you're right.

ELEANOR: You listen to *him*. When I say—all right, I mean, I get a little bit perturbed about it. And when you say everybody has guilt. I don't feel one iota of guilt about being gay and bringing Tom up. I think it is going to be fine.

DONNA: That's impossible.

FRANCES: That's ridiculous. I mean you give me this bullshit. Why do you tell me you want to move out of the neighborhood because "Archie Bunker" lives up the street?

ELEANOR: Because he's sick—

(General laughter from the group)

DONNA: But there's one in every neighborhood.

But the Archie Bunkers don't make you any sicker, do they?

FRANCES: No, they don't.

ELEANOR: I've been wanting to move for a lot of reasons—not having to do with my being gay.

FRANCES: Yeah, well, Archie Bunker lives up the street and she's about to pick up and leave—I mean, not really leave but—

ELEANOR: And you're about to go up and break his leg.

DONNA: *(Mother of six)* Listen, Frances, I mean, they're everywhere. He's our school principal.

(General laughter from the group)

What do you do in school—I mean, about school?

DONNA: Well, Cleo wrote some notes for the children last week—

This is your daughter?

> (*General laughter from the group*)

DONNA: No, it's my lover with whom I live.

> (*More laughter*)

DONNA: I was sick in bed with tonsillitis, so she wrote the notes and signed her name.

CLEO: Sure I wrote the notes, and excused them for not being there, and I signed my name.

DONNA: No one at school ever says anything—they all seem to know who Cleo is. I mean, you know, I ran into this friend of mine when I was with Cleo, and my friend, she's straight, said, "Oh, so you're Cleo!" So, I'm dying of curiosity of what the children are saying—and what the other children are saying to their parents . . . I don't know what's going on.

FRANCES: I know what my kids say.

DONNA: Well, what?

FRANCES: He's saying well, you're his aunt (*indicating her lover Eleanor*).

ELEANOR: Oh, yeah.

FRANCES: I'm saying, don't tell him anything different.

DONNA: It's like mommy's honey—

CLEO: Yeah.

DONNA: It's cute, tell them the story, honey.

CLEO: Well, they wanted to fix the washing machine, so they called to talk to Donna, my lover, and her oldest daughter answered the phone and said, "Well, mommy's not home." And he said, "Well, is there any adult in the house?" And she said, "Yes, Mommy's honey" . . . and I picked up the phone (*general laughter*), and I just about floored the guy.

Did he fix your washing machine?

DONNA: He fixed the washing machine.
CLEO: He came right over—he couldn't wait to see!

A lot of younger people I've talked with say that they feel the situation is very much different now with, say, the college kids than it was in the forties or fifties, or even five years ago. They say we don't feel that oppression, we don't hear that. It's a whole different generation with a whole different attitude. Do you think this is true?

BETH: Well, you're not really dealing with that generation. Most of the people who are in power, in control, are the ones from the forties and fifties.

But these children are going to be—a few years hence—the younger generation now that's saying, "Look, people love each other and they're together, and we don't care what your life style is."

BETH: Yeah, that may be very cool, but—
FRANCES: They don't live on my block.
GEORGETTE: They don't live in my neighborhood either.
DONNA: Yeah, but they're also saying one thing in a group, but they're expressing a lot of fears at the other times. My baby-sitter is eighteen years old and she has, or was, for some reason very, very curious, about homosexuality—enough to do some reading. Well, she came up with all the stereotyped answers. I don't think that she has the same

prejudice herself but she has been fed that same prejudice.

THERAPIST: I think there is another point too. And that is even with the college kids, you're dealing with the adult, two adults. The problem is that the family style in our country is still a nuclear family; it's man/woman and two and a half children. I think the other chance is that that is changing, but at the moment that is the accepted family pattern, and everybody in here is saying or living another pattern that is very threatening.

The question I'm asking—and I agree with you—but the question I'm asking is, The children that you, all of you in this room, are bringing up now, are you going to accept that yourselves, and allow them to accept it and perpetrate it?

FRANCES: No! I'll sure as hell try to see to that. But if the kid has the fear, I can't just say you can't have the fear, kid—let the fear go away because it's not real. I mean, he's got it! You know, I have to deal with that fear—and I have to somehow help him to work that out. And baby, that ain't going to happen overnight!

GEORGETTE: (*Mother of five*) But it's the fault of your own perception of your fear in a situation—

FRANCES: Yeah, but I'm less fearful now than I've ever been.

GEORGETTE: Fine.

FRANCES: And like I said, time is a great healer, and I think it is not going to happen, you know, tomorrow.

GEORGETTE: I think there is a difference among younger kids—and it also depends on what they pick up from you.

BETH: You know what's very interesting? We have a baby-sitter—I mean, my lover has the baby-sitter, I don't.

(*Laughter*)

ANNA: (*Jokingly*) I'm just along for the ride.

(*Laughter*)

DONNA: Don't mistake me for a mother, huh?

(*More laughter*)

BETH: Yeah, okay! But I mean we had this baby-sitter. We had his brother first, and he's orthodox Jewish. You can compare it to a priest—I mean, same thing. And he had his older brother coming over—and we had gay signs hanging every place, and I've been there since Anna's son has been a year old, and he knows practically nothing of men. He knows that I'm his Beth—that's who I am. We're the family: Mommy, Beth and him. And we had this baby-sitter and he was a college kid and he didn't say anything, but I didn't expect him to because he was a little older. But then we got his brother for a baby-sitter, and then all of a sudden we found their sister coming up, who was around ten or eleven years old. And I mean, she accepts it.

ANNA: Well, I don't even know if they even notice.

BETH: Even if they don't notice anything else, I'm sure that they notice that it's a strange thing for a woman with a child to have a roommate. I mean, it is not a usual thing. I mean, you know—

THERAPIST: You know what?

ELEANOR: (*Imitating "butch" type*) I mean what you look like, Beth—

BETH: Yeah, sure, the way I look—they call me a masculine nickname and all—but so what! What I'm saying is the younger sister is just very accepting of the whole thing. And that is—I mean, especially in an orthodox Jewish family— that's really wild! I mean, I would expect somebody who is a little bit more "with it" to understand, but as far as I can see, the people in the building understand, too.

ANNA: Yeah, and my son is taken care of by welfare. My caseworker seems to understand—and my lover and I have gone to see the caseworker together, as a family, and we discussed the child as a family, and there haven't been any problems there. But I worry that someone may try to cause problems, or try to get my child away from me as being an unfit mother or something like that—those are my own fears.

You mean the Welfare Department?

ANNA: Yeah, the Welfare Department or the child's father, or anybody.

GEORGETTE: Well, you live in an apartment and you probably have a lot more younger people in an apartment than we do out in the suburbs.

BETH: Yeah, but it's a whole 'nother thing with the kids. I went to pick up Don and this eight-year-old girl came over and said, "Are you Don's father?" And I said no. And then she walked away, and then she came back and she said, "Are you Don's mother?" And I said no, and then she said, "Then how are you related to Don?" So then I said, "I'm related to him because I love him." And she sort of didn't like the answer because it didn't fit into any role, but she had to accept it and then she walked away—and I think that's the way to deal with it, you know.

HENRIETTA: That's beautiful.

BETH: Yes. But like strange things happen in our building—like these old men come up and they say weird things to him. Like one day a guy came over to me and I was waiting for Anna, who went up to get something. And Don is very attached to me like I am his other parent—like, I've been living with him like for three fourths of his life, and the guy wanted to take me away. And he said, "Look, I'm taking Beth away"—putting Don on—and Don got very upset. And he said to me, "Well, he's not your son—did you give birth to him?" I said, "No—did you give birth to your son?" And so he had to stop at that.

(Laughter)

BETH: I mean they don't understand this—because I didn't have a sexual relation that made this little person, then I shouldn't have any feelings toward him, and I do.

Have any of you had any personal experiences with children that you'd like to talk about?

DONNA: Well, I've been thinking of moving, and a neighbor—a friend of mine—is aware of the school . . . and the needs of my children. This friend said to us last night—I mean, we were talking of the pros and cons of moving out of where I live now—and she said, "Well, a big plus we have in this neighborhood is the fact that the neighborhood does accept your relationship with Cleo."

This is a straight person?

DONNA: Yeah, a friend of my father—everybody knows.

FRANCES: If this happened in my neighborhood a bomb would go off . . . and you live less than a fourth of a mile away from me.

Where do you live?

ANNA: I live in New Jersey.

DONNA: And you know something—I don't know why—the block is not unprejudiced or whatever, but for some unknown reason—

CLEO: The only prejudice is from the older people—and even then it's tolerant.

ANNA: Listen, my aunt bought a new dress, and Cleo and I were over there returning my mother's car. My son came out and said "Cleo, Aunt Ruth wants to see you"—and Cleo was all afraid. What did they have in mind? But it was very simple: she had bought a new dress and she wanted to show it to Cleo. This is my mother's sister, who is seventy years old.

FRANCES: Well, you're doing great—because I can't even get my mother to talk to Eleanor on the phone. She doesn't even want to have her around! She doesn't even want to know from it, you know—out of sight, out of mind. She doesn't even want to hear about it.

ELEANOR: But she's pretty nice to me.

BETH: My mother isn't even a grandmother, and she wants them to come around. At least Anna's Jewish, right, and my mother's Jewish, so at least there's something there. Somehow, in her mind she has a little grandchild . . . so it's not all a total loss that she had me.

DONNA: Yeah, my mother would be so much happier if she accepted the children as her own grandchildren—all six of them.

Why did you have so many children?

(General laughter)

BETH: That's a right-on question.
CLEO: *I* had nothing to do with it.

(More laughter)

DONNA: Well, I was married then—
CLEO: And she wasn't Catholic.

Did you ever hear of contraception?

(*Laughter*)

DONNA: Very vague kind of thing—it didn't apply to me because I thought I wouldn't get pregnant.

Well, weren't the first three times enough to tell you something?

(*Laughter*)

DONNA: I changed methods.
BETH: Why did you have six children?
ELEANOR: Do you know why?
CLEO: She doesn't know.

Are you glad you had them?

DONNA: On sunny days when they can go out and play, yes—on rainy days like yesterday, no.

(*Laughter and agreement*)

Can we get back to the point—why did you have six children?

DONNA: To try to make myself fit in; to fence myself in; to make myself normal and extra-normal, and the super-mother, and—

Where did you get those ideas?

DONNA: My own mother.
ELEANOR: Did you have gay feelings before?

DONNA: No, I don't think so.

FRANCES: No?

ANNA: Did you have any feelings before?

DONNA: Not that I let myself be aware of.

GEORGETTE: You just did what somebody expected you to do?

DONNA: Yeah, and then went them one even better.

> You mean you outdid what you were supposed to do?

DONNA: Right.

> Why did you suddenly change?

DONNA: I don't know. I mean, I knew I was very unhappy, and I tried to start listening to myself and doing what *I* wanted to do—not what normal mothers do.

> Do you feel that you are abnormal?

DONNA: I don't play mah-jong, that's abnormal.

> (*General laughter*)

FRANCES: I played mah-jong—it didn't help.

> (*More laughter*)

> Do you feel now that you're abnormal?

DONNA: Well, I've always felt that I was abnormal.

> When you were married and having children, did you feel abnormal?

DONNA: Yeah.

Why?

DONNA: Because I wasn't happy to sit home, I wasn't happy to just—you know—

Do you resent your children?

DONNA: Sure.

Does anyone else here resent their children?

(*All answer a strong affirmative; all laugh meaningfully*)
THERAPIST: We recently had a whole session on that subject.

Do you think it's your fault, or the man you were married to, or the system or what—that you had them, and you now resent them?

FRANCES: I think part of it is that children are just resentful little things sometimes—because they're just like a very heavy load to carry around. And to carry both the children and this life style—and the life that we have to go through— it's just a heavy thing, and so we just tend to resent.

BETH: I find that people who don't have children don't really know what it's like. I mean we have friends who say, "Well, why don't you back-pack them and take them camping on a safari to the middle of the mountains?" A three-year-old who is being toilet trained, you can't do this with.

ANNA: I mean they think it's not so hard. We have neighbors upstairs—they're a straight couple—and we're very, very friendly with them; in fact, I think they're just about our best friends. We see them very often. They don't have any kids, so they've sort of adopted Don. And they say, "You know, my friend takes hers along with her"—but they don't understand how hard it is.

BETH: Especially to be accepted in places.

ANNA: Our gay friends have more of a problem accepting—the ones that don't have any children. They can't accept that we can't just pick up and go running around. Our straight friends seem to understand it more because they seem to have been around children more, taken care of them and so forth.

HENRIETTA: (*Mother of two children*) I sort of wanted to speak to that too. I feel that there are three communities: there's the place you live; your own family; and there's the gay community. I find much the most acceptance in the first —the straight community with which I live. I live in Manhattan, and there are a lot of gay people in the block, just to begin with. I don't have a lover; I'm not living with anybody at the moment. Although I do share an apartment with a woman who is straight and has a child. But it's, like, I mean, there isn't a sense of censure there. With my mother, who is very old, I don't think I could talk to her about it. I may be able to, I don't know, but my one conversation with her about gayness occurred when I was a senior in high school, and I asked her whether one of the teachers was the lover of another teacher—and they were both women—and she said, "Oh, of course not, they're both intelligent women."

FRANCES: Oh wow!

(*Reaction and laughter of disbelief from the group*)

HENRIETTA: On the other hand, I've been able to talk to two of my sisters a little bit around the subject. One of them seemed sympathetic—I didn't go into it a lot, I just said that I had had a homosexual experience. She didn't fall on the floor. They've been very supportive during my current crisis. (*She was in the midst of a difficult divorce action.*) But the third community, the gay community, I've had a great deal of trouble with . . . and I finally just recently left a consciousness-raising group—a gay consciousness-raising group—I'd been in for a year.

(*Entire group cheers her for having left the group*)

FRANCES: Why did you leave?

HENRIETTA: Because they could not relate to the reality problems I had with the divorce and with the children. They don't come around on Saturdays and say, "Let's all go to the park and throw a ball around," you know. I mean, they just aren't there. They understand why I can't go out at night with them—and socialize and so on—very often, but they don't care either. But I was with them for a year, and I love them very much, and I resent this tremendously, just tremendously.

You, I take it, had homosexual affairs before you were married?

HENRIETTA: No.

Did you feel inclinations?

HENRIETTA: Not consciously, not so that I knew what it was about.

Did it happen while you were married?

HENRIETTA: It happened just over a year ago.

Why?

HENRIETTA: The marriage had been very much bankrupt, I would say for about four years. My eleventh anniversary was the last. There had been difficulties in communication before that, but there was a progressive shutting out. And I fell very deeply in love with a woman, and I acted on it.

Are you glad?

HENRIETTA: I didn't make a very good choice. I was very much rejected by her. I am now reconsidering my gayness. If I've lived this long without it, and it causes me this much fear, such as I'm going through now—with harassment from my husband—I wonder if it is worth it? And yet it is very important to me, and I don't repudiate it. It's just that I don't know whether or not I can.

What will you do?

HENRIETTA: I don't know if I have a choice. This is one of the things I meant when I said I can't identify with me, I can't find out who I am. This is one of the things.

I repeat, what will you do?

HENRIETTA: I don't know.

Do you feel at this stage that you'd like to try a relationship with a man again?

HENRIETTA: Yes, but not just any man. Just as I wouldn't relate to just any woman. I keep saying I'm in to human beings, and that's where I think I am. But this point of view, at the moment, is dominated by fear.

Fear of what, exactly?

HENRIETTA: Fear that if my divorce came to a court battle we might both lose the children. He's gay too.

He is gay too?

HENRIETTA: Yes.

Did you know this when you married him?

HENRIETTA: No.

When did you find out about him?

HENRIETTA: When I told him that I'd come out.

So he wants the children, and you're afraid he'll take them away from you?

HENRIETTA: He can't take them away, and he doesn't even want them.

It seems that he has a problem too?

HENRIETTA: He has a tremendous problem. But if he chose to sling garbage, he could get them taken away from both of us.

It is a vindictive thing—so long as you don't have them, it suits him?

HENRIETTA: I don't know, but I'm afraid.

You have a big thing set up for yourself, don't you?

HENRIETTA: What are you saying?

It seems that the problem is too big. It's easier to sit there and say *he* will take them away, or *they* will take them away from us. I doubt that. You're obviously a responsible and concerned mother. If it came to a fight, you'd likely get them in any event, but can you live in constant fear of what he might do?

THERAPIST: Some people do—

Of course, I don't know, but I'm asking you, Henrietta, is the fear really realistic?

HENRIETTA: I'm afraid that my choices might be dictated.

You don't think you have recourse—someone like a psychologist helping you with the problem, testifying to your fitness and your love of your children?

HENRIETTA: I think probability is on my side, but I'm still frightened.

GEORGETTE: (*Mother of five children*) I'm not living with any-body right now, and my children don't have the problem of seeing me in a relationship with anybody. I have had people come into the house occasionally, but I don't know how it would really be if I were in a relationship with somebody. I really don't know how much my son knows. He is thirteen. I have Archie Bunker next door, too, but I don't think Archie Bunker knows.

If you had a choice to have your children be either gay or straight, what would you choose?

FRANCES: Are you asking me?

Anybody, everybody—

GEORGETTE: Whatever makes them happy, whatever they are.
(*General agreement*)

FRANCES: I don't feel I can choose for them; I had really bad feelings about my son Larry, bad in the sense that he had these—what I saw as kind of tendencies, and this was when I was into my own thing, too. He has, you know—he has these little schticks which are very feminine. I used to see him do these little things, and I would like say to myself, get out of here, you know—

DONNA: When did you notice that?

FRANCES: Oh, this was years ago.

DONNA: Because I have one child that's like that, and I've noticed it since he was about two or three years old.

FRANCES: Yeah, well anyway, this was like when Larry was about six or seven, and things like that, and I was, you know, really upset about him. And I went to my psychologist, the one I went to before I came here, and he said, "Well, there's nothing you can do about it; just leave him alone. The worst thing you could do about it would be to tell him not to do the things he's doing, because then you're going to drive it underground. If it's going to come out, let it come out; then however you want to deal with it, you can deal with it then." From that point on, I stopped reacting to it. It was almost like the psychologist had said the magic words—my whole concern disappeared. It was almost as if I needed this authority—for someone to say, "Don't worry, stay away from it, don't do anything with it."

ELEANOR: He smoked a cigarette the other day, did you know?

FRANCES: No. Well, I guess he had to find out.

DONNA: My son smoked a cigarette recently, but then he announced that he was going to be a singer and wasn't going to smoke any more.

(*General laughter*)

HENRIETTA: I have two sets of feelings about my children. One is my rhetorical feelings, my idealistic feelings. I want my kids to have maximum choice, that is very important to me. Not only in sexual preference, but anything else. My other set of feelings are, like, I don't have any objections to my daughter being gay, but I do object to my son being gay.

Why?

HENRIETTA: My feeling about this is that from my own experience, and this is only my own experience. My feelings for women are based on love, and from my experience, most, but not all, male homosexuals I know—it seems to me their feelings for men are based on hatred of women. I think that is the fundamental difference. I don't know if I'm right, but I feel it.

You feel the relationship of woman to woman is more constructive than man-to-man feelings?

THERAPIST: She's also saying something more basic. She's saying that she feels one is a constructive, positive relationship, and the other is based on a negative relationship with women —therefore, men choose men. The first love object in the child is its mother. Females, therefore, are automatically in a homosexual position immediately, whereas men are in a heterosexual one and then they shift. I'm also curious whether or not your feeling doesn't have something to do with *your* husband, Henrietta.

To what extent do you feel that your individual guilts and fears are based on church influence upon you and upon society? Do you feel that the church contributed to your guilt feelings?

ELEANOR: Well, the church has certainly affected society, but I was never into religion. I've never gone to a synagogue or a church. I'm an atheist, and my son will just learn. I won't tell him he has to believe in God or in the Bible; I will teach him everything.

What do you mean by everything?

ELEANOR: I will let him see everything—all the different religions. I'm into the Ethical Culture Society, which I think is beautiful.
HENRIETTA: It seems to me that churches exist to support the social order through a system of guilt and reward, and I

think that's how they affect it. I'm not into church at all; I have a very loose Buddhist affiliation, but I don't know what the Buddhist position on homosexuality is.

ELEANOR: They're not negative about it. I know a gay couple that are Buddhist, and they had a Buddhist marriage ceremony.

DONNA: That must be very new.

HENRIETTA: I want to get back to the children question. I don't hide relationships from my kids—heterosexual, homosexual, anything else. I believe in being open with them, because I believe I can't be anything but honest with them.

GEORGETTE: Children are so sensitive, they pick up on things anyway.

ELEANOR: If you're hiding it, they're going to think you're doing something wrong.

(General agreement)

GEORGETTE: It's much more destructive if you're hiding it, because they know—and then it becomes a thing like, why don't you trust them—and it goes into a whole thing.

(General agreement)

NORA: I have two children, one is seventeen and my other will be twenty-two. My older son was told by his father about me, when he was eighteen and I was still married, that I was involved with a woman—whom I now live with.

What happened?

NORA: We separated because of it—or rather that really precipitated the separation, which had been coming a long time. He knew about it, openly knew about it, just a short time before he told my son. The younger son, who is going to be eighteen, has been living with me and my lover since we've been living together.

How long is that?

NORA: Well, we've only been living under the same roof for eight months, but we spent a great deal of time together before. I've been separated over three years. I think my younger son knows; we've never discussed it. My older son and I have discussed it, of course, on and off a great deal since his father told him. The only time the younger ever made any comment was because of something I said to him because I thought he ought to say something about it. I asked him if there was anything he wanted to tell me about what he feels about living with Mona and me. He said, "Mother, the only thing I really care about is what I get from both of you in relationship to me. Otherwise, whatever you do is your business." Kids today are very hip, and I'm sure he understands it and has accepted it, or integrated it, or whatever—and just decided that's not his affair, and only his relationship with me is what's important, or his relationship with Mona as a person—who she is in the house. So, I don't think that's any particular problem. My older son—it's been no problem with him since he worked it out. It took him about three months of not talking to me and going into therapy, and then he worked it out rather quickly. So, it's really been very easy. I've done exactly as I've always done, I'm the same person that I've always been, and I relate to the children exactly the same way. There's not been any change in our relationship except that the marriage is broken up. But then my husband was not a very strong figure and so the children always related more to me than they did to him. And I don't think that it had anything to do with the fact that I'm a Lesbian, I think it had to do with the kind of person I am. I've always felt very strongly that people who are aware of the choices are free to make them. I'm not into a particular homosexual bag, or heterosexual bag; I've related to men, I still do a great deal; both my sons are males. I have no desire to throw them out with bath water.

ANNA: Like?

NORA: We went to a gay movement meeting, and one of the speakers, a well-known Lesbian who has a son, whipped her son out at that meeting while he was standing there. I couldn't believe it. However, that's a particular kind of bag which I've never been into. I'm not a particularly free soul. I'm probably a very middle-class Jewish mother, and that's one of my roles—which I enjoy, by the way. I like keeping my children close enough to me to know what they're doing. Where are your children tonight? I know where mine are, I think. I certainly know where one of them is; the other is living by himself. But I think because I have been more honest with them within the last three years. It's been very good for them. My oldest does not hide, nor does he make any general announcements to the fact of my preferred life style. He is totally accepting of how I live and he is extremely fond of Mona. He also has some personal problems with Mona, but that's because he has personal problems with her on a personality basis and has nothing to do with our relationship. I think I made a serious error for many years by not being more honest with my children in terms of what my preference was. But in not letting them know that their judgment was correct in that I was unhappily married. But then I like to make everything look nice.

Why do you think you made a mistake?

NORA: I made a mistake because with both of my children in therapy at this point, both of them have come back with, "Why did you ever do what you did? Why did we always get double messages?" Particularly the older one, who was even more aware of it. It hampered their own sense of their own judgment for a long time.

In other words, they were confused as to what was going on?

NORA: Really.

MONA: I don't think that is the point. I think the point she is making is that she interfered with their judgment, their ego ability, their perceptive ability. They perceived something and she kept interfering with it by not being honest with them.

NORA: And I don't mean being honest with them in telling them about my sex life, because I really don't believe in seducing children . . . because that is one way of doing it. What I do with myself is my business—I'm a separate person apart from the children. Their only part of my life is in terms of their relationship to me as a mother, and that's the role I would choose to play again. I like my children, I like to see that they're now grown up to the age that they have reached. I think they're about as good as you're going to get these days—but then, I am a very proud Jewish mother. I think most of all, and I get a lot of this from my older son, there is still a lot of anger at how many years he had to juggle things, how he really was made to believe that things were all right when he would feel underneath that things really weren't all right. The choice of life style doesn't seem to have any bearing on it at all. As a matter of fact, he's extremely fond of Mona—sometimes to the point of where the two of them can gang up on me together. This goes on a lot around here, and it's good. And I find that mostly I enjoy the fact that I can do what I can do comfortably. Because I do pretty much the same thing, even though it seems to be a far-out kind of life style. I'm really a nesting person, I like being in a house. I cook, but I am also a painter, and I am involved in my work. So a lot of things can go at the same time, and one comes to the conclusion that people are people. I think the best thing was when I heard my oldest son say that he was not any longer frightened of his own homosexual fantasies.

His?

NORA: Yes, his. He lived with a woman for two years—from the time he was about eighteen until twenty, or twenty-one. He said just recently that he was no longer afraid of his homosexual fantasies.

Is he, in fact, homosexual?

NORA: No, I don't think he is. I think that he is probably like me, bisexual. People who really find out there are choices to be made are probably bisexual. I mean, one relates to people, and acting it out to the ultimate is a matter of choice. I think all relationships are sexual—including not only on a lateral level but in an up-and-down level: mothers and children, parents and children, children to parents, and so forth. I know that I like my kids, and I know that I dig them, and they can turn me on—but I chose not to go to bed with them. That is a choice I make, because I am aware of it. Hopefully, by knowing that, I don't have to take that feeling, not recognize it, and use it overprotectively, or in some other destructive way. Because it is there, it's always there between mothers and children—and it is always there from children to mothers.

I gather that your children were old enough that when your lesbianism became an issue they did

not feel pressures from outside, from their friends, their peers?

NORA: No. I lived in Brooklyn at that time, in a very middle-class Jewish neighborhood.

MONA: I think the best example, though, is one day with Nora's seventeen-year-old—he had his friends over here at the house. I was in the other room, and I really wasn't paying that much attention, but they were talking among themselves. They're teen-agers, and somebody said about a girl, "Well, she's trisexual." And one of his friends said, "Well, what's that mean?" He answered, "She'll try anything." (*General laughter*) And I really think that kids are not hung into the same kind of "You gotta do this and you gotta do that"—you know, you don't gotta do anything. I mean it's really doing your *own* thing. I know one day, before I was living with Nora and Carl, I was in my own apartment, and one day Carl asked me if he could bring a girl friend of his from school over. And I said of course. And they came over and they stayed, and I said something about I was glad that Carl had brought her over and stuff like that. And he said, "Well, I sorta wanted her to see how our family works." It was kind of his way—I mean, like he couldn't quite explain it, so he figured he'd show it. So he used to bring his friends over and say, "Well, like this is the way it is."

NORA: Now, he's going to Europe for the summer, and his friend is going, and I got together with his friend's parents; they came here, they wanted to see the paintings, and they wanted to meet me, and of course I wanted to talk to them, because the boy is going away for the first time. And I find that first of all, since the cliché doesn't hold well with me, people don't categorize me very easily. It is very difficult. I am obviously very much a mother, I am also a painter. My background is obviously very middle class, and I like certain little class comforts and so forth and so on—and have certain middle-class values. So that the old categories fly out the window, in terms of Lesbians.

In other words, you don't seem that different?

NORA: I'm just like everybody else, and I'm Carl's mother—so that there has never been any problem in terms of the children. My other son is an artist, a graphic designer, and he really digs the whole business, he thinks it's cool—and I know that's where his head is now. While he will still entreat me not to act as his mother—he would prefer me not to be motherly around him, because he is going to be twenty-two—he's the first one to say, "This is my mother," in any given situation. I'll come in on his friends, and I'm nobody's mother, and the first thing he will do is say, "This is *my* mother." So I think in my case I am extremely fortunate, I really do, I don't think that this is the usual thing. I think that my own sense of myself is very strong, my own needs are so strong—and they really have been in one sense all of my life, although I did all the proper things all the way through. But who I was was really what was most important. I have homosexual friends I know since before I was married, and who knew me all through my marriage. They were shocked when they found out that I had started an affair with another woman. I had already been categorized by people in a situation, and I stepped out of all the types. But the point is, I really didn't, I remained—

Your lesbianism was just an extension of yourself and not a change?

NORA: That's right.

How did you happen to do it, having come from that background?

NORA: I think I always knew. First of all, I was always attracted to both sexes. The reason that I got married was that was what my Jewish goals were—to get married and have children. Of course, remember that was twenty-five years ago we're talking about.

MONA: Well, that was a big oppressive trip—

NORA: And then I knew that my attraction to other people, both males and females—and this has been all through my life—has been based on who the other person was. When I acted out with a woman for the first time in my life, my children were six and eleven, and it was with another married woman, who had two children, who had been actively homosexual since before her second child was born. It was a very convenient set-up. She was married and had no intention of leaving her husband; I was married and had no intention of leaving my husband. We could socialize—we had very middle-class lives. We did a lot of things together. We went away to camp in the summer. She was a singer and taught dramatics, and I did arts and crafts, and my children were little and that was a way we could send them to camp—we all got out of the city for the summer . . . four children and two women.

At what point did you decide to make a choice to live with another woman?

NORA: Well, when I met Mona. I told her that we'd have to wait until I thought Carl was old enough—and I thought that would be around eighteen. And my husband found out and accused me of it. I admitted that it was true, but said that I had no intention of hurting him, nor did I have any intention of leaving him until Carl was old enough—*he* had no intention of leaving me, which is where it really came out. I was okay, you know, that was it. And I told him I would not leave him until Carl was old enough; there was no reason to. We had a home, and I saw no reason to change that part of my life. But when he dragged my older son into it there was really no choice, and I left him. And I lived alone with my younger son, Carl, for about a year and a half, we found this house, and so on.

But you would have made the choice when he became old enough?

NORA: Yes. I would have left; I don't know if I would have made the choice to live with someone. I mean, I think either way, whether or not I was involved with someone or not, I would have left, because it was just no marriage. It had really deteriorated until there was really no marriage at all. I guess I had really made my choice a long time ago. And I really was angry at him. I had spent about fifteen years of my married life trying to make a good marriage, a reasonably good marriage, considering all the things that we have to work with. I was faithful for fifteen years, but there was just nothing—it was like— Well, you'd have to know my husband to know he was a very nice guy, very sweet, very passive—it was like punching a marshmallow. There was nothing—and I think probably if he was rotten or mean, or mean to the children, I would have left him earlier. You know the tyranny of the weak, they hold you with a loose rope—there was no reason to leave. I was doing what I wanted to do anyway, and I wasn't neglecting the family.

How did he get up the guts to oppose you with your eldest son? To strike out at you?

NORA: Well, that's the whole emotional thing and psychological involvement with our son Edward. He was always threatened by Edward. From the day Edward was born he was threatened by him.

Are you saying he was getting even with Edward?

NORA: Oh yeah, he was getting even with Edward. Edward was bright, talented, and verbal, and communicated with me.

And like you?

NORA: Very much like me.
MONA: Like a carbon copy.

So, bang, you gave him ammunition against you both—what he couldn't do to you, he did to Edward?

NORA: Right! And he knew that was the only area in which he could attack me. Even if he had attacked me, literally violently attacked me, I could have understood his anger at me—because in a sense I did use him.

You did use him?

NORA: There's no question about it. You know, I have to take on my own guilt in this, but the children—that is *verboten!* And that finished it! That was just all! I left, I'm glad—I just should have done it long before.

Chapter 10

Lesbian Sexuality

This group met on July 13, 1972, for the express purpose of discussing lesbian sexuality. They ranged in age from early twenties to late forties, and represented a total scale of socio-economic class and educational level. Some of the women had been married, some had children, and some had never been married. With one or two exceptions all had had relationships with men at one time or another.

> How do you respond to the theory that lesbian sexuality is more involved with caressing, holding, and comforting affection in their relationships than in actual physical sexual activity culminating in orgasm?

(General laughter)

BEVERLY: Oh boy, that old saw.

(More laughter)

DONNA: Well, I think it is true that Lesbians value caressing and tenderness, but I think that sexuality is just as important. I think it is on an equal basis, where I think sometimes with men, sex is more important.

HALLIE: I think that women relating to women tends to come more from strong feelings of love than sex per se. I think women are more socialized to be nurturing, tender, and so on, so it is not surprising that women behave this way toward other women, but I don't think this is at the expense of sexuality. In my own experience, I know it is not true. I only came out a little over a year ago, and up until that time my sexual behavior with men was much less satisfactory to me. When I came out with women, I had a sort of sexual flowering which accompanied coming out. I don't know whether this happened because it was accompanied with greater tenderness or not, but I'm sure it was accompanied by greater sexual understanding of the needs of women. I think men tend to get further divorced from their feelings than women do, and that's part of the socialization of both men and women.

BEVERLY: I think that whole concept of lesbian sexuality as you stated the question is an erroneous concept to begin with. I think sexuality involves a tremendous range of feelings and attitudes and sensation. Maybe it would be better to talk about sensuality, which would be much more basic. I think that men and women are capable of being tender— but I think that men have been told in much stronger terms that this is not what you're supposed to do, but I do think they're capable of it.

DONNA: When I came out I had a discovery of my own sexual being. I'd been relating to men for close to ten years, and I never felt sexual; sensual, yes, but I never saw myself as a sexual being at all. I could have sex, but I never felt turned on. The sexual feeling just wouldn't be there; it was enjoyable, but it wasn't anything I desired beforehand.

Are you saying that you didn't really feel desire? It was something that just happened?

DONNA: It was something that I could walk out in the middle of. I never had an orgasm. Maybe I didn't identify as a woman because I wasn't being sexual as a woman. I don't really understand it; all I know is, I just didn't think of myself as sexual, I really considered myself asexual until I started relating to women.

CAMELLA: My experience has been different. I find that I am primarily sexual, in relationships with both men and women. I had an extremely good sexual relationship with my husband—for fifteen years, as a matter of fact—until I fell in love with a woman. The sexuality was a continuance; it was a part of my own feelings that continued right on into my relationship with the woman. I didn't find that I was feeling any different in terms of sex to the woman than I had felt in terms of the man. I could get turned on even now by both men and women. I have never had a problem in terms of dealing with the role—it's very clear to me when I'm sleeping with a man that I'm sleeping with a man, and that it is a certain kind of sex that I'm enjoying. The other is that when it is a woman, it is never— I never imagine sleeping with a woman while I was sleeping with a man, nor the reverse. I never imagined when sleeping with a woman that I was role-playing as a male or my partner being male to me. I find that I'm attracted to— I think if it's breathing, I can be sexual about practically anyone. I say that very specifically because I know that I'm sexually attracted to my children, but I choose not to sleep with my children.

You are saying that sexually you are a very well-evolved woman?

CAMELLA: Yeah. But, it's never in a role-playing sense. If it's with a woman, it's woman to woman; I'm very conscious of breasts and vagina and the rest of the thing. It's never like I wish she had a penis or I wish I did—none of that ever enters into it. If it's with a man, it's always penis to vagina contact and it's the whole thing, and it's neither disturbing nor do I go into any kind of fantasy about it.

Why do you choose to live with a woman if either satisfies you?

CAMELLA: It just happened, and it just happened in the sense that the relationship that I've had with men whom I think that I could have been involved with more seriously than I was, has always been, for some reason or another, married and other kinds of things. I didn't cheat on my husband, literally, for fifteen years because I didn't want to, and somehow getting involved with a woman I didn't quite feel like I was cheating.

ABBIE: Oh, wow!

(General uproar)

GALE: What a cop-out, baby!

CAMELLA: Oh sure, but I worked that out.

GALE: That's some double standard.

CAMELLA: Of course, but I'm talking about ten years ago. And I've been through a lot of therapy since then and a lot of understanding about why. I think that analytically I was still involved with my mother, and that was part of it. The first relation I had with a woman almost destroyed me because of my emotional problem, which was a psychotic one.

I think that the relationship with my friend Beverly is— She is who she is, and I relate to her—and who she is as the kind of person I would like . . . the sensitivity, the brains, the involvement, and so forth, all the pieces that go. I'm attracted to that kind of man, but the fact that Beverly is a woman, that's fine, and part of my relationship with her is sexual, but part of my relationship with a man would be sexual too, and so that the feelings go in all directions. And I find living like that—and I'm not promiscuous in the true sense—is what I choose at this point, because I am committed not to get involved with someone else male or female. But that doesn't mean that I'm dead, so I can still get turned on. It's like not going to bed with my own boys; I choose not to do that. After seeing *Murmur of the Heart* I was wondering whether or not a little thing couldn't be done there—

(General laughter)

CAMELLA: But, seriously—it made me very nervous; I came home from that movie very nervous. I said no, no, Camella, cut that out.

ABBIE: You know this is what makes me very angry, because why should it make you very nervous? It's society that's putting up all the boundaries—a society that says we have to be straight rather than gay, we have to be monogamous rather than polygamous. You know, to be in tune with what's going on in your head and your own body is fine, but society doesn't think it is. And you're using the word making a choice, that's the distinction *you* make. Now, if you made the choice to go to bed with your son, okay, that's cool if that's what you want.

CAMELLA: Well, it may be pretty cool for me, but I don't know how cool it would be for him.

ABBIE: No, I'm talking about how I feel if you related to me that you were having an affair with your son. If we were very close friends I would want to know if you could handle it, if you took on the responsibility of it and made more choices after the initial choice. But my response to it would be, let's get out there somewhere. You know, there's a whole lot out there somewhere that somebody's touching—and what they're doing is going through weeks of anxiety because they saw something and related to it.

CAMELLA: But what I was saying really is that in knowing that and choosing not to do it, I don't have to put a lot of other shit on him. Because that's the thing I wouldn't want to do. I mean, that's the thing that I feel, but I wouldn't want to do it, I make that as a conscious choice. When one doesn't make it as a conscious choice is when you get fucked up with the parent and the kid because you're using that as all kinds of overprotective holding on.

HALLIE: That would be a misuse of power, which is like therapists fucking their patients.

CAMELLA: Absolutely.

DONNA: Like teacher and student.

BEVERLY: That's the reason. It's not a moralistic issue, it's not any kind of issue except that the child, or the patient, is not in an equal position to make a choice.

ABBIE: Why don't you say that the *dependent* is not?

BEVERLY: The dependent is in the power of the person who is in authority, and that means there is not a consent, that there's not a choice. Between consenting adults, fine—any choice that consenting adults want to make is truly up to them. But the minute you move into areas where you are dealing with children . . . Or like in a therapeutic situation where there is so much that goes to the therapist that really doesn't belong to the therapist—if the therapist used that it would be totally oppressive.

Could we get back to lesbian sexuality?

ESTHER: My sexuality trip is in line with yours, Camella, the men-women situation. I had what I call pleasant sexual experiences with men. There was a period when I was really pretty crazy. In fact, I'd come home at night and hop into the shower and get dressed and go to one of the singles bars. You take a look around the bar, and say okay, that one, to yourself, and you walk over to the guy and somehow—however it is—you make contact, and you arrange to get to a motel room. I couldn't care less if I ever saw him again. Now, I say it runs and it doesn't run. I think that that may have been very callous of me at the time, but that's what I wanted, and that's what I needed, and all that. And people would say to me *what* are you doing? I don't know what I'm doing—I'm just getting my rocks off and that's it! It was shortly after that that I went from that to falling in love with a straight woman. The relationship was very difficult for me, and then I finally went into full-blown acceptance of my homosexuality, and was very, very happy and more re-laxed when I went to a Daughters of Bilitis meeting than when I went to a straight bar. Whatever reasons there were, I don't know yet—and I really don't care because I don't think I've felt this good as I feel today in my whole life. I was married for twelve years, and while I thought it was a good thing . . .

HALLIE: You mean you didn't feel as good in your whole life as you feel today?

ESTHER: Yes. As far as a relationship with another human being, as far as the way I feel toward . . . the way I'm *capable* of feeling toward another human being. If Deborah did not exist, if she went away, there would be somebody else, but I feel at this point that I am capable of caring and loving in a way that I've never been able to do before.

Do you think that age has anything to do with greater ability to care and to enjoy and relax with sexuality? For example, can you say "I feel more today than I felt at, say, twenty-five, and today I'm thirty-five"? That your own feelings and your own sexuality have so developed that your appreciation, your enjoyment and your involvement is greater?

DONNA: I would agree one hundred per cent with that. I was trying to tell this guy in the office today how I've been affected since I've been gay—how I've changed, or expanded, or what. And I was going through some things about my personality— how it's different from when I was straight—and every time I would discuss some aspect of myself and how I've changed, I would always add, of course I'm older now, it can't be only because I'm gay now. Because I'm older and I've had more experience.

HALLIE: I don't feel it is a function of numerical experiences. I think it may be a function of growth in the individual, but this can happen at age X, Y or Z.

GALE: Oh, I don't agree with you, I don't think it can happen at sixteen—

DONNA: Right—

BEVERLY: I'd like to comment on something Donna said about when she was straight and then when she was gay. I think that is a trip that is laid on by society—you're the same person today that you were all your life.

DONNA: I'm aware of that, but I'm saying it's not only because now I am relating to women—I'm saying it is also because I've grown in terms of what I've gotten out of experiences. Just in living, in daily living, and learning. That's the thing I'm talking about—that's the numerical goals I'm talking about: the experience of life that I live every day, and I just learn more, more about myself—and that's maturity.

HALLIE: Where I'm trying to place it is in relation to your-self and not to the other people to whom you've related.

DONNA: Of course.

GALE: Children don't automatically love. They learn by the love shown to them, and that happens all through our lives from the beginning; so our experiences have to advance us in areas of feeling and loving.

CAMELLA: Well, if I had to assort it out in terms of learning how to love because I'm homosexual or not—the most destructive experience I ever had was my first homosexual experience which lasted for five years and almost killed me. And taking that particular experience only and learning from it only, I would have said that's it—forget it, who needs it.

DONNA: Well, didn't you learn from it?

CAMELLA: Yes, I did, but one learns from all kinds of experiences.

DONNA: Well, that's what I'm talking about. When I say "experiences" that's what I mean. I learn about myself through everything I relate to.

BEVERLY: Well, I think we're a little off the subject which I think needs to be looked at, and I'm not sure it just doesn't fit into just the whole woman thing first and then the lesbian piece on top of that. And that is, the myth that women are not sexual. I think this is caught up with the concept of woman as a passive person rather than aggressive, and I think it also has to do with people saying, What do they do, those Lesbians? I think it's terribly important to say that by and large women are very sexual. I think the fact that there have been so many frigid women heterosexually is because they have been forced into a position that is not really within their natural feelings and inclinations—and that is to be passive, to be totally receptive, to be available.

HALLIE: I think there is another piece to that. I think that men, as they get out of touch with other feelings through the culture, get out of touch with their sensuality, and they really do not understand female sexuality, and they do not make an effort. I'm being very general, but it's certainly very strongly my experience with a number of men, that they are much less understanding and giving. They satisfy their own urges at the expense of the women very often.

GALE: Well, not to put you down, but I think that's a little simplistic. I think they don't really think it's not necessary to satisfy a woman—I don't think it really comes down to that. I think they think they're really doing women a favor. I don't think they go through the mental process of saying it's not necessary to satisfy a woman, but they have this idea that what women need is men, and however men do it is okay.

HALLIE: A lot of men go on the assumption that they must ke a woman come. This is a scalp on their belt; it has nothing to do with a woman's wants, needs, and so on.

DONNA: It's for their own ego.

HALLIE: Yeah.

ESTHER: Mostly my feeling has been that they really don't care whether you do or not.

HALLIE: Well, how can so many women lie about coming?

FEONA: Because they don't want to be considered frigid. They think it indicates that they're a failure as a woman.

ESTHER: Well, I've had experiences with men and I've spoken to them concerning this particular area, and I've asked, and in a lot of cases they don't know whether the woman has an orgasm or not, and they haven't bothered enough to find out whether she has or not. I had this at the beginning of my marriage—where one night I just lay still, perfectly still—and finally it got to him, and he said, "What are you doing?" And I said, "I'm doing what you're doing—because you don't ask, and you don't care, and you're not interested, and if you're not interested, then why the hell should I be?" But I don't know how many women can say that. Because first of all, I think they feel that their main thing is to go ahead and satisfy the guy. Many women have told me, "Oh, let him get off and leave me alone."

CAMELLA: But I don't think that's exclusive to men.

GALE: I don't either.

CAMELLA: I've known frigidity between lesbian couples, between male homosexuals. I cannot help but try to say over and over again that it is the person with whom you are dealing. From the time that we got married my husband was patient, kind, inventive, and creative in our sex life. He was also a very passive man in every other way, and it was incredible. And it was because he needed me so much on so many other levels that he wanted me to be happy and to enjoy sex. I had a very difficult time physically because, believe it or not, I was very small; the doctor said I was like a thirteen-year-old when I got married. His patience and kindness and courting—he didn't care how long it took. I think that the women build up the myth about frigidity and the attitudes as much as men do.

FEONA: I agree.

HALLIE: I do not agree, and the reason I don't agree is that, I think that since women tend to be so dependent on men, and to have to stay with the man, or have the man stay with them, that they go through this whole thing of lying about orgasm in order to keep the man interested, because he will lose interest faster if they do not come. It is a survival mechanism. It's unconscious, I'm sure.

GALE: In a way you're contradicting yourself.

CAMELLA: Yeah.

BEVERLY: I don't think men by and large either know or in many instances care whether a woman has orgasm or not. I mean they don't have any way of telling. There are many women who don't know whether they have orgasms. And the other thing is that there is such a myth about orgasm in our society that it is absolutely incredible—I mean, it's like the shrine is built and the orgasm is upon it—and I think that's what has inhibited everyone. Then there is the big argument about the clitoral orgasm or the vaginal orgasm.

HALLIE: I think a man cares only about a woman being satisfied from his own ego point of view, but he does not care from the point of view of the woman as a human being.

CAMELLA: But you said before that because the woman wants to hold onto him, she makes him think that he has done it, so it seems to me that they're both doing the same thing, don't you think?

BEVERLY: It's the nature of role-playing.

DONNA: They're both socialized into that.

HALLIE: As opposed to peer relationships—

CAMELLA: I think there's more game-playing than role-playing.

DONNA: Well, I think the same game-playing happens between women.

GALE: Absolutely.

BEVERLY: Well, this is the problem.

ESTHER: Yeah, yeah. Well, I was gay and then I went into a twelve-year marriage and then I came out again. So, I experienced both, and this was the irritating thought I had right from the beginning. I found that there was some kind of a relative thing between the men that don't care and some of the male-oriented Lesbians I know who behave the same way. And when you talk to them about sex, they talk in terms of "Well, I can't get it up for her," and "balling," and "Every time I pick up some broad she looks like a whore," and the same bullshit from the male point of view. This is very irritating to me. Being around in the fifties and coming out then, I would have to say that I was very "butch," but it stopped at a certain point—my clothes, my behavior, but in my relationship with another woman, the only place that I found it got me into trouble was, I could not receive from the other woman. Somehow, in my head, I couldn't do this; I could give, but I couldn't take.

CAMELLA: That's the whole male *schtick*.

GALE: I'm hearing something very interesting in what you just said—that you were afraid the woman would no suffer you to go through the same thing you had to go through to achieve orgasm, the same as the man would not suffer you to either—so you were conditioned to the idea that it had to happen very fast. And therefore, your ego did not allow you to allow for the fact that the woman may not have been able to satisfy you—and you couldn't believe that she would be willing to try, and not be disturbed if it took you longer, and you didn't—and she would have gone on being interested in you, having failed.

ESTHER: I think it had something to do with my self-worth, and my feelings about myself.

GALE: Well, that's part of what I meant.

ESTHER: I think that's where it was really at. And, as I began to feel more of a woman, and more proud that I was a woman, I then could share with another woman.

ABBIE: And dare to enjoy it. This is another thing too.

GALE: Straight on—

ABBIE: You can't be into a fantasy of being a male, or half a male, and have a woman touch you, and be touching a woman's body.

ESTHER: Well, I can only tell you of the feelings that I had at the time, and they were extremely frightening to me. When they began to talk about feelings for me, I would back away, and I would feel very guilty that I did, because in my own head I knew that I was cheating somebody of something they wanted—because I was on the receiving end of that, and how would she feel if we reversed the situation? So I felt very bad, but I just could not overcome that one thing. But some of the "butch" women, they used to slap their women around, push them around—and it was a total thing—and when I went down there to the bars where they hung out, it was like another world to me. And the only thing about me, like I said, was my come-on, my outer exterior, but otherwise—

ABBIE: You know, I went through my whole "stone-butch" number, for all the reasons that have been said, and I couldn't deal with being a woman, because the way I grew up—what was a woman? A nothing, an absolute nothing—certainly not a sexual being, certainly nothing to be proud about, nothing to be aggressive about. I wasn't a "stone butch" in 1941. That's where I lucked out, because I would have been a little boy all my life—and I would have had some floozy "femme" who would have been a little girl all her life.

BEVERLY: I think there's something else that's very important, and I don't think we're there yet because we're just beginning to explore sexuality without this kind of role-playing, but I think what happened in those days of the "butch" and the "femme"—and I think it is still true of women and men—is that there was no place to fit—like, you were one thing or the other. So, that the only way you could experience certain kinds of feelings was through another person. In other words, if you were feeling aggressive and you were female—somehow in order to experience that, you had to have another person; you had to have someone else involved in the whole thing. I think that's the problem with men, too. I think men don't know what to do with their passive feelings—and that's why I think they use women in the way that they do.

ABBIE: It's like Hallie was saying—the more you get into the role-playing, the more you lose that sensuality, and without it, it becomes an act which you can't do anything with. And therefore, talking about being frigid— I mean, if you're going to be a "stone butch," you've got to have a woman who is going to be frigid all through the motions. There's no flowing back and forth.

BEVERLY: I remember the time an analyst friend of mine was saying that she had a male patient who was extremely jealous of the fact that she was a woman. And I looked at her and said, you're kidding. And she said no, I'm not kidding at all. But in my head the concept of being jealous of being a woman was like the most alien idea possible.

Why was he jealous?

BEVERLY: Well, she had him in analysis so it was a very intensive kind of thing. He was very jealous because she could have a child.

DONNA: I work for a magazine, and I check manuscripts. The other day we got this manuscript from a guy who was doing his thesis on sex, and he was talking about warriors and spears and penis and vagina—and the penis is like a spear and the vagina is like a carnivore and he evolved the whole thing into why women are put down in society and why there is no respect for them—and it all had to do with the sex act.

Why was there no respect?

DONNA: It had to do with religion and taboos, and things like that.

CAMELLA: I hate to take us back twenty-five years ago, but I have to because it's interesting in terms of my own head. I was always an aggressive girl—and I'm an aggressive woman —but never male in that sense. My parents wanted a girl, my brother was eight years old, and she had two other miscarriages, and I was like the Virgin Mary, in a Jewish family. Because my brother was eight years old, and ill, I was treated like an only child. I was allowed to be very aggressive as a girl. Now, while all the quiet underneath pushing was going on because my brother was ill and wasn't functioning as a boy (that's another whole thing I won't go into), I had an idea that I liked both men and women. I was having crushes on women teachers and all kinds of sexual fantasies, and also the same thing with men teachers. Teachers always liked me because I was always into the brain thing. In one sense I didn't fit any place, because I was a woman who could relate to both men and women, and there was hardly any such thing around. My homosexual friends would tell me, once you act out homosexually, that's it, you're gay— because if you're not straight you've got to be gay, and there is no alternative ever. Well, for a lot of social reasons, I decided to go through with the whole marriage bit.

GALE: But you picked a passive man who did not threaten you.

CAMELLA: That's right, because then I could do my whole thing. I could be an aggressive woman, I could bear children, I could act—I'm very much a mother type—I could run the household. My father was the same kind of man my husband was—passive. My mother was an aggressive woman. But what I'm saying about sexuality—was that at the time there was no real place for me in terms of my own feelings, which were directed both to men and women.

HALLIE: There's still very little place. I feel very much ostracized as a woman who relates to both men and women.

GALE: You're not accepted by straights and you're not accepted by gays?

HALLIE: That's right.

BEVERLY: It's very hard. It's a big trip coming down on everybody's head.

HALLIE: That's absolutely right. And a very bright and enlightened gay woman whom I love very much always refers to gays and bisexuals—so I'm beyond the pale either way.

GALE: You ain't nowhere!

HALLIE: That's exactly right, and that's where Carmella was. And this is my whole life experience, this being neither here nor there, neither radical or conservative—a little of both maybe, but whatever it is.

CAMELLA: But we can't be sexual. We are not really allowed, in our society; it's like if you're not Jewish, then you're—

ABBIE: Is it that you can't be sexual or you can't be social?

CAMELLA: You're not allowed to be sexual. You're allowed to be homosexual—and on one level, if that's your thing you find your own milieu, your own ghetto. You're certainly allowed to be heterosexual, but somewhere in limbo are the sexual people. Very strongly, however, twenty-five years ago, my children don't feel that way. You're still relating to people who haven't gotten away from that—people who have been acting out one role or another for all their lives, and won't give up that very secure piece.

BEVERLY: Or you have people who are in the gay movement, and are coming out, and for the first time are beginning to feel like they're making it, in a sense. And anybody whose threat does not fit the image has got to go. I mean, that is a movement position.

HALLIE: That's right.

BEVERLY: It's not very humanistic.

ABBIE: That's right. But I think what I've always heard is people putting down people who claim to be bisexual and say they're claiming to be bisexual because they can't make a commitment to being gay. Okay now, this is the stand I've heard. Now the people in the movement who can't, or won't, deal in their heads with bisexuality—

They can't make a commitment to being gay, or they don't want to give up feeling that they're partially heterosexual?

ABBIE: Yeah, the movement people say it's a cop-out.

BEVERLY: But that's what the heterosexuals have been saying for years.

ABBIE: Yeah, but the gays are just beginning to recover from the heterosexual oppression, and they're just beginning to feel pride in being gay. Of course it's false.

BEVERLY: But the real problem has to do with a very basic concept of sameness and difference. The more secure one is with oneself—the total self, including one's sexuality, which is not a separate entity—the less it is necessary for people around you to be the same as you are. It's possible to be associated with somebody who is bisexual, heterosexual, asexual—whatever. It doesn't threaten you. And I think it's the threat—it's like people want to put people immediately into boxes. It's like with the black movement or any minority movement, there's such a hangover problem.

What part do you think the father played in the sexual preference of Lesbians?

BEVERLY: There are three ways one learns to be oneself. One has something simply to do with your constitution and how you're born—your own individuality—and then what happens to you in relation to your mother and father, but the mother is much more key in the relationship initially. That's what Hallie was saying—the more positive aspects of lesbian relationships, I think, are related to the fact that the first loving person is one's mother. Females are born into a homosexual position, males are born into a heterosexual position—and this is a very significant point—and in terms of development no one has ever really figured out significantly how the female develops. Because they have to make at least three different changes. But the reality is that the mother is the first connection to the child. But for every homosexual who had a certain kind of relationship to a mother, you can find a heterosexual who had the same relationship. There's no connection—

ESTHER: I don't like my mother. I didn't like her then, and I don't like her now, and the chances are I never will. And my father—I remember feeling very good about him up until a certain age, and then he went by the boards. I don't know, my piece doesn't fit in here—but that's my piece, whatever it is. But since I didn't like my mother, I patterned myself as much as possible after my father, as long as he was around. His position as a man seemed better to me than my mother's. Of course, I didn't like her anyway.

DONNA: You know the Lesbian that plays the "femme" role also has the feeling that the man's position is better and doesn't feel capable of being a man; therefore she runs after a male image. She's just as male-identified as the "butch."

CAMELLA: I had a mother who was the greatest thing that ever lived, and my father was a kind, sweet, gentle, passive loving father. But my mother, wow, what a woman, I was going to be just like her. I had been working at it all my life. My mother was my role model and she was a strong, aggressive, controlling, domineering, warm, loving, delicious, funny, kind woman.

GALE: I did not have a good relationship with my father. I admired him in certain ways, but I really didn't like him. He was cold, remote, authoritarian and primarily disinterested in children. My mother was passive, submissive, hypochondriacal, and affectionate in a way that made you draw back from it because she tended to infantilize you. But my paternal grandparents were terrific and I spent a lot of time with them. There my grandmother was the major influence, but my grandfather, too, was influential. They had the most equal kind of relationship I've ever seen between man and woman. Grandfather had his farms, which he loved, and Grandmother had her investments and her dairy and her chicken farm—and they never asked each other for money, nor interfered with each other's business. They loved each other and enjoyed each other, and you could feel it being around them. Grandmother was a particularly handsome-looking woman, and grandfather was a fine-looking man. Grandmother was affectionate, warm, kind, permissive, loving and funny. She exuded a marvelous kind of expansive warmth, and zest for life that made her attractive to people of all ages. Grandfather was kind, gentle, instructive and affectionate after the fashion of the patriarch of his generation, patient, sometimes funny with a sense of humor that bordered on being whimsical. I loved and admired them both and adored being with them. I think they had such a perfect relationship together that they didn't need anyone else. I suspect that my father, who was an only child, felt somewhat left out—and he was really fucked up. I, on the other hand—not being their child, and enough removed from the parent-child thing—found it perfect for me. They were enough removed to be objective and giving with me.

BEVERLY: You're saying something terribly important, something that is really the key thing in child rearing or dealing with children—and that is giving the child enough room to find out who they are, different from anybody around them. And consistency is the key to that. In other words, even if you make mistakes, or you're wrong. For instance, my mother was a royal pain in the ass—she's *still* a royal pain in the ass—but the thing about her was that she was consistent—consistently lousy—but that allowed me to separate from her. It's when a mother is one way one time and another way another time—and the child is totally confused, because you keep trying to hold onto the good pieces and you don't want to let go. Whereas if somebody is consistent, it gives you something to push against, and you're allowed to move away from it and say, I don't like this or like that—and develop your ego capacity, your judgment, perception. But if you're not consistent, you constantly interfere with the child, who perceives one thing one minute and another thing another minute and thinks he can't deal with reality, and thinks, God, I'll never make it myself, I've got to stay in a dependent position.

DONNA: I was constantly moving—going from my grandparents

down to my first father's house, to my second parents, and then with my mother alone and her new husband—who used to come home every year. I didn't know anything.

CAMELLA: But on the other side, what Gale was saying . . . You were lucky it was your grandparents and not your parents.

GALE: Yes, they were enough removed.

CAMELLA: Because the best couples I know, the most happily married, contained units I know have the most fucked-up kids, because the kids have a sense of exclusion. Nothing is really that perfect, but the kid perceives it that way. Like, "if they're having such a good time with each other, they really don't need me."

HALLIE: My parents were always denying and rejecting. Mother was always overpraising, as I perceived it growing up, and father was overcritical. It occurs to me at this moment that what she was doing was saying, you were great, you were that, taking credit for it. She didn't say you did a good thing, you did great; she said, you are great, which is a whole different trip—and it is a trip. So, I was negated in both cases. One was my father's fantasy of me, and one was my mother's fantasy—and they had nothing to do with me. Whereas, if they had addressed themselves to the things I did, it would have been me.

ESTHER: It was always made quite clear to me that I was not a human being, even as a child. Anything I did related to how they were going to be looked at by the neighbors, the community, the family—and this was verbalized very strongly. Whatever I chose to do, wherever I wanted to go to school, whatever I wanted to be, became a thing in relation to what it would do for them. I was very unhappy with that, and I really wanted to do something for me. So, in spite of what they thought, I did what I had to do, but I had a tremendous guilt feeling about the whole thing—you know, I was not going to get approval—and the older I got the further I got away from approval and the more guilt I had I knew it was never going to happen, I could see the seas between us getting wider and wider. It's really a very lonely position.

This is all very interesting, and meaningful in the total scope of it all, but could we return to the discussion of sexuality, and possibly pick up where Hallie was talking about being betwixt and between the straight world and the gay world in being bisexual?

HALLIE: Although both tend to put me down, I feel that gays put me down more than straights do at this point. Straight women seem to be accepting of me if I talk to them about it; straight men seem to be stimulated by the challenge. I won't even go into gay men . . . but gay women— My first love relationship with a woman was as much of a disaster as yours, Camella, although it didn't last as long, and it damned near killed me in about four months. She kept telling me that I was a straight woman fucking her over, putting her in a male position. I don't think I was doing that.

GALE: In other words, you were using her like a man?

HALLIE: That's what she thought—not sexually, but in terms of roles. And I don't think I was; if I was it was very, very fractional.

GALE: How can you do that? I mean, how can you make a woman play the masculine role socially if she doesn't play the masculine role sexually, too? Are they separate?

HALLIE: Well, we weren't role-playing in bed.

GALE: Why did she attach such importance to it?

HALLIE: Well, I think she was full of constructs. At first she thought I was, as she put it, "a wop," then she discovered that I was a WASP and—

GALE: What does that have to do with it?

HALLIE: She was full of these categories.

CAMELLA: She was playing the roles, you weren't.

HALLIE: Yeah, I was a married woman, and I was a mother, and I was this and I was that, and she was dumping her constructs back on me.

CAMELLA: She was projecting the whole thing.

BEVERLY: I think one of the problems is defining what bisexuality is. What do you think it is?

HALLIE: I don't know what bisexuality is. I think I'm beginning to know what I am, which is a person who relates to other human beings—and I'm not really into categorizing. And I think it is possible to relate to human beings who are only of the opposite sex, or of the same sex, but I happen to relate to human beings who are two different sexes.

BEVERLY: But there is a difference—or *is* there a different sexual experience with a man than there is with a woman?

HALLIE: In my experience the men that I have related to are in general a great deal more inept, a great deal more self-gratifying. I think there was a good deal of variation in whether they cared or not about whether I came, and how they cared—whether it was caring for me, or for their own ego. But when I came out and began relating to women I did experience this kind of opening up of sexuality, sensuality, myself as a valid sexual human being who could be either active or passive, could be both at once. All kinds of things. And I found that the women I related to. even if they weren't kind out of bed, they were damned kind in bed. And this could be the exact opposite of a lot of my experiences with men.

GALE: You do need somebody to be kind to you.

HALLIE: Yeah, I like that a lot, I do need it, and I also need to be kind. It's a two-way street, and that's when I feel best. But what I wanted further to say was that this sensualization and opening up of feeling then fed back into my relationships with men and I was better, in my own terms, in bed with men thereafter.

GALE: You mean the women had given you a good feeling of yourself so that you were able then to experience more sexually?

HALLIE: They didn't give it to me, but I gained it through the experiences with them, so that my sexuality has improved. But I don't think the men have improved—although the best male lover I ever had was exactly the same as you described your husband being, Camella. One of the most passive males I've ever come across . . . who needed my approval, and cared so much that he was tremendous; in fact, he actually said that one time. He said that this was part of why he cared if I came, and not only once but two or three times— because he needed me so much. I once wrote a poem which said, "How do you tell a man he makes love as good as a woman"—the point being that the male ego is so involved in making love as good as a man that how could a woman—

GALE: Why did you make that comparison—that he made love as good as a woman? Why didn't you reverse it to the woman and say you make love as good as a man, or better than a man?

HALLIE: Because as good as a man wasn't as good as a woman.

(*Laughter*)

GALE: Then what you're really saying is that you enjoy it more with a woman?

HALLIE: Yes—and still do.

BEVERLY: I really think that the further we've moved sexuality away from reproduction the more potential and creativity and possibility there really is in the whole thing. That means that you have to call into play not only the genitals, but one's total body, psyche, mind and emotions. And I think that when women love each other— I mean, sex calls into play all the primitive emotions; and the most primitive emotions and the most primitive relationships, and the most sensual and total one is between the child and the mother. It's like women in love are immediately moved back to this, and it has a great deal of depth.

FEONA: My first experience with a woman happened only a few years ago after many years of marriage. This thing happened, I was enormously attracted, and when I first went to bed with her I was a little bit shook up by the whole experience. I said to myself, good God, what have I gotten into now, what am I doing now? The lady was very funny in a way; she said, "Look, you haven't done anything. You've just added a new dimension to your whole experience, and I think it's good for you. I think it's good that it happened and you should be very happy about it." I thought about that and I finally said to myself—you know, this hasn't cut off my feelings of sexuality for men; although I felt enormous feelings of sexuality toward this woman, I still feel very much the same way—this is also a kind of added dimension. It all depends on who you're involved with, to my way of thinking.

BEVERLY: I think that's true, and I've been to bed with men, but I find that I do not have the same kind of emotional attachment. It just doesn't do the same thing for me. Those of you who are bisexual, I think you're great; you've got you the whole world. But I think sexuality is on a continuum. I think some of us are in one place, and some of us are in other places, and some people are more fortunate in terms of adding—

ESTHER: My experience is that I am more sexually aroused when I'm in bed with a woman—and in fact, a woman arouses me sexually more on sight. But men don't turn me off now; it's just that they don't turn me on. I don't know what it means, it's not a rejection of men—but it's just like there are so many flavors of ice cream and some you like and some you don't like.

GALE: It's not that you've stopped liking ice cream. You may just like chocolate better than strawberry.

ESTHER: Right.

DONNA: I consider myself a homosexual bisexual—or a bisexual who leans more toward women. I put it in three categories: a bisexual who has no preference, a homosexual-bisexual, and a heterosexual-bisexual. I think that's the way it is.

GALE: Here we go again, putting labels on people.

DONNA: You can, people do make preferences. But I wanted to talk about the mental part of homosexuality. Why do I prefer women? I think we should look into the physical part of it. There's a difference between the physical make-up of a man and a woman—and one I consider hard and one I consider soft—and that is part of my preference.

What part do you feel the psyche plays in preference? Is what turns you on, what you're able to love?

BEVERLY: A lot.

(General agreement)

HALLIE: Well, I engage with a woman at more levels simultaneously than I do with a man, there's no question about that, and that it is a much more complete and a much more satisfying experience. And if I have continued, or reverted to, relating with a man a good deal in the past few months it has to do with my peculiar position in terms of my divorce and my children, and fear and so on. And I think given absolutely free choice, if anyone ever is, I would be tending much more toward women. Certainly much more than I am right now.

GALE: I think sometimes it's a question of having the guts to be what you really derive the most pleasure from, and are most happy with—saying, the hell with what the rest of society thinks, it's my life, I've only got one as far as I know, and I'm going to do what's good for me. It's like somebody continuing to claim they're bisexual—well, straight on, let them claim they're bisexual—but they claim it while at the same time preferring a homosexual relationship and living within that framework. I think what they're really hanging onto is the society part of saying, yes, I'm still into the men thing; I still want to say that I'm a bisexual, or I'm partly heterosexual—like half a loaf. It's a big status thing. Not being able to say okay, I'm doing this, and I think this is where I am and I'll give it the respect it's due and honor it as a valid part of myself, and why do I keep bringing up the bisexual bit, and hanging onto it. Well, the bisexual person may be again bisexual sometime, but for that time which they are acting out and living a homosexual situation, then I think they should acknowledge it and pay it the due respect.

BEVERLY: That's fine, but I think you have to be careful not to put a trip on other people. There are people who are truly into both at the same time; I know people like that. It is really truly a different experience—like wherever their head is, they are truly turned on by both men and women. I think it's great, there's much more, but you've really got to be honest with yourself and say where am I.

GALE: Okay, if you've got to have both at the same time, and you're doing both, but if you're not and you're committed to a woman and your intentions—at present, at least—are to remain within that situation, then stop the bisexual claims, because that's really not what you're doing then. You're being homosexual.

DONNA: A while ago a lot of us got together and had a big discussion on bisexuality—and they were putting down bisexuality. Somebody got up and said she was bisexual and they put her down. I got up and I was feeling a little annoyed and I said that I was bisexual and they blasted me. So, I turned around in anger and I said, I'm a homosexual when I'm in a homosexual relationship, and a heterosexual when in a heterosexual relationship and if you don't like it you can shove it.

What about responsibility toward a relationship to which you are committed? Particularly in terms of other attractions?

BEVERLY: It has nothing to do with it.

ESTHER: Right, we're not married and we're not forced into a legal situation. Look, what's so different? Many heterosexual men and women have broken up marriages. If there is going to be another person that's to come along, whether that be a man or a woman—the fact that one is homosexual is not related to that happening.

HALLIE: One thing that I find very exciting as a potential in homosexual relationships— Well, let me put it another way. I find it very depressing when a homosexual couple goes through a marriage ceremony. Because I think the great potential is toward this other kind of relating and it does not have to reproduce the monogamous heterosexual life style.

CAMELLA: Well, that's what Donna said; when she's in a homosexual relationship she is a homosexual acting as a homosexual. That's all very good, but you can sometimes get into a homosexual relationship where they don't let you act like a homosexual because they're the partners and they insist on the role and force you into it. So what you're doing is acting out a heterosexual relationship in a homosexual situation. And that's like really fucked up—that's like nowhere . . . But I reject the word bisexual, and homosexual, and heterosexual, because it all boils down to sexual. And particularly everyone is born sexual—beyond that knowing what all the choices are, you make choices— But that's the hard part, to make people understand that they are sexual. Once the labels start flowing there is really no way to deal with it.

BEVERLY: Yeah, and they've got to stay together, otherwise you're dealing with—I mean you could do it with a machine if you developed one. But it's so hard to talk about just sexuality because it is so integrated into everything else . . . unless you talk technique, or—

ABBIE: Well, you can tell people a hundred times—what Lesbians really do in bed—you tell them that they do whatever you could imagine two people who are sexually attracted and in love doing—that's never going to satisfy them. You could give them a very graphic description, and that isn't going to satisfy them either. The only thing that is going to satisfy them is having the experience themselves. Which of course they're never going to do.

CAMELLA: You know as far back as Kinsey—he went up the social ladder in terms of what people did in bed.

ABBIE: Well, the thing with the labels is how people deal with their fears.

(*General agreement*)

Could we come back to lesbian sexuality—we keep getting away from it—we keep getting away from the sexual interaction that is going on between women—

BEVERLY: I think we are a very oral society, we are very orally oriented—and again this is the most primitive, the most satisfying— "You'd better watch the baby, everything goes immediately into the mouth." And I think that sometimes in heterosexual relationships since there is more vaginal focus, vaginal to genital focus; there is not enough of all the other aspects of sexuality—the oral aspects.

HALLIE: And just generalized touching. The lower on the social ladder, the faster the act was done and the darker the room, and under the covers. And that it was primarily for the man; it was on again, off again Charlie. The higher economically, socially, educationally up on the scale, the more inventive—of course he was talking primarily about heterosexual sex—the more open, the more erotic, the more creative it became.

CAMELLA: You know, I think that is absolute bullshit. I was raised in New England, however, which is a very inhibited culture, but I related to some upper-middle-class boys and some upper-class boys who would never do any of *those* things. And later on with grown middle-class men, I was never gone down on until about halfway through my second marriage by my second husband. I didn't like it—and it really took coming out as a Lesbian to experience this in a pleasurable way.

ABBIE: Of course, two women could not be in the same situation of not enjoying it, finding it very ugly, making all kinds of defenses about it, about any kind of oral love, or any kind of—

CAMELLA: My grown son was talking about that the other day. Talking about oral, not anal genital sex. There are homosexuals who are saying they can't have anal sex. It's that whole toilet-training shit literally. I'm sorry, but it's true. Some guys are so anal, they're so uptight about it, that they can't relax enough to have anal genital relations.

ESTHER: That's very interesting, because when I was relating heterosexually I had anal intercourse—and I don't know, but I don't think it's just a homosexual thing.

HALLIE: Well, the way I was raised, one had to wash oneself in the bath. And I always had a problem with it. I had to wash my face first and then down to my bottom that was dirty—and you couldn't put the rag on your face after it had been down there. On the other hand, I never could imagine why one was allowed to sit in the same bath water. It really always confused me.

(General laughter)

ABBIE: What's coming into my mind are some experiences where you realize that there have been taboos that somehow— I never remember having been taught them, and probably most women don't—but I think a lot of women, whether they're heterosexual or homosexual, will not have sex when they menstruate—and why is that? I was certainly never taught that.

BEVERLY: Oh, but it's a very primitive, early taboo.

CAMELLA: It's very much part of the religion— There's a whole book that the Jews have written about sexual practices.

ABBIE: Yes, but where would I get it, out of the air?

BEVERLY: No, it's a very Judeo-Christian ethic—and those ancient taboos are read right into the present-day society.

ABBIE: Okay, so that's one of the things I've run into—and that's like osmosis as far as I'm concerned; it comes from all the cultural things—

BEVERLY: But it also comes from the whole attitude about menstruation: it was unclean.

ABBIE: Of course, too, sex was always associated with having babies.

CAMELLA: Always—I just thought that things didn't open up until you had your period. I didn't think you could have sex until then.

GALE: A lot of women are glad to have their period because it keeps them from having to have sex with their husbands; it's a rest period.

BEVERLY: Yeah, most men don't want to touch a woman then; they're afraid of it. It's the bleeding wound, and brings up the whole fear of castration thing.

Do you think the period is used as an excuse not to have sex in a lesbian relationship as well?

BEVERLY: I've heard of the same thing happening.

ABBIE: A lot of Lesbians resent it; they think it gets in the way of sex. But I don't see why that should stop anything—stop them from enjoying any sexual contact. And the other thing I have found is that I don't think there are many Lesbians who have anal contact; I think this is something that has always been left to gay men. I thought this was the way gay men made love; that was the picture in my mind and that's where it stayed—never thinking, of course, that the human body reacts to anal stimulation, period, that's all.

CAMELLA: That's one of the great erotic pleasures.

BEVERLY: Well, are you saying that you think most women don't—

ABBIE: I had never heard women talking about their sexual relationships and about what is enjoyable sexually, ever mention anal sex.

CAMELLA: You were in the wrong group.

(General laughter)

BEVERLY: There seems to be the same problem among Lesbians and male homosexuals to do with anal love-making. There are such taboos in our society in terms of bowel control, and "you never *make* in your bed" kind of thing, and this gets transmitted. If you happen to be in bed sexually, and it comes to that, it brings back all the feelings about it when they were kids.

GALE: Odd too, because you hear so many stories about babies and young children who smear it all over the walls, draw pictures with it, and things like that.

ABBIE: We used to play doctor when we were kids and stick sticks up the backside. But I find most of the dirty jokes, about oral sex, the most obscene are always in terms of, like,

"Do you swallow it or spit it out," both men and women. "Well, it's only thirty-four calories."

(General laughter)

CAMELLA: But that was also part of the taboo—just the fact that you were having oral genital sex is like— Well, starting from scratch, it's illegal—and let me take it from there—

DONNA: It is illegal both homosexually and heterosexually.

ESTHER: But enforced it never will be—

CAMELLA: Unless you happen to be black and white and then—

BEVERLY: Well, they'll use the law in terms of prejudice.

CAMELLA: Yeah. New Jersey has an action pending for revision of the penal code, and the thing about oral genital sex would be that it is legal for heterosexuals and illegal for homosexuals. But they might get specific about it.

FEONA: In New Jersey as it exists right now in the sodomy law, women are free—the way the interpretation is.

CAMELLA: Nobody thinks anything about women—because their sexuality doesn't exist, of course—

HALLIE: I always thought that sodomy was anal intercourse— and therefore excluded women.

DONNA: I always thought it was when the woman was on top and the man on the bottom—in heterosexual sex.

GALE: No. Originally it was considered a form of idolatry, but it is not really defined in the Bible. The Jewish laws forbade genital sex between the same sexes; that's about as specific as it ever gets. The rest is loose interpretation for reasons of convenience and prejudice, I think.

BEVERLY: Technically, sodomy does not apply to females; they never thought there was such a thing as female homosexuality—

HALLIE: Female homosexuality had to be rampant from the beginning, given the polygamous situation. Lesbianism was accepted in the harem—no one thought anything about it— as long as the woman was available for the man when he desired her. Whatever else she did was not important.

ABBIE: Which is exactly where we're still at. The only time society is going to put it down is if we are obviously not available for men.

DONNA: In my conversation with the man in my office on lesbianism, he said it was a shame—a woman who is a Lesbian is a waste. I asked him what he meant, and he said, "Well, if you're a Lesbian, you'll never be able to go for men." I agreed, and he said, "Well, some guy won't be able to have you. You won't be able to have a relationship with a man." I said, "Yeah, but if I'm not a Lesbian some woman won't be able to have me, and I won't be available for her. Are you saying that the man has priority? That he's more important?"

I was talking to this woman about how natural it is to have oral sex. She was putting lesbianism down, and saying that men and women *fit* and that's the way it's supposed to be. And one woman had her child in a very radical day-care center, and she said that the kids are let free, and sometimes they take off their clothes, and sometimes they actually have oral contact with the other child's genitals. Of course, this other woman got all upset and said, "How disgusting! Why do you let that happen? It's not right!" And the woman replied, "It's natural; kids put things in their mouths, and they don't find that part of the body any more disgusting than the thumb."

GALE: Depends on how you use it.

(General laughter)

CAMELLA: We tried to point out to this woman that it was a natural thing, but of course, she couldn't accept it.

ABBIE: Sounds like the bit in *Auntie Mame*—spreading the sperm—

GALE: Playing leapfrog—

(Laughter)

ABBIE: It must be a very frightening world for women who have not broken away at all from that very narrow—whether straight or gay—thinking of themselves as the women they've been taught to be. I've been waiting for backlash—a whole sexual revolution—what the media has talked about as a sexual revolution for so many years. And now that it's here, it's a very quiet thing because it's developing inside.

BEVERLY: I think we're going to have some trouble before it's over. I think in our particular society we're so homophobic that it's really going to be very difficult. I think that is one reason why men also attempt to keep women in the position they're in—it is to protect themselves from their own homosexual fantasies. You know, I think it's going to be a little rough before we make it.

ABBIE: I think women—up until the last two to five years— have kept their sexuality so separate that they're now having to deal with the freedom of a new sexuality—they're having an experience that happened to me . . . last weekend is like something that I've seen over and over in miniature. We were in the country and had a to-do with neighbors across the lake. Here was this family out on their little boat dock with their binoculars, and we're all paddling around at the other end of the lake, naked, and having a marvelous time. The reaction of the women there was mixed. One half was the sort of simpering waving, this kind of thing—and the other half of the women were very angry. They got into their clothes and yelled across and said, "What are you doing there with your binoculars, little man?" And there was much shouting and great cursing and so forth. Then the man came around to our side—he had a young child there and she shouldn't be hearing obscene words. But there he was, and he walked onto the property, and he walked into the house, and he walked through the house—with people saying to him, "You go back out to the road and we'll speak to you." But total blankness from him—and walking into the house. People were screaming at him: "But you're walking into our house!"

But whatever was said, this was a total blank face—still saying, "I can't have you screaming those words." Finally someone said to him, "If you're going to stay here and keep violating our privacy, we're just going to have to call the state troopers." It finally dawned on him that he was actually somewhere that he had no right to be. But he kept saying, "But you can't." And someone in our house would say, "You can't talk to us that way." And we'd all scream at him, "Don't you tell her that she can't talk that way!" I mean, he was just another world out there somewhere, you know.

GALE: How did he get into the house in the first place?

ABBIE: Just opened the door and walked in.

GALE: But that's trespassing.

ABBIE: Well, of course—but no, he thinks he has the priority.

BEVERLY: He's the man.

GALE: I don't think that he thought they'd react that way.

ABBIE: Exactly! He was there to say why he was aggravated.

BEVERLY: He was the authority.

ABBIE: Right—and what were the voices doing bothering him, the man, right? And he presented his thing—and what we were supposed to do was say, "Oh, yes, we're really sorry," and "It'll never happen again," and all that. Instead what he got was a herd of females screaming, charging at him, accusing him, being angry, being defiant—and he was blank—he couldn't seem to comprehend what was happening.

BEVERLY: It was beyond his experience.

ABBIE: Exactly, it was beyond his experience. This is no fool, you know; an educated man, and he's completely utterly wrong.

CAMELLA: He just naturally assumed that you would feel that he was superior, as he felt he was superior, and that was that. It's very similar to what you had with the blacks in the south—who had grown up a whole generation of people which simply cannot— Their whole existence depends on the concept of the black as an inferior; as nonresistance first, and then it's inferior. And so their whole ego is caught up with that concept. Therefore, you have people who cannot deal with solving problems, and that's the same kind of thing that happens with men and women; and many men have not got the equipment to deal with this kind of behavior. It's like talking another language.

Do you think that women tend to be in their relationships more sexual with each other than they might be with a man? In other words, might two women be more sexually active than they would with a man in a heterosexual relationship?

GALE: No man and woman can ever really be as close as two women, because after all, who can better understand a woman than another woman?

I hate to return to the original discussion, but statements have been made by psychologists that women are more interested in the comforting, holding affectionate aspects of a relationship than in actual sexual activity—

BEVERLY: You see, that is a very male-oriented concept.

ABBIE: But here's a thing, too. If you are relegating sex to the sexual act, then you spend more time, possibly and probably, on the sexual act with a man, than with a woman—physically speaking.

CAMELLA: Yeah, but the man is physically set up to be aroused and to have to have immediate gratification.

ABBIE: Or to think that he does—

I'm wondering why I can't really get anyone to answer directly to this question, or to discuss the theory—or to refute the theory—of the importance of sex between two women.

CAMELLA: I had sex for five years three times a day with a woman. I had sex with my husband, which was very good, three times a week, approximately. I would have had it more than three times a day with my woman friend if I could have found how, and where and when—since between us we had four children, it got to be a little difficult, but we did manage to have it around three times a day for five years. That's my own story—

BEVERLY: I think the question has been answered several times, and it's an improper question because the holding and the sensuality is part of sexuality and obviously the whole thing is important.

DONNA: I would agree with the theory if you were satisfied with just sensuality—and it was never completed.

ABBIE: That's playing with your panda bear—

CAMELLA: How do they define "sex act"? From the waist down?

HALLIE: Genital sex culminating in orgasm, I guess is the comparison, and if that is what they're talking about, the question is sheer out-and-out horseshit!

ABBIE: Okay, but what has to be part of that question is the realization that men make the *myths* about women.

GALE: Oh, come on, let's get off that kick with men—

BEVERLY: Okay, let's forget about men altogether. Let's move to women . . . and change the question.

CAMELLA: Yeah, let me pose it. Do women as Lesbians prefer to have sensuous, loving contact more than the final completion of either oral or genital sex, or finger sex, or whatever, that's supposed to emulate, or supposed to be in somebody's terms, the "sex act"? And the answer is *no,* I don't think so. I don't think women to women, given reasonably good circumstances, and a reasonably good healthy relationship, desire just to be comforted, handled, stroked, and not finish off in an orgasm.

BEVERLY: And we know that because people have come in for help with that problem—saying that they are dissatisfied with not having orgasm.

HALLIE: I think orgasm is fantastically important.

DONNA: Yeah, I started masturbating at nine years old to have an orgasm—and I really just couldn't think of giving that up.

(*Laughter*)

DONNA: I think girls masturbate as much as boys do—to orgasm, and that is pure "sex act" in the literal sense. There is no other scale in which you can weigh that. It's not genital, it's not penis to vagina, it's not mouth to vagina—it's not anything else.

> I really don't expect anyone in this room to answer the question in terms of a clinical study—I'm interested in your personal experience. Is it, or is it not so, this theory—people who have been in relationships of duration and know. Do they, for example, find that it may be sexual in the beginning of attraction, but then after a time calms down into more of a comforting, holding relationship than a sexual one?

CAMELLA: You know, when I was married and went on my honeymoon we had sex three times a day, four times a day—but by the time I was married twenty-four years, about once a week—hardly then, because by that time I was with women. But let's say up until the fifteenth year I was having sex about three times a week with my husband. I think that any relationship evolves, depending on the needs of the particular person. I needed to have sex with the woman I was involved with three times a day. If for some reason, I missed out on one, I was going up the wall—and I was masturbating at the same time—so that my particular need was to have that damned orgasm at least three times a day.

ESTHER: I get the feeling that I have foreplay, at times, all day long and at night when I come together with my lover I have the final orgasm.

HALLIE: Foreplay being fantasy?

ESTHER: Oh no. I mean hugging and kissing is foreplay as far as I'm concerned.

CAMELLA: Oh, yeah, I know what you mean.

ESTHER: I'm talking about really touching the right areas all day long. I don't mean every five minutes, but sometimes we'll be around the house all day and I won't hesitate to touch her anywhere, anyhow.

GALE: That's being sexually aware of her all the time.

ESTHER: That's right—so I certainly couldn't agree with whatever psychiatrists made those statements about Lesbians not being sexually active.

GALE: I know what they're trying to say: they're trying to say that a lesbian relationship is infantile, and that is a lot of hogwash.

CAMELLA: They're saying there's no sex in the relationship because it isn't penis to vagina, and that's exactly what they're saying.

BEVERLY: Well, of course that's what they're saying.

HALLIE: And it's pure horseshit.

CAMELLA: I think the only answer to that theory, really, is, What do you consider the sex act? If you're going to go to a straight heterosexual, you're going to get the answer that it has to be penis and vagina—and there ain't no such thing among women; it's impossible. So naturally, if that's the only sex they think works, then they're going to say—

BEVERLY: You see, I think women's sexuality is much more complicated than male sexuality. First of all, in terms of location of the genitals and so forth, that it is much more complicated, and much more difficult for a little girl to locate—like, where is it? For a little boy, it is very clear, there it is! And that's part of the problem.

HALLIE: That's why the question as phrased—from other people phrasing it—is improper. I'd like to say that the first orgasm I ever had with a female was when I was nursing my infant daughter. And it was very nice.

Women have said that they've had their first experience of real orgasm with a woman after having lived with a man for several years and having had sexual relations with him. The question is, What were they having with the man? Some, not you here, have said, "Well, that's what I thought it was—or I had my own sort of fantasy thing going on while he was working, and I thought that was orgasm until I had a real orgasm." In other words, they were doing their own sort of head thing with this, and what they were having was not really an orgasm. But when they had the orgasm with the woman, they were surprised, delighted, and mad as hell that they'd been missing that all along.

CAMELLA: That fascinates me; I can't imagine that women never masturbated.

GALE: I've heard a lot of women say they never masturbated.

BEVERLY: That happens to be true. There happen to be more

women who do not masturbate than men, and this is the thing that women have to learn to do. As a matter of fact, in terms of helping people with their sexual difficulties, one of the things that's terribly important is helping people to masturbate. I mean, that's really—

DONNA: I had a psychologist who asked me to masturbate in front of him, and that was the last time I ever went to him.

GALE: A friend told me a story once. She'd been married three times, and she'd never masturbated ever in her life, nor had she ever had an orgasm. Then she met this guy, and they spent a weekend together, and things just weren't going very well in bed. He asked her if she'd ever masturbated. She said no. And he said, "Well, how did you ever find out where it was, and what it was all supposed to be about?" So he showed her how to do it. So after he went to sleep, she got up and dressed, wrote him a note, and left. The note said, "Have gone home to masturbate and find out what it's all about."

ESTHER: I started to masturbate very early. And I brought my brother into it. I was the oldest and I told him I was going to teach him something. I had him conned into believing that I was going to teach *him* something about sex—but I was really trying to get off, and I did. I never repeated the scene.

CAMELLA: Well, I know that I always had a clitoral orgasm first. My husband always went through a lot of sex play and made sure that I had a clitoral orgasm first—but I never had a vaginal one. What I did have was a very pleasurable feeling against the vaginal walls, but I never had an orgasm that way. I've always really believed that women can only have clitoral orgasms; I don't believe that they can have vaginal orgasms. I think that what happens is that there is contact with the clitoris sometimes in the process, and that's what is really bringing on the orgasm.

BEVERLY: And the feeling of clitoral orgasm can be different if the penis is inserted into the vagina than it would be if it wasn't, so the sensation is different. But I am absolutely convinced that one only has a clitoral orgasm. There is nothing in the vagina, physiologically speaking, to make a vaginal orgasm possible. And the other thing is that in terms of "health" if a man ever displaced his sexuality from his penis, he'd be in a lot of trouble, but women are supposed to disassociate from the clitoris to the vagina.

GALE: Well, I think proof of the fact that there is only clitoral orgasm is the fact that certain primitive societies still remove the clitoris from little girls—to keep them from enjoying sex, and therefore to keep them the property of that certain man whom they are wedded to.

CAMELLA: You'd better believe it.

FEONA: There is a contemporary psychologist in this town who has gone on and on about the joys of the vaginal orgasm. She doesn't believe there is any other kind.

(General laughter)

GALE: She bought the myth. I wonder if she's ever really had an orgasm?

FEONA: I think she's afraid of men and of women.

CAMELLA: Well, I'll tell you something. I don't know about everybody else, but I know from myself that the only kind of masturbation that I could ever conceive of would be a clitoral masturbation. You might go into the vagina because the whole area is erotic, but for orgasm, it's got to be on the clitoris. I remember once long ago I was sitting talking to my friend—and her little one-and-a-half-year-old girl was lying under the couch, and she was masturbating—and boy, it was clitoral! Now she was only one and a half so she didn't know from the head what she was doing, but she went through the whole thing and had an orgasm while she had her thumb in her mouth—her finger in her crotch, and her thumb in her mouth, and she was masturbating. Her mother said that she did that very often—which was surprising in a child so young. She was a very precocious child. She still is very precocious, and she is married now. But back then, I saw her very clearly producing a clitoral orgasm at one and a half, and I think that proves very clearly where it's at. And men don't really know that, because women don't tell them.

HALLIE: Well, I would say to amplify that. I mean, I don't deny that when one is having deeper sensations because of something in the vagina, but the clitoris is also being stimulated. Certainly, the thing that is the most satisfying to me is the mouth on the clitoris and finger in the vagina.

CAMELLA: Well, it's very erotic—and then there's a finger inserted in the anus, too—

HALLIE: Yes, that is fantastic.

ESTHER: When you have anal stimulation, too—well, that's fantastic. I've had sex with some women who find that to be really the most pleasurable thing, and I get really turned on doing it—very excited myself—and part of that is the fact that they are. Sometimes I can get off myself, at the same time, if I get excited enough.

CAMELLA: I really like sex in the morning.

ESTHER: I like it during the day, at night, in the middle of the night, in the morning—anytime. I like sex—with someone I love.

CAMELLA: One thing, when I was relating to men—let's say the man was doing something to me, touching me, then I would be feeling pleasure; but if I was just doing something to him I felt nothing. But relating to women, when I'm in the position of doing something for her, I am also very sexually stimulated.

GALE: Well, you're equals—and allowed to be aggressive and expressive. Classically that is not woman's role with a man— unless, of course, she's a prostitute, in which case that's all right, but not a *nice* woman.

BEVERLY: It's funny—the only time I was interested in being with men at all was when I was doing something to him.

(Laughter)

GALE: You've got a problem there, kid—

(*Laughter*)

ESTHER: Well, I have to tell you that I had both experiences in both directions and in both ways—with men and with women—and again, it becomes an individual thing. It all has to do with the male you're dealing with. If I was very turned on to the guy it was very exciting to me what I was doing to that guy; but if I wasn't really turned on to the guy, then it wasn't exciting to me—and the same thing with women.

ABBIE: Well, I have to say that I haven't related to men since I've been gay—and since I've been having orgasms . . . and since I've become aware of my sexuality. It's possible now that if I did—relate to men, that is—I might possibly feel sexual, because I never had a sexual identity before I related to women. I might now relate to both—or better to a man, if I wanted to.

HALLIE: My preference is still for women.

CAMELLA: Well, I don't think that mine will ever change, not really. I'm happy with women—the way I am.

Notes

CHAPTER I

1. Joseph Fletcher, *Situation Ethics* (Philadelphia: The Westminster Press, 1966), p. 18–19 (Formerly Dean of St. Paul's Cathedral, Cincinnati; Professor of Social Ethics, Episcopal Theology School, Cambridge, Mass.; Professor of Medical Ethics, University of Virginia).
2. *Ibid.*, p. 18.
3. Robert L. Treese, "Toward a Theology of Homosexuality," from a paper delivered before the Department of Ministry Special Needs Seminar, Boston University, October 28–29, 1966.
4. William H. Masters and Virginia E. Johnson, *Human Sexual Inadequacy* (Boston: Little, Brown, 1970), p. 137.
5. *Ibid.*, p. 139.
6. *Ibid.*, p. 139–40.
7. *Ibid.*, p. 252.
8. Ronald Mazur, from a paper presented at the annual meeting of the National Council on Family Relations, Chicago, Illinois, on October 7, 1970.
9. W. Norman Pittenger, *Making Sexuality Human* (Philadelphia: Pilgrim Press, 1970), p. 72.
10. *Ibid.*, pp. 13–14.
11. Louis M. Epstein, *Sex Laws and Customs in Judaism*, revised edition (New York: 1967, KTAV Publishing, Inc.), p. 4.
12. *Ibid.*, pp. 5–6.

13. *Ibid.*, pp. 9–10.
14. Erich Neumann, *The Origins and History of Consciousness* (Princeton, N. J.: Princeton University Press, 1954, Bollingen Series XLII; Princeton Bollingen Paperback, 1970), p. 57.
15. *Making Sexuality Human*, pp. 80–81.
16. *Ibid.*, p. 81.
17. *Sex Laws and Customs in Judaism*, p. 144.
18. *Ibid.*, pp. 146–147.
19. *Ibid.*, p. 144.
20. Alfred Kinsey, *et al*, *Sexual Behavior in the Human Female* (Philadelphia: W. B. Saunders Co., 1953), p. 164.
21. *Ibid.*, p. 165.
22. *Ibid.*, p. 154.
23. Bertrand Russell, *Why I Am Not a Christian* (New York: Simon and Schuster, Inc., 1957), p. 33.
24. *Situation Ethics*, p. 139.

CHAPTER 2

1. Derrick Sherwin Bailey, *Homosexuality and the Western Christian Tradition* (New York: Longman, Green & Co., 1955), p. 3.
2. *Ibid.*, p. 9.
3. *Ibid.*, p. 10.
4. *Ibid.*, pp. 10–26.
5. *Ibid.*, p. 155.
6. Robert L. Treese, from the paper "Toward a Theology of Homosexuality," p. 3.
7. *Ibid.*, pp. 59–60.
8. Helmut Thielicke, *The Ethics of Sex*, trans. by John W. Doberstein (New York: Harper & Row, 1964), p. 279.
9. "Toward a Theology of Homosexuality," pp. 8–9.
10. Louis M. Epstein, *Sex Laws and Customs in Judaism*, pp. 134–35.
11. *Ibid.*, pp. 135–36.
12. *Ibid.*, p. 136.
13. *Ibid.*, pp. 137–38.
14. *Ibid.*, p. 138.
15. Neal A. Secor, "A Brief for a New Homosexual Ethic," from Ralph W. Weltge, ed., *The Same Sex* (Pilgrim Press; Boston, 1969), pp. 70–71.
16. *Ibid.*, p. 72.
17. Ralph W. Weltge, "The Paradox of Man & Woman," from *The Same Sex*, pp. 56–57.
18. Paul Lehmann, *Ethics in a Christian Context* (New York: Harper & Row, 1963), p. 119.

19. *Ibid.,* p. 119.
20. *Ibid.*
21. *Ibid.,* p. 121.
22. Emil Brunner, *The Divine Imperative* (Philadelphia: Westminister Press, 1947), p. 133.
23. Joseph Fletcher, *Situation Ethics,* p. 133.
24. Martin Luther, "Sermon, Eighteenth Sunday after Trinity," in J. N. Linker, ed., *The Church Postil,* Vol. V (Cluther House, 1905), p. 175.
25. *Enchiridon,* Ch. 117 in M. Dods., ed., *Works,* Vol. IX (Edinburgh: T. T. Clark, 1973), p. 256.

CHAPTER 3

1. Anthony Grey, "Christian Society and the Homosexual," from *Faith and Freedom,* Vol. 19, no. 56 (Spring 1966), Manchester College, Oxford.
2. William Dempsey, from *Dublin Review,* no. 504 (Summer 1965), also contained in the Grey article.
3. Roger L. Shinn, "Homosexuality: Christian Conviction and Inquiry," from *The Same Sex,* Ralph W. Weltge, ed., pp. 45–46.
4. *Ibid.,* p. 47.
5. *Ibid.,* p. 54.
6. Wardell B. Pomeroy, "Homosexuality" from *The Same Sex,* Ralph Weltge, ed., p. 8.
7. Judd Marmor, ed., *Sexual Inversion* (New York: Basic Books, 1965), p. 19.
8. C. A. Tripp, "Who Is A Homosexual?" from Sex Disorders in Clinical Practice (a course for physicians, University of California, School of Medicine, March 19–21, 1965) pp. 1–2.

CHAPTER 4

1. Frank A. Beach and Priscilla Rasquin, "Masculine Copulatory Behavior in Intact and Castrated Females Rats," from *Endocrinology,* Vol. 31, no. 4 (October 1942), p. 393.
2. "Factors Involved in the Control of Mounting Behavior by Female Mammals," from *Perspectives in Reproduction and Sexual Behavior,* Milton Diamond, ed. (Bloomington: University of Indiana Press, 1968), p. 83.
3. *Ibid.,* p. 87.
4. *Ibid.,* p. 149.
5. *Ibid.,* p. 150.
6. *Ibid.,* p. 151.

7. *Ibid.*, p. 87.
8. *Ibid.*
9. *Ibid.*, p. 112.
10. *Ibid.*, p. 125.
11. Judith Blake, "Population Policy for Americans: Is the Government Being Misled?" reprinted from *Science* magazine, Vol. 164 (May 2, 1969).
12. S. E. Willis, *Understanding and Counseling The Male Homosexual* (Boston: Little, Brown, 1967).
13. John Money, "Components of Eroticism in Man: I. The Hormones in Relation to Sexual Morphology and Sexual Desire," from the *Journal of Nervous and Mental Diseases* (1961), p. 132.
14. John Money, "Factors in the Genesis of Homosexuality," from *Determinants of Human Sexual Behavior,* G. Winokur, *et al.* (Springfield, Ill.: Charles C. Thomas), Chapter 2.
15. Alfred Auerback, from G. M. Cantor, *Brief of The Homosexual Law Reform Society of America's Curiae before the Supreme Court of the United States,* October Term, No. 44 (1966), Clive Michael Boutilier, Petitioner, vs. The Immigration and Naturalization Service, Respondent (Philadelphia: The Janus Society, 1966).
16. M. B. Clinard, *Sociology of Deviant Behavior* (New York: Holt, Rinehart & Winston, 1968).
17. John Money, "Matched Pairs of Hermaphrodites: Behavioral Biology of Sexual Differentiation from Chromosomes to Gender Identity," from *Engineering and Science,* California Institute of Technology, Vol. 33 (1970), pp. 34–39. Special Issue: Biological Bases of Human Behavior.
18. John Money, in an article by Faubion Bowers, "Homosex: Living The Life" *Saturday Review* (Feb. 12, 1972), p. 23.
19. Père de Finance, extract from Robert Johann, ed., *Building the Human* (New York: Herder & Herder, 1968).

CHAPTER 5

1. Irving Bieber, *et al., Homosexuality: A Psychoanalytic Study of Male Homosexuals* (New York: Basic Books, 1962), conclusion.
2. Bernard Riess, "A New Psychology of Women or a Psychology for the New Woman, Active or Passive." *International Mental Health Research Newsletter,* published by Postgraduate Center for Mental Health, New York, Vol. XIV, no. 4 (Winter 1971), pp. 1, 4.
3. Ralph H. Gundlach and Bernard F. Riess, "Self and Sexual Identity in the Female: A Study of Female Homosexuals," from *New Directions in Mental Health* (New York: Grune & Stratton, Inc., 1968), pp. 205–206.

4. *Ibid.*, p. 211.
5. Judd Marmor, "Normal and Deviant Sexual Behavior," *Journal of the American Medical Association,* Vol. 217 (2) (1971), 165–67.
6. L. K. Frank, R. Harrison, E. Hellerberg, K. Machover and M. Steiner, *Personality Development in Adolescent Girls,* Monographs of Society for Research in Child Development, XVI, No. 53 (1953).
7. Gundlach and Riess, "Sex and Sexual Identity in the Female: A Study of Female Homosexuality."
8. Simone de Beauvoir, *The Second Sex* (New York: Bantam Books, 1961).
9. Gundlach and Riess, "Sex and Sexual Identity in the Female: A Study of Female Homosexuality."
10. C. A. Tripp, "Who Is A Homosexual?" From *Sex Disorders In Clinical Practice,* a course for physicians at the University of California School of Medicine, March 19–21, 1965, pp. 4–5 (portions of which will be included in his forthcoming book on male and female homosexuality, to be published by Atheneum).
11. *Ibid.*, p. 5.
12. *Ibid.*, pp. 6–7.
13. Ralph H. Gundlach, "Who Is A Lesbian?" *International Mental Health Research Newsletter,* published by Postgraduate Center for Mental Health, Vol. XIV, no. 4 (Winter 1971), p. 3.
14. *Ibid.*, p. 5.
15. June H. Hopkins, "The Lesbian Personality," *The British Journal of Psychiatry,* Vol. 115, no. 529 (December 1969), p. 1433.
16. *Ibid.*, p. 1436.
17. W. H. Perloff, "The Role of Hormones in Homosexuality," *Journal of The Albert Einstein Medical Center,* Philadelphia (July 11, 1963).
18. C. A. Tripp paper, pp. 1–12.
19. *Ibid.*, p. 8.
20. *Ibid.*, pp. 8–11.
21. *Ibid.*, p. 12.
22. Judd Marmor, "Normal and Deviant Sexual Behavior," pp. 13–14.
23. DeSavitsch, from *Cantor Brief,* presented before the U.S. Supreme Court.
24. Ernest Van Den Haag, from *Cantor Brief.*
25. Judd Marmor, from *Cantor Brief.*
26. Judd Marmor, ed., *Sexual Inversion: The Multiple Roots of Homosexuality* (New York: Basic Books, 1965).
27. D. Curran and D. Parr, "Homosexuality: An Analysis of 100 Male Cases Seen in Private Practice," *British Medical Journal* (April 6, 1957).
28. D. W. Hastings, *Impotence And Frigidity* (Boston: Little, Brown, 1963).

29. S. E. Willis, *Understanding and Counseling The Male Homosexual,* (Boston: Little, Brown, 1967).

30. A. C. Kinsey, *et al., Sexual Behavior in the Human Female* (Philadelphia: W. B. Saunders, 1953).

31. John Money, cited in G. Winokur, ed., *Determinants of Human Sexual Behavior* (Springfield, Ill.: Charles C. Thomas, 1963).

32. S. Freud, *Three Essays on the Theory of Sexuality* (London: Hogarth, 1953).

33. S. Freud, "A Letter To A Grateful Mother," dated April 9, 1935, *International Journal of Psychoanalysis,* Vol. 32 (1951).

34. *Ibid.*

35. P. Gebbhard, reported in *The Chicago Sun Times,* April 21, 1969.

36. *Modern Medicine* (April 1969), p. 20.

37. G. Weinberg, *Society And The Healthy Homosexual* (New York: St. Martins, 1972).

CHAPTER 6

1. J. M. Edmonds, translator, *The Songs of Sappho* (Mt. Vernon, N.Y.: The Peter Pauper Press), pp. 9–11.

2. *Ibid.,* p. 30.

3. *Ibid.,* p. 38.

4. *Ibid.,* pp. 59–60.

5. *Ibid.,* p. 93.

6. Jeannette H. Foster, *Sex Variant Women In Literature* (New York: Vantage Press, 1956), p. 18.

7. *Ibid.,* p. 20.

8. *Ibid.,* p. 19.

9. Philip Sidney, *The Countess of Pembroke's Arcadia* (Cambridge University Press, 1912).

10. Jeannette H. Foster, *Sex Variant Women In Literature,* p. 55.

11. *Modern Woman, The Lost Sex* (New York: Harper, 1947).

12. William Godwin, *Memoirs of Mary Wollenstonecraft* (New York: Richard Smith, 1930).

13. Jeannette H. Foster, *Sex Variant Women In Literature,* p. 60.

14. *Ibid.,* p. 63.

15. *Ibid.,* p. 64.

16. *Ibid.,* p. 65.

17. *Ibid.,* p. 109.

18. *Ibid.,* p. 112.

19. *Ibid.,* p. 114.

20. Pierre Louÿs, *The Songs of Bilitis* (privately issued for subscribers, 1928), LII.

21. *Ibid.,* LIII.

22. *Ibid.*, LV.
23. *Ibid.*, LXI.
24. *Ibid.*, LXIII.
25. *The Collected Works of Pierre Louÿs* (New York: Liveright Publishing Company, 1932).
26. *Ibid.*, from the foreword by Michael S. Buck.
27. *Ibid.*
28. Jeannette H. Foster, *Sex Variant Women In Literature*, p. 117.
29. *Ibid.*, p. 154.
30. *Ibid.*, p. 158.
31. *Ibid.*, p. 173.
32. *Amy Lowell* (Boston: Houghton, 1912).
33. *Ibid.*
34. Edna St. Vincent Millay, *Renascence Interim* (New York: Kennerly, 1924).
35. Jeannette H. Foster, *Sex Variant Women In Literature*, p. 184.
36. Edna St. Vincent Millay, *The Harp Weaver And Other Poems* (New York: Harper, 1923).
37. Jeannette H. Foster, *Sex Variant Women In Literature*, pp. 185–186.
38. *Ibid.*, p. 192.
39. *Ibid.*, p. 200.
40. Vera Brittain, *Radclyffe Hall: A Case Of Obscenity?* (London: A Femina Book, Ltd., 1968) pp. 52–55.
41. *Ibid.*, p. 85.
42. *Ibid.*, p. 102.
43. *Ibid.*, p. 102.
44. *Ibid.*, p. 148.
45. Djuna Barnes, *Ladies Almanack* (New York: Harper & Row, 1972), foreword.
46. *Ibid.*, p. 8.
47. *Ibid.*, p. 18.
48. Gertrude Stein, *Fernherst, Q.E.D., And Other Early Writings* (New York: Liveright, 1971), p. 49.
49. *Ibid.*, Introduction.

A Bibliography
of Lesbianism
in Literature

(This bibliography could not have been compiled without the aid of a publication issued by *The Ladder*, entitled *The Lesbian in Literature**; Jeannette H. Foster's book *Sex Variant Women in Literature*, Vantage Press; and university sources.)

Amis, Kingsley, *Take a Girl Like You*. New York: Harcourt Brace and World, Inc., 1961; Signet paperback, 1963.

Andreyev, Leonid, "The Abyss," in *Strange Desires* (New York: Lion paperback, 1954). Also available in *A Treasure of Russian Life and Humor* (New York: Coward-McCann, 1943) and in *A World of Great Stories* (New York: Crown Publishers, Inc., 1947).

Ansell, Helen Essary, "The Threesome," in Whit Burnett, ed., *Best College Writing 1961* (New York: Random House, 1962). Also in Richard Poirier, ed., *Prize Stories, 1963* (Garden City, New York: Doubleday, 1963).

Aristo, Ludovico, *Orlando Furioso*, 2 volumes. London: Bell, 1907; Bloomington: Indiana University Press, 1963 (available in both hardcover and paperback).

* *The Lesbian in Literature*, by Gene Damon and Lee Stuart, is published by *The Ladder*, P.O. Box 5025, Washington Station, Reno, Nevada 89503.

Balzac, Honoré de, *Cousin Betty* (1847). Available in many English and American editions.

———, *The Girl with the Golden Eyes* (1835). Available in many English and American editions.

———, *Seraphita* (1842). Available in many English and American editions.

Bannon, Ann, *Beebo Brinker*. New York: Fawcett Gold Medal paperback, 1962.

———, *I Am a Woman*. New York: Fawcett Gold Medal paperback, 1959.

———, *Journey to a Woman*. New York: Fawcett Gold Medal paperback, 1960.

———, *The Marriage*. New York: Fawcett Gold Medal paperback, 1960.

———, *Odd Girl Out*. New York: Fawcett Gold Medal paperback, 1957.

———, *Woman in the Shadows*. New York: Fawcett Gold Medal paperback, 1959.

Barnes, Djuna, "Dusie," in *American Esoterica* (New York: Macy-Masius, 1927).

———, *Ladies Almanack*. Paris, 1928 (First edition limited to 1,050 copies. Supposedly written by "A Lady of Fashion.") Reissued by Harper & Row (New York) in 1972.

———, *Nightwood*. New York: Harcourt Brace and World, Inc., 1937; New Directions paperback, 1946.

Barney, Natalie Clifford, *Poems and Poemes: Autres Alliances*. New York: George H. Doran; Paris: Emile-Paul Freres, 1920.

Barry, Philip, *War in Heaven*. New York: Coward, 1938.

Bartlett, Paul, *When the Owl Cries*. New York: Macmillan, 1960.

Bates, H. E., "Breeze Anstey" in *The Best of H. E. Bates*. Boston: Little, Brown, 1963.

Baudelaire, Charles, *The Flowers of Evil* (*Les Fleurs Du Mal*). New York: Harper, 1936; Washington Square Press, 1962.

Beauvoir, Simone de, *She Came to Stay*. New York: Dell Books, 1963.

Bell, G. H., ed., *The Hamwood Papers of the Ladies of Llangollen and Caroline Hamilton*. London: Macmillan, 1930.

Berkman, Sylvia, "Blackberry Wilderness" in *Blackberry Wilderness and Other Stories*. New York: Doubleday, 1962.

Bertin, Celia, *The Last Innocence*. New York: McGraw-Hill, 1955.

Bishop, Leonard, *Creep Into Thy Narrow Bed*. New York: Dial, 1954.

Blackburn, Paul, "The Proposition" and "Once Over" in *Erotic Poetry*, ed. by William Cole. New York: Random House, 1963. Originally published in *Brooklyn-Manhattan Transit*. New York: Totem Press, 1960.

Bodenheim, Maxwell, *My Life and Loves in Greenwich Village*. New York: Bridgehead Books, 1954.

Burdet, Edouard, *The Captive*. New York: Brentano, 1926.

———, *Replenishing Jessica*. New York: Liveright, 1925.

Bowen, Elizabeth, *Friends and Relations*. London: Constable, 1931; New York: Dial, 1931.

———, "Happy Autumn Fields" in *Ivy Gripped the Steps and Other Stories*. New York: Knopf, 1946.

———, *The Hotel*. New York: Dial, 1928; Popular Library, 1966.

———, *The Little Girls*. New York: Knopf, 1963, 1964.

———, "Mrs. Windemere" in *Encounters*. London: Sedgwick, 1928. Also in *Early Stories*. New York: Knopf, 1950.

Boyle, Kay, "Bridegroom's Body" in *The Crazy Hunter*. New York: Harcourt, 1938, 1940; Boston: Beacon Press, 1958.

———, *Monday Night*. New York: Harcourt, 1938.

———, "Your Body Is a Jewel Box" in *Thirty Stories*. New York: Simon & Schuster, 1946.

Bradley, Marion Zimmer, "Centaurus Changeling" in *Magazine of Fantasy and Science Fiction*, April, 1954.

———, *The Sword of Aldones*. New York: Ace Books, 1962.

———, (As Lee Chapman, pseud.) *I Am a Lesbian*. New York: Monarch Press, 1962.

———, (As Mariam Gardner, pseud.) *My Sister, My Love*. New York: Monarch Press, 1962.

———, (As Mariam Gardner, pseud.) *The Twilight Lovers*. New York: Monarch Press, 1962.

———, (As Mariam Gardner, pseud.) *The Strange Woman*. New York: Monarch Press, 1962.

Bromfield, Louis, *The Rains Came*. New York: Collier, 1937; Bantam, 1952.

Brontë, Emily, *Complete Poems*. New York: Columbia University Press, 1941.

Brophy, Brigid, *The Finishing Touch*. London: Secker & Warburg, 1963. Also in *The Snow Ball and the Finishing Touch*. New York: World, 1964.

————, *Flesh*. New York: World, 1963; Popular Library, 1964.

————, *The King of Rainy Country*. New York: Knopf, 1957.

Burgess, Anthony, *Honey For the Bears*. New York: Norton, 1964; Ballantine, 1964.

————, *The Wanting Seed*. New York: Norton, 1963; Ballantine, 1964.

Caldwell, Erskine, *Tragic Ground*. Boston: Little, Brown, 1944.

Capote, Truman, *Breakfast At Tiffany's*. New York: Random House, 1958.

————, "The Headless Hawk" in *Best American Short Stories*. Boston: Houghton-Mifflin, 1948. Also in *The Tree of Night and Other Stories*. New York: Random House, 1949.

Casanova de Seingalt, *G. J.*, *Memoirs*. New York: Regency House, 1938.

Christian, Paula, *Amanda*. New York: Belmont, 1965.

————, *Another Kind of Love*. New York: Fawcett Crest, 1961.

————, *Edge of Twilight*. New York: Fawcett Crest, 1959, 1961, 1963.

————, *Love Is Where You Find It*. New York: Avon, 1961.

————, *The Other Side of Desire*. New York: Belmont, 1965.

————, *This Side of Love*. New York: Avon, 1963.

Christie, Agatha, *Murder Is Announced*. New York: Dodd, Mead, 1950.

Coleridge, Samuel Taylor, *Christabel*. 1798. (Available in dozens of English literature anthologies).

Colette, Sidonie Gabrielle, "Bella-Vista" in *The Tender Shoot and Other Stories*. New York: Farrar, Straus and Giroux, 1958, 1959.

————, *Claudine At School*. New York: Farrar, Straus and Giroux, 1930, 1957; Berkley, 1965.

————, *Earthly Paradise*. New York: Farrar, Straus & Giroux, 1966.

————, "Gitanette" in *Mitsou and Music Hall Delights*. New York: Farrar, Straus & Giroux, 1958.

————, *The Indulgent Husband*. New York: Farrar, Straus & Giroux, 1935. Also in *Short Novels of Colette*. New York: Dial, 1951.

————, *Claudine Married*. New York: Farrar, Straus & Giroux, 1960; Avon, 1961; Berkley, 1965.

————, *The Pure and the Impure (Ces Plaisirs)*. New York: Farrar, Straus & Giroux, 1933.

————, *Young Lady of Paris*. New York: Farrar, Straus & Giroux, 1931, 1958.

————, *Claudine In Paris*. New York: Avon, 1958, 1959; Belmont, 1964. Also, *Claudine*. New York: Berkley, 1965.

Craigin, Elizabeth, *Either Is Love*. New York: Harcourt, 1937; Lion, 1952, 1966; Pyramid, 1960.

Creal, Margaret, *A Lesson In Love*. New York: Simon and Schuster, 1957.

Dane, Clemence, *Regiment of Women*. New York: Macmillan, 1917.

Davenport, Marcia, *Of Lena Geyer*. New York: Scribner, 1936.

Dennis, Patrick, *Little Me*. New York: Dutton, 1961; Fawcett Crest, 1962.

De Vries, Peter, *The Tents of Wickedness*. Boston: Little, Brown, 1969; Signet, 1960.

Dickinson, Emily, *Bolts of Melody*. New York: Harper, 1945.

Dinesen, Isak, "The Invincible Slave Owners" in *A Winter's Tales*. New York: Random House, 1942.

————, *Seven Gothic Tales*. New York: Harrison Smith and Robert Haas, 1934; Modern Library.

Durrell, Lawrence, *The Alexandria Quartet—Justine, Balthazar, Mountolive, Clea*. New York: Dutton.

Ellis, Havelock, *The Sage of Sex by Arthur Calder-Marshall*. New York: Putnam, 1960.

————, *Havelock Ellis: Artist of Life* by John Steward Collis. New York: Sloane, 1959.

Emerson, Jill, *Enough of Sorrow*. Midwood Flower, 1965.

————, *Warm and Willing*. Boston: Beacon Press, 1957.

Firbank, Ronald, *The Complete Works of Ronald Firbank*. New York: New Directions, 1961.

————, *The Flower Beneath the Foot*. New York: Brentano's, 1923. Also in *Five Novels*. New York: New Directions, 1951.

————, *The New Rhythm* (sic). London: Duckworth, 1962; New York: New Directions, 1963.

————, "Inclinations" in *Three Novels*. New York: New Directions, 1951.

————, *The Princess Zoubaroff*. London: Gerald Duckworth, 1930, 1940.

Fitzgerald, F. Scott, *Tender Is the Night*. New York: Scribner, 1934; Bantam, 1950.

Flaubert, Gustave, *Salammbo* (1862). Available in both English and American editions. Current paperback edition from Berkley.

Fleming, Ian, *From Russia With Love*. New York: Macmillan, 1957; Signet, 1958. Also in *Filtedge Bonds*. New York: Macmillan, 1961.

———, *Goldfinger*. New York: Macmillan, 1959; Signet, 1960.

Flynn, Errol, *My Wicked, Wicked Ways*. New York: Putnam, 1959; Pocketbooks, 1960.

Foster, Jeannette, *Sex Variant Women in Literature*. New York: Vantage, 1956.

Fox, Stella, *Lesbian Love In Literature*. New York: Avon, 1962. Note: An anthology containing: *The Ode* by Sappho; *Monday Night* (excerpt) by Kay Boyle; *Paul's Mistress* by Guy de Maupassant; *The Illusionist* (excerpt) by Francoise Mallet-Joris; *Ann Vickers* (excerpt) by Sinclair Lewis; *Mlle. de Maupin* (excerpt) by Theophile Gautier; *The Sum of Two Angels* by Rosamond Lehmann; *The Rainbow* (excerpt) by D. H. Lawrence; *Bliss* by Katherine Mansfield; and *Friend of the Family* by Feodor Dostoevsky.

Gide, André, *The School For Wives, Robert and Genevieve*. New York: Knopf, 1950.

Godden, Rumer, *The Greengage Summer*. New York: Viking, 1957.

Graves, Robert, "But It Still Goes On" in *But It Still Goes On*. New York: Cape & Smith, 1931.

Greene, Graham, *Orient Express*. New York: Doubleday, 1932; Bantam, 1955.

Gunn, Peter, *Vernon Lee*. London: Oxford University Press, 1964.

Haggard, Henry Rider, *Allan's Wife*. 1889. Available in many English and American editions, including *Five Adventure Novels of H. Rider Haggard*. New York: Dover, 1951.

Hall, Radclyffe, *The Forgotten Island*. London: Chapman & Hall, 1915.

———, "Miss Ogilvy Finds Herself" in *Miss Ogilvy Finds Herself*. New York: Harcourt, 1924.

———, *Poems of the Past and Present*. London, Chapman & Hall, 1910.

———, *A Saturday Life*. London: Arrowsmith, 1925; Falcon, 1952.

———, *A Sheaf of Verses*. London: John & Edward Bumpus, 1905.

———, *Song of Three Countries and Other Poems*. London: Chapman & Hall, 1913.

———, *Twixt Earth and Stars*. London: John & Edward Bumpus, 1906.

————, *The Unlit Lamp*. London: Jonathan Cape and Harrison Smith, 1929.

————, *The Well of Loneliness*. London: Jonathan Cape, 1928; New York: Covici-Friede, 1928.

Hecht, Ben, *The Sensualists*. New York: Messner, 1959; Dell, 1959, 1964.

Hellman, Lillian, *The Children's Hour*. New York: Knopf, 1934; Signet, 1962.

Hemingway, Ernest, "The Sea Change" in *The Fifth Column and the First Forty-Nine Stories*. New York: Collier, 1938.

Hesse, Hermann, *Steppenwolf*. New York: Holt, 1929.

Holmes, Oliver Wendell, *Elsie Venner*. New York: Burt, 1850; Doubleday Dolphin, 1961; Signet, 1961.

————, *A Guardian Angel*. Boston: Houghton-Mifflin, 1890.

————, *A Moral Antipathy*. Boston: Houghton-Mifflin, 1892.

Hurst, Fannie, *Lonely Parade*. New York: Harper, 1942.

Jackson, Shirley, *Hangsman*. New York: Farrar, Straus & Giroux, 1951; Ace, 1964.

————, *The Haunting of Hill House*. New York: Viking, 1959; Popular Library, 1962, 1966.

————, *We Have Always Lived in the Castle*. New York: Viking, 1962; Eagle, 1964.

James, Henry, *The Bostonians*. Century Magazine, 1885. New York: Dial, 1945.

————, *The Turn of the Screw*. New York: Macmillan, 1898. (Paperback editions by Apollo, Dell and Signet.)

La Farge, Christopher, *The Sudden Guest*. New York: Coward-McCann, 1946.

Lamarr, Hedy, *Ecstasy and Me*. New York: Bartholomew House, 1966.

Lawrence, D. H., *The Fox*. Dial Magazine, May–August, 1922.

————, *The Rainbow*. New York: Modern Library, 1915, 1943; Avon, 1959, 1960.

Leduc, Violette, *La Batarde*. New York: Farrar, Straus & Giroux, 1965; Dell, 1966.

Lee, Gypsy Rose, *Gypsy*. New York: Harper, 1957; Dell, 1959.

Lehmann, Rosamond, *Dusty Answer*. London: Reynal and Hitchcock, 1927; New York: Holt, 1927.

Lewis, Sinclair, *Ann Vickers*. New York: Doubleday, 1932; Dell, 1962.

Lewis, Wyndham, *The Apes of God*. London: Arthur Press, 1930; Arco, 1955; Penguin, 1965.

Louÿs, Pierre, *The Adventures of King Pausole*. 1899. Available in many English and American editions.

———, *Aphrodite*. 1896. Available in many editions, including *The Collected Works of Pierre Loüys*. New York: Liveright, 1926; Avon, 1955.

———, *The Songs of Bilitis*. 1894. Available in many editions, some of them illustrated.

Lowell, Amy, *The Complete Poetical Works of Amy Lowell*. Boston: Houghton-Mifflin, 1955.

Lucian, *Dialogues of a Petaerae*. Many editions available, including *A Treasury of Ribaldry*, edited by Louis Untermeyer. New York: Doubleday, 1956. (The pertinent dialogues are "The Lesbian," Dialogue V, and "A Curious Deception," Dialogue XII. These were written between 120 A.D. and 200 A.D.)

MacKenzie, Compton, *Extraordinary Women*. London: Martin Secker, 1928, 1932; New York: Macy-Masius, 1928.

———, *Vestal Fire*. New York: George H. Doran, 1927.

Mailer, Norman, *The Barbary Shore*. New York: Holt, 1951; Signet 1953, 1960.

Mallet, Francoise (later Mallet-Joris, Francoise), *The Illusionist*. New York: Farrar, Straus & Giroux, 1952.

———, *The Loving and the Daring*. New York: Popular Library, 1953.

———, *The Red Room*. New York: Farrar, Straus & Cudahy, 1956.

———, "Jimmy" in *Cordelia and Other Stories*. New York: Farrar, Straus & Giroux, 1965.

Mansfield, Katherine, "Bliss" in *Bliss and Other Stories*. New York: Knopf, 1920. Also in *Short Stories of Katherine Mansfield*. New York: Knopf, 1937.

———, *The Journal of Katherine Mansfield*. New York: Knopf, 1928; McGraw Hill, 1964.

———, *The Scrapbook of Katherine Mansfield*. New York: Knopf, 1939, 1940.

Margueritte, Victor, *The Bachelor Girl*. London: Philpot, 1924.

Marks, Elaine, *Colette*. New Jersey: Rutger's University Press, 1960.

Masefield, John, *Multitude and Solitude*. New York: Macmillan, 1909, 1916.

Masters, Edgar Lee, *Doomesday Book*. New York: Macmillan, 1920.

———, *The Fate of the Jury*. New York: Appleton, 1929.

McCarthy, Mary, *The Group*. New York: Harcourt, 1963; Signet, 1964.

Mendes, Catulle, *Mephistophela*. 1890.

Millay, Edna St. Vincent, *Collected Poems*. New York: Harper, 1956.

————, *The Lamp and the Bell*. New York: Harper, 1921.

Miller, Henry, *Plexus*. Paris: Olympia, 1953; New York: Grove, 1964.

————, *Sexus*. Paris: Obelisk, 1949; New York: Grove, 1964.

————, *The Tropic of Cancer*. Paris: Obelisk, 1933. New York: Grove, 1961.

Moravia, Alberto, *The Conformist*. New York: Farrar, Straus & Giroux, 1951; Signet, 1954.

Murdoch, Iris, *The Italian Girl*. New York: Viking, 1964; Avon, 1965.

————, *The Unicorn*. New York: Viking, 1963; Avon, 1964.

————, *An Unofficial Rose*. New York: Viking, 1962.

Nabokov, Vladimir, *Lolita*. New York: Putnam, 1958; Fawcett Crest, 1959.

Nin, Anaïs, *Collages*. London: Peter Owen, 1963.

————, *The Diary of Anaïs Nin: 1931–1934*, New York: Harcourt, 1966.

————, *House of Incest*. San Francisco: Centaur, 1949.

————, *Ladders to Fire*. New York: Dutton, 1945.

————, *Seduction of the Minotaur*. Denver: Alan Swallow, 1961.

————, *Spy In the House of Love*. New York: British Book Centre, 1954; Denver: Alan Swallow, 1966.

————, *Under a Glass Bell*. New York: Dutton, 1948.

O'Hara, John, "Clayton Bunter" in *The Horse Knows the Way*. New York: Random House, 1963; Bantam, 1966.

————, "James Francis and the Star" in *Waiting For Winter*. New York: Random House, 1966; Bantam, 1966.

————, "Jurge Dulrumple" in *Cape Cod Lighter*. New York: Random House, 1962; Bantam, 1964.

————, *The Lockwood Concern*. New York: Random House, 1965; Signet, 1966.

————, "The Skeletons" in *Waiting For Winter*. New York: Random House, 1966.

————, "Yucca Knolls" in *The Hat On the Bed*. New York: Random House, 1963; Bantam, 1965. (Note: John O'Hara presents a problem in entry, since he has begun to sprinkle his stories and novels with casual mention of Lesbians and homosexuals. There are at least six other possible entries here which seem so casual and insignificant in the story or the novel concerned that I have deliberately deleted them.)

Pavese, Cesare, *Among Women Only*. Noonday Press, 1959.

Purdy, James, "Encore" in *Children Is All*. New York: New Directions, 1962.

———, "Mrs. Benson" in *Children Is All*. New York: New Directions, 1962.

Remarque, Erich Maria, *Arch of Triumph*. New York: Pantheon, 1962; Pocketbooks, 1963.

Renault, Mary, *The Bull From the Sea*. New York: Pantheon, 1962; Pocketbooks, 1963.

———, *Kind Are Her Answers*. New York: Morrow, 1940; Dell, 1950.

———, *The Mask of Apollo*. New York: Pantheon, 1966.

———, *Friendly Young Ladies*. London: Longmans, Green, 1944. New York: Morrow, 1945; Avon, 1962. (Note: American hardcover and paperback editions under the title, *The Middle Mist*.)

———, *Purposes of Love*. London: Longmans, Green, 1939. New York: Morrow, 1939; Popular Library, 1963 from editions under the title, *Promise of Love*.

Rice, Elmer, *Imperial City*. London: Gollancz, 1937. New York: Coward-McCann, 1937.

Rochefort, Christine, *Cats Don't Care for Money*. New York: Doubleday, 1965.

———, *Warrior's Rest*. New York: David McKay, 1959; Fawcett Crest, 1960.

Rolland, Romain, *Annette and Sylvie*. New York: Holt, 1925.

Rule, Jane, *The Desert of the Heart*. London: Secker and Warburg, 1954. New York: World, 1965.

Sackville-West, Victoria, *The Dark Island*. New York: Doubleday, 1934.

———, *King's Daughter*. New York: Doubleday, 1930.

Sand, George, *Gabriel-Gabrielle* (1834). Various English and American editions available—primarily in old sets of her complete works. Issued by various obscure publishers without dates around 1890 to 1910.

Sappho, *Works* (600 B.C.). Many translations in existence, among them, *The Poems of Sappho*, translation by Mary Barnard. University of California Press, 1958.

Sarton, May, *Cloud, Stone, Sun, Vine.* New York: Norton, 1962.

———, *Encounter In April.* Boston: Houghton-Mifflin, 1937.

———, *In Time Like Air.* New York: Holt, Rinehart & Winston, 1958.

———, *Inner Landscape.* Boston: Houghton-Mifflin, 1939.

———, *The Land of Silence.* New York: Holt, Rinehart & Winston, 1953.

———, *The Lion and the Rose.* New York: Holt, Rinehart & Winston, 1948.

———, *Mrs. Stevens Hears the Mermaids Singing.* New York Norton, 1965. London: Peter Owen, 1966.

———, *A Shower of Summer Days.* New York: Holt, Rinehart & Winston, 1952.

———, *The Small Room.* New York: Norton, 1961.

Sartre, Jean-Paul, *No Exit.* New York: Knopf, 1947.

Shakespeare, William, *As You Like It.* Hundreds of editions available in England and America.

———, *Twelfth Night.* Hundreds of editions available in England and America.

Sontag, Susan, *The Benefactor.* New York: Farrar, Straus & Giroux, 1963; Avon, 1964.

Sparks, Muriel, *The Mandelbaum Gate.* New York: Knopf, 1965.

Sprigge, Elizabeth, *The Strange Life of August Strindberg.* New York: Macmillan, 1949.

Stein, Gertrude, "Miss Furr and Miss Skeene" in *Selected Writings of Gertrude Stein.* New York: Random House, 1946.

———, *Things As They Are.* Vermont: Banyan Press, 1950.

Stone, Irving, *Pageant of Youth.* New York: Alfred H. King, 1933.

Strindberg, August, *The Confessions of a Fool* (1899). New York: Viking, 1925. (Many other editions available.)

———, "Lady Julie" in *Lucky Peter's Travels and Other Tales.* London: Jonathan Cape, 1930.

Susann, Jacqueline, *Valley of the Dolls.* New York: Bernard Geis, 1966.

Tolstoi, Leo, *Anna Karenina.* New York: World, 1931.

Uris, Leon M., *Armageddon.* New York: Doubleday, 1964; Dell, 1965.

———, *Exodus.* New York: Doubleday, 1958; Bantam, 1960.

Verlaine, Paul, Poetry. Various single poems and sections of poetry available in anthologies of French literature. Six overt poems plus eleven variant poems are known to exist. The largest single group that has been located is in *Baudelaire, Rimbaud, Verlaine,* ed. by Joseph M. Bernstein. New York: Citadel, 1947.

Vidal, Gore, *Death In the Fifth Position.* New York: Dutton, 1952; Signet, 1953.

Voltaire, *Candide* (1760). Available in many English and American editions, many expurgated. Various Modern Library editions during the 1930's to 1950's, usually complete. Also various complete paperback editions, including St. Martin's Library, 1966.

Wedekind, Frank, "Earth Spirit" in *Five Tragedies of Sex.* London: G. T. Wray, 1953.

———, "Pandora's Box" in *Five Tragedies of Sex.* London: G. T. Wray, 1953.

West, Anthony, *The Trend Is Up.* New York: Random House, 1960; Fawcett Crest, 1961, 1964.

White, Antonia, *Frost In May.* London: Eyre & Spottiswoode, 1933, 1957.

Wilde, Oscar, *Teleny: Or the Reverse of the Medal* (1833). Paris: Olympia, 1958.

Williams, Tennessee, *The Night of the Iguana.* New York: Signet, 1964.

———, "Something Unspoken" in *27 Wagons Full of Cotton.* New York: New Directions, 1953 (third ed.). Also in *Best Short Plays of 1955–56.* New York: Dodd, Mead, 1956, 1957.

Wilson, Edmund, *Memoirs of Hecate Country.* New York: Doubleday, 1946; Signet, 1961.

Woolf, Virginia, *Geraldine and Jane.* Essay in *Bookman Magazine,* 1928.

———, *Mrs. Dalloway.* New York: Modern Library, 1928; Harcourt, 1964.

———, *Orlando.* New York: Harcourt, 1928; Signet, 1960.

———, *The Lighthouse.* New York: Harcourt, 1927, 1964.

Wouk, Herman, *Don't Stop the Carnival.* New York: Doubleday, 1965. Pocketbooks, 1966.

———, *Marjorie Morningstar.* New York: Doubleday, 1955; Signet, 1956.

Wylie, Philip, *The Disappearance.* New York: Holt, Rinehart & Winston, 1951; Pocketbooks, 1958.

————, *Opus 21.* New York: Holt, Rinehart & Winston, 1949; Pocketbooks, 1958.

Zola, Emile, *La Curee* (1874). Many editions available, including several cheaply printed "sets" of the author's works.

————, *Nana* (1880). Many editions available.

————, *Pot Bouille* (1883). Many editions available.

Zweig, Stefan, *Marie Antoinette.* New York: Garden City Publications, 1933.

————, *Mary Queen of Scotland and the Isles.* New York: Viking, 1935.

Index

ABOUT THE AUTHOR

BETTIE WYSOR was born in Virginia, where she attended college. Ms. Wysor has been a newspaper reporter, assistant television producer, and an award-winning writer for major television advertising agencies. A past art and antiques editor for *Town and Country* Magazine, she is presently a free-lance writer, contributing feature articles to *Vogue, Harper's Bazaar, Ladies' Home Journal* and other magazines here and abroad.